Rethinking
the
Western
Tradition

*The volumes in this series
seek to address the present debate
over the Western tradition
by reprinting key works of
that tradition along with essays
that evaluate each text from
different perspectives.*

Discourse on the Method and Meditations on First Philosophy

RENÉ DESCARTES

Edited by David Weissman

with essays by

William T. Bluhm

Lou Massa

Thomas Pavel

John F. Post

Stephen Toulmin

David Weissman

Yale University Press

New Haven & London

Designed by Rich Hendel.
Set in Times Roman type by
Keystone Typesetting, Inc.,
Orwigsburg, Pennsylvania.
Printed in the United States of America by Vail-Ballou Press,
Binghamton, New York.

Library of Congress Cataloging-in-Publication Data
Descartes, René, 1596–1650.
[Discours de la méthode. English]
Discourse on the method ; and, Meditations on first philosophy /
René Descartes ; edited by David Weissman ; with essays by
William T. Bluhm . . . [et al.]
p. cm. — (Rethinking the Western tradition)
Includes bibliographical references.
978-0-300-06773-6
I. Methodology. 2. Knowledge, Theory of. 3. Science — Methodology.
4. First philosophy. I. Weissman, David, 1936– . II. Bluhm,
William Theodore, 1923– III. Descartes, René, 1596–1650.
Meditationes de prima philosophia. English. IV. Title.
V. Title: Meditations on first philosophy. VI. Series.
B1846.W4513 1996
194 — dc20 96–5885
CIP

A catalogue record for this book is available from the
British Library.

The paper in this book meets the guidelines for
permanence and durability of the Committee on
Production Guidelines for Book Longevity of the
Council on Library Resources.

10 9 8 7 6 5 4

Contributors

William T. Bluhm is Professor of Political Science Emeritus at the University of Rochester.

Lou Massa is Professor of Chemistry and Physics at Hunter College and the Graduate School of the City University of New York.

Thomas Pavel is Professor of French and Comparative Literature at Princeton University.

John F. Post is Professor of Philosophy at Vanderbilt University.

Stephen Toulmin is Henry Luce Professor at the Center for Multiethnic and Transnational Studies at the University of Southern California.

David Weissman is Professor of Philosophy at the City College of the City University of New York.

Contents

Preface

Our Western intellectual tradition has many roots, but none stronger or more consequential than philosophic theory. It asks questions such as these: What are we? What is the world, and our place in it? What could (or should) we do or be? The essays of this book consider René Descartes' answers and the uses still made of them. The volume contains his *Discourse* and *Meditations*, and nine essays that describe the elaboration of his ideas in physical science, psychoanalysis, literature, and political theory, as well as metaphysics, theology, and epistemology. Descartes is a principal determinant of theory and practice in our time. Thinking about his ideas makes us more comprehensible to ourselves.

Abbreviations

The translations of Descartes' *Discourse* and *Meditations* reprinted here are by Elizabeth S. Haldane, and G. R. T. Ross, first published in *The Philosophical Works of Descartes* (Cambridge: Cambridge University Press, 1911), volume I.

Citations of Descartes' texts observe the following conventions. References to the *Discourse* and *Meditations* are followed by a parenthetic expression with these components: page number in this volume; an abbreviation for *The Philosophical Writings of Descartes*, trans. John Cottingham, Robert Stoothoff, and Dugald Murdoch, vol. I and II – *CSM* – or by them and Anthony Kenny, vol. III – *CSMK* – published by Cambridge University Press in 1985–91, *CSM* being followed by a volume and page number, *CSMK* by a page number only; the abbreviation *AT* for *Oeuvres des Descartes*, ed. Charles Adam and Paul Tannery, rev. edition, 12 vol. (Paris: Vrin/CNRS, 1964–76), followed by a volume and page number – citations thus: oo; *CSM*, I or II (or *CSMK*), oo; *AT*, I (through XII), oo.

Descartes' *Geometry* (New York: Dover, 1954) does not appear in *CSM* or *CSMK*. References to this volume read: Descartes [1637] 1954, p. oo. *AT* is not cited because this volume includes Descartes' French text.

Texts

Discourse on the Method of Rightly Conducting the Reason and Seeking for Truth in the Sciences

If this Discourse appears too long to be read all at once, it may be separated into six portions. And in the first there will be found various considerations respecting the sciences; in the second, the principal rules regarding the Method which the author has sought out; while in the third are some of the rules of morality which he has derived from this Method. In the fourth are the reasons by which he proves the existence of God and of the human soul, which form the foundation of his Metaphysic. In the fifth, the order of the questions regarding physics which he has investigated, and particularly the explanation of the movement of the heart, and of some other difficulties which pertain to medicine, as also the difference between the soul of man and that of the brutes. And in the last part the questions raised relate to those matters which the author believes to be requisite in order to advance further in the investigation of nature, in addition to the reasons that caused him to write.

PART I

Good sense is of all things in the world the most equally distributed, for everybody thinks himself so abundantly provided with it, that even those most difficult to please in all other matters do not commonly desire more of it than they already possess. It is unlikely that this is an error on their part; it seems rather to be evidence in support of the view that the power of forming a good judgment and of distinguishing the true from the false, which is properly speaking what is called Good sense or Reason, is by nature equal in all men. Hence too it will show that the diversity of our opinions does not proceed from some men being more rational than others, but solely from the fact that our thoughts pass through diverse channels and the same objects are not considered by all. For to be possessed of good mental powers is not sufficient; the principal matter is to apply them well. The greatest minds are capable of the greatest vices as well as of the greatest virtues, and those who proceed very slowly may, provided they always follow the straight road, really advance much faster than those who, though they run, forsake it.

For myself I have never ventured to presume that my mind was in any way more perfect than that of the ordinary man; I have even longed to possess thought as quick, or an imagination as accurate and distinct, or a memory as comprehensive or ready, as some others. And besides these I do not know any other qualities that make for the perfection of the human mind. For as to reason or sense, inasmuch as it is the only thing that constitutes us men and distinguishes us from the brutes, I would fain believe that it is to be found complete in each individual, and in this I follow the common opinion of the philosophers, who say that the question of more or less occurs only in the sphere of the *accidents* and does not affect the *forms* or natures of the *individuals* in the same *species.*

But I shall not hesitate to say that I have had great good fortune from my youth up, in lighting upon and pursuing certain paths which have conducted me to considerations and maxims from which I have formed a Method, by whose assistance it appears to me I have the means of gradually increasing my knowledge and of little by little raising it to the highest possible point which the mediocrity of my talents and the brief duration of my life can permit me to reach. For I have already reaped from it fruits of such a nature that, even though I always try in the judgments I make on myself to lean to the side of self-depreciation rather than to that of arrogance, and though, looking with the eye of a philosopher on the diverse actions and enterprises of all mankind, I find scarcely any which do not seem to me vain and useless, I do not cease to receive extreme satisfaction in the progress which I seem to have already made in the search after truth, and to form such hopes for the future as to venture to believe that, if amongst the occupations of men, simply as men, there is some one in particular that is excellent and important, that is the one which I have selected.

It must always be recollected, however, that possibly I deceive myself, and that what I take to be gold and diamonds is perhaps no more than copper and glass. I know how subject we are to delusion in whatever touches ourselves, and also how much the judgments of our friends ought to be suspected when they are in our favour. But in this Discourse I shall be very happy to show the paths I have followed, and to set forth my life as in a picture, so that everyone may judge of it for himself; and thus in learning from the common talk what are the opinions which are held of it, a new means of obtaining self-instruction will be reached, which I shall add to those which I have been in the habit of using.

Thus my design is not here to teach the Method which everyone should follow in order to promote the good conduct of his Reason, but only to show in what manner I have endeavoured to conduct my own. Those who set about giving precepts must esteem themselves more skilful than those to whom they advance them, and if they fall short in the smallest matter they must of course take the blame for it. But regarding this Treatise simply as a history, or, if you prefer it, a fable in which, amongst certain things which may be imitated, there are possibly others also which it would not be right to follow, I hope that it will be of use to some without being hurtful to any, and that all will thank me for my frankness.

I have been nourished on letters since my childhood, and since I was given to believe that by their means a clear and certain knowledge could be obtained of all that is useful in life, I had an extreme desire to acquire instruction. But so soon as I had achieved the entire course of study at the close of which one is usually received into the ranks of the learned, I entirely changed my opinion. For I found myself embarrassed with so many doubts and errors that it seemed to me that the effort to instruct myself had no effect other than the increasing discovery of my own ignorance. And yet I was studying at one of the most celebrated Schools in Europe, where I thought that there must be men of learning if they were to be found anywhere in the world. I learned there all that others learned; and not being satisfied with the sciences that we were taught, I even read through all the books which fell into my hands, treating of what is considered most curious and rare. Along with this I knew the judgments that others had formed of me, and I did not feel that I was esteemed inferior to my fellow-students, although there were amongst them some destined to fill the places of our masters. And finally our century seemed to me as flourishing, and as fertile in great minds, as any which had preceded. And this made me take the liberty of judging all others by myself and of coming to the conclusion that there was no learning in the world such as I was formerly led to believe it to be.

I did not omit, however, always to hold in esteem those exercises which are the occupation of the Schools. I knew that the Languages which one learns there are essential for the understanding of all ancient literature; that fables with their charm stimulate the mind and histories of memorable deeds exalt it; and that, when read with discretion, these books assist in forming a sound judgment. I was aware that the reading of all good books is indeed like a conversation with the noblest men of past centuries who were the authors of them, nay a carefully studied conversation, in which they reveal to us none but the best of their thoughts. I deemed Eloquence to have a power and beauty beyond compare; that Poesy has most ravishing delicacy and sweetness; that in Mathematics there are the subtlest discoveries and inventions which may accomplish much, both in satisfying the curious, and in furthering all the arts, and in diminishing man's labour; that those writings that deal with Morals contain much that is instructive, and many exhortations to virtue which are most useful; that Theology points out the way to Heaven; that Philosophy teaches us to speak with an appearance of truth on all things, and causes us to be admired by the less learned; that Jurisprudence, Medicine and all other sciences bring honour and riches to those who cultivate them; and finally that it is good to have examined all things, even those most full of superstition and falsehood, in order that we may know their just value, and avoid being deceived by them.

But I considered that I had already given sufficient time to languages and likewise even to the reading of the literature of the ancients, both their histories and their fables. For to converse with those of other centuries is almost the same thing as to travel. It is good to know something of the customs of different peoples in order to judge more sanely of our own, and not to think that everything of a fashion not ours is absurd and contrary to reason, as do those who have seen nothing. But when one employs too much time in travelling, one becomes a stranger in one's own country, and when one is too curious about things which were practised in past centuries, one is usually very ignorant about those which are practised in our own time. Besides, fables make one imagine many events possible which in reality are not so, and even the most accurate of histories, if they do not exactly misrepresent or exaggerate the value of things in order to render them more worthy of being read, at least omit in them all the circumstances which are basest and least notable; and from this fact it follows that what is retained is not portrayed as it really is, and that those who regulate their conduct by examples which they derive from such a source, are liable to fall into the extravagances of the knights-errant of Romance, and form projects beyond their power of performance.

I esteemed Eloquence most highly and I was enamoured of Poesy, but I thought that both were gifts of the mind rather than fruits of study. Those who have the strongest power of reasoning, and who most skilfully arrange their thoughts in order to render them clear and intelligible, have the best power of persuasion even if they can but speak the language of Lower Brittany and have never learned Rhetoric. And those who have the most delightful original ideas and who know how to express them with the maximum of style and suavity, would not fail to be the best poets even if the art of Poetry were unknown to them.

Most of all was I delighted with Mathematics because of the certainty of its demonstrations and the evidence of its reasoning; but I did not yet understand its true use, and, believing that it was of service only in the mechanical arts, I was astonished that, seeing how firm and solid was its basis, no loftier edifice had been reared thereupon. On the other hand I compared the works of the ancient pagans which deal with Morals to palaces most superb and magnificent, which are yet built on sand and mud alone. They praise the virtues most highly and show them to be more worthy of being prized than anything else in the world, but they do not sufficiently teach us to become acquainted with them, and often that which is called by a fine name is nothing but insensibility, or pride, or despair, or parricide.

I honoured our Theology and aspired as much as anyone to reach to heaven, but having learned to regard it as a most highly assured fact that the road is not less open to the most ignorant than to the most learned, and that the revealed truths which conduct thither are quite above our intelligence, I should not have dared to submit them to the feebleness of my reasonings; and I thought that, in order to undertake to examine them and succeed in so doing, it was necessary to have some extraordinary assistance from above and to be more than a mere man.

I shall not say anything about Philosophy, but that, seeing that it has been cultivated for many centuries by the best minds that have ever lived, and that nevertheless no single thing is to be found in it which is not subject of dispute, and in consequence which is not dubious, I had not enough presumption to hope to fare better there than other men had done. And also, considering how many conflicting opinions there may be regarding the self-same matter, all supported by learned people, while there can never be more than one which is true, I esteemed as well-nigh false all that only went as far as being probable.

Then as to the other sciences, inasmuch as they derive their principles from Philosophy, I judged that one could have built nothing solid on foundations so far from firm. And neither the honour nor the promised gain was sufficient to persuade me to cultivate them, for, thanks be to God, I did not find myself in a condition which obliged me to make a merchandise of science for the improvement of my fortune; and, although I did not pretend to scorn all glory like the Cynics, I yet had very small esteem for what I could not hope to acquire, excepting through fictitious titles. And, finally, as to false doctrines, I thought that I already knew well enough what they were worth to be subject to deception neither by the promises of an alchemist, the predictions of an astrologer, the impostures of a magician, the artifices or the empty boastings of any of those who make a profession of knowing that of which they are ignorant.

This is why, as soon as age permitted me to emerge from the control of my tutors, I entirely quitted the study of letters. And resolving to seek no other science than that which could be found in myself, or at least in the great book of the world, I employed the rest of my youth in travel, in seeing courts and armies, in intercourse with men of diverse temperaments and conditions, in collecting varied experiences, in proving myself in the various predicaments in which I was placed by fortune, and under all circumstances bringing my mind to bear on the things which came before it, so that I might derive some profit from my experience. For it seemed to me that I might meet with much more truth in the reasonings that each man makes on the matters that specially concern him, and the issue of which would very soon punish him if he made a wrong judgment, than in the case of those made by a man of letters in his study touching speculations which lead to no result, and which bring about no other consequences to himself excepting that he will be all the more vain the more they are removed from common sense, since in this case it proves him to have employed so much the more ingenuity and skill in trying to make them seem probable. And I always had an excessive desire to learn to distinguish the true from the false, in order to see clearly in my actions and to walk with confidence in this life.

It is true that while I only considered the manners of other men I found in them nothing to give me settled convictions; and I remarked in them almost as much diversity as I had formerly seen in the opinions of philosophers. So much was this the case that the greatest profit which I derived from their study was that, in seeing many things which, although they seem to us very extravagant and ridiculous, were yet commonly received and approved by other great nations, I learned to believe nothing too certainly of which I had only been convinced by example and custom. Thus little by little I was delivered from many errors which might have obscured our natural vision and rendered us less capable of listening to Reason. But after I had employed several years in thus studying the book of the world and trying to acquire some experience, I one day formed the resolution of also making myself an object of study and of employing all the strength of my mind in choosing the road I should follow. This succeeded much better, it appeared to me, than if I had never departed either from my country or my books.

PART II

I was then in Germany, to which country I had been attracted by the wars which are not yet at an end. And as I was returning from the coronation of the Emperor to join the army, the setting in of winter detained me in a quarter where, since I found no society to divert me, while fortunately I had also no cares or passions to trouble me, I remained the whole day shut up alone in a stove-heated room, where I had complete leisure to occupy myself with my own thoughts. One of the first of the considerations that occurred to me was that there is very often less perfection in works composed of several portions, and carried out by the hands of various masters, than in those on which one individual alone has worked. Thus we see that buildings planned and carried out by one architect alone are usually more beautiful and better proportioned than those which many have tried to put in order and improve, making use of old walls which were built with other ends in view. In the same way also, those ancient cities which, originally mere villages, have become in the process of time great towns, are usually badly constructed in comparison with those which are regularly laid out on a plain by a surveyor who is free to follow his own ideas. Even though, considering their buildings each one apart, there is often as much or more display of skill in the one case than in the other, the former have large buildings and small buildings indiscriminately placed together, thus rendering the streets crooked and irregular, so that it might be said that it was chance rather than the will of men guided by reason that led to such an arrangement. And if we consider that this happens despite the fact that from all time there have been certain officials who have had the special duty of looking after the buildings of private individuals in order that they may be public ornaments, we shall understand how difficult it is to bring about much that is satisfactory in operating only upon the works of others. Thus I imagined that those people who were once half-savage, and who have become civilized only by slow degrees, merely forming their laws as the disagreeable necessities of their crimes and quarrels constrained them, could not succeed in establishing so good a system of government as those who, from the time they first came together as communities, carried into effect the constitution laid down by some prudent legislator. Thus it is quite certain that the constitution of the true Religion whose ordinances are of God alone is incomparably better regulated than any other. And, to come down to human affairs, I believe that if Sparta was very flourishing in former times, this was not because of the excellence of each and every one of its laws, seeing that many were very strange and even contrary to good morals, but because, being drawn up by one individual, they all tended towards the same end. And similarly I thought that the sciences found in books – in those at least whose reasonings are only probable and which have no demonstrations, composed as they are of the gradually accumulated opinions of many different individuals – do not approach so near to the truth as the simple reasoning which a man of common sense can quite naturally carry out respecting the things which come immediately before him. Again I thought that since we have all been children before being men, and since it has for long fallen to us to be governed by our appetites and by our teachers (who often enough contradicted one another, and none of whom perhaps counselled us always for the best), it is almost impossible that our judgments should be so excellent or solid as they should have been had we had complete use of our reason since our birth, and had we been guided by its means alone.

It is true that we do not find that all the houses in a town are rased to the ground for the sole reason that the town is to be rebuilt in another fashion, with streets made more beautiful; but at the same time we see that many people cause their own houses to be knocked down in order to rebuild them, and that sometimes they are forced so to do where there is danger of the houses falling of themselves, and when the foundations are not secure. From such examples I argued to myself that there was no plausibility in the claim of any private individual to reform a state by altering everything, and by overturning it throughout, in order to set it right again. Nor is it likewise probable that the whole body of the Sciences, or the order of teaching established by the Schools, should be reformed. But as regards all the opinions which up to this time I had embraced, I thought I could not do better than endeavour once for all to sweep them completely away, so that they might later on be replaced, either by others which were better, or by the same, when I had made them conform to the uniformity of a rational scheme. And I firmly believed that by this means I should succeed in directing my life much better than if I had only built on old foundations, and relied on principles of which I allowed myself to be in youth persuaded without having inquired into their truth. For although in so doing I recognised various difficulties, these were at the same time not unsurmountable, nor comparable to those which are found in reformation of the most insignificant kind in matters which concern the public. In the case of great bodies it is too difficult a task to raise them again when they are once thrown down, or even to keep them in their places when once thoroughly shaken; and their fall cannot be otherwise than very violent. Then as to any imperfections that they may possess (and the very diversity that is found between them is sufficient to tell us that these in many cases exist) custom has doubtless greatly mitigated them, while it has also helped us to avoid, or insensibly corrected a number against which mere foresight would have found it difficult to guard. And finally the imperfections are almost always more supportable than would be the process of removing them, just as the great roads which wind about amongst the mountains become, because of being frequented, little by little so well-beaten and easy that it is much better to follow them than to try to go more directly by climbing over rocks and descending to the foot of precipices.

This is the reason why I cannot in any way approve of those turbulent and unrestful spirits who, being called neither by birth nor fortune to the management of public affairs, never fail to have always in their minds some new reforms. And if I thought that in this treatise there was contained the smallest justification for this folly, I should be very sorry to allow it to be published. My design has never extended beyond trying to reform my own opinion and to build on a foundation which is entirely my own. If my work has given me a certain satisfaction, so that I here present to you a draft of it, I do not so do because I wish to advise anybody to imitate it. Those to whom God has been most beneficent in the bestowal of His graces will perhaps form designs which are more elevated; but I fear much that this particular one will seem too venturesome for many. The simple resolve to strip oneself of all opinions and beliefs formerly received is not to be regarded as an example that each man should follow, and the world may be said to be mainly composed of two classes of minds neither of which could prudently adopt it. There are those who, believing themselves to be cleverer than they are, cannot restrain themselves from being precipitate in judgment and have not sufficient patience to arrange their thoughts in proper order; hence, once a man of this description had taken the liberty of doubting the principles he formerly accepted, and had deviated from the beaten track, he would never be able to maintain the path which must be followed to reach the appointed end more quickly, and he would hence remain wandering astray all through his life. Secondly, there are those who having reason or modesty enough to judge that they are less capable of distinguishing truth from falsehood than some others from whom instruction might be obtained, are right in contenting themselves with following the opinions of these others rather than in searching better ones for themselves.

For myself I should doubtless have been of these last if I had never had more than a single master, or had I never known the diversities which have from all time existed between the opinions of men of the greatest learning. But I had been taught, even in my College days, that there is nothing imaginable so strange or so little credible that it has not been maintained by one philosopher or other, and I further recognised in the course of my travels that all those whose sentiments are very contrary to ours are yet not necessarily barbarians or savages, but may be possessed of reason in as great or even a greater degree than ourselves. I also considered how very different the self-same man, identical in mind and spirit, may become, according as he is brought up from childhood amongst the French or Germans, or has passed his whole life amongst Chinese or cannibals. I likewise noticed how even in the fashions of one's clothing the same thing that pleased us ten years ago, and which will perhaps please us once again before ten years are passed, seems at the present time extravagant and ridiculous. I thus concluded that it is much more custom and example that persuade us than any certain knowledge, and yet in spite of this the voice of the majority does not afford a proof of any value in truths a little difficult to discover, because such truths are much more likely to have been discovered by one man than by a nation. I could not, however, put my finger on a single person whose opinions seemed preferable to those of others, and I found that I was, so to speak, constrained myself to undertake the direction of my procedure.

But like one who walks alone and in the twilight I resolved to go so slowly, and to use so much circumspection in all things, that if my advance was but very small, at least I guarded myself well from falling. I did not wish to set about the final rejection of any single opinion which might formerly have crept into my beliefs without having been introduced there by means of Reason, until I had first of all employed sufficient time in planning out the task which I had undertaken, and in seeking the true Method of arriving at a knowledge of all the things of which my mind was capable.

Among the different branches of Philosophy, I had in my younger days to a certain extent studied Logic; and in those of Mathematics, Geometrical Analysis and Algebra – three arts or sciences which seemed as though they ought to contribute something to the design I had in view. But in examining them I observed in respect to Logic that the syllogisms and the greater part of the other teaching served better in explaining to others those things that one knows (or like the art of Lully, in enabling one to speak without judgment of those things of which one is ignorant) than in learning what is new. And although in reality Logic contains many precepts which are very true and very good, there are at the same time mingled with them so many others which are hurtful or superfluous, that it is almost as difficult to separate the two as to draw a Diana or a Minerva out of a block of marble which is not yet roughly hewn. And as to the Analysis of the ancients and the Algebra of the moderns, besides the fact that they embrace only matters the most abstract, such as appear to have no actual use, the former is always so restricted to the consideration of symbols that it cannot exercise the Understanding without greatly fatiguing the Imagination; and in the latter one is so subjected to certain rules and formulas that the result is the construction of an art which is confused and obscure, and which embarrasses the mind, instead of a science which contributes to its cultivation. This made me feel that some other Method must be found, which, comprising the advantages of the three, is yet exempt from their faults. And as a multiplicity of laws often furnishes excuses for evil-doing, and as a State is hence much better ruled when, having but very few laws, these are most strictly observed; so, instead of the great number of precepts of which Logic is composed, I believed that I should find the four which I shall state quite sufficient, provided that I adhered to a firm and constant resolve never on any single occasion to fail in their observance.

1. The first of these was to accept nothing as true which I did not clearly recognise to be so: that is to say, carefully to avoid precipitation and prejudice in judgments, and to accept in them nothing more than what was presented to my mind so clearly and distinctly that I could have no occasion to doubt it.

2. The second was to divide up each of the difficulties which I examined into as many parts as possible, and as seemed requisite in order that it might be resolved in the best manner possible.

3. The third was to carry on my reflections in due order, commencing with objects that were the most simple and easy to understand, in order to rise little by little, or by degrees, to knowledge of the most complex, assuming an order, even if a fictitious one, among those which do not follow a natural sequence relatively to one another.

4. The last was in all cases to make enumerations so complete and reviews so general that I should be certain of having omitted nothing.

Those long chains of reasoning, simple and easy as they are, of which geometricians make use in order to arrive at the most difficult demonstrations, had caused me to imagine that all those things which fall under the cognizance of man might very likely be mutually related in the same fashion; and that, provided only that we abstain from receiving anything as true which is not so, and always retain the order which is necessary in order to deduce the one conclusion from the other, there can be nothing so remote that we cannot reach to it, nor so recondite that we cannot discover it. And I had not much trouble in discovering which objects it was necessary to begin with, for I already knew that it was with the most simple and those most easy to apprehend. Considering also that of all those who have hitherto sought for the truth in the Sciences, it has been the mathematicians alone who have been able to succeed in making any demonstrations, that is to say producing reasons which are evident and certain, I did not doubt that it had been by means of a similar kind that they carried on their investigations. I did not at the same time hope for any practical result in so doing, except that my mind would become accustomed to the nourishment of truth and would not content itself with false reasoning. But for all that I had no intention of trying to master all those particular sciences that receive in common the name of Mathematics; but observing that, although their objects are different, they do not fail to agree in this, that they take nothing under consideration but the various relationships or proportions which are present in these objects, I thought that it would be better if I only examined these proportions in their general aspect, and without viewing them otherwise than in the objects which would serve most to facilitate a knowledge of them. Not that I should in any way restrict them to these objects, for I might later on all the more easily apply them to all other objects to which they were applicable. Then, having carefully noted that in order to comprehend the proportions I should sometimes require to consider each one in particular, and sometimes merely keep them in mind, or take them in groups, I thought that, in order the better to consider them in detail, I should picture them in the form of lines, because I could find no method more simple nor more capable of being distinctly represented to my imagination and senses. I considered, however, that in order to keep them in my memory or to embrace several at once, it would be essential that I should explain them by means of certain formulas, the shorter the better. And for this purpose it was requisite that I should borrow all that is best in Geometrical Analysis and Algebra, and correct the errors of the one by the other.

As a matter of fact, I can venture to say that the exact observation of the few precepts which I had chosen gave me so much facility in sifting out all the questions embraced in these two sciences, that in the two or three months which I employed in examining them – commencing with the most simple and general, and making each truth that I discovered a rule for helping me to find others – not only did I arrive at the solution of many questions which I had hitherto regarded as most difficult, but, towards the end, it seemed to me that I was able to determine in the case of those of which I was still ignorant, by what means, and in how far, it was possible to solve them. In this I might perhaps appear to you to be very vain if you did not remember that having but one truth to discover in respect to each matter, whoever succeeds in finding it knows in its regard as much as can be known. It is the same as with a child, for instance, who has been instructed in Arithmetic and has made an addition according to the rule prescribed; he may be sure of having found as regards the sum of figures given to him all that the human mind can know. For, in conclusion, the Method which teaches us to follow the true order and enumerate exactly every term in the matter under investigation contains everything which gives certainty to the rules of Arithmetic.

But what pleased me most in this Method was that I was certain by its means of exercising my reason in all things, if not perfectly, at least as well as was in my power. And besides this, I felt in making use of it that my mind gradually accustomed itself to conceive of its objects more accurately and distinctly; and not having restricted this Method to any particular matter, I promised myself to apply it as usefully to the difficulties of other sciences as I had done to those of Algebra. Not that on this account I dared undertake to examine just at once all those that might present themselves; for that would itself have been contrary to the order which the Method prescribes. But having noticed that the knowledge of these difficulties must be dependent on principles derived from Philosophy in which I yet found nothing to be certain, I thought that it was requisite above all to try to establish certainty in it. I considered also that since this endeavour is the most important in all the world, and that in which precipitation and prejudice were most to be feared, I should not try to grapple with it till I had attained to a much riper age than that of three and twenty, which was the age I had reached. I thought, too, that I should first of all employ much time in preparing myself for the work by eradicating from my mind all the wrong opinions which I had up to this time accepted, and accumulating a variety of experiences fitted later on to afford matter for my reasonings, and by ever exercising myself in the Method which I had prescribed, in order more and more to fortify myself in the power of using it.

PART III

And finally, as it is not sufficient, before commencing to rebuild the house which we inhabit, to pull it down and provide materials and an architect (or to act in this capacity ourselves, and make a careful drawing of its design), unless we have also provided ourselves with some other house where we can be comfortably lodged during the time of rebuilding, so in order that I should not remain irresolute in my actions while reason obliged me to be so in my judgments, and that I might not omit to carry on my life as happily as I could, I formed for myself a code of morals for the time being which did not consist of more than three or four maxims, which maxims I should like to enumerate to you.

The first was to obey the laws and customs of my country, adhering constantly to the religion in which by God's grace I had been instructed since my childhood, and in all other things directing my conduct by opinions the most moderate in nature, and the farthest removed from excess in all those which are commonly received and acted on by the most judicious of those with whom I might come in contact. For since I began to count my own opinions as nought, because I desired to place all under examination, I was convinced that I could not do better than follow those held by people on whose judgment reliance could be placed. And although such persons may possibly exist amongst the Persians and Chinese as well as amongst ourselves, it seemed to me that it was most expedient to bring my conduct into harmony with the ideas of those with whom I should have to live; and that, in order to ascertain that these were their real opinions, I should observe what they did rather than what they said, not only because in the corrupt state of our manners there are few people who desire to say all that they believe, but also because many are themselves ignorant of their beliefs. For since the act of thought by which we believe a thing is different from that by which we know that we believe it, the one often exists without the other. And amongst many opinions all equally received, I chose only the most moderate, both because these are always most suited for putting into practice, and probably the best (for all excess has a tendency to be bad), and also because I should have in a less degree turned aside from the right path, supposing that I was wrong, than if, having chosen an extreme course, I found that I had chosen amiss. I also made a point of counting as excess all the engagements by means of which we limit in some degree our liberty. Not that I hold in low esteem those laws which, in order to remedy the inconstancy of feeble souls, permit, when we have a good object in our view, that certain vows be taken, or contracts made, which oblige us to carry out that object. This sanction is even given for security in commerce where designs are wholly indifferent. But because I saw nothing in all the world remaining constant, and because for my own part I promised myself gradually to get my judgments to grow better and never to grow worse, I should have thought that I had committed a serious sin against commonsense if, because I approved of something at one time, I was obliged to regard it similarly at a later time, after it had possibly ceased to meet my approval, or after I had ceased to regard it in a favourable light.

My second maxim was that of being as firm and resolute in my actions as I could be, and not to follow less faithfully opinions the most dubious, when my mind was once made up regarding them, than if these had been beyond doubt. In this I should be following the example of travellers, who, finding themselves lost in a forest, know that they ought not to wander first to one side and then to the other, nor, still less, to stop in one place, but understand that they should continue to walk as straight as they can in one direction, not diverging for any slight reason, even though it was possibly chance alone that first determined them in their choice. By this means if they do not go exactly where they wish, they will at least arrive somewhere at the end, where probably they will be better off than in the middle of a forest. And thus since often enough in the actions of life no delay is permissible, it is very certain that, when it is beyond our power to discern the opinions which carry most truth, we should follow the most probable; and even although we notice no greater probability in the one opinion than in the other, we at least should make up our minds to follow a particular one and afterwards consider it as no longer doubtful in its relationship to practice, but as very true and very certain, inasmuch as the reason which caused us to determine upon it is known to be so. And henceforward this principle was sufficient to deliver me from all the penitence and remorse which usually affect the mind and agitate the conscience of those weak and vacillating creatures who allow themselves to keep changing their procedure, and practise as good, things which they afterwards judge to be evil.

My third maxim was to try always to conquer myself rather than fortune, and to alter my desires rather than change the order of the world, and generally to accustom myself to believe that there is nothing entirely within our power but our own thoughts: so that after we have done our best in regard to the things that are without us, our ill-success cannot possibly be failure on our part.[1] And this alone seemed to me sufficient to prevent my desiring anything in the future beyond what I could actually obtain, hence rendering me content; for since our will does not naturally induce us to desire anything but what our understanding represents to it as in some way possible of attainment, it is certain that if we consider all good things which are outside of us as equally outside of our power, we should not have more regret in resigning those goods which appear to pertain to our birth, when we are deprived of them for no fault of our own, than we have in not possessing the kingdoms of China or Mexico. In the same way, making what is called a virtue out of a necessity, we should no more desire to be well if ill, or free, if in prison, than we now do to have our bodies formed of a substance as little corruptible as diamonds, or to have wings to fly with

---

1. "So that whatever does not eventuate after we have done all in our power that it should happen is to be accounted by us as among the things which evidently cannot be done and which in philosophical phrase are called impossible." Latin Version.

like birds. I allow, however, that to accustom oneself to regard all things from this point of view requires long exercise and meditation often repeated; and I believe that it is principally in this that is to be found the secret of those philosophers who, in ancient times, were able to free themselves from the empire of fortune, or, despite suffering or poverty, to rival their gods in their happiness. For, ceaselessly occupying themselves in considering the limits which were prescribed to them by nature, they persuaded themselves so completely that nothing was within their own power but their thoughts, that this conviction alone was sufficient to prevent their having any longing for other things. And they had so absolute a mastery over their thoughts that they had some reason for esteeming themselves as more rich and more powerful, and more free and more happy than other men, who, however favoured by nature or fortune they might be, if devoid of this philosophy, never could arrive at all at which they aim.

And last of all, to conclude this moral code, I felt it incumbent on me to make a review of the various occupations of men in this life in order to try to choose out the best; and without wishing to say anything of the employment of others I thought that I could not do better than continue in the one in which I found myself engaged, that is to say, in occupying my whole life in cultivating my Reason, and in advancing myself as much as possible in the knowledge of the truth in accordance with the method which I had prescribed myself. I had experienced so much satisfaction since beginning to use this method, that I did not believe that any sweeter or more innocent could in this life be found, – every day discovering by its means some truths which seemed to me sufficiently important, although commonly ignored by other men. The satisfaction which I had so filled my mind that all else seemed of no account. And, besides, the three preceding maxims were founded solely on the plan which I had formed of continuing to instruct myself. For since God has given to each of us some light with which to distinguish truth from error, I could not believe that I ought for a single moment to content myself with accepting the opinions held by others unless I had in view the employment of my own judgment in examining them at the proper time; and I could not have held myself free of scruple in following such opinions, if nevertheless I had not intended to lose no occasion of finding superior opinions, supposing them to exist; and finally, I should not have been able to restrain my desires nor to remain content, if I had not followed a road by which, thinking that I should be certain to be able to acquire all the knowledge of which I was capable, I also thought I should likewise be certain of obtaining all the best things which could ever come within my power. And inasmuch as our will impels us neither to follow after nor to flee from anything, excepting as our understanding represents it as good or evil, it is sufficient to judge wisely in order to act well, and the best judgment brings the best action – that is to say, the acquisition of all the virtues and all the other good things that it is possible to obtain. When one is certain that this point is reached, one cannot fail to be contented.

Having thus assured myself of these maxims, and having set them on one side along with the truths of religion which have always taken the first place in my creed, I judged that as far as the rest of my opinions were concerned, I could safely undertake to rid myself of them. And inasmuch as I hoped to be able to reach my end more successfully in converse with man than in living longer shut up in the warm room where these reflections had come to me, I hardly awaited the end of winter before I once more set myself to travel. And in all the nine following years I did nought but roam hither and thither, trying to be a spectator rather than an actor in all the comedies the world displays. More especially did I reflect in each matter that came before me as to anything which could make it subject to suspicion or doubt, and give occasion for mistake, and I rooted out of my mind all the errors which might have formerly crept in. Not that indeed I imitated the sceptics, who only doubt for the sake of doubting, and pretend to be always uncertain; for, on the contrary, my design was only to provide myself with good ground for assurance, and to reject the quicksand and mud in order to find the rock or clay. In this task it seems to me, I succeeded pretty well, since in trying to discover the error or uncertainty of the propositions which I examined, not by feeble conjectures, but by clear and assured reasonings, I encountered nothing so dubious that I could not draw from it some conclusion that was tolerably secure, if this were no more than the inference that it contained in it nothing that was certain. And just as in pulling down an old house we usually preserve the debris to serve in building up another, so in destroying all those opinions which I considered to be ill-founded, I made various observations and acquired many experiences, which have since been of use to me in establishing those which are more certain. And more than this, I continued to exercise myself in the method which I had laid down for my use; for besides the fact that I was careful as a rule to conduct all my thoughts according to its maxims, I set aside some hours from time to time which I more especially employed in practising myself in the solution of mathematical problems according to the Method, or in the solution of other problems which though pertaining to other sciences, I was able to make almost similar to those of mathematics, by detaching them from all principles of other sciences which I found to be not sufficiently secure. You will see the result in many examples which are expounded in this volume.[2] And hence, without living to all appearance in any way differently from those who, having no occupation beyond spending their lives in ease and innocence, study to separate pleasure from vice, and who, in order to enjoy their leisure without weariness, make use of all distractions that are innocent and good, I did not cease to prosecute my design, and to profit perhaps even more in my study of Truth than if I had done nothing but read books or associate with literary people.

These nine years thus passed away before I had taken any definite part in regard to the difficulties as to which the learned are in the habit of disputing, or had commenced to seek the foundation of any philosophy more certain than the vulgar. And the example of many excellent men who had tried to do the same before me, but, as it appears to me, without success, made me imagine it to be so hard that possibly I should not have dared to undertake the task, had I not discovered that someone had spread abroad the report that I had already reached its conclusion. I cannot tell on what they based this opinion; if my conversation has contributed anything to it, this must have arisen from my confessing my ignorance more ingenuously than those who have studied a little usually do. And perhaps it was also due to my having shown forth my reasons for doubting many things which were held by others to be certain, rather than from having boasted of any special philosophic system. But being at heart honest enough not to desire to be esteemed as different from what I am, I thought that I must try by every means in my power to render myself worthy of the reputation which I had gained. And it is just eight years ago that this desire made me resolve to remove myself from all places where any acquaintances were possible, and to retire to a country such as this,[3] where the long-continued war has caused such order to be established that the armies which are maintained seem only to be of use in allowing the inhabitants to enjoy the fruits of peace with so much the more security; and where, in the crowded throng of a great and very active nation, which is more concerned with its own affairs than curious about those of others, without missing any of the conveniences of the most populous towns, I can live as solitary and retired as in deserts the most remote.

2. The Dioptrics, Meteors and Geometry were published originally in the same volume.

3. i.e., Holland, where Descartes settled in 1629.

PART IV

I do not know that I ought to tell you of the first meditations there made by me, for they are so metaphysical and so unusual that they may perhaps not be acceptable to everyone. And yet at the same time, in order that one may judge whether the foundations which I have laid are sufficiently secure, I find myself constrained in some measure to refer to them. For a long time I had remarked that it is sometimes requisite in common life to follow opinions which one knows to be most uncertain, exactly as though they were indisputable, as has been said above. But because in this case I wished to give myself entirely to the search after Truth, I thought that it was necessary for me to take an apparently opposite course, and to reject as absolutely false everything as to which I could imagine the least ground of doubt, in order to see if afterwards there remained anything in my belief that was entirely certain. Thus, because our senses sometimes deceive us, I wished to suppose that nothing is just as they cause us to imagine it to be; and because there are men who deceive themselves in their reasoning and fall into paralogisms, even concerning the simplest matters of geometry, and judging that I was as subject to error as was any other, I rejected as false all the reasons formerly accepted by me as demonstrations. And since all the same thoughts and conceptions which we have while awake may also come to us in sleep, without any of them being at that time true, I resolved to assume that everything that ever entered into my mind was no more true than the illusions of my dreams. But immediately afterwards I noticed that whilst I thus wished to think all things false, it was absolutely essential that the 'I' who thought this should be somewhat, and remarking that this truth *'I think, therefore I am'* was so certain and so assured that all the most extravagant suppositions brought forward by the sceptics were incapable of shaking it, I came to the conclusion that I could receive it without scruple as the first principle of the Philosophy for which I was seeking.

And then, examining attentively that which I was, I saw that I could conceive that I had no body, and that there was no world nor place where I might be; but yet that I could not for all that conceive that I was not. On the contrary, I saw from the very fact that I thought of doubting the truth of other things, it very evidently and certainly followed that I was; on the other hand if I had only ceased from thinking, even if all the rest of what I had ever imagined had really existed, I should have no reason for thinking that I had existed. From that I knew that I was a substance the whole essence or nature of which is to think, and that for its existence there is no need of any place, nor does it depend on any material thing; so that this 'me,' that is to say, the soul by which I am what I am, is entirely distinct from body, and is even more easy to know than is the latter; and even if body were not, the soul would not cease to be what it is.

After this I considered generally what in a proposition is requisite in order to be true and certain; for since I had just discovered one which I knew to be such, I thought that I ought also to know in what this certainty consisted. And having remarked that there was nothing at all in the statement '*I think, therefore I am*' which assures me of having thereby made a true assertion, excepting that I see very clearly that to think it is necessary to be, I came to the conclusion that I might assume, as a general rule, that the things which we conceive very clearly and distinctly are all true – remembering, however, that there is some difficulty in ascertaining which are those that we distinctly conceive.

Following upon this, and reflecting on the fact that I doubted, and that consequently my existence was not quite perfect (for I saw clearly that it was a greater perfection to know than to doubt), I resolved to inquire whence I had learnt to think of anything more perfect than I myself was; and I recognised very clearly that this conception must proceed from some nature which was really more perfect. As to the thoughts which I had of many other things outside of me, like the heavens, the earth, light, heat, and a thousand others, I had not so much difficulty in knowing whence they came, because, remarking nothing in them which seemed to render them superior to me, I could believe that, if they were true, they were dependencies upon my nature, in so far as it possessed some perfection; and if they were not true, that I held them from nought, that is to say, that they were in me because I had something lacking in my nature. But this could not apply to the idea of a Being more perfect than my own, for to hold it from nought would be manifestly impossible; and because it is no less contradictory to say of the more perfect that it is what results from and depends on the less perfect, than to say that there is something which proceeds from nothing, it was equally impossible that I should hold it from myself. In this way it could but follow that it had been placed in me by a Nature which was really more perfect than mine could be, and which even had within itself all the perfections of which I could form any idea – that is to say, to put it in a word, which was God. To which I added that since I knew some perfections which I did not possess, I was not the only being in existence (I shall here use freely, if you will allow, the terms of the School); but that there was necessarily some other more perfect Being on which I depended, or from which I acquired all that I had. For if I had existed alone and independent of any others, so that I should have had from myself all that perfection of being in which I participated to however small an extent, I should have been able for the same reason to have had all the remainder which I knew that I lacked; and thus I myself should have been infinite, eternal, immutable, omniscient, all-powerful, and, finally, I should have all the perfections which I could discern in God. For, in pursuance of the reasonings which I have just carried on, in order to know the nature of God as far as my nature is capable of knowing it, I had only to consider in reference to all these things of which I found some idea in myself, whether it was a perfection to possess them or not. And I was assured that none of those which indicated some imperfection were in Him, but that all else was present; and I saw that doubt, inconstancy, sadness, and such things, could not be in Him considering that I myself should have been glad to be without them. In addition to this, I had ideas of many things which are sensible and corporeal, for, although I might suppose that I was dreaming, and that all that I saw or imagined was false, I could not at the same time deny that the ideas were really in my thoughts. But because I had already recognised very clearly in myself that the nature of the intelligence is distinct from that of the body, and observing that all composition gives evidence of dependency, and that dependency is manifestly an imperfection, I came to the conclusion that it could not be a perfection in God to be composed of these two natures, and that consequently He was not so composed. I judged, however, that if there were any bodies in the world, or even any intelligences or other natures which were not wholly perfect, their existence must depend on His power in such a way that they could not subsist without Him for a single moment.

After that I desired to seek for other truths, and having put before myself the object of the geometricians, which I conceived to be a continuous body, or a space indefinitely extended in length, breadth, height or depth, which was divisible into various parts, and which might have various figures and sizes, and might be moved or transposed in all sorts of ways (for all this the geometricians suppose to be in the object of their contemplation), I went through some of their simplest demonstrations, and having noticed that this great certainty which everyone attributes to these demonstrations is founded solely on the fact that they are conceived of with clearness, in accordance with the rule which I have just laid down, I also noticed that there was nothing at all in them to assure me of the existence of their object. For, to take an example, I saw very well that if we suppose a triangle to be given, the three angles must certainly be equal to two right angles; but for all that I saw no reason to be assured that there was any such triangle in existence, while on the contrary, on reverting to the examination of the idea which I had of a Perfect Being, I found that in this case existence was implied in it in the same manner in which the equality of its three angles to two right angles is implied in the idea of a triangle; or in the idea of a sphere, that all the points on its surface are equidistant from its centre, or even more evidently still. Consequently it is at least as certain that God, who is a Being so perfect, is, or exists, as any demonstration of geometry can possibly be.

What causes many, however, to persuade themselves that there is difficulty in knowing this truth, and even in knowing the nature of their soul, is the fact that they never raise their minds above the things of sense, or that they are so accustomed to consider nothing excepting by imagining it, which is a mode of thought specially adapted to material objects, that all that is not capable of being imagined appears to them not to be intelligible at all. This is manifest enough from the fact that even the philosophers in the Schools hold it as a maxim that there is nothing in the understanding which has not first of all been in the senses, in which there is certainly no doubt that the ideas of God and of the soul have never been. And it seems to me that those who desire to make use of their imagination in order to understand these ideas, act in the same way as if, to hear sounds or smell odours, they should wish to make use of their eyes: excepting that there is indeed this difference, that the sense of sight does not give us less assurance of the truth of its objects, than do those of scent or of hearing, while neither our imagination nor our senses can ever assure us of anything, if our understanding does not intervene.

If there are finally any persons who are not sufficiently persuaded of the existence of God and of their soul by the reasons which I have brought forward, I wish that they should know that all other things of which they perhaps think themselves more assured (such as possessing a body, and that there are stars and an earth and so on) are less certain. For, although we have a moral assurance of these things which is such that it seems that it would be extravagant in us to doubt them, at the same time no one, unless he is devoid of reason, can deny, when a metaphysical certainty is in question, that there is sufficient cause for our not having complete assurance, by observing the fact that when asleep we may similarly imagine that we have another body, and that we see other stars and another earth, without there being anything of the kind. For how do we know that the thoughts that come in dreams are more false than those that we have when we are awake, seeing that often enough the former are not less lively and vivid than the latter? And though the wisest minds may study the matter as much as they will, I do not believe that they will be able to give any sufficient reason for removing this doubt, unless they presuppose the existence of God. For to begin with, that which I have just taken as a rule, that is to say, that all the things that we very clearly and very distinctly conceive of are true, is certain only because God is or exists, and that He is a Perfect Being, and that all that is in us issues from Him. From this it follows that our ideas or notions, which to the extent of their being clear or distinct are ideas of real things issuing from God, cannot but to that extent be true. So that though we often enough have ideas which have an element of falsity, this can only be the case in regard to those which have in them somewhat that is confused or obscure, because in so far as they have this character they participate in negation – that is, they exist in us as confused only because we are not quite perfect. And it is evident that there is no less repugnance in the idea that error or imperfection, inasmuch as it is imperfection, proceeds from God, than there is in the idea of truth or perfection proceeding from nought. But if we did not know that all that is in us of reality and truth proceeds from a perfect and infinite Being, however clear and distinct were our ideas, we should not have any reason to assure ourselves that they had the perfection of being true.

But after the knowledge of God and of the soul has thus rendered us certain of this rule, it is very easy to understand that the dreams which we imagine in our sleep should not make us in any way doubt the truth of the thoughts which we have when awake. For even if in sleep we had some very distinct idea such as a geometrician might have who discovered some new demonstration, the fact of being asleep would not militate against its truth. And as to the most ordinary error in our dreams, which consists in their representing to us various objects in the same way as do our external senses, it does not matter that this should give us occasion to suspect the truth of such ideas, because we may be likewise often enough deceived in them without our sleeping at all, just as when those who have the jaundice see everything as yellow, or when stars or other bodies which are very remote appear much smaller than they really are. For, finally, whether we are awake or asleep, we should never allow ourselves to be persuaded excepting by the evidence of our Reason. And it must be remarked that I speak of our Reason and not of our imagination nor of our senses; just as though we see the sun very clearly, we should not for that reason judge that it is of the size of which it appears to be; likewise we could quite well distinctly imagine the head of a lion on the body of a goat, without necessarily concluding that a chimera exists. For Reason does not insist that whatever we see or imagine thus is a truth, but it tells us clearly that all our ideas or notions must have some foundation of truth. For otherwise it could not be possible that God, who is all perfection and truth, should have placed them within us. And because our reasonings are never so evident nor so complete during sleep as during wakefulness, although sometimes our imaginations are then just as lively and acute, or even more so, Reason tells us that since our thoughts cannot possibly be all true, because we are not altogether perfect, that which they have of truth must infallibly be met with in our waking experience rather than in that of our dreams.

PART V

I should be very glad to proceed to show forth the complete chain of truths which I have deduced from these first, but because to do this it would have been necessary now to speak of many matters of dispute among the learned, with whom I have no desire to embroil myself, I think that it will be better to abstain. I shall only state generally what these truths are, so that it may be left to the decision of those best able to judge whether it would be of use for the public to be more particularly informed of them or not. I always remained firm in the resolution which I had made, not to assume any other principle than that of which I have just made use, in order to demonstrate the existence of God and of the Soul, and to accept nothing as true which did not appear to be more clear and more certain than the demonstrations of the geometricians had formerly seemed. And nevertheless I venture to say that not only have I found the means of satisfying myself in a short time as to the more important of those difficulties usually dealt with in philosophy, but I have also observed certain laws which God has so established in Nature, and of which He has imprinted such ideas on our minds, that, after having reflected sufficiently upon the matter, we cannot doubt their being accurately observed in all that exists or is done in the world. Further, in considering the sequence of these laws, it seems to me that I have discovered many truths more useful and more important than all that I had formerly learned or even hoped to learn.

But because I tried to explain the most important of these in a Treatise[4] which certain considerations prevented me from publishing, I cannot do better, in making them known, than here summarise briefly what that Treatise contains. I had planned to comprise in it all that I believed myself to know regarding the nature of material objects, before I set myself to write. However, just as the painters who cannot represent equally well on a plain surface all the various sides of a solid body, make selection of one of the most important, which alone is set in the light, while the others are put in

4. i.e., 'Le Monde,' suppressed on hearing of Galileo's condemnation.

shadow and made to appear only as they may be seen in looking at the former, so, fearing that I could not put in my Treatise all that I had in my mind, I undertook only to show very fully my conceptions of light. Later on, when occasion occurred, I resolved to add something about the sun and fixed stars, because light proceeds almost entirely from them; the heavens would be dealt with because they transmit light, the planets, the comets and the earth because they reflect it, and more particularly would all bodies which are on the earth, because they are either coloured or transparent, or else luminous; and finally I should deal with man because he is the spectator of all. For the very purpose of putting all these topics somewhat in shadow, and being able to express myself freely about them, without being obliged to adopt or to refute the opinions which are accepted by the learned, I resolved to leave all this world to their disputes, and to speak only of what would happen in a new world if God now created, somewhere in an imaginary space, matter sufficient wherewith to form it, and if He agitated in diverse ways, and without any order, the diverse portions of this matter, so that there resulted a chaos as confused as the poets ever feigned, and concluded His work by merely lending His concurrence to Nature in the usual way, leaving her to act in accordance with the laws which He had established. So, to begin with, I described this matter and tried to represent it in such a way, that it seems to me that nothing in the world could be more clear or intelligible, excepting what has just been said of God and the Soul. For I even went so far as expressly to assume that there was in it none of these forms or qualities which are so debated in the Schools, nor anything at all the knowledge of which is not so natural to our minds that none could even pretend to be ignorant of it. Further I pointed out what are the laws of Nature, and, without resting my reasons on any other principle than the infinite perfections of God, I tried to demonstrate all those of which one could have any doubt, and to show that they are of such a nature that even if God had created other worlds, He could not have created any in which these laws would fail to be observed. After that, I showed how the greatest part of the matter of which this chaos is constituted, must, in accordance with these laws, dispose and arrange itself in such a fashion as to render it similar to our heavens; and how meantime some of its parts must form an earth, some planets and comets, and some others a sun and fixed stars. And, enlarging on the subject of light, I here explained at length the nature of the light which would be found in the sun and stars, and how from these it crossed in an instant the immense space of the heavens, and how it was reflected from the planets and comets to the earth. To this I also added many things touching the substance, situation, movements, and all the different qualities of these heavens and stars, so that I thought I had said enough to make it clear that there is nothing to be seen in the heavens and stars pertaining to our system which must not, or at least may not, appear exactly the same in those of the system which I described. From this point I came to speak more particularly of the earth, showing how, though I had expressly presupposed that God had not placed any weight in the matter of which it is composed, its parts did not fail all to gravitate exactly to its centre; and how, having water and air on its surface, the disposition of the heavens and of the stars, more particularly of the moon, must cause a flux or reflux, which in all its circumstances is similar to that which is observed in our seas, and besides that, a certain current both of water and air from east to west, such as may also be observed in the tropics. I also showed how the mountains, seas, fountains and rivers, could naturally be formed in it, how the metals came to be in the mines and the plants to grow in the fields; and generally how all bodies, called mixed or composite, might arise. And because I knew nothing but fire which could produce light, excepting the stars, I studied amongst other things to make very clear all that pertains to its nature, how it is formed, how nourished, how there is sometimes only heat without light, and sometimes light without heat; I showed, too, how different colours might by it be induced upon different bodies and qualities of diverse kinds, how some of these were liquefied and others solidified, how nearly all can be consumed or converted into ashes and smoke by its means, and finally how of these ashes, by the intensity of its action alone, it forms glass. Since this transformation of ashes into glass seemed to me as wonderful as any other process in nature, I took particular pleasure in describing it.

I did not at the same time wish to infer from all these facts that this world has been created in the manner which I described; for it is much more probable that at the beginning God made it such as it was to be. But it is certain, and it is an opinion commonly received by the theologians, that the action by which He now preserves it is just the same as that by which He at first created it. In this way, although He had not, to begin with, given this world any other form than that of chaos, provided that the laws of nature had once been established and that He had lent His aid in order that its action should be according to its wont, we may well believe, without doing outrage to the miracle of creation, that by this means alone all things which are purely material might in course of time have become such as we observe them to be at present; and their nature is much easier to understand when we see them coming to pass little by little in this manner, than were we to consider them as all complete to begin with.

From a description of inanimate bodies and plants I passed on to that of animals, and particularly to that of men. But since I had not yet sufficient knowledge to speak of them in the same style as of the rest, that is to say, demonstrating the effects from the causes, and showing from what beginnings and in what fashion Nature must produce them, I contented myself with supposing that God formed the body of man altogether like one of ours, in the outward figure of its members as well as in the interior conformation of its organs, without making use of any matter other than that which I had described, and without at the first placing in it a rational soul, or any other thing which might serve as a vegetative or as a sensitive soul; excepting that He kindled in the heart one of these fires without light, which I have already described, and which I did not conceive of as in any way different from that which makes the hay heat when shut up before it is dry, and which makes new wine grow frothy when it is left to ferment over the fruit. For, examining the functions which might in accordance with this supposition exist in this body, I found precisely all those which might exist in us without our having the power of thought, and consequently without our soul – that is to say, this part of us, distinct from the body, of which it has just been said that its nature is to think – contributing to it, functions which are identically the same as those in which animals lacking reason may be said to resemble us. For all that, I could not find in these functions any which, being dependent on thought, pertain to us alone, inasmuch as we are men; while I found all of them afterwards, when I assumed that God had created a rational soul and that He had united it to this body in a particular manner which I described.

But in order to show how I there treated of this matter, I wish here to set forth the explanation of the movement of heart and arteries which, being the first and most general movement that is observed in animals, will give us the means of easily judging as to what we ought to think about all the rest. And so that there may be less difficulty in understanding what I shall say on this matter, I should like that those not versed in anatomy should take the trouble, before reading this, of having cut up before their eyes the heart of some large animal which has lungs (for it is in all respects sufficiently similar to the heart of a man), and cause that there be demonstrated to them the two chambers or cavities which are within it. There is first of all that which is on the right side, with which two very large tubes or channels correspond, viz. the *vena cava*, which is the principal receptacle of the blood, and so to speak the trunk of a tree of which all the other veins of the body are the branches; and there is the arterial vein which has been badly named because it is nothing but an artery which, taking its origin from the heart, divides, after having issued from it, into many branches which proceed to disperse themselves all through the lungs. Then there is secondly the cavity on the left side with which there again correspond two tubes which are as large or larger than the preceding, viz. the venous artery, which has also been badly named, because it is nothing but a vein which comes from the lungs, where it is divided into many branches, interlaced with those of the arterial vein, and with those of the tube which is called the windpipe, through which enters the air which we breathe; and the great artery which, issuing from the heart, sends its branches throughout the body. I should also wish that the eleven little membranes, which, like so many doors, open and shut the four entrances which are in these two cavities, should be carefully shown. There are of these three at the entrance of the *vena cava*, where they are so arranged that they can in nowise prevent the blood which it contains from flowing into the right cavity of the heart and yet exactly prevent its issuing out; there are three at the entrance to the arterial vein, which, being arranged quite the other way, easily allow the blood which is in this cavity to pass into the lungs, but not that which is already in the lungs to return to this cavity. There are also two others at the entrance of the venous artery, which allow the blood in the lungs to flow towards the left cavity of the heart, but do not permit its return; and three at the entrance of the great artery, which allow the blood to flow from the heart, but prevent its return. There is then no cause to seek for any other reason for the number of these membranes, except that the opening of the venous artery being oval, because of the situation where it is met with, may be conveniently closed with two membranes, while the others, being round, can be better closed with three. Further, I should have my readers consider that the grand artery and the arterial vein are much harder and firmer than are the venous artery and the *vena cava*; and that these two last expand before entering the heart, and there form so to speak two pockets called the auricles of the heart, which are composed of a tissue similar to its own; and also that there is always more heat in the heart than in any other part of the body; and finally that this heat is capable of causing any drop of blood that enters into its cavities promptly to expand and dilate, as liquids usually do when they are allowed to fall drop by drop into some very hot vessel.

After this I do not need to say anything with a view to explaining the movement of the heart, except that when its cavities are not full of blood there necessarily flows from the *vena cava* into the right cavity, and from the venous artery into the left, enough blood to keep these two vessels always full, and being full, that their orifices, which are turned towards the heart, cannot then be closed. But as soon as two drops of blood have thus entered, one into each of the cavities, these drops, which cannot be otherwise than very large, because the openings by which they enter are very wide and the vessels from whence they come are very full of blood, rarefy and dilate because of the heat which they find there. By this means, causing the whole heart to expand, they force home and close the five little doors which are at the entrances of the two vessels whence they flow, thus preventing any more blood from coming down into the heart; and becoming more and more rarefied, they push open the six doors which are in the entrances of the two other vessels through which they make their exit, by this means causing all the branches of the arterial vein and of the great artery to expand almost at the same instant as the heart. This last immediately afterward contracts as do also the arteries, because the blood which has entered them has cooled; and the six little doors close up again, and the five doors of the *vena cava* and of the venous artery re-open and make a way for two other drops of blood which cause the heart and the arteries once more to expand, just as we saw before. And because the blood which then enters the heart passes through these two pouches which are called auricles, it comes to pass that their movement is contrary to the movement of the heart, and that they contract when it expands. For the rest, in order that those who do not know the force of mathematical demonstration and are unaccustomed to distinguish true reasons from merely probable reasons, should not venture to deny what has been said without examination, I wish to acquaint them with the fact that this movement which I have just explained follows as necessarily from the very disposition of the organs, as can be seen by looking at the heart, and from the heat which can be felt with the fingers, and from the nature of the blood of which we can learn by experience, as does that of a clock from the power, the situation, and the form, of its counterpoise and of its wheels.

But if we ask how the blood in the veins does not exhaust itself in thus flowing continually into the heart, and how the arteries do not become too full of blood, since all that passes through the heart flows into them, I need only reply by stating what has already been written by an English physician,[5] to whom the credit of having broken the ice in this matter must be ascribed, as also of being the first to teach that there are many little tubes at the extremities of the arteries whereby the blood that they receive from the heart enters the little branches of the veins, whence it returns once more to the heart; in this way its course is just a perpetual circulation. He proves this very clearly by the common experience of surgeons, who, by binding the arm moderately firmly above the place where they open the vein, cause the

5. Harvey (Latin Tr.).

blood to issue more abundantly than it would have done if they had not bound it at all; while quite a contrary result would occur if they bound it below, between the hand and the opening, or if they bound it very firmly above. For it is clear that when the bandage is moderately tight, though it may prevent the blood already in the arm from returning to the heart by the veins, it cannot for all that prevent more blood from coming anew by the arteries, because these are situated below the veins, and their walls, being stronger, are less easy to compress; and also that the blood which comes from the heart tends to pass by means of the arteries to the hand with greater force than it does to return from the hand to the heart by the veins. And because this blood escapes from the arm by the opening which is made in one of the veins, there must necessarily be some passages below the ligature, that is to say, towards the extremities of the arm, through which it can come thither from the arteries. This physician likewise proves very clearly the truth of that which he says of the course of the blood, by the existence of certain little membranes or valves which are so arranged in different places along the course of the veins, that they do not permit the blood to pass from the middle of the body towards the extremities, but only to return from the extremities to the heart; and further by the experiment which shows that all the blood which is in the body may issue from it in a very short time by means of one single artery that has been cut, and this is so even when it is very tightly bound very near the heart, and cut between it and the ligature, so that there could be no ground for supposing that the blood which flowed out of it could proceed from any other place but the heart.

But there are many other things which demonstrate that the true cause of this motion of the blood is that which I have stated. To begin with, the difference which is seen between the blood which issues from the veins, and that which issues from the arteries, can only proceed from the fact, that, being rarefied, and so to speak distilled by passing through the heart, it is more subtle and lively and warmer immediately after leaving the heart (that is to say, when in the arteries) than it is a little while before entering it (that is, when in the veins). And if attention be paid, we shall find that this difference does not appear clearly, excepting in the vicinity of the heart, and is not so clear in those parts which are further removed from it. Further, the consistency of the coverings of which the arterial vein and the great artery are composed, shows clearly enough that the blood beats against them with more force than it does in the case of the veins. And why should the left cavity of the heart and the great artery be larger and wider than the right cavity and the arterial vein, if it is not that the blood of the venous artery having only been in the lungs since it had passed through the heart, is more subtle and rarefies more effectively and easily than that which proceeds immediately from the *vena cava*? And what is it that the physicians can discover in feeling the pulse, unless they know that, according as the blood changes its nature, it may be rarefied by the warmth of the heart in a greater or less degree, and more or less quickly than before? And if we inquire how this heat is communicated to the other members, must it not be allowed that it is by means of the blood which, passing through the heart, is heated once again and thence is spread throughout all the body? From this it happens that if we take away the blood from any particular part, by that same means we take away from it the heat; even if the heart were as ardent as a red hot iron it would not suffice to heat up the feet and hands as it actually does, unless it continually sent out to them new blood. We further understand from this that the true use of respiration is to carry sufficient fresh air into the lungs to cause the blood, which comes there from the right cavity of the heart, where it has been rarefied and so to speak transformed into vapours, to thicken, and become anew converted into blood before falling into the left cavity, without which process it would not be fit to serve as fuel for the fire which there exists. We are confirmed in this statement by seeing that the animals which have no lungs have also but one cavity in their hearts, and that in children, who cannot use them while still within their mother's wombs, there is an opening by which the blood flows from the *vena cava* into the left cavity of the heart, and a conduit through which it passes from the arterial vein into the great artery without passing through the lung. Again, how could digestion be carried on in the stomach if the heart did not send heat there by the arteries, and along with this some of the more fluid parts of the blood which aid in dissolving the foods which have been there placed? And is not the action which converts the juice of foods into blood easy to understand if we consider that it is distilled by passing and repassing through the heart possibly more than one or two hundred times in a day? What further need is there to explain the process of nutrition and the production of the different humours which are in the body, if we can say that the force with which the blood, in being rarefied, passes from the heart towards the extremities of the arteries, causes some of its parts to remain among those of the members where they are found and there to take the place of others which they oust; and that according to the situation or form or smallness of the little pores which they encounter, certain ones proceed to certain parts rather than others, just as a number of different sieves variously perforated, as everyone has probably seen, are capable of separating different species of grain? And finally what in all this is most remarkable of all, is the generation of the animal spirits, which resemble a very subtle wind, or rather a flame which is very pure and very vivid, and which, continually rising up in great abundance from the heart to the brain, thence proceeds through the nerves to the muscles, thereby giving the power of motion to all the members. And it is not necessary to suppose any other cause to explain how the particles of blood, which, being most agitated and most penetrating, are the most proper to constitute these spirits, proceed towards the brain rather than elsewhere, than that the arteries which carry them thither are those which proceed from the heart in the most direct lines, and that according to the laws of Mechanics, which are identical with those of Nature, when many objects tend to move together to the same point, where there is not room for all (as is the case with the particles of blood which issue from the left cavity of the heart and tend to go towards the brain), the weakest and least agitated parts must necessarily be turned aside by those that are stronger, which by this means are the only ones to reach it.

I had explained all these matters in some detail in the Treatise which I formerly intended to publish. And afterwards I had shown there, what must be the fabric of the nerves and muscles of the human body in order that the animal spirits therein contained should have the power to move the members, just as the heads of animals, a little while after decapitation, are still observed to move and bite the earth, notwithstanding that they are no longer animate; what changes are necessary in the brain to cause wakefulness, sleep and dreams; how light, sounds, smells, tastes, heat and all other qualities pertaining to external objects are able to imprint on it various ideas by the intervention of the senses; how hunger, thirst and other internal affections can also convey their impressions upon it; what should be regarded as the 'common sense' by which these ideas are received, and what is meant by the memory which retains them, by the fancy which can change them in diverse ways and out of them constitute new ideas, and which, by the same means, distributing the animal spirits through the muscles, can cause the members of such a body to move in as many diverse ways, and in a manner as suitable to the objects which present themselves to its senses and to its internal passions, as can happen in our own case apart from the direction of our free will. And this will not seem strange to those, who, knowing how many different *automata* or moving machines can be made by the industry of man, without employing in so doing more than a very few parts in comparison with the great multitude of bones, muscles, nerves, arteries, veins, or other parts that are found in the body of each animal. From this aspect the body is regarded as a machine which, having been made by the hands of God, is incomparably better arranged, and possesses in itself movements which are much more admirable, than any of those which can be invented by man. Here I specially stopped to show that if there had been such machines, possessing the organs and outward form of a monkey or some other animal without reason, we should not have had any means of ascertaining that they were not of the same nature as those animals. On the other hand, if there were machines which bore a resemblance to our body and imitated our actions as far as it was morally possible to do so, we should always have two very certain tests by which to recognise that, for all that, they were not real men. The first is, that they could never use speech or other signs as we do when placing our thoughts on record for the benefit of others. For we can easily understand a machine's being constituted so that it can utter words, and even emit some responses to action on it of a corporeal kind, which brings about a change in its organs; for instance, if it is touched in a particular part it may ask what we wish to say to it; if in another part it may exclaim that it is being hurt, and so on. But it never happens that it arranges its speech in various ways, in order to reply appropriately to everything that may be said in its presence, as even the lowest type of man can do. And the second difference is, that although machines can perform certain things as well as or perhaps better than any of us can do, they infallibly fall short in others, by the which means we may discover that they did not act from knowledge, but only from the disposition of their organs. For while reason is a universal instrument which can serve for all contingencies, these organs have need of some special adaptation for every particular action. From this it follows that it is morally impossible that there should be sufficient diversity in any machine to allow it to act in all the events of life in the same way as our reason causes us to act.

By these two methods we may also recognise the difference that exists between men and brutes. For it is a very remarkable fact that there are none so depraved and stupid, without even excepting idiots, that they cannot arrange different words together, forming of them a statement by which they make known their thoughts; while, on the other hand, there is no other animal, however perfect and fortunately circumstanced it may be, which can do the same. It is not the want of organs that brings this to pass, for it is evident that magpies and parrots are able to utter words just like ourselves, and yet they cannot speak as we do, that is, so as to give evidence that they think of what they say. On the other hand, men who, being born deaf and dumb, are in the same degree, or even more than the brutes, destitute of the organs which serve the others for talking, are in the habit of themselves inventing certain signs by which they make themselves understood by those who, being usually in their company, have leisure to learn their language. And this does not merely show that the brutes have less reason than men, but that they have none at all, since it is clear that very little is required in order to be able to talk. And when we notice the inequality that exists between animals of the same species, as well as between men, and observe that some are more capable of receiving instruction than others, it is not credible that a monkey or a parrot, selected as the most perfect of its species, should not in these matters equal the stupidest child to be found, or at least a child whose mind is clouded, unless in the case of the brute the soul were of an entirely different nature from ours. And we ought not to confound speech with natural movements which betray passions and may be imitated by machines as well as be manifested by animals; nor must we think, as did some of the ancients, that brutes talk, although we do not understand their language. For if this were true, since they have many organs which are allied to our own, they could communicate their thoughts to us just as easily as to those of their own race. It is also a very remarkable fact that although there are many animals which exhibit more dexterity than we do in some of their actions, we at the same time observe that they do not manifest any dexterity at all in many others. Hence the fact that they do better than we do, does not prove that they are endowed with mind, for in this case they would have more reason than any of us, and would surpass us in all other things. It rather shows that they have no reason at all, and that it is nature which acts in them according to the disposition of their organs, just as a clock, which is only composed of wheels and weights is able to tell the hours and measure the time more correctly than we can do with all our wisdom.

I had described after this the rational soul and shown that it could not be in any way derived from the power of matter, like the other things of which I had spoken, but that it must be expressly created. I showed, too, that it is not sufficient that it should be lodged in the human body like a pilot in his ship, unless perhaps for the moving of its members, but that it is necessary that it should also be joined and united more closely to the body in order to have sensations and appetites similar to our own, and thus to form a true man. In conclusion, I have here enlarged a little on the subject of the soul, because it is one of the greatest importance. For next to the error of those who deny God, which I think I have already sufficiently refuted, there is none which is more effectual in leading feeble spirits from the straight path of virtue, than to imagine that the soul of the brute is of the same nature as our own, and that in consequence, after this life we have nothing to fear or to hope for, any more than the flies and ants. As a matter of fact, when one comes to know how greatly they differ, we understand much better the reasons which go to prove that our soul is in its nature entirely independent of body, and in consequence that it is not liable to die with it. And then, inasmuch as we observe no other causes capable of destroying it, we are naturally inclined to judge that it is immortal.

PART VI

It is three years since I arrived at the end of the Treatise which contained all these things; and I was commencing to revise it in order to place it in the hands of a printer, when I learned that certain persons, to whose opinions I defer, and whose authority cannot have less weight with my actions than my own reason has over my thoughts, had disapproved of a physical theory published a little while before by another person.[6] I will not say that I agreed with this opinion, but only that before their censure I observed in it nothing which I could possibly imagine to be prejudicial either to Religion or the State, or consequently which could have prevented me from giving expression to it in writing, if my reason had persuaded me to do so: and this made me fear that among my own opinions one might be found which should be misunderstood, notwithstanding the great care which I have always taken not to accept any new beliefs unless I had very certain proof of their truth, and not to give expression to what could tend to the disadvantage of any person. This sufficed to cause me to alter the resolution which I had made to publish. For, although the reasons for my former resolution were very strong, my inclination, which always made me hate the profession of writing books, caused me immediately to find plenty of other reasons for excusing myself from doing so. And these reasons, on the one side and on the other, are of such a nature that not only have I here some interest in giving expression to them, but possibly the public may also have some interest in knowing them.

I have never made much of those things which proceed from my own mind, and so long as I culled no other fruits from the Method which I use, beyond that of satisfying myself respecting certain difficulties which pertain to the speculative sciences, or trying to regulate my conduct by the reasons which it has taught me, I never believed myself to be obliged to write anything about it. For as regards that which concerns conduct, everyone is so confident of his own common sense, that there might be found as many reformers as heads, if it were permitted that others than those whom God has established as the sovereigns of his people, or at least to whom He

6. i.e., Galileo.

has given sufficient grace and zeal to be prophets, should be allowed to make any changes in that. And, although my speculations give me the greatest pleasure, I believed that others also had speculations which possibly pleased them even more. But so soon as I had acquired some general notions concerning Physics, and as, beginning to make use of them in various special difficulties, I observed to what point they might lead us, and how much they differ from the principles of which we have made use up to the present time, I believed that I could not keep them concealed without greatly sinning against the law which obliges us to procure, as much as in us lies, the general good of all mankind. For they caused me to see that it is possible to attain knowledge which is very useful in life, and that, instead of that speculative philosophy which is taught in the Schools, we may find a practical philosophy by means of which, knowing the force and the action of fire, water, air, the stars, heavens and all other bodies that environ us, as distinctly as we know the different crafts of our artisans, we can in the same way employ them in all those uses to which they are adapted, and thus render ourselves the masters and possessors of nature. This is not merely to be desired with a view to the invention of an infinity of arts and crafts which enable us to enjoy without any trouble the fruits of the earth and all the good things which are to be found there, but also principally because it brings about the preservation of health, which is without doubt the chief blessing and the foundation of all other blessings in this life. For the mind depends so much on the temperament and disposition of the bodily organs that, if it is possible to find a means of rendering men wiser and cleverer than they have hitherto been, I believe that it is in medicine that it must be sought. It is true that the medicine which is now in vogue contains little of which the utility is remarkable; but, without having any intention of decrying it, I am sure that there is no one, even among those who make its study a profession, who does not confess that all that men know is almost nothing in comparison with what remains to be known; and that we could be free of an infinitude of maladies both of body and mind, and even also possibly of the infirmities of age, if we had sufficient knowledge of their causes, and of all the remedies with which nature has provided us. But, having the intention of devoting all my life to the investigation of a knowledge which is so essential, and having discovered a path which appears to me to be of such a nature that we must by its means infallibly reach our end if we pursue it, unless, indeed, we are prevented by the shortness of life or by lack of experience, I judged that there was no better provision against these two impediments than faithfully to communicate to the public the little which I should myself have discovered, and to beg all well-inclined persons to proceed further by contributing, each one according to his own inclination and ability, to the experiments which must be made, and then to communicate to the public all the things which they might discover, in order that the last should commence where the preceding had left off; and thus, by joining together the lives and labours of many, we should collectively proceed much further than any one in particular could succeed in doing.

I remarked also respecting experiments, that they become so much the more necessary the more one is advanced in knowledge, for to begin with it is better to make use simply of those which present themselves spontaneously to our senses, and of which we could not be ignorant provided that we reflected ever so little, rather than to seek out those which are more rare and recondite; the reason of this is that those which are more rare often mislead us so long as we do not know the causes of the more common, and the fact that the circumstances on which they depend are almost always so particular and so minute that it is very difficult to observe them. But in this the order which I have followed is as follows: I have first tried to discover generally the principles or first causes of everything that is or that can be in the world, without considering anything that might accomplish this end but God Himself who has created the world, or deriving them from any source excepting from certain germs of truths which are naturally existent in our souls. After that I considered which were the primary and most ordinary effects which might be deduced from these causes, and it seems to me that in this way I discovered the heavens, the stars, an earth, and even on the earth, water, air, fire, the minerals and some other such things, which are the most common and simple of any that exist, and consequently the easiest to know. Then, when I wished to descend to those which were more particular, so many objects of various kinds presented themselves to me, that I did not think it was possible for the human mind to distinguish the forms or species of bodies which are on the earth from an infinitude of others which might have been so if it had been the will of God to place them there, or consequently to apply them to our use, if it were not that we arrive at the causes by the effects, and avail ourselves of many particular experiments. In subsequently passing over in my mind all the objects which have ever been presented to my senses, I can truly venture to say that I have not there observed anything which I could not easily explain by the principles which I had discovered. But I must also confess that the power of nature is so ample and so vast, and these principles are so simple and general, that I observed hardly any particular effect as to which I could not at once recognise that it might be deduced from the principles in many different ways; and my greatest difficulty is usually to discover in which of these ways the effect does depend upon them. As to that, I do not know any other plan but again to try to find experiments of such a nature that their result is not the same if it has to be explained by one of the methods, as it would be if explained by the other. For the rest, I have now reached a position in which I discern, as it seems to me, sufficiently clearly what course must be adopted in order to make the majority of the experiments which may conduce to carry out this end. But I also perceive that they are of such a nature, and of so great a number, that neither my hands nor my income, though the latter were a thousand times larger than it is, could suffice for the whole; so that just in proportion as henceforth I shall have the power of carrying out more of them or less, shall I make more or less progress in arriving at a knowledge of nature. This is what I had promised myself to make known by the Treatise which I had written, and to demonstrate in it so clearly the advantage which the public might receive from it, that I should induce all those who have the good of mankind at heart – that is to say, all those who are really virtuous in fact, and not only by a false semblance or by opinion – both to communicate to me those experiments that they have already carried out, and to help me in the investigation of those that still remain to be accomplished.

But I have since that time found other reasons which caused me to change my opinion, and consider that I should indeed continue to put in writing all the things which I judged to be of importance whenever I discovered them to be true, and that I should bestow on them the same care as I should have done had I wished to have them printed. I did this because it would give me so much the more occasion to examine them carefully (for there is no doubt that we always scrutinize more closely what we think will be seen by many, than what is done simply for ourselves, and often the things which have seemed true to me when I began to think about them, seemed false when I tried to place them on paper); and because I did not desire to lose any opportunity of benefiting the public if I were able to do so, and in order that if my works have any value, those into whose hands they will fall after my death, might have the power of making use of them as seems best to them. I, however, resolved that I should not consent to their being published during my lifetime, so that neither the contradictions and controversies to which they might possibly give rise, nor even the reputation, such as it might be, which they would bring to me, should give me any occasion to lose the time which I meant to set apart for my own instruction. For although it is true that each man is obliged to procure, as much as in him lies, the good of others, and that to be useful to nobody is popularly speaking to be worthless, it is at the same time true that our cares should extend further than the present time, and that it is good to set aside those things which may possibly be adapted to bring profit to the living, when we have in view the accomplishment of other ends which will bring much more advantage to our descendants. In the same way I should much like that men should know that the little which I have learned hitherto is almost nothing in comparison with that of which I am ignorant, and with the knowledge of which I do not despair of being able to attain. For it is much the same with those who little by little discover the truth in the Sciences, as with those who, commencing to become rich, have less trouble in obtaining great acquisitions than they formerly experienced, when poorer, in arriving at those much smaller in amount. Or we might compare them to the Generals of our armies, whose forces usually grow in proportion to their victories, and who require more leadership in order to hold together their troops after the loss of a battle, than is needed to take towns and provinces after having obtained a success. For he really gives battle who attempts to conquer all the difficulties and errors which prevent him from arriving at a knowledge of the truth, and it is to lose a battle to admit a false opinion touching a matter of any generality and importance. Much more skill is required in order to recover the position that one beforehand held, than is necessary to make great progress when one already possesses principles which are assured. For myself, if I have succeeded in discovering certain truths in the Sciences (and I hope that the matters contained in this volume will show that I have discovered some), I may say that they are resultant from, and dependent on, five or six principal difficulties which I have surmounted, and my encounter with these I look upon as so many battles in which I have had fortune on my side. I will not even hesitate to say that I think I shall have no need to win more than two or three other victories similar in kind in order to reach the accomplishment of my plans. And my age is not so advanced but that, in the ordinary course of nature, I may still have sufficient leisure for this end. But I believe myself to be so much the more bound to make the most of the time which remains, as I have the greater hope of being able to employ it well. And without doubt I should have many chances of being robbed of it, were I to publish the foundations of my Physics; for though these are nearly all so evident that it is only necessary to understand them in order to accept them, and although there are none of them as to which I do not believe myself capable of giving demonstration, yet because it is impossible that they should accord with all the various opinions of other men, I foresee that I should often be diverted from my main design by the opposition which they would bring to birth.

    We may say that these contradictions might be useful both in making me aware of my errors, and, supposing that I had reached some satisfactory conclusion, in bringing others to a fuller understanding of my speculations; and, as many can see more than can a single man, they might help in leading others who from the present time may begin to avail themselves of my system, to assist me likewise with their discoveries. But though I recognise that I am extremely liable to err, and though I almost never trust the first reflections that I arrive at, the experience which I have had of the objections which may be made to my system prevents my having any hope of deriving profit from them. For I have often had experience of the judgments both of those whom I have esteemed as my friends, and of some others to whom I believed myself to be indifferent, and even, too, of some whose ill-feeling and envy would, I felt sure, make them endeavour to reveal what affection concealed from the eyes of my friends. But rarely has it happened that any objection has been made which I did not in some sort foresee, unless where it was something very far removed from my subject. In this way hardly ever have I encountered any censor of my opinions who did not appear to me to be either less rigorous or less judicial than myself. And I certainly never remarked that by means of disputations employed by the Schools any truth has been discovered of which we were formerly ignorant. And so long as each side attempts to vanquish his opponent, there is a much more serious attempt to establish probability than to weigh the reasons on either side; and those who have for long been excellent pleaders are not for that reason the best judges.

As to the advantage which others may receive from the communication of my reflections, it could not be very great, inasmuch as I have not yet carried them so far as that it is not necessary to add many things before they can be brought into practice. And I think I can without vanity say that if anyone is capable of doing this, it should be myself rather than another – not indeed that there may not be in the world many minds incomparably superior to my own, but because no one can so well understand a thing and make it his own when learnt from another as when it is discovered for himself. As regards the matter in hand there is so much truth in this, that although I have often explained some of my opinions to persons of very good intelligence, who, while I talked to them appeared to understand them very clearly, yet when they recounted them I remarked that they had almost always altered them in such a manner that I could no longer acknowledge them as mine. On this account I am very glad to have the opportunity here of begging my descendants never to believe that what is told to them proceeded from myself unless I have myself divulged it. And I do not in the least wonder at the extravagances attributed to all the ancient philosophers whose writings we do not possess, nor do I judge from these that their thoughts were very unreasonable, considering that theirs were the best minds of the time they lived in, but only that they have been imperfectly represented to us. We see, too, that it hardly ever happens that any of their disciples surpassed them, and I am sure that those who most passionately follow Aristotle now-a-days would think themselves happy if they had as much knowledge of nature as he had, even if this were on the condition that they should never attain to any more. They are like the ivy that never tries to mount above the trees which give it support, and which often even descends again after it has reached their summit; for it appears to me that such men also sink again – that is to say, somehow render themselves more ignorant than they would have been had they abstained from study altogether. For, not content with knowing all that is intelligibly explained in their author, they wish in addition to find in him the solution of many difficulties of which he says nothing, and in regard to which he possibly had no thought at all. At the same time their mode of philosophising is very convenient for those who have abilities of a very mediocre kind, for the obscurity of the distinctions and principles of which they make use, is the reason of their being able to talk of all things as boldly as though they really knew about them, and defend all that they say against the most subtle and acute, without any one having the means of convincing them to the contrary. In this they seem to me like a blind man who, in order to fight on equal terms with one who sees, would have the latter to come into the bottom of a very dark cave. I may say, too, that it is in the interest of such people that I should abstain from publishing the principles of philosophy of which I make use, for, being so simple and evident as they are, I should, in publishing them, do the same as though I threw open the windows and caused daylight to enter the cave into which they have descended in order to fight. But even the best minds have no reason to desire to be acquainted with these principles, for if they wish to be able to talk of everything and acquire a reputation for learning, they will more readily attain their end by contenting themselves with the appearance of truth which may be found in all sorts of things without much trouble, than in seeking for truth which only reveals itself little by little in certain spheres, and which, when others come into question, obliges one to confess one's ignorance. If, however, they prefer the knowledge of some small amount of truth to the vanity of seeming to be ignorant of nothing, which knowledge is doubtless preferable, or if they desire to follow a course similar to my own, it is not necessary that I should say any more than what I have already said in this Discourse. For if they are capable of passing beyond the point I have reached, they will also so much the more be able to find by themselves all that I believe myself to have discovered; since, not having examined anything but in its order, it is certain that what remains for me to discover is in itself more difficult and more recondite than anything that I have hitherto been able to meet with, and they would have much less pleasure in learning from me than from themselves. Besides, the habit which they will acquire of seeking first things that are simple and then little by little and by degrees passing to others more difficult, will be of more use than could be all my instructions. For, as regards myself, I am persuaded that if from my youth up I had been taught all the truths of which I have since sought the demonstrations, or if I had not had any difficulty in learning them, I should perhaps never have known any others, or at least I should never have acquired the habit or facility which I think I have obtained, of ever finding them anew, in proportion as I set myself to seek for them. And, in a word, if there is any work at all which cannot be so well achieved by another as by him who has begun it, it is that at which I labour.

It is true as regards the experiments which may conduce to this end, that one man could not possibly accomplish all of them. But yet he could not, to good advantage, employ other hands than his own, excepting those of artisans or persons of that kind whom he could pay, and whom the hope of gain – which is a very effectual incentive – might cause to perform with exactitude all the things they were directed to accomplish. As to those who, whether by curiosity or desire to learn, might possibly offer him their voluntary assistance, not only are they usually more ready with promises than with performance, planning out fine sounding projects, none of which are ever realised, but they will also infallibly demand payment for their trouble by requesting the explanation of certain difficulties, or at least by empty compliments and useless talk, which could not occupy any of the student's time without causing it to be lost. And as to the experiments already made by others, even if they desired to communicate these to him – which those who term them secrets would never do – they are for the most part accompanied by so many circumstances or superfluous matter, that it would be very difficult for him to disentangle the truth. In addition to this he would find nearly all so badly explained, or even so false (because those who carried them out were forced to make them appear to be in conformity with their principles), that if there had been some which might have been of use to him, they would hardly be worth the time that would be required in making the selection. So true is this, that if there were anywhere in the world a person whom one knew to be assuredly capable of discovering matters of the highest importance and those of the greatest possible utility to the public, and if for this reason all other men were eager by every means in their power to help him in reaching the end which he set before him, I do not see that they could do anything for him beyond contributing to defray the expenses of the experiments which might be requisite, or, for the rest, seeing that he was not deprived of his leisure by the importunities of anyone. But, in addition to the fact that I neither esteem myself so highly as to be willing to promise anything extraordinary, nor give scope to an imagination so vain as to conceive that the public should interest itself greatly in my designs, I do not yet own a soul so base as to be willing to accept from anyone whatever a favour which it might be supposed I did not merit.

All those considerations taken together were, three years ago, the cause of my not desiring to publish the Treatise which I had on hand, and the reason why I even formed the resolution of not bringing to light during my life any other of so general a kind, or one by which the foundations of Physics could be understood. But since then two other reasons came into operation which compelled me to bring forward certain attempts, as I have done here, and to render to the public some account of my actions and designs. The first is that if I failed to do so, many who knew the intention I formerly had of publishing certain writings, might imagine that the causes for which I abstained from so doing were more to my disadvantage than they really were; for although I do not care immoderately for glory, or, if I dare say so, although I even hate it, inasmuch as I judge it to be antagonistic to the repose which I esteem above all other things, at the same time I never tried to conceal my actions as though they were crimes, nor have I used many precautions against being known, partly because I should have thought it damaging to myself, and partly because it would have given me a sort of disquietude which would again have militated against the perfect repose of spirit which I seek. And forasmuch as having in this way always held myself in a condition of indifference as regards whether I was known or was not known, I have not yet been able to prevent myself from acquiring some sort of reputation, I thought that I should do my best at least to prevent myself from acquiring an evil reputation. The other reason which obliged me to put this in writing is that I am becoming every day more and more alive to the delay which is being suffered in the design which I have of instructing myself, because of the lack of an infinitude of experiments, which it is impossible that I should perform without the aid of others: and although I do not flatter myself so much as to hope that the public should to any large degree participate in my interest, I yet do not wish to be found wanting, both on my own account, and as one day giving occasion to those who will survive me of reproaching me for the fact that I might have left many matters in a much better condition than I have done, had I not too much neglected to make them understand in what way they could have contributed to the accomplishment of my designs.

And I thought that it was easy for me to select certain matters which would not be the occasion for many controversies, nor yet oblige me to propound more of my principles than I wish, and which yet would suffice to allow a pretty clear manifestation of what I can do and what I cannot do in the sciences. In this I cannot say whether I have succeeded or have not succeeded, and I do not wish to anticipate the judgment of any one by myself speaking of my writings; but I shall be very glad if they will examine them. And in order that they may have the better opportunity of so doing, I beg all those who have any objections to offer to take the trouble of sending them to my publishers, so that, being made aware of them, I may try at the same time to subjoin my reply. By this means, the reader, seeing objections and reply at the same time, will the more easily judge of the truth; for I do not promise in any instance to make lengthy replies, but just to avow my errors very frankly if I am convinced of them; or, if I cannot perceive them, to say simply what I think requisite for the defence of the matters I have written, without adding the exposition of any new matter, so that I may not be endlessly engaged in passing from one side to the other.

If some of the matters of which I spoke in the beginning of the *Dioptrics* and *Meteors* should at first sight give offence because I call them hypotheses and do not appear to care about their proof, let them have the patience to read these in entirety, and I hope that they will find themselves satisfied. For it appears to me that the reasonings are so mutually interwoven, that as the later ones are demonstrated by the earlier, which are their causes, the earlier are reciprocally demonstrated by the later which are their effects. And it must not be imagined that in this I commit the fallacy which logicians name arguing in a circle, for, since experience renders the greater part of these effects very certain, the causes from which I deduce them do not so much serve to prove their existence as to explain them; on the other hand, the causes are explained by the effects. And I have not named them hypotheses with any other object than that it may be known that while I consider myself able to deduce them from the primary truths which I explained above, yet I particularly desired not to do so, in order that certain persons may not for this reason take occasion to build up some extravagant philosophic system on what they take to be my principles, and thus cause the blame to be put on me. I refer to those who imagine that in one day they may discover all that another has arrived at in twenty years of work, so soon as he has merely spoken to them two or three words on the subject; while they are really all the more subject to err, and less capable of perceiving the truth as they are the more subtle and lively. For as regards the opinions that are truly mine I do not apologise for them as being new, inasmuch as if we consider the reasons of them well, I assure myself that they will be found to be so simple and so conformable to common sense, as to appear less extraordinary and less paradoxical than any others which may be held on similar subjects. And I do not even boast of being the first discoverer of any of them, but only state that I have adopted them, not because they have been held by others, nor because they have not been so held, but only because Reason has persuaded me of their truth.

Even if artisans are not at once able to carry out the invention[7] explained in the *Dioptrics*, I do not for that reason think that it can be said that it is to be condemned; for, inasmuch as great address and practice is required to make and adjust the mechanism which I have described without omitting any detail, I should not be less astonished at their succeeding at the first effort than I should be supposing some one were in one day to learn to play the guitar with skill, just because a good sheet of musical notation were set up before him. And if I write in French which is the language of my country, rather than in Latin which is that of my teachers, that is because I hope that those who avail themselves only of their natural reason in its purity may be better judges of my opinions than those who believe only in the writings of the ancients; and as to those who unite good sense with study, whom alone I crave for my judges, they will not, I feel sure, be so partial to Latin as to refuse to follow my reasoning because I expound it in a vulgar tongue.

For the rest, I do not desire to speak here more particularly of the progress which I hope in the future to make in the sciences, nor to bind myself as regards the public with any promise which I shall not with certainty be able to fulfil. But I will just say that I have resolved not to employ the time which remains to me in life in any other matter than in endeavouring to acquire some knowledge of nature, which shall be of such a kind that it will enable us to arrive at rules for Medicine more assured than those which have as yet been attained; and my inclination is so strongly opposed to any other kind of pursuit, more especially to those which can only be useful to some by being harmful to others, that if certain circumstances had constrained me to employ them, I do not think that I should have been capable of succeeding. In so saying I make a declaration that I know very

---

7. Doubtless the machine for the purpose of cutting lenses which Descartes so minutely describes.

well cannot help me to make myself of consideration in the world, but to this end I have no desire to attain; and I shall always hold myself to be more indebted to those by whose favour I may enjoy my leisure without hindrance, than I shall be to any who may offer me the most honourable position in all the world.

Meditations on First Philosophy

TO THE MOST WISE AND ILLUSTRIOUS THE DEAN
AND DOCTORS OF THE SACRED FACULTY
OF THEOLOGY IN PARIS.

The motive which induces me to present to you this Treatise is so excellent, and, when you become acquainted with its design, I am convinced that you will also have so excellent a motive for taking it under your protection, that I feel that I cannot do better, in order to render it in some sort acceptable to you, than in a few words to state what I have set myself to do.

I have always considered that the two questions respecting God and the Soul were the chief of those that ought to be demonstrated by philosophical rather than theological argument. For although it is quite enough for us faithful ones to accept by means of faith the fact that the human soul does not perish with the body, and that God exists, it certainly does not seem possible ever to persuade infidels of any religion, indeed, we may almost say, of any moral virtue, unless, to begin with, we prove these two facts by means of the natural reason. And inasmuch as often in this life greater rewards are offered for vice than for virtue, few people would prefer the right to the useful, were they restrained neither by the fear of God nor the expectation of another life; and although it is absolutely true that we must believe that there is a God, because we are so taught in the Holy Scriptures, and, on the other hand, that we must believe the Holy Scriptures because they come from God (the reason of this is, that, faith being a gift of God, He who gives the grace to cause us to believe other things can likewise give it to cause us to believe that He exists), we nevertheless could not place this argument before infidels, who might accuse us of reasoning in a circle. And, in truth, I have noticed that you, along with all the theologians, did not only affirm that the existence of God may be proved by the natural reason, but also that it may be inferred from the Holy Scriptures, that knowledge about Him is much clearer than that which we have of many created things, and, as a matter of fact, is so easy to acquire, that those who have it not are culpable in their ignorance. This indeed appears from the Wisdom of Solomon, chapter xiii, where it is said *'Howbeit they are not to be excused; for if their understanding was so great that they could discern the world and the creatures, why did they not rather find out the Lord thereof?'* and in Romans, chapter i, it is said that they are *'without excuse'*; and again in the same place, by these words *'that which may be known of God is manifest in them,'* it seems as though we were shown that all that which can be known of God may be made manifest by means which are not derived from anywhere but from ourselves, and from the simple consideration of the nature of our minds. Hence I thought it not beside my purpose to inquire how this is so, and how God may be more easily and certainly known than the things of the world.

And as regards the soul, although many have considered that it is not easy to know its nature, and some have even dared to say that human reasons have convinced us that it would perish with the body, and that faith alone could believe the contrary, nevertheless, inasmuch as the Lateran Council held under Leo X (in the eighth session) condemns these tenets, and as Leo expressly ordains Christian philosophers to refute their arguments and to employ all their powers in making known the truth, I have ventured in this treatise to undertake the same task.

More than that, I am aware that the principal reason which causes many impious persons not to desire to believe that there is a God, and that the human soul is distinct from the body, is that they declare that hitherto no one has been able to demonstrate these two facts; and although I am not of their opinion but, on the contrary, hold that the greater part of the reasons which have been brought forward concerning these two questions by so many great men are, when they are rightly understood, equal to so many demonstrations, and that it is almost impossible to invent new ones, it is yet in my opinion the case that nothing more useful can be accomplished in philosophy than once for all to seek with care for the best of these reasons, and to set them forth in so clear and exact a manner, that it will henceforth be evident to everybody that they are veritable demonstrations. And, finally, inasmuch as it was desired that I should undertake this task by many who were aware that I had cultivated a certain Method for the resolution of difficulties of every kind in the Sciences – a method which it is true is not novel, since there is nothing more ancient than the truth, but of which they were aware that I had made use successfully enough in other matters of difficulty – I have thought that it was my duty also to make trial of it in the present matter.

Now all that I could accomplish in the matter is contained in this Treatise. Not that I have here drawn together all the different reasons which might be brought forward to serve as proofs of this subject: for that never seemed to be necessary excepting when there was no one single proof that was certain. But I have treated the first and principal ones in such a manner that I can venture to bring them forward as very evident and very certain demonstrations. And more than that, I will say that these proofs are such that I do not think that there is any way open to the human mind by which it can ever succeed in discovering better. For the importance of the subject, and the glory of God to which all this relates, constrain me to speak here somewhat more freely of myself than is my habit. Nevertheless, whatever certainty and evidence I find in my reasons, I cannot persuade myself that all the world is capable of understanding them. Still, just as in Geometry there are many demonstrations that have been left to us by Archimedes, by Apollonius, by Pappus, and others, which are accepted by everyone as perfectly certain and evident (because they clearly contain nothing which, considered by itself, is not very easy to understand, and as all through that which follows has an exact connection with, and dependence on that which precedes), nevertheless, because they are somewhat lengthy, and demand a mind wholly devoted to their consideration, they are only taken in and understood by a very limited number of persons. Similarly, although I judge that those of which I here make use are equal to, or even surpass in certainty and evidence, the demonstrations of Geometry, I yet apprehend that they cannot be adequately understood by many, both because they are also a little lengthy and dependent the one on the other, and principally because they demand a mind wholly free of prejudices, and one which can be easily detached from the affairs of the senses. And, truth to say, there are not so many in the world who are fitted for metaphysical speculations as there are for those of Geometry. And more than that; there is still this difference, that in Geometry, since each one is persuaded that nothing must be advanced of which there is not a certain demonstration, those who are not entirely adepts more frequently err in approving what is false, in order to give the impression that they understand it, than in refuting the true. But the case is different in philosophy where everyone believes that all is problematical, and few give themselves to the search after truth; and the greater number, in their desire to acquire a reputation for boldness of thought, arrogantly combat the most important of truths.[1]

That is why, whatever force there may be in my reasonings, seeing they belong to philosophy, I cannot hope that they will have much effect on the

1. The French version is followed here.

minds of men, unless you extend to them your protection. But the estimation in which your Company is universally held is so great, and the name of SORBONNE carries with it so much authority, that, next to the Sacred Councils, never has such deference been paid to the judgment of any Body, not only in what concerns the faith, but also in what regards human philosophy as well: everyone indeed believes that it is not possible to discover elsewhere more perspicacity and solidity, or more integrity and wisdom in pronouncing judgment. For this reason I have no doubt that if you deign to take the trouble in the first place of correcting this work (for being conscious not only of my infirmity, but also of my ignorance, I should not dare to state that it was free from errors), and then, after adding to it these things that are lacking to it, completing those which are imperfect, and yourselves taking the trouble to give a more ample explanation of those things which have need of it, or at least making me aware of the defects so that I may apply myself to remedy them[2] – when this is done and when finally the reasonings by which I prove that there is a God, and that the human soul differs from the body, shall be carried to that point of perspicuity to which I am sure they can be carried in order that they may be esteemed as perfectly exact demonstrations, if you deign to authorise your approbation and to render public testimony to their truth and certainty, I do not doubt, I say, that henceforward all the errors and false opinions which have ever existed regarding these two questions will soon be effaced from the minds of men. For the truth itself will easily cause all men of mind and learning to subscribe to your judgment; and your authority will cause the atheists, who are usually more arrogant than learned or judicious, to rid themselves of their spirit of contradiction or lead them possibly themselves to defend the reasonings which they find being received as demonstrations by all persons of consideration, lest they appear not to understand them. And, finally, all others will easily yield to such a mass of evidence, and there will be none who dares to doubt the existence of God and the real and true distinction between the human soul and the body. It is for you now in your singular wisdom to judge of the importance of the establishment of such beliefs [you who see the disorders produced by the doubt of them].[3] But it would not become me to say more in consideration of the cause of God and religion to those who have always been the most worthy supports of the Catholic Church.

2. The French version is followed here.

3. When it is thought desirable to insert additional readings from the French version, this will be indicated by the use of square brackets.

PREFACE TO THE READER

I have already slightly touched on these two questions of God and the human soul in the Discourse on the Method of rightly conducting the Reason and seeking truth in the Sciences, published in French in the year 1637. Not that I had the design of treating these with any thoroughness, but only so to speak in passing, and in order to ascertain by the judgment of the readers how I should treat them later on. For these questions have always appeared to me to be of such importance that I judged it suitable to speak of them more than once; and the road which I follow in the explanation of them is so little trodden, and so far removed from the ordinary path, that I did not judge it to be expedient to set it forth at length in French and in a Discourse which might be read by everyone, in case the feebler minds should believe that it was permitted to them to attempt to follow the same path.

But, having in this Discourse on Method begged all those who have found in my writings somewhat deserving of censure to do me the favour of acquainting me with the grounds of it, nothing worthy of remark has been objected to in them beyond two matters: to these two I wish here to reply in a few words before undertaking their more detailed discussion.

The first objection is that it does not follow from the fact that the human mind reflecting on itself does not perceive itself to be other than a thing that thinks, that its nature or its essence consists only in its being a thing that thinks, in the sense that this word *only* excludes all other things which might also be supposed to pertain to the nature of the soul. To this objection I reply that it was not my intention in that place to exclude these in accordance with the order that looks to the truth of the matter (as to which I was not then dealing), but only in accordance with the order of my thought [perception]; thus my meaning was that so far as I was aware, I knew nothing clearly as belonging to my essence, excepting that I was a thing that thinks, or a thing that has in itself the faculty of thinking. But I shall show hereafter how from the fact that I know no other thing which pertains to my essence, it follows that there is no other thing which really does belong to it.

The second objection is that it does not follow from the fact that I have in myself the idea of something more perfect than I am, that this idea is more perfect than I, and much less that what is represented by this idea exists. But I reply that in this term *idea* there is here something equivocal, for it may either be taken materially, as an act of my understanding, and in this sense it cannot be said that it is more perfect than I; or it may be taken objectively, as the thing which is represented by this act, which, although we do not suppose it to exist outside of my understanding, may, none the less, be more perfect than I, because of its essence. And in following out this Treatise I shall show more fully how, from the sole fact that I have in myself the idea of a thing more perfect than myself, it follows that this thing truly exists.

In addition to these two objections I have also seen two fairly lengthy works on this subject, which, however, did not so much impugn my reasonings as my conclusions, and this by arguments drawn from the ordinary atheistic sources. But, because such arguments cannot make any impression on the minds of those who really understand my reasonings, and as the judgments of many are so feeble and irrational that they very often allow themselves to be persuaded by the opinions which they have first formed, however false and far removed from reason they may be, rather than by a true and solid but subsequently received refutation of these opinions, I do not desire to reply here to their criticisms in case of being first of all obliged to state them. I shall only say in general that all that is said by the atheist against the existence of God, always depends either on the fact that we ascribe to God affections which are human, or that we attribute so much strength and wisdom to our minds that we even have the presumption to desire to determine and understand that which God can and ought to do. In this way all that they allege will cause us no difficulty, provided only we remember that we must consider our minds as things which are finite and limited, and God as a Being who is incomprehensible and infinite.

Now that I have once for all recognised and acknowledged the opinions of men, I at once begin to treat of God and the human soul, and at the same time to treat of the whole of the First Philosophy, without however expecting any praise from the vulgar and without the hope that my book will have many readers. On the contrary, I should never advise anyone to read it excepting those who desire to meditate seriously with me, and who can detach their minds from affairs of sense, and deliver themselves entirely from every sort of prejudice. I know too well that such men exist in a very small number. But for those who, without caring to comprehend the order and connections of my reasonings, form their criticisms on detached portions arbitrarily selected, as is the custom with many, these, I say, will not obtain much profit from reading this Treatise. And although they perhaps in several parts find occasion of cavilling, they can for all their pains make no objection which is urgent or deserving of reply.

And inasmuch as I make no promise to others to satisfy them at once, and as I do not presume so much on my own powers as to believe myself capable of foreseeing all that can cause difficulty to anyone, I shall first of all set forth in these Meditations the very considerations by which I persuade myself that I have reached a certain and evident knowledge of the truth, in order to see if, by the same reasons which persuaded me, I can also persuade others. And, after that, I shall reply to the objections which have been made to me by persons of genius and learning to whom I have sent my Meditations for examination, before submitting them to the press. For they have made so many objections and these so different, that I venture to promise that it will be difficult for anyone to bring to mind criticisms of any consequence which have not been already touched upon. This is why I beg those who read these Meditations to form no judgment upon them unless they have given themselves the trouble to read all the objections as well as the replies which I have made to them.[4]

SYNOPSIS OF THE SIX FOLLOWING MEDITATIONS

In the first Meditation I set forth the reasons for which we may, generally speaking, doubt about all things and especially about material things, at least so long as we have no other foundations for the sciences than those which we have hitherto possessed. But although the utility of a Doubt which is so general does not at first appear, it is at the same time very great, inasmuch as it delivers us from every kind of prejudice, and sets out for us a very simple way by which the mind may detach itself from the senses; and finally it makes it impossible for us ever to doubt those things which we have once discovered to be true.

In the second Meditation, mind, which making use of the liberty which pertains to it, takes for granted that all those things of whose existence it has the least doubt, are non-existent, recognises that it is however absolutely impossible that it does not itself exist. This point is likewise of the greatest moment, inasmuch as by this means a distinction is easily drawn between the things which pertain to mind – that is to say to the intellectual nature – and those which pertain to body.

But because it may be that some expect from me in this place a statement of the reasons establishing the immortality of the soul, I feel that I should here make known to them that having aimed at writing nothing in all this

---

4. Between the *Præfatio ad Lectorem* and the *Synopsis*, the Paris Edition (1st Edition) interpolates an *Index* which is not found in the Amsterdam Edition (2nd Edition). Since Descartes did not reproduce it, he was doubtless not its author. Mersenne probably composed it himself, adjusting it to the paging of the first Edition. (Note in Adam and Tannery's Edition.)

Treatise of which I do not possess very exact demonstrations, I am obliged to follow a similar order to that made use of by the geometers, which is to begin by putting forward as premises all those things upon which the proposition that we seek depends, before coming to any conclusion regarding it. Now the first and principal matter which is requisite for thoroughly understanding the immortality of the soul is to form the clearest possible conception of it, and one which will be entirely distinct from all the conceptions which we may have of body; and in this Meditation this has been done. In addition to this it is requisite that we may be assured that all the things which we conceive clearly and distinctly are true in the very way in which we think them; and this could not be proved previously to the Fourth Meditation. Further we must have a distinct conception of corporeal nature, which is given partly in this Second, and partly in the Fifth and Sixth Meditations. And finally we should conclude from all this, that those things which we conceive clearly and distinctly as being diverse substances, as we regard mind and body to be, are really substances essentially distinct one from the other; and this is the conclusion of the Sixth Meditation. This is further confirmed in this same Meditation by the fact that we cannot conceive of body excepting in so far as it is divisible, while the mind cannot be conceived of excepting as indivisible. For we are not able to conceive of the half of a mind as we can do of the smallest of all bodies; so that we see that not only are their natures different but even in some respects contrary to one another. I have not however dealt further with this matter in this treatise, both because what I have said is sufficient to show clearly enough that the extinction of the mind does not follow from the corruption of the body, and also to give men the hope of another life after death, as also because the premises from which the immortality of the soul may be deduced depend on an elucidation of a complete system of Physics. This would mean to establish in the first place that all substances generally – that is to say all things which cannot exist without being created by God – are in their nature incorruptible, and that they can never cease to exist unless God, in denying to them his concurrence, reduce them to nought; and secondly that body, regarded generally, is a substance, which is the reason why it also cannot perish, but that the human body, inasmuch as it differs from other bodies, is composed only of a certain configuration of members and of other similar accidents, while the human mind is not similarly composed of any accidents, but is a pure substance. For although all the accidents of mind be changed, although, for instance, it think certain things, will others, perceive others, etc., despite all this it does not emerge from these changes another mind: the human body on the other hand becomes a different thing from the sole fact that the figure or form of any of its portions is found to be changed. From this it follows that the human body may indeed easily enough perish, but the mind [or soul of man (I make no distinction between them)] is owing to its nature immortal.

In the third Meditation it seems to me that I have explained at sufficient length the principal argument of which I make use in order to prove the existence of God. But none the less, because I did not wish in that place to make use of any comparisons derived from corporeal things, so as to withdraw as much as I could the minds of readers from the senses, there may perhaps have remained many obscurities which, however, will, I hope, be entirely removed by the Replies which I have made to the Objections which have been set before me. Amongst others there is, for example, this one, 'How the idea in us of a being supremely perfect possesses so much objective reality [that is to say participates by representation in so many degrees of being and perfection] that it necessarily proceeds from a cause which is absolutely perfect. This is illustrated in these Replies by the comparison of a very perfect machine, the idea of which is found in the mind of some workman. For as the objective contrivance of this idea must have some cause, i.e., either the science of the workman or that of some other from whom he has received the idea, it is similarly impossible that the idea of God which is in us should not have God himself as its cause.

In the fourth Meditation it is shown that all these things which we very clearly and distinctly perceive are true, and at the same time it is explained in what the nature of error or falsity consists. This must of necessity be known both for the confirmation of the preceding truths and for the better comprehension of those that follow. (But it must meanwhile be remarked that I do not in any way there treat of sin – that is to say of the error which is committed in the pursuit of good and evil, but only of that which arises in the deciding between the true and the false. And I do not intend to speak of matters pertaining to the Faith or the conduct of life, but only of those which concern speculative truths, and which may be known by the sole aid of the light of nature.)

In the fifth Meditation corporeal nature generally is explained, and in addition to this the existence of God is demonstrated by a new proof in which there may possibly be certain difficulties also, but the solution of these will be seen in the Replies to the Objections. And further I show in what sense it is true to say that the certainty of geometrical demonstrations is itself dependent on the knowledge of God.

Finally in the Sixth I distinguish the action of the understanding[5] from that of the imagination[6]; the marks by which this distinction is made are described. I here show that the mind of man is really distinct from the body, and at the same time that the two are so closely joined together that they form, so to speak, a single thing. All the errors which proceed from the senses are then surveyed, while the means of avoiding them are demonstrated, and finally all the reasons from which we may deduce the existence of material things are set forth. Not that I judge them to be very useful in establishing that which they prove, to wit, that there is in truth a world, that men possess bodies, and other such things which never have been doubted by anyone of sense; but because in considering these closely we come to see that they are neither so strong nor so evident as those arguments which lead us to the knowledge of our mind and of God; so that these last must be the most certain and most evident facts which can fall within the cognizance of the human mind. And this is the whole matter that I have tried to prove in these Meditations, for which reason I here omit to speak of many other questions with which I dealt incidentally in this discussion.

MEDITATIONS ON THE FIRST PHILOSOPHY
IN WHICH THE EXISTENCE OF GOD
AND THE DISTINCTION BETWEEN MIND
AND BODY ARE DEMONSTRATED[7]

MEDITATION I

Of the things which may be brought within the sphere of the doubtful.

It is now some years since I detected how many were the false beliefs that I had from my earliest youth admitted as true, and how doubtful was everything I had since constructed on this basis; and from that time I was convinced that I must once for all seriously undertake to rid myself of all the opinions which I had formerly accepted, and commence to build anew from the foundation, if I wanted to establish any firm and permanent structure in

5. *intellectio.*

6. *imaginatio.*

7. In place of this long title at the head of the page, the first Edition had immediately after the Synopsis, and on the same page 7, simply 'First Meditation.' (Adam's Edition.)

the sciences. But as this enterprise appeared to be a very great one, I waited until I had attained an age so mature that I could not hope that at any later date I should be better fitted to execute my design. This reason caused me to delay so long that I should feel that I was doing wrong were I to occupy in deliberation the time that yet remains to me for action. To-day, then, since very opportunely for the plan I have in view I have delivered my mind from every care [and am happily agitated by no passions] and since I have procured for myself an assured leisure in a peaceable retirement, I shall at last seriously and freely address myself to the general upheaval of all my former opinions.

Now for this object it is not necessary that I should show that all of these are false – I shall perhaps never arrive at this end. But inasmuch as reason already persuades me that I ought no less carefully to withhold my assent from matters which are not entirely certain and indubitable than from those which appear to me manifestly to be false, if I am able to find in each one some reason to doubt, this will suffice to justify my rejecting the whole. And for that end it will not be requisite that I should examine each in particular, which would be an endless undertaking; for owing to the fact that the destruction of the foundations of necessity brings with it the down-fall of the rest of the edifice, I shall only in the first place attack those principles upon which all my former opinions rested.

All that up to the present time I have accepted as most true and certain I have learned either from the senses or through the senses; but it is some-times proved to me that these senses are deceptive, and it is wiser not to trust entirely to any thing by which we have once been deceived.

But it may be that although the senses sometimes deceive us concerning things which are hardly perceptible, or very far away, there are yet many others to be met with as to which we cannot reasonably have any doubt, although we recognise them by their means. For example, there is the fact that I am here, seated by the fire, attired in a dressing gown, having this paper in my hands and other similar matters. And how could I deny that these hands and this body are mine, were it not perhaps that I compare myself to certain persons, devoid of sense, whose cerebella are so troubled and clouded by the violent vapours of black bile, that they constantly assure us that they think they are kings when they are really quite poor, or that they are clothed in purple when they are really without covering, or who imagine that they have an earthenware head or are nothing but pumpkins or are made of glass. But they are mad, and I should not be any the less insane were I to follow examples so extravagant.

At the same time I must remember that I am a man, and that consequently I am in the habit of sleeping, and in my dreams representing to myself the same things or sometimes even less probable things, than do those who are insane in their waking moments. How often has it happened to me that in the night I dreamt that I found myself in this particular place, that I was dressed and seated near the fire, whilst in reality I was lying undressed in bed! At this moment it does indeed seem to me that it is with eyes awake that I am looking at this paper; that this head which I move is not asleep, that it is deliberately and of set purpose that I extend my hand and perceive it; what happens in sleep does not appear so clear nor so distinct as does all this. But in thinking over this I remind myself that on many occasions I have in sleep been deceived by similar illusions, and in dwelling carefully on this reflection I see so manifestly that there are no certain indications by which we may clearly distinguish wakefulness from sleep that I am lost in astonishment. And my astonishment is such that it is almost capable of persuading me that I now dream.

Now let us assume that we are asleep and that all these particulars, e.g. that we open our eyes, shake our head, extend our hands, and so on, are but false delusions; and let us reflect that possibly neither our hands nor our whole body are such as they appear to us to be. At the same time we must at least confess that the things which are represented to us in sleep are like painted representations which can only have been formed as the counterparts of something real and true, and that in this way those general things at least, i.e. eyes, a head, hands, and a whole body, are not imaginary things, but things really existent. For, as a matter of fact, painters, even when they study with the greatest skill to represent sirens and satyrs by forms the most strange and extraordinary, cannot give them natures which are entirely new, but merely make a certain medley of the members of different animals; or if their imagination is extravagant enough to invent something so novel that nothing similar has ever before been seen, and that then their work represents a thing purely fictitious and absolutely false, it is certain all the same that the colours of which this is composed are necessarily real. And for the same reason, although these general things, to wit, [a body], eyes, a head, hands, and such like, may be imaginary, we are bound at the same time to confess that there are at least some other objects yet more simple and more universal, which are real and true; and of these just in the same way as with certain real colours, all these images of things which dwell in our thoughts, whether true and real or false and fantastic, are formed.

To such a class of things pertains corporeal nature in general, and its extension, the figure of extended things, their quantity or magnitude and number, as also the place in which they are, the time which measures their duration, and so on.

That is possibly why our reasoning is not unjust when we conclude from this that Physics, Astronomy, Medicine and all other sciences which have as their end the consideration of composite things, are very dubious and uncertain; but that Arithmetic, Geometry and other sciences of that kind which only treat of things that are very simple and very general, without taking great trouble to ascertain whether they are actually existent or not, contain some measure of certainty and an element of the indubitable. For whether I am awake or asleep, two and three together always form five, and the square can never have more than four sides, and it does not seem possible that truths so clear and apparent can be suspected of any falsity [or uncertainty].

Nevertheless I have long had fixed in my mind the belief that an all-powerful God existed by whom I have been created such as I am. But how do I know that He has not brought it to pass that there is no earth, no heaven, no extended body, no magnitude, no place, and that nevertheless [I possess the perceptions of all these things and that] they seem to me to exist just exactly as I now see them? And, besides, as I sometimes imagine that others deceive themselves in the things which they think they know best, how do I know that I am not deceived every time that I add two and three, or count the sides of a square, or judge of things yet simpler, if anything simpler can be imagined? But possibly God has not desired that I should be thus deceived, for He is said to be supremely good. If, however, it is contrary to His goodness to have made me such that I constantly deceive myself, it would also appear to be contrary to His goodness to permit me to be sometimes deceived, and nevertheless I cannot doubt that He does permit this.

There may indeed be those who would prefer to deny the existence of a God so powerful, rather than believe that all other things are uncertain. But let us not oppose them for the present, and grant that all that is here said of a God is a fable; nevertheless in whatever way they suppose that I have arrived at the state of being that I have reached – whether they attribute it to fate or to accident, or make out that it is by a continual succession of antecedents, or by some other method – since to err and deceive oneself is a defect, it is clear that the greater will be the probability of my being so imperfect as to deceive myself ever, as is the Author to whom they assign my origin the less powerful. To these reasons I have certainly nothing to reply, but at the end I feel constrained to confess that there is nothing in all that I formerly believed to be true, of which I cannot in some measure doubt, and that not merely through want of thought or through levity, but for reasons which are very powerful and maturely considered; so that henceforth I ought not the less carefully to refrain from giving credence to these opinions than to that which is manifestly false, if I desire to arrive at any certainty [in the sciences].

But it is not sufficient to have made these remarks, we must also be careful to keep them in mind. For these ancient and commonly held opinions still revert frequently to my mind, long and familiar custom having given them the right to occupy my mind against my inclination and rendered them almost masters of my belief; nor will I ever lose the habit of deferring to them or of placing my confidence in them, so long as I consider them as they really are, i.e. opinions in some measure doubtful, as I have just shown, and at the same time highly probable, so that there is much more reason to believe in than to deny them. That is why I consider that I shall not be acting amiss, if, taking of set purpose a contrary belief, I allow myself to be deceived, and for a certain time pretend that all these opinions are entirely false and imaginary, until at last, having thus balanced my former prejudices with my latter [so that they cannot divert my opinions more to one side than to the other], my judgment will no longer be dominated by bad usage or turned away from the right knowledge of the truth. For I am assured that there can be neither peril nor error in this course, and that I cannot at present yield too much to distrust, since I am not considering the question of action, but only of knowledge.

I shall then suppose, not that God who is supremely good and the fountain of truth, but some evil genius not less powerful than deceitful, has employed his whole energies in deceiving me; I shall consider that the heavens, the earth, colours, figures, sound, and all other external things are nought but the illusions and dreams of which this genius has availed himself in order to lay traps for my credulity; I shall consider myself as having no hands, no eyes, no flesh, no blood, nor any senses, yet falsely believing myself to possess all these things; I shall remain obstinately attached to this idea, and if by this means it is not in my power to arrive at the knowledge of any truth, I may at least do what is in my power [i.e. suspend my judgment], and with firm purpose avoid giving credence to any false thing, or being imposed upon by this arch deceiver, however powerful and deceptive he may be. But this task is a laborious one, and insensibly a certain lassitude leads me into the course of my ordinary life. And just as a captive who in sleep enjoys an imaginary liberty, when he begins to suspect that his liberty is but a dream, fears to awaken, and conspires with these agreeable illusions that the deception may be prolonged, so insensibly of my own accord I fall back into my former opinions, and I dread awakening from this slumber, lest the laborious wakefulness which would follow the tranquillity of this repose should have to be spent not in daylight, but in the excessive darkness of the difficulties which have just been discussed.

MEDITATION II

Of the Nature of the Human Mind; and that it is more easily known than the Body.

The Meditation of yesterday filled my mind with so many doubts that it is no longer in my power to forget them. And yet I do not see in what manner I can resolve them; and, just as if I had all of a sudden fallen into very deep water, I am so disconcerted that I can neither make certain of setting my feet on the bottom, nor can I swim and so support myself on the surface. I shall nevertheless make an effort and follow anew the same path as that on which I yesterday entered, i.e. I shall proceed by setting aside all that in which the least doubt could be supposed to exist, just as if I had discovered that it was absolutely false; and I shall ever follow in this road until I have met with something which is certain, or at least, if I can do nothing else, until I have learned for certain that there is nothing in the world that is certain. Archimedes, in order that he might draw the terrestrial globe out of its place, and transport it elsewhere, demanded only that one point should be fixed and immoveable; in the same way I shall have the right to conceive high hopes if I am happy enough to discover one thing only which is certain and indubitable.

I suppose, then, that all the things that I see are false; I persuade myself that nothing has ever existed of all that my fallacious memory represents to me. I consider that I possess no senses; I imagine that body, figure, extension, movement and place are but the fictions of my mind. What, then, can be esteemed as true? Perhaps nothing at all, unless that there is nothing in the world that is certain.

But how can I know there is not something different from those things that I have just considered, of which one cannot have the slightest doubt? Is there not some God, or some other being by whatever name we call it, who puts these reflections into my mind? That is not necessary, for is it not possible that I am capable of producing them myself? I myself, am I not at least something? But I have already denied that I had senses and body. Yet I hesitate, for what follows from that? Am I so dependent on body and senses that I cannot exist without these? But I was persuaded that there was nothing in all the world, that there was no heaven, no earth, that there were no minds, nor any bodies: was I not then likewise persuaded that I did not exist? Not at all; of a surety I myself did exist since I persuaded myself of something [or merely because I thought of something]. But there is some deceiver or other, very powerful and very cunning, who ever employs his ingenuity in deceiving me. Then without doubt I exist also if he deceives me, and let him deceive me as much as he will, he can never cause me to be nothing so long as I think that I am something. So that after having reflected well and carefully examined all things, we must come to the definite conclusion that this proposition: I am, I exist, is necessarily true each time that I pronounce it, or that I mentally conceive it.

But I do not yet know clearly enough what I am, I who am certain that I am; and hence I must be careful to see that I do not imprudently take some other object in place of myself, and thus that I do not go astray in respect of this knowledge that I hold to be the most certain and most evident of all that I have formerly learned. That is why I shall now consider anew what I believed myself to be before I embarked upon these last reflections; and of my former opinions I shall withdraw all that might even in a small degree be invalidated by the reasons which I have just brought forward, in order that there may be nothing at all left beyond what is absolutely certain and indubitable.

What then did I formerly believe myself to be? Undoubtedly I believed myself to be a man. But what is a man? Shall I say a reasonable animal? Certainly not; for then I should have to inquire what an animal is, and what is reasonable; and thus from a single question I should insensibly fall into an infinitude of others more difficult; and I should not wish to waste the little time and leisure remaining to me in trying to unravel subtleties like these. But I shall rather stop here to consider the thoughts which of themselves spring up in my mind, and which were not inspired by anything beyond my own nature alone when I applied myself to the consideration of my being. In the first place, then, I considered myself as having a face, hands, arms, and all that system of members composed of bones and flesh as seen in a corpse which I designated by the name of body. In addition to this I considered that I was nourished, that I walked, that I felt, and that I thought, and I referred all these actions to the soul: but I did not stop to consider what the soul was, or if I did stop, I imagined that it was something extremely rare and subtle like a wind, a flame, or an ether, which was spread throughout my grosser parts. As to body I had no manner of doubt about its nature, but thought I had a very clear knowledge of it; and if I had desired to explain it according to the notions that I had then formed of it, I should have described it thus: By the body I understand all that which can be defined by a certain figure: something which can be confined in a certain place, and

which can fill a given space in such a way that every other body will be
excluded from it; which can be perceived either by touch, or by sight, or by
hearing, or by taste, or by smell: which can be moved in many ways not, in
truth, by itself, but by something which is foreign to it, by which it is
touched [and from which it receives impressions]: for to have the power of
self-movement, as also of feeling or of thinking, I did not consider to
appertain to the nature of body: on the contrary, I was rather astonished to
find that faculties similar to them existed in some bodies.

But what am I, now that I suppose that there is a certain genius which is
extremely powerful, and, if I may say so, malicious, who employs all his
powers in deceiving me? Can I affirm that I possess the least of all those
things which I have just said pertain to the nature of body? I pause to
consider, I revolve all these things in my mind, and I find none of which I
can say that it pertains to me. It would be tedious to stop to enumerate them.
Let us pass to the attributes of soul and see if there is any one which is in
me? What of nutrition or walking [the first mentioned]? But if it is so that I
have no body it is also true that I can neither walk nor take nourishment.
Another attribute is sensation. But one cannot feel without body, and besides I have thought I perceived many things during sleep that I recognised
in my waking moments as not having been experienced at all. What of
thinking? I find here that thought is an attribute that belongs to me; it alone
cannot be separated from me. I am, I exist, that is certain. But how often?
Just when I think; for it might possibly be the case if I ceased entirely to
think, that I should likewise cease altogether to exist. I do not now admit
anything which is not necessarily true: to speak accurately I am not more
than a thing which thinks, that is to say a mind or a soul, or an understanding, or a reason, which are terms whose significance was formerly unknown
to me. I am, however, a real thing and really exist; but what thing? I have
answered: a thing which thinks.

And what more? I shall exercise my imagination [in order to see if I am
not something more]. I am not a collection of members which we call the
human body: I am not a subtle air distributed through these members, I am
not a wind, a fire, a vapour, a breath, nor anything at all which I can imagine
or conceive; because I have assumed that all these were nothing. Without
changing that supposition I find that I only leave myself certain of the fact
that I am somewhat. But perhaps it is true that these same things which I
supposed were non-existent because they are unknown to me, are really not
different from the self which I know. I am not sure about this, I shall not
dispute about it now; I can only give judgment on things that are known to
me. I know that I exist, and I inquire what I am, I whom I know to exist. But

it is very certain that the knowledge of my existence taken in its precise significance does not depend on things whose existence is not yet known to me; consequently it does not depend on those which I can feign in imagination. And indeed the very term *feign* in imagination[8] proves to me my error, for I really do this if I image myself a something, since to imagine is nothing else than to contemplate the figure or image of a corporeal thing. But I already know for certain that I am, and that it may be that all these images, and, speaking generally, all things that relate to the nature of body are nothing but dreams [and chimeras]. For this reason I see clearly that I have as little reason to say, 'I shall stimulate my imagination in order to know more distinctly what I am,' than if I were to say, 'I am now awake, and I perceive somewhat that is real and true: but because I do not yet perceive it distinctly enough, I shall go to sleep of express purpose, so that my dreams may represent the perception with greatest truth and evidence.' And, thus, I know for certain that nothing of all that I can understand by means of my imagination belongs to this knowledge which I have of myself, and that it is necessary to recall the mind from this mode of thought with the utmost diligence in order that it may be able to know its own nature with perfect distinctness.

But what then am I? A thing which thinks. What is a thing which thinks? It is a thing which doubts, understands, [conceives], affirms, denies, wills, refuses, which also imagines and feels.

Certainly it is no small matter if all these things pertain to my nature. But why should they not so pertain? Am I not that being who now doubts nearly everything, who nevertheless understands certain things, who affirms that one only is true, who denies all the others, who desires to know more, is averse from being deceived, who imagines many things, sometimes indeed despite his will, and who perceives many likewise, as by the intervention of the bodily organs? Is there nothing in all this which is as true as it is certain that I exist, even though I should always sleep and though he who has given me being employed all his ingenuity in deceiving me? Is there likewise any one of these attributes which can be distinguished from my thought, or which might be said to be separated from myself? For it is so evident of itself that it is I who doubts, who understands, and who desires, that there is no reason here to add anything to explain it. And I have certainly the power of imagining likewise; for although it may happen (as I formerly supposed) that none of the things which I imagine are true, nevertheless this power of imagining does not cease to be really in use, and it forms part of my thought.

8. Or 'form an image' (effingò).

Finally, I am the same who feels, that is to say, who perceives certain things, as by the organs of sense, since in truth I see light, I hear noise, I feel heat. But it will be said that these phenomena are false and that I am dreaming. Let it be so; still it is at least quite certain that it seems to me that I see light, that I hear noise and that I feel heat. That cannot be false; properly speaking it is what is in me called feeling;[9] and used in this precise sense that is no other thing than thinking.

From this time I begin to know what I am with a little more clearness and distinction than before; but nevertheless it still seems to me, and I cannot prevent myself from thinking, that corporeal things, whose images are framed by thought, which are tested by the senses, are much more distinctly known than that obscure part of me which does not come under the imagination. Although really it is very strange to say that I know and understand more distinctly these things whose existence seems to me dubious, which are unknown to me, and which do not belong to me, than others of the truth of which I am convinced, which are known to me and which pertain to my real nature, in a word, than myself. But I see clearly how the case stands: my mind loves to wander, and cannot yet suffer itself to be retained within the just limits of truth. Very good, let us once more give it the freest rein, so that, when afterwards we seize the proper occasion for pulling up, it may the more easily be regulated and controlled.

Let us begin by considering the commonest matters, those which we believe to be the most distinctly comprehended, to wit, the bodies which we touch and see; not indeed bodies in general, for these general ideas are usually a little more confused, but let us consider one body in particular. Let us take, for example, this piece of wax: it has been taken quite freshly from the hive, and it has not yet lost the sweetness of the honey which it contains; it still retains somewhat of the odour of the flowers from which it has been culled; its colour, its figure, its size are apparent; it is hard, cold, easily handled, and if you strike it with the finger, it will emit a sound. Finally all the things which are requisite to cause us distinctly to recognise a body, are met with in it. But notice that while I speak and approach the fire what remained of the taste is exhaled, the smell evaporates, the colour alters, the figure is destroyed, the size increases, it becomes liquid, it heats, scarcely can one handle it, and when one strikes it, no sound is emitted. Does the same wax remain after this change? We must confess that it remains; none would judge otherwise. What then did I know so distinctly in this piece of wax? It could certainly be nothing of all that the senses brought to my

9. Sentire.

notice, since all these things which fall under taste, smell, sight, touch, and hearing, are found to be changed, and yet the same wax remains.

Perhaps it was what I now think, viz. that this wax was not that sweetness of honey, nor that agreeable scent of flowers, nor that particular whiteness, nor that figure, nor that sound, but simply a body which a little while before appeared to me as perceptible under these forms, and which is now perceptible under others. But what, precisely, is it that I imagine when I form such conceptions? Let us attentively consider this, and, abstracting from all that does not belong to the wax, let us see what remains. Certainly nothing remains excepting a certain extended thing which is flexible and movable. But what is the meaning of flexible and movable? Is it not that I imagine that this piece of wax being round is capable of becoming square and of passing from a square to a triangular figure? No, certainly it is not that, since I imagine it admits of an infinitude of similar changes, and I nevertheless do not know how to compass the infinitude by my imagination, and consequently this conception which I have of the wax is not brought about by the faculty of imagination. What now is this extension? Is it not also unknown? For it becomes greater when the wax is melted, greater when it is boiled, and greater still when the heat increases; and I should not conceive [clearly] according to truth what wax is, if I did not think that even this piece that we are considering is capable of receiving more variations in extension than I have ever imagined. We must then grant that I could not even understand through the imagination what this piece of wax is, and that it is my mind[10] alone which perceives it. I say this piece of wax in particular, for as to wax in general it is yet clearer. But what is this piece of wax which cannot be understood excepting by the [understanding or] mind? It is certainly the same that I see, touch, imagine, and finally it is the same which I have always believed it to be from the beginning. But what must particularly be observed is that its perception is neither an act of vision, nor of touch, nor of imagination, and has never been such although it may have appeared formerly to be so, but only an intuition[11] of the mind, which may be imperfect and confused as it was formerly, or clear and distinct as it is at present, according as my attention is more or less directed to the elements which are found in it, and of which it is composed.

Yet in the meantime I am greatly astonished when I consider [the great feebleness of mind] and its proneness to fall [insensibly] into error; for although without giving expression to my thoughts I consider all this in my

10. entendement Fr., mens L.

11. inspectio.

own mind, words often impede me and I am almost deceived by the terms of ordinary language. For we say that we see the same wax, if it is present, and not that we simply judge that it is the same from its having the same colour and figure. From this I should conclude that I knew the wax by means of vision and not simply by the intuition of the mind; unless by chance I remember that, when looking from a window and saying I see men who pass in the street, I really do not see them, but infer that what I see is men, just as I say that I see wax. And yet what do I see from the window but hats and coats which may cover automatic machines? Yet I judge these to be men. And similarly solely by the faculty of judgment which rests in my mind, I comprehend that which I believed I saw with my eyes.

A man who makes it his aim to raise his knowledge above the common should be ashamed to derive the occasion for doubting from the forms of speech invented by the vulgar; I prefer to pass on and consider whether I had a more evident and perfect conception of what the wax was when I first perceived it, and when I believed I knew it by means of the external senses or at least by the common sense[12] as it is called, that is to say by the imaginative faculty, or whether my present conception is clearer now that I have most carefully examined what it is, and in what way it can be known. It would certainly be absurd to doubt as to this. For what was there in this first perception which was distinct? What was there which might not as well have been perceived by any of the animals? But when I distinguish the wax from its external forms, and when, just as if I had taken from it its vestments, I consider it quite naked, it is certain that although some error may still be found in my judgment, I can nevertheless not perceive it thus without a human mind.

But finally what shall I say of this mind, that is, of myself, for up to this point I do not admit in myself anything but mind? What then, I who seem to perceive this piece of wax so distinctly, do I not know myself, not only with much more truth and certainty, but also with much more distinctness and clearness? For if I judge that the wax is or exists from the fact that I see it, it certainly follows much more clearly that I am or that I exist myself from the fact that I see it. For it may be that what I see is not really wax, it may also be that I do not possess eyes with which to see anything; but it cannot be that when I see, or (for I no longer take account of the distinction) when I think I see, that I myself who think am nought. So if I judge that the wax exists from the fact that I touch it, the same thing will follow, to wit, that I am; and if I judge that my imagination, or some other cause, whatever it is,

12. sensus communis.

persuades me that the wax exists, I shall still conclude the same. And what I have here remarked of wax may be applied to all other things which are external to me [and which are met with outside of me]. And further, if the [notion or] perception of wax has seemed to me clearer and more distinct, not only after the sight or the touch, but also after many other causes have rendered it quite manifest to me, with how much more [evidence] and distinctness must it be said that I now know myself, since all the reasons which contribute to the knowledge of wax, or any other body whatever, are yet better proofs of the nature of my mind! And there are so many other things in the mind itself which may contribute to the elucidation of its nature, that those which depend on body such as these just mentioned, hardly merit being taken into account.

But finally here I am, having insensibly reverted to the point I desired, for, since it is now manifest to me that even bodies are not properly speaking known by the senses or by the faculty of imagination, but by the understanding only, and since they are not known from the fact that they are seen or touched, but only because they are understood, I see clearly that there is nothing which is easier for me to know than my mind. But because it is difficult to rid oneself so promptly of an opinion to which one was accustomed for so long, it will be well that I should halt a little at this point, so that by the length of my meditation I may more deeply imprint on my memory this new knowledge.

MEDITATION III

Of God: that He exists.

I shall now close my eyes, I shall stop my ears, I shall call away all my senses, I shall efface even from my thoughts all the images of corporeal things, or at least (for that is hardly possible) I shall esteem them as vain and false; and thus holding converse only with myself and considering my own nature, I shall try little by little to reach a better knowledge of and a more familiar acquaintanceship with myself. I am a thing that thinks, that is to say, that doubts, affirms, denies, that knows a few things, that is ignorant of many [that loves, that hates], that wills, that desires, that also imagines and perceives; for as I remarked before, although the things which I perceive and imagine are perhaps nothing at all apart from me and in themselves, I am nevertheless assured that these modes of thought that I call perceptions and imaginations, inasmuch only as they are modes of thought, certainly reside [and are met with] in me.

And in the little that I have just said, I think I have summed up all that I really know, or at least all that hitherto I was aware that I knew. In order to try to extend my knowledge further, I shall now look around more carefully and see whether I cannot still discover in myself some other things which I have not hitherto perceived. I am certain that I am a thing which thinks; but do I not then likewise know what is requisite to render me certain of a truth? Certainly in this first knowledge there is nothing that assures me of its truth, excepting the clear and distinct perception of that which I state, which would not indeed suffice to assure me that what I say is true, if it could ever happen that a thing which I conceived so clearly and distinctly could be false; and accordingly it seems to me that already I can establish as a general rule that all things which I perceive[13] very clearly and very distinctly are true.

At the same time I have before received and admitted many things to be very certain and manifest, which yet I afterwards recognised as being dubious. What then were these things? They were the earth, sky, stars and all other objects which I apprehended by means of the senses. But what did I clearly [and distinctly] perceive in them? Nothing more than that the ideas or thoughts of these things were presented to my mind. And not even now do I deny that these ideas are met with in me. But there was yet another thing which I affirmed, and which, owing to the habit which I had formed of believing it, I thought I perceived very clearly, although in truth I did not perceive it at all, to wit, that there were objects outside of me from which these ideas proceeded, and to which they were entirely similar. And it was in this that I erred, or, if perchance my judgment was correct, this was not due to any knowledge arising from my perception.

But when I took anything very simple and easy in the sphere of arithmetic or geometry into consideration, e.g. that two and three together made five, and other things of the sort, were not these present to my mind so clearly as to enable me to affirm that they were true? Certainly if I judged that since such matters could be doubted, this would not have been so for any other reason than that it came into my mind that perhaps a God might have endowed me with such a nature that I may have been deceived even concerning things which seemed to me most manifest. But every time that this preconceived opinion of the sovereign power of a God presents itself to my thought, I am constrained to confess that it is easy to Him, if He wishes it, to cause me to err, even in matters in which I believe myself to have the best evidence. And, on the other hand, always when I direct my attention to

13. Percipio, Fr. nous concevons.

things which I believe myself to perceive very clearly, I am so persuaded of their truth that I let myself break out into words such as these: Let who will deceive me, He can never cause me to be nothing while I think that I am, or some day cause it to be true to say that I have never been, it being true now to say that I am, or that two and three make more or less than five, or any such thing in which I see a manifest contradiction. And, certainly, since I have no reason to believe that there is a God who is a deceiver, and as I have not yet satisfied myself that there is a God at all, the reason for doubt which depends on this opinion alone is very slight, and so to speak metaphysical. But in order to be able altogether to remove it, I must inquire whether there is a God as soon as the occasion presents itself; and if I find that there is a God, I must also inquire whether He may be a deceiver; for without a knowledge of these two truths I do not see that I can ever be certain of anything.

And in order that I may have an opportunity of inquiring into this in an orderly way [without interrupting the order of meditation which I have proposed to myself, and which is little by little to pass from the notions which I find first of all in my mind to those which I shall later on discover in it] it is requisite that I should here divide my thoughts into certain kinds, and that I should consider in which of these kinds there is, properly speaking, truth or error to be found. Of my thoughts some are, so to speak, images of the things, and to these alone is the title 'idea' properly applied; examples are my thought of a man or of a chimera, of heaven, of an angel, or [even] of God. But other thoughts possess other forms as well. For example in willing, fearing, approving, denying, though I always perceive something as the subject of the action of my mind,[14] yet by this action I always add something else to the idea[15] which I have of that thing; and of the thoughts of this kind some are called volitions or affections, and others judgments.

Now as to what concerns ideas, if we consider them only in themselves and do not relate them to anything else beyond themselves, they cannot properly speaking be false; for whether I imagine a goat or a chimera, it is not less true that I imagine the one than the other. We must not fear likewise that falsity can enter into will and into affections, for although I may desire evil things, or even things that never existed, it is not the less true that I desire them. Thus there remains no more than the judgments which we make, in which I must take the greatest care not to deceive myself. But the

14. The French version is followed here as being more explicit. In it 'action de mon esprit' replaces 'mea cogitatio.'

15. In the Latin version 'similitudinem.'

principal error and the commonest which we may meet with in them, consists in my judging that the ideas which are in me are similar or conformable to the things which are outside me; for without doubt if I considered the ideas only as certain modes of my thoughts, without trying to relate them to anything beyond, they could scarcely give me material for error.

⌊But among these ideas, some appear to me to be innate, some adventitious, and others to be formed [or invented] by myself; for, as I have the power of understanding what is called a thing, or a truth, or a thought, it appears to me that I hold this power from no other source than my own nature. But if I now hear some sound, if I see the sun, or feel heat, I have hitherto judged that these sensations proceeded from certain things that exist outside of me; and finally it appears to me that sirens, hippogryphs, and the like, are formed out of my own mind. But again I may possibly persuade myself that all these ideas are of the nature of those which I term adventitious, or else that they are all innate, or all fictitious: for I have not yet clearly discovered their true origin.⌉

And my principal task in this place is to consider, in respect to those ideas which appear to me to proceed from certain objects that are outside me, what are the reasons which cause me to think them similar to these objects. It seems indeed in the first place that I am taught this lesson by nature; and, secondly, I experience in myself that these ideas do not depend on my will nor therefore on myself – for they often present themselves to my mind in spite of my will. Just now, for instance, whether I will or whether I do not will, I feel heat, and thus I persuade myself that this feeling, or at least this idea of heat, is produced in me by something which is different from me, i.e. by the heat of the fire near which I sit. And nothing seems to me more obvious than to judge that this object imprints its likeness rather than anything else upon me.

Now I must discover whether these proofs are sufficiently strong and convincing. When I say that I am so instructed by nature, I merely mean a certain spontaneous inclination which impels me to believe in this connection, and not a natural light which makes me recognise that it is true. But these two things are very different; for I cannot doubt that which the natural light causes me to believe to be true, as, for example, it has shown me that I am from the fact that I doubt, or other facts of the same kind. And I possess no other faculty whereby to distinguish truth from falsehood, which can teach me that what this light shows me to be true is not really true, and no other faculty that is equally trustworthy. But as far as [apparently] natural impulses are concerned, I have frequently remarked, when I had to make active choice between virtue and vice, that they often enough led me to the part that was worse; and this is why I do not see any reason for following them in what regards truth and error.

And as to the other reason, which is that these ideas must proceed from objects outside me, since they do not depend on my will, I do not find it any the more convincing. For just as these impulses of which I have spoken are found in me, notwithstanding that they do not always concur with my will, so perhaps there is in me some faculty fitted to produce these ideas without the assistance of any external things, even though it is not yet known by me; just as, apparently, they have hitherto always been found in me during sleep without the aid of any external objects.

And finally, though they did proceed from objects different from myself, it is not a necessary consequence that they should resemble these. On the contrary, I have noticed that in many cases there was a great difference between the object and its idea. I find, for example, two completely diverse ideas of the sun in my mind; the one derives its origin from the senses, and should be placed in the category of adventitious ideas; according to this idea the sun seems to be extremely small; but the other is derived from astronomical reasonings, i.e. is elicited from certain notions that are innate to me, or else it is formed by me in some other manner; in accordance with it the sun appears to be several times greater than the earth. These two ideas cannot, indeed, both resemble the same sun, and reason makes me believe that the one which seems to have originated directly from the sun itself, is the one which is most dissimilar to it.

All this causes me to believe that until the present time it has not been by a judgment that was certain [or premeditated], but only by a sort of blind impulse that I believed that things existed outside of, and different from me, which, by the organs of my senses, or by some other method whatever it might be, conveyed these ideas or images to me [and imprinted on me their similitudes].

But there is yet another method of inquiring whether any of the objects of which I have ideas within me exist outside of me. If ideas are only taken as certain modes of thought, I recognise amongst them no difference or inequality, and all appear to proceed from me in the same manner; but when we consider them as images, one representing one thing and the other another, it is clear that they are very different one from the other. There is no doubt that those which represent to me substances are something more, and contain so to speak more objective reality within them [that is to say, by representation participate in a higher degree of being or perfection] than those that simply represent modes or accidents; and that idea again by which I understand a supreme God, eternal, infinite, [immutable], omniscient, omnipotent, and Creator of all things which are outside of Himself, has certainly more objective reality in itself than those ideas by which finite substances are represented.

Now it is manifest by the natural light that there must at least be as much reality in the efficient and total cause as in its effect. For, pray, whence can the effect derive its reality, if not from its cause? And in what way can this cause communicate this reality to it, unless it possessed it in itself? And from this it follows, not only that something cannot proceed from nothing, but likewise that what is more perfect – that is to say, which has more reality within itself – cannot proceed from the less perfect. And this is not only evidently true of those effects which possess actual or formal reality, but also of the ideas in which we consider merely what is termed objective reality. To take an example, the stone which has not yet existed not only cannot now commence to be unless it has been produced by something which posssesses within itself, either formally or eminently, all that enters into the composition of the stone [i.e. it must possess the same things or other more excellent things than those which exist in the stone [and heat can only be produced in a subject in which it did not previously exist by a cause that is of an order [degree or kind] at least as perfect as heat, and so in all other cases. But further, the idea of heat, or of a stone, cannot exist in me unless it has been placed within me by some cause which possesses within it at least as much reality as that which I conceive to exist in the heat or the stone.] For although this cause does not transmit anything of its actual or formal reality to my idea, we must not for that reason imagine that it is necessarily a less real cause; we must remember that [since every idea is a work of the mind] its nature is such that it demands of itself no other formal reality than that which it borrows from my thought, of which it is only a mode [i.e. a manner or way of thinking]. But in order that an idea should contain some one certain objective reality rather than another, it must without doubt derive it from some cause in which there is at least as much formal reality as this idea contains of objective reality. For if we imagine that something is found in an idea which is not found in the cause, it must then have been derived from nought; but however imperfect may be this mode of being by which a thing is objectively [or by representation] in the understanding by its idea, we cannot certainly say that this mode of being is nothing, nor, consequently, that the idea derives its origin from nothing.

Nor must I imagine that, since the reality that I consider in these ideas is only objective, it is not essential that this reality should be formally in the causes of my ideas, but that it is sufficient that it should be found objectively. For just as this mode of objective existence pertains to ideas by their proper nature, so does the mode of formal existence pertain to the causes of those ideas (this is at least true of the first and principal) by the nature peculiar to them. And although it may be the case that one idea gives birth to another idea, that cannot continue to be so indefinitely; for in the end we must reach an idea whose cause shall be so to speak an archetype, in which the whole reality [or perfection] which is so to speak objectively [or by representation] in these ideas is contained formally [and really]. Thus the light of nature causes me to know clearly that the ideas in me are like [pictures or] images which can, in truth, easily fall short of the perfection of the objects from which they have been derived, but which can never contain anything greater or more perfect.

And the longer and the more carefully that I investigate these matters, the more clearly and distinctly do I recognise their truth. But what am I to conclude from it all in the end? It is this, that if the objective reality of any one of my ideas is of such a nature as clearly to make me recognise that it is not in me either formally or eminently, and that consequently I cannot myself be the cause of it, it follows of necessity that I am not alone in the world, but that there is another being which exists, or which is the cause of this idea. On the other hand, had no such an idea existed in me, I should have had no sufficient argument to convince me of the existence of any being beyond myself; for I have made very careful investigation everywhere and up to the present time have been able to find no other ground.

But of my ideas, beyond that which represents me to myself, as to which there can here be no difficulty, there is another which represents a God, and there are others representing corporeal and inanimate things, other angels, other animals, and others again which represent to me men similar to myself.

As regards the ideas which represent to me other men or animals, or angels, I can however easily conceive that they might be formed by an admixture of the other ideas which I have of myself, of corporeal things, and of God, even although there were apart from me neither men nor animals, nor angels, in all the world.

And in regard to the ideas of corporeal objects, I do not recognise in them anything so great or so excellent that they might not have possibly proceeded from myself; for if I consider them more closely, and examine them individually, as I yesterday examined the idea of wax, I find that there is very little in them which I perceive clearly and distinctly. Magnitude or extension in length, breadth, or depth, I do so perceive; also figure which results from a termination of this extension, the situation which bodies of different figure preserve in relation to one another, and movement or change of situation; to which we may also add substance, duration and number. As to other things such as light, colours, sounds, scents, tastes, heat, cold and the other tactile qualities, they are thought by me with so much obscurity and confusion that I do not even know if they are true or false, i.e. whether the ideas which I form of these qualities are actually the ideas of real objects or not [or whether they only represent chimeras which cannot exist in fact]. For although I have before remarked that it is only in judgments that falsity, properly speaking, or formal falsity, can be met with, a certain material falsity may nevertheless be found in ideas, i.e. when these ideas represent what is nothing as though it were something. For example, the ideas which I have of cold and heat are so far from clear and distinct that by their means I cannot tell whether cold is merely a privation of heat, or heat a privation of cold, or whether both are real qualities, or are not such. And inasmuch as [since ideas resemble images] there cannot be any ideas which do not appear to represent some things, if it is correct to say that cold is merely a privation of heat, the idea which represents it to me as something real and positive will not be improperly termed false, and the same holds good of other similar ideas.

To these it is certainly not necessary that I should attribute any author other than myself. For if they are false, i.e. if they represent things which do not exist, the light of nature shows me that they issue from nought, that is to say, that they are only in me in so far as something is lacking to the perfection of my nature. But if they are true, nevertheless because they exhibit so little reality to me that I cannot even clearly distinguish the thing represented from non-being, I do not see any reason why they should not be produced by myself.

As to the clear and distinct idea which I have of corporeal things, some of them seem as though I might have derived them from the idea which I possess of myself, as those which I have of substance, duration, number, and such like. For [even] when I think that a stone is a substance, or at least a thing capable of existing of itself, and that I am a substance also, although I conceive that I am a thing that thinks and not one that is extended, and that the stone on the other hand is an extended thing which does not think, and that thus there is a notable difference between the two conceptions – they seem, nevertheless, to agree in this, that both represent substances. In the same way, when I perceive that I now exist and further recollect that I have in former times existed, and when I remember that I have various thoughts of which I can recognise the number, I acquire ideas of duration and number which I can afterwards transfer to any object that I please. But as to all the other qualities of which the ideas of corporeal things are composed, to wit, extension, figure, situation and motion, it is true that they are not formally in me, since I am only a thing that thinks; but because they are merely certain modes of substance [and so to speak the vestments under which corporeal substance appears to us] and because I myself am also a substance, it would seem that they might be contained in me eminently.

Hence there remains only the idea of God, concerning which we must consider whether it is something which cannot have proceeded from me myself. By the name God I understand a substance that is infinite [eternal, immutable], independent, all-knowing, all-powerful, and by which I myself and everything else, if anything else does exist, have been created. Now all these characteristics are such that the more diligently I attend to them, the less do they appear capable of proceeding from me alone; hence, from what has been already said, we must conclude that God necessarily exists.

[For although the idea of substance is within me owing to the fact that I am substance, nevertheless I should not have the idea of an infinite substance – since I am finite – if it had not proceeded from some substance which was veritably infinite.]

Nor should I imagine that I do not perceive the infinite by a true idea, but only by the negation of the finite, just as I perceive repose and darkness by the negation of movement and of light; for, on the contrary, I see that there is manifestly more reality in infinite substance than in finite, and therefore that in some way I have in me the notion of the infinite earlier than the finite – to wit, the notion of God before that of myself. (For how would it be possible that I should know that I doubt and desire, that is to say, that something is lacking to me, and that I am not quite perfect, unless I had within me some idea of a Being more perfect than myself, in comparison with which I should recognise the deficiencies of my nature?)

And we cannot say that this idea of God is perhaps materially false and that consequently I can derive it from nought [i.e. that possibly it exists in me because I am imperfect], as I have just said is the case with ideas of heat, cold and other such things; for, on the contrary, as this idea is very clear and distinct and contains within it more objective reality than any other, there can be none which is of itself more true, nor any in which there can be less suspicion of falsehood. The idea, I say, of this Being who is absolutely perfect and infinite, is entirely true; for although, perhaps, we can imagine that such a Being does not exist, we cannot nevertheless imagine that His idea represents nothing real to me, as I have said of the idea of cold. This idea is also very clear and distinct; since all that I conceive clearly and distinctly of the real and the true, and of what conveys some perfection, is in its entirety contained in this idea. [And this does not cease to be true although I do not comprehend the infinite, or though in God there is an infinitude of things which I cannot comprehend, nor possibly even reach in any way by thought; for it is of the nature of the infinite that my nature, which is finite and limited, should not comprehend it; and it is sufficient that I should understand this, and that I should judge that all things which I clearly perceive and in which I know that there is some perfection, and possibly likewise an infinitude of properties of which I am ignorant, are in God formally or eminently, so that the idea which I have of Him may become the most true, most clear, and most distinct of all the ideas that are in my mind.]

But possibly I am something more than I suppose myself to be, and perhaps all those perfections which I attribute to God are in some way potentially in me, although they do not yet disclose themselves, or issue in action. As a matter of fact I am already sensible that my knowledge increases [and perfects itself] little by little, and I see nothing which can prevent it from increasing more and more into infinitude; nor do I see, after it has thus been increased [or perfected], anything to prevent my being able to acquire by its means all the other perfections of the Divine nature; nor finally why the power I have of acquiring these perfections, if it really exists in me, shall not suffice to produce the ideas of them.

At the same time I recognise that this cannot be. For, in the first place, although it were true that every day my knowledge acquired new degrees of perfection, and that there were in my nature many things potentially which are not yet there actually, nevertheless these excellences do not pertain to [or make the smallest approach to] the idea which I have of God in whom there is nothing merely potential [but in whom all is present really and actually]; for it is an infallible token of imperfection in my knowledge that it increases little by little. And further, although my knowledge grows more and more, nevertheless I do not for that reason believe that it can ever be actually infinite, since it can never reach a point so high that it will be unable to attain to any greater increase. But I understand God to be actually infinite, so that He can add nothing to His supreme perfection. And finally I perceive that the objective being of an idea cannot be produced by a being that exists potentially only, which properly speaking is nothing, but only by a being which is formal or actual.]

To speak the truth, I see nothing in all that I have just said which by the light of nature is not manifest to anyone who desires to think attentively on the subject; but when I slightly relax my attention, my mind, finding its vision somewhat obscured and so to speak blinded by the images of sensible objects, I do not easily recollect the reason why the idea that I possess of a being more perfect than I, must necessarily have been placed in me by a being which is really more perfect; and this is why I wish here to go on to inquire whether I, who have this idea, can exist if no such being exists.

And I ask, from whom do I then derive my existence? Perhaps from myself or from my parents, or from some other source less perfect than God; for we can imagine nothing more perfect than God, or even as perfect as He is.

But [were I independent of every other and] were I myself the author of my being, I should doubt nothing and I should desire nothing, and finally no perfection would be lacking to me; for I should have bestowed on myself every perfection of which I possessed any idea and should thus be God. And it must not be imagined that those things that are lacking to me are perhaps more difficult of attainment than those which I already possess; for, on the contrary, it is quite evident that it was a matter of much greater difficulty to bring to pass that I, that is to say, a thing or a substance that thinks, should emerge out of nothing, than it would be to attain to the knowledge of many things of which I am ignorant, and which are only the accidents of this thinking substance. But it is clear that if I had of myself possessed this greater perfection of which I have just spoken [that is to say, if I had been the author of my own existence], I should not at least have denied myself the things which are the more easy to acquire [to wit, many branches of knowledge of which my nature is destitute]; nor should I have deprived myself of any of the things contained in the idea which I form of God, because there are none of them which seem to me specially difficult to acquire, and if there were any that were more difficult to acquire, they would certainly appear to me to be such (supposing I myself were the origin of the other things which I possess) since I should discover in them that my powers were limited.

(But though I assume that perhaps I have always existed just as I am at present, neither can I escape the force of this reasoning, and imagine that the conclusion to be drawn from this is, that I need not seek for any author of my existence) For all the course of my life may be divided into an infinite number of parts, none of which is in any way dependent on the other; and thus from the fact that I was in existence a short time ago it does not follow that I must be in existence now, unless some cause at this instant, so to speak, produces me anew, that is to say, conserves me. It is as a matter of fact perfectly clear and evident to all those who consider with attention the nature of time, that, in order to be conserved in each moment in which it endures, a substance has need of the same power and action as would be necessary to produce and create it anew, supposing it did not yet exist, so that the light of nature shows us clearly that the distinction between creation and conservation is solely a distinction of the reason.

All that I thus require here is that I should interrogate myself, if I wish to know whether I possess a power which is capable of bringing it to pass that I who now am shall still be in the future; for since I am nothing but a thinking thing, or at least since thus far it is only this portion of myself which is precisely in question at present, if such a power did reside in me, I should certainly be conscious of it. But I am conscious of nothing of the kind, and by this I know clearly that I depend on some being different from myself.

Possibly, however, this being on which I depend is not that which I call God, and I am created either by my parents or by some other cause less perfect than God. This cannot be, because, as I have just said, it is perfectly evident that there must be at least as much reality in the cause as in the effect; and thus since I am a thinking thing, and possess an idea of God within me, whatever in the end be the cause assigned to my existence, it must be allowed that it is likewise a thinking thing and that it possesses in itself the idea of all the perfections which I attribute to God. We may again inquire whether this cause derives its origin from itself or from some other thing. For if from itself, it follows by the reasons before brought forward, that this cause must itself be God; for since it possesses the virtue of self-existence, it must also without doubt have the power of actually possessing all the perfections of which it has the idea, that is, all those which I conceive as existing in God. But if it derives its existence from some other cause than itself, we shall again ask, for the same reason, whether this second cause exists by itself or through another, until from one step to another, we finally arrive at an ultimate cause, which will be God.

And it is perfectly manifest that in this there can be no regression into infinity, since what is in question is not so much the cause which formerly created me, as that which conserves me at the present time.

Nor can we suppose that several causes may have concurred in my production, and that from one I have received the idea of one of the perfections which I attribute to God, and from another the idea of some other, so that all these perfections indeed exist somewhere in the universe, but not as complete in one unity which is God. On the contrary, the unity, the simplicity or the inseparability of all things which are in God is one of the principal perfections which I conceive to be in Him. And certainly the idea of this unity of all Divine perfections cannot have been placed in me by any cause from which I have not likewise received the ideas of all the other perfections; for this cause could not make me able to comprehend them as joined together in an inseparable unity without having at the same time caused me in some measure to know what they are [and in some way to recognise each one of them].

Finally, so far as my parents [from whom it appears I have sprung] are concerned, although all that I have ever been able to believe of them were true, that does not make it follow that it is they who conserve me, nor are they even the authors of my being in any sense, in so far as I am a thinking being; since what they did was merely to implant certain dispositions in that matter in which the self – i.e. the mind, which alone I at present identify with myself – is by me deemed to exist. And thus there can be no difficulty in their regard, but we must of necessity conclude from the fact alone that I exist, or that the idea of a Being supremely perfect – that is of God – is in me, that the proof of God's existence is grounded on the highest evidence.

It only remains to me to examine into the manner in which I have acquired this idea from God; for I have not received it through the senses, and it is never presented to me unexpectedly, as is usual with the ideas of sensible things when these things present themselves, or seem to present themselves, to the external organs of my senses; nor is it likewise a fiction of my mind, for it is not in my power to take from or to add anything to it; and consequently the only alternative is that it is innate in me, just as the idea of myself is innate in me.

And one certainly ought not to find it strange that God, in creating me, placed this idea within me to be like the mark of the workman imprinted on his work; and it is likewise not essential that the mark shall be something different from the work itself. For from the sole fact that God created me it is most probable that in some way he has placed his image and similitude upon me, and that I perceive this similitude (in which the idea of God is contained) by means of the same faculty by which I perceive myself – that is to say, when I reflect on myself I not only know that I am something [imperfect], incomplete and dependent on another, which incessantly as-pires after something which is better and greater than myself, but I also know that He on whom I depend possesses in Himself all the great things towards which I aspire [and the ideas of which I find within myself], and that not indefinitely or potentially alone, but really, actually and infinitely; and that thus He is God. And the whole strength of the argument which I have here made use of to prove the existence of God consists in this, that I recognise that it is not possible that my nature should be what it is, and indeed that I should have in myself the idea of a God, if God did not veritably exist – a God, I say, whose idea is in me, i.e. who possesses all those supreme perfections of which our mind may indeed have some idea but without understanding them all, who is liable to no errors or defect [and who has none of all those marks which denote imperfection]. From this it is manifest that He cannot be a deceiver, since the light of nature teaches us that fraud and deception necessarily proceed from some defect.

But before I examine this matter with more care, and pass on to the consideration of other truths which may be derived from it, it seems to me right to pause for a while in order to contemplate God Himself, to ponder at leisure His marvellous attributes, to consider, and admire, and adore, the beauty of this light so resplendent, at least as far as the strength of my mind, which is in some measure dazzled by the sight, will allow me to do so. For just as faith teaches us that the supreme felicity of the other life consists only in this contemplation of the Divine Majesty, so we continue to learn by experience that a similar meditation, though incomparably less perfect, causes us to enjoy the greatest satisfaction of which we are capable in this life.

MEDITATION IV

Of the True and the False.

I have been well accustomed these past days to detach my mind from my senses, and I have accurately observed that there are very few things that one knows with certainty respecting corporeal objects, that there are many more which are known to us respecting the human mind, and yet more still regarding God Himself; so that I shall now without any difficulty abstract my thoughts from the consideration of [sensible or] imaginable objects, and carry them to those which, being withdrawn from all contact with matter, are purely intelligible. And certainly the idea which I possess of the human mind inasmuch as it is a thinking thing, and not extended in length, width and depth, nor participating in anything pertaining to body, is incomparably more distinct than is the idea of any corporeal thing. And when I consider that I doubt, that is to say, that I am an incomplete and dependent being, the idea of a being that is complete and independent, that is of God, presents itself to my mind with so much distinctness and clearness – and from the fact alone that this idea is found in me, or that I who possess this idea exist, I conclude so certainly that God exists, and that my existence depends entirely on Him in every moment of my life – that I do not think that the human mind is capable of knowing anything with more evidence and certitude. And it seems to me that I now have before me a road which will lead us from the contemplation of the true God (in whom all the treasures of science and wisdom are contained) to the knowledge of the other objects of the universe.

For, first of all, I recognise it to be impossible that He should ever deceive me; for in all fraud and deception some imperfection is to be found, and although it may appear that the power of deception is a mark of subtilty or power, yet the desire to deceive without doubt testifies to malice or feebleness, and accordingly cannot be found in God.

In the next place I experienced in myself a certain capacity for judging which I have doubtless received from God, like all the other things that I possess; and as He could not desire to deceive me, it is clear that He has not given me a faculty that will lead me to err if I use it aright.

And no doubt respecting this matter could remain, if it were not that the consequence would seem to follow that I can thus never be deceived; for if I hold all that I possess from God, and if He has not placed in me the capacity for error, it seems as though I could never fall into error. And it is true that when I think only of God [and direct my mind wholly to Him],[16] I discover [in myself] no cause of error, or falsity; yet directly afterwards, when recurring to myself, experience shows me that I am nevertheless subject to an infinitude of errors, as to which, when we come to investigate them more closely, I notice that not only is there a real and positive idea of God or of a Being of supreme perfection present to my mind, but also, so to speak, a certain negative idea of nothing, that is, of that which is infinitely removed from any kind of perfection; and that I am in a sense something intermediate between God and nought, i.e. placed in such a manner between the supreme Being and non-being, that there is in truth nothing in me that can lead to error in so far as a sovereign Being has formed me; but that, as I in some degree participate likewise in nought or in non-being, i.e. in so far as I am not myself the supreme Being, and as I find myself subject to an infinitude of imperfections, I ought not to be astonished if I should fall into error. Thus do I recognise that error, in so far as it is such, is not a real thing depending on God, but simply a defect; and therefore, in order to fall into it, that I have no need to possess a special faculty given me by God for this very purpose, but that I fall into error from the fact that the power given me by God for the purpose of distinguishing truth from error is not infinite.

Nevertheless this does not quite satisfy me; for error is not a pure negation [i.e. is not the simple defect or want of some perfection which ought not

16. Not in the French version.

to be mine], but it is a lack of some knowledge which it seems that I ought to possess. And on considering the nature of God it does not appear to me possible that He should have given me a faculty which is not perfect of its kind, that is, which is wanting in some perfection due to it. For if it is true that the more skilful the artizan, the more perfect is the work of his hands, what can have been produced by this supreme Creator of all things that is not in all its parts perfect? And certainly there is no doubt that God could have created me so that I could never have been subject to error; it is also certain that He ever wills what is best; is it then better that I should be subject to err than that I should not?

In considering this more attentively, it occurs to me in the first place that I should not be astonished if my intelligence is not capable of comprehending why God acts as He does; and that there is thus no reason to doubt of His existence from the fact that I may perhaps find many other things besides this as to which I am able to understand neither for what reason nor how God has produced them. For, in the first place, knowing that my nature is extremely feeble and limited, and that the nature of God is on the contrary immense, incomprehensible, and infinite, I have no further difficulty in recognising that there is an infinitude of matters in His power, the causes of which transcend my knowledge; and this reason suffices to convince me that the species of cause termed final, finds no useful employment in physical [or natural] things; for it does not appear to me that I can without temerity seek to investigate the [inscrutable] ends of God.

It further occurs to me that we should not consider one single creature separately, when we inquire as to whether the works of God are perfect, but should regard all his creations together. For the same thing which might possibly seem very imperfect with some semblance of reason if regarded by itself, is found to be very perfect if regarded as part of the whole universe; and although, since I resolved to doubt all things, I as yet have only known certainly my own existence and that of God, nevertheless since I have recognised the infinite power of God, I cannot deny that He may have produced many other things, or at least that He has the power of producing them, so that I may obtain a place as a part of a great universe.

Whereupon, regarding myself more closely, and considering what are my errors (for they alone testify to there being any imperfection in me), I answer that they depend on a combination of two causes, to wit, on the faculty of knowledge that rests in me, and on the power of choice or of free will – that is to say, of the understanding and at the same time of the will. For by the understanding alone I [neither assert nor deny anything, but] apprehend[17] the ideas of things as to which I can form a judgment. But no error is properly speaking found in it, provided the word error is taken in its proper signification; and though there is possibly an infinitude of things in the world of which I have no idea in my understanding, we cannot for all that say that it is deprived of these ideas [as we might say of something which is required by its nature], but simply it does not possess these; because in truth there is no reason to prove that God should have given me a greater faculty of knowledge than He has given me; and however skilful a workman I represent Him to be, I should not for all that consider that He was bound to have placed in each of His works all the perfections which He may have been able to place in some. I likewise cannot complain that God has not given me a free choice or a will which is sufficient, ample and perfect, since as a matter of fact I am conscious of a will so extended as to be subject to no limits. And what seems to me very remarkable in this regard is that of all the qualities which I possess there is no one so perfect and so comprehensive that I do not very clearly recognise that it might be yet greater and more perfect. For, to take an example, if I consider the faculty of comprehension which I possess, I find that it is of very small extent and extremely limited, and at the same time I find the idea of another faculty much more ample and even infinite, and seeing that I can form the idea of it, I recognise from this very fact that it pertains to the nature of God. If in the same way I examine the memory, the imagination, or some other faculty, I do not find any which is not small and circumscribed, while in God it is immense [or infinite]. It is free-will alone or liberty of choice which I find to be so great in me that I can conceive no other idea to be more great; it is indeed the case that it is for the most part this will that causes me to know that in some manner I bear the image and similitude of God. For although the power of will is incomparably greater in God than in me, both by reason of the knowledge and the power which, conjoined with it, render it stronger and more efficacious, and by reason of its object, inasmuch as in God it extends to a great many things; it nevertheless does not seem to me greater if I consider it formally and precisely in itself: for the faculty of will consists alone in our having the power of choosing to do a thing or choosing not to do it (that is, to affirm or deny, to pursue or to shun it), or rather it consists alone in the fact that in order to affirm or deny, pursue or shun those things placed before us by the understanding, we act so that we are unconscious that any outside force constrains us in doing so. For in order that I should be free it is not necessary that I should be indifferent as to the choice of one or

17. percipio.

the other of two contraries; but contrariwise the more I lean to the one – whether I recognise clearly that the reasons of the good and true are to be found in it, or whether God so disposes my inward thought – the more freely do I choose and embrace it. And undoubtedly both divine grace and natural knowledge, far from diminishing my liberty, rather increase it and strengthen it. Hence this indifference which I feel, when I am not swayed to one side rather than to the other by lack of reason, is the lowest grade of liberty, and rather evinces a lack or negation in knowledge than a perfection of will: for if I always recognised clearly what was true and good, I should never have trouble in deliberating as to what judgment or choice I should make, and then I should be entirely free without ever being indifferent.

From all this I recognise that the power of will which I have received from God is not of itself the source of my errors – for it is very ample and very perfect of its kind – any more than is the power of understanding; for since I understand nothing but by the power which God has given me for understanding, there is no doubt that all that I understand, I understand as I ought, and it is not possible that I err in this. Whence then come my errors? They come from the sole fact that since the will is much wider in its range and compass than the understanding, I do not restrain it within the same bounds, but extend it also to things which I do not understand: and as the will is of itself indifferent to these, it easily falls into error and sin, and chooses the evil for the good, or the false for the true.

For example, when I lately examined whether anything existed in the world, and found that from the very fact that I considered this question it followed very clearly that I myself existed, I could not prevent myself from believing that a thing I so clearly conceived was true: not that I found myself compelled to do so by some external cause, but simply because from great clearness in my mind there followed a great inclination of my will; and I believed this with so much the greater freedom or spontaneity as I possessed the less indifference towards it. Now, on the contrary, I not only know that I exist, inasmuch as I am a thinking thing, but a certain representation of corporeal nature is also presented to my mind; and it comes to pass that I doubt whether this thinking nature which is in me, or rather by which I am what I am, differs from this corporeal nature, or whether both are not simply the same thing; and I here suppose that I do not yet know any reason to persuade me to adopt the one belief rather than the other. From this it follows that I am entirely indifferent as to which of the two I affirm or deny, or even whether I abstain from forming any judgment in the matter.

And this indifference does not only extend to matters as to which the understanding has no knowledge, but also in general to all those which are not apprehended with perfect clearness at the moment when the will is deliberating upon them: for, however probable are the conjectures which render me disposed to form a judgment respecting anything, the simple knowledge that I have that those are conjectures alone and not certain and indubitable reasons, suffices to occasion me to judge the contrary. Of this I have had great experience of late when I set aside as false all that I had formerly held to be absolutely true, for the sole reason that I remarked that it might in some measure be doubted.

But if I abstain from giving my judgment on any thing when I do not perceive it with sufficient clearness and distinctness, it is plain that I act rightly and am not deceived. But if I determine to deny or affirm, I no longer make use as I should of my free will, and if I affirm what is not true, it is evident that I deceive myself; even though I judge according to truth, this comes about only by chance, and I do not escape the blame of misusing my freedom; for the light of nature teaches us that the knowledge of the understanding should always precede the determination of the will. And it is in the misuse of the free will that the privation which constitutes the characteristic nature of error is met with. Privation, I say, is found in the act, in so far as it proceeds from me, but it is not found in the faculty which I have received from God, nor even in the act in so far as it depends on Him.

For I have certainly no cause to complain that God has not given me an intelligence which is more powerful, or a natural light which is stronger than that which I have received from Him, since it is proper to the finite understanding not to comprehend a multitude of things, and it is proper to a created understanding to be finite; on the contrary, I have every reason to render thanks to God who owes me nothing and who has given me all the perfections I possess, and I should be far from charging Him with injustice, and with having deprived me of, or wrongfully withheld from me, these perfections which He has not bestowed upon me.

I have further no reason to complain that He has given me a will more ample than my understanding, for since the will consists only of one single element, and is so to speak indivisible, it appears that its nature is such that nothing can be abstracted from it [without destroying it]; and certainly the more comprehensive it is found to be, the more reason I have to render gratitude to the giver.

And, finally, I must also not complain that God concurs with me in forming the acts of the will, that is the judgment in which I go astray, because these acts are entirely true and good, inasmuch as they depend on God; and in a certain sense more perfection accrues to my nature from the fact that I can form them, than if I could not do so. As to the privation in which alone the formal reason of error or sin consists, it has no need of any concurrence from God, since it is not a thing [or an existence], and since it is not related to God as to a cause, but should be termed merely a negation [according to the significance given to these words in the Schools]. For in fact it is not an imperfection in God that He has given me the liberty to give or withhold my assent from certain things as to which He has not placed a clear and distinct knowledge in my understanding; but it is without doubt an imperfection in me not to make a good use of my freedom, and to give my judgment readily on matters which I only understand obscurely. I nevertheless perceive that God could easily have created me so that I never should err, although I still remained free, and endowed with a limited knowledge, viz. by giving to my understanding a clear and distinct intelligence of all things as to which I should ever have to deliberate; or simply by His engraving deeply in my memory the resolution never to form a judgment on anything without having a clear and distinct understanding of it, so that I could never forget it. And it is easy for me to understand that, in so far as I consider myself alone, and as if there were only myself in the world, I should have been much more perfect than I am, if God had created me so that I could never err. Nevertheless I cannot deny that in some sense it is a greater perfection in the whole universe that certain parts should not be exempt from error as others are than that all parts should be exactly similar. And I have no right to complain if God, having placed me in the world, has not called upon me to play a part that excels all others in distinction and perfection.

And further I have reason to be glad on the ground that if He has not given me the power of never going astray by the first means pointed out above, which depends on a clear and evident knowledge of all the things regarding which I can deliberate, He has at least left within my power the other means, which is firmly to adhere to the resolution never to give judgment on matters whose truth is not clearly known to me; for although I notice a certain weakness in my nature in that I cannot continually concentrate my mind on one single thought, I can yet, by attentive and frequently repeated meditation, impress it so forcibly on my memory that I shall never fail to recollect it whenever I have need of it, and thus acquire the habit of never going astray.

And inasmuch as it is in this that the greatest and principal perfection of man consists, it seems to me that I have not gained little by this day's Meditation, since I have discovered the source of falsity and error. And certainly there can be no other source than that which I have explained; for as often as I so restrain my will within the limits of my knowledge that it

forms no judgment except on matters which are clearly and distinctly represented to it by the understanding, I can never be deceived; for every clear
and distinct conception[18] is without doubt something, and hence cannot
derive its origin from what is nought, but must of necessity have God as its
author – God, I say, who being supremely perfect, cannot be the cause of
any error; and consequently we must conclude that such a conception [or
such a judgment] is true. Nor have I only learned to-day what I should avoid
in order that I may not err, but also how I should act in order to arrive at a
knowledge of the truth; for without doubt I shall arrive at this end if I devote
my attention sufficiently to those things which I perfectly understand; and if
I separate from these that which I only understand confusedly and with
obscurity. To these I shall henceforth diligently give heed.

MEDITATION V

Of the essence of material things, and, again, of God, that He exists.

Many other matters respecting the attributes of God and my own nature
or mind remain for consideration; but I shall possibly on another occasion
resume the investigation of these. Now (after first noting what must be done
or avoided, in order to arrive at a knowledge of the truth) my principal task
is to endeavour to emerge from the state of doubt into which I have these
last days fallen, and to see whether nothing certain can be known regarding
material things.

But before examining whether any such objects as I conceive exist
outside of me, I must consider the ideas of them in so far as they are in my
thought, and see which of them are distinct and which confused.

In the first place, I am able distinctly to imagine that quantity which
philosophers commonly call continuous, or the extension in length, breadth,
or depth, that is in this quantity, or rather in the object to which it is
attributed. Further, I can number in it many different parts, and attribute to
each of its parts many sorts of size, figure, situation and local movement,
and, finally, I can assign to each of these movements all degrees of duration.

And not only do I know these things with distinctness when I consider
them in general, but, likewise [however little I apply my attention to the
matter], I discover an infinitude of particulars respecting numbers, figures,
movements, and other such things, whose truth is so manifest, and so well
accords with my nature, that when I begin to discover them, it seems to me

18. perceptio.

that I learn nothing new, or recollect what I formerly knew – that is to say, that I for the first time perceive things which were already present to my mind, although I had not as yet applied my mind to them.

And what I here find to be most important is that I discover in myself an infinitude of ideas of certain things which cannot be esteemed as pure negations, although they may possibly have no existence outside of my thought, and which are not framed by me, although it is within my power either to think or not to think them, but which possess natures which are true and immutable. For example, when I imagine a triangle, although there may nowhere in the world be such a figure outside my thought, or ever have been, there is nevertheless in this figure a certain determinate nature, form, or essence, which is immutable and eternal, which I have not invented, and which in no wise depends on my mind, as appears from the fact that diverse properties of that triangle can be demonstrated, viz. that its three angles are equal to two right angles, that the greatest side is subtended by the greatest angle, and the like, which now, whether I wish it or do not wish it, I recognise very clearly as pertaining to it, although I never thought of the matter at all when I imagined a triangle for the first time, and which therefore cannot be said to have been invented by me.

Nor does the objection hold good that possibly this idea of a triangle has reached my mind through the medium of my senses, since I have sometimes seen bodies triangular in shape; because I can form in my mind an infinitude of other figures regarding which we cannot have the least conception of their ever having been objects of sense, and I can nevertheless demonstrate various properties pertaining to their nature as well as to that of the triangle, and these must certainly all be true since I conceive them clearly. Hence they are something, and not pure negation; for it is perfectly clear that all that is true is something, and I have already fully demonstrated that all that I know clearly is true. And even although I had not demonstrated this, the nature of my mind is such that I could not prevent myself from holding them to be true so long as I conceive them clearly; and I recollect that even when I was still strongly attached to the objects of sense, I counted as the most certain those truths which I conceived clearly as regards figures, numbers, and the other matters which pertain to arithmetic and geometry, and, in general, to pure and abstract mathematics.

But now, if just because I can draw the idea of something from my thought, it follows that all which I know clearly and distinctly as pertaining to this object does really belong to it, may I not derive from this an argument demonstrating the existence of God? It is certain that I no less find the idea of God, that is to say, the idea of a supremely perfect Being, in me, than that of any figure or number whatever it is; and I do not know any less clearly and distinctly that an [actual and] eternal existence pertains to this nature than I know that all that which I am able to demonstrate of some figure or number truly pertains to the nature of this figure or number, and therefore, although all that I concluded in the preceding Meditations were found to be false, the existence of God would pass with me as at least as certain as I have ever held the truths of mathematics (which concern only numbers and figures) to be.

This indeed is not at first manifest, since it would seem to present some appearance of being a sophism. For being accustomed in all other things to make a distinction between existence and essence, I easily persuade myself that the existence can be separated from the essence of God, and that we can thus conceive God as not actually existing. But, nevertheless, when I think of it with more attention, I clearly see that existence can no more be separated from the essence of God than can its having its three angles equal to two right angles be separated from the essence of a [rectilinear] triangle, or the idea of a mountain from the idea of a valley; and so there is not any less repugnance to our conceiving a God (that is, a Being supremely perfect) to whom existence is lacking (that is to say, to whom a certain perfection is lacking), than to conceive of a mountain which has no valley.

But although I cannot really conceive of a God without existence any more than a mountain without a valley, still from the fact that I conceive of a mountain with a valley, it does not follow that there is such a mountain in the world; similarly although I conceive of God as possessing existence, it would seem that it does not follow that there is a God which exists; for my thought does not impose any necessity upon things, and just as I may imagine a winged horse, although no horse with wings exists, so I could perhaps attribute existence to God, although no God existed.

But a sophism is concealed in this objection; for from the fact that I cannot conceive a mountain without a valley, it does not follow that there is any mountain or any valley in existence, but only that the mountain and the valley, whether they exist or do not exist, cannot in any way be separated one from the other. While from the fact that I cannot conceive God without existence, it follows that existence is inseparable from Him, and hence that He really exists; not that my thought can bring this to pass, or impose any necessity on things, but, on the contrary, because the necessity which lies in the thing itself, i.e. the necessity of the existence of God determines me to think in this way. For it is not within my power to think of God without existence (that is of a supremely perfect Being devoid of a supreme perfection) though it is in my power to imagine a horse either with wings or without wings.

And we must not here object that it is in truth necessary for me to assert that God exists after having presupposed that He possesses every sort of perfection, since existence is one of these, but that as a matter of fact my original supposition was not necessary, just as it is not necessary to consider that all quadrilateral figures can be inscribed in the circle; for supposing I thought this, I should be constrained to admit that the rhombus might be inscribed in the circle since it is a quadrilateral figure, which, however, is manifestly false [We must not, I say, make any such allegations because] although it is not necessary that I should at any time entertain the notion of God, nevertheless whenever it happens that I think of a first and a sovereign Being, and, so to speak, derive the idea of Him from the storehouse of my mind, it is necessary that I should attribute to Him every sort of perfection, although I do not get so far as to enumerate them all, or to apply my mind to each one in particular. And this necessity suffices to make me conclude (after having recognised that existence is a perfection) that this first and sovereign Being really exists; just as though it is not necessary for me ever to imagine any triangle, yet, whenever I wish to consider a rectilinear figure composed only of three angles, it is absolutely essential that I should attribute to it all those properties which serve to bring about the conclusion that its three angles are not greater than two right angles, even although I may not then be considering this point in particular. But when I consider which figures are capable of being inscribed in the circle, it is in no wise necessary that I should think that all quadrilateral figures are of this number; on the contrary, I cannot even pretend that this is the case, so long as I do not desire to accept anything which I cannot conceive clearly and distinctly. And in consequence there is a great difference between the false suppositions such as this, and the true ideas born within me, the first and principal of which is that of God. For really I discern in many ways that this idea is not something factitious, and depending solely on my thought, but that it is the image of a true and immutable nature; first of all, because I cannot conceive anything but God himself to whose essence existence [necessarily] pertains; in the second place because it is not possible for me to conceive two or more Gods in this same position; and, granted that there is one such God who now exists, I see clearly that it is necessary that He should have existed from all eternity, and that He must exist eternally; and finally, because I know an infinitude of other properties in God, none of which I can either diminish or change.

For the rest, whatever proof or argument I avail myself of, we must always return to the point that it is only those things which we conceive clearly and distinctly that have the power of persuading me entirely. And although amongst the matters which I conceive of in this way, some indeed are manifestly obvious to all, while others only manifest themselves to those who consider them closely and examine them attentively; still, after they have once been discovered, the latter are not esteemed as any less certain than the former. For example, in the case of every right-angled triangle, although it does not so manifestly appear that the square of the base is equal to the squares of the two other sides as that this base is opposite to the greatest angle; still, when this has once been apprehended, we are just as certain of its truth as of the truth of the other. And as regards God, if my mind were not pre-occupied with prejudices, and if my thought did not find itself on all hands diverted by the continual pressure of sensible things, there would be nothing which I could know more immediately and more easily than Him. For is there anything more manifest than that there is a God, that is to say, a Supreme Being, to whose essence alone existence pertains?[19]

And although for a firm grasp of this truth I have need of a strenuous application of mind, at present I not only feel myself to be as assured of it as of all that I hold as most certain, but I also remark that the certainty of all other things depends on it so absolutely, that without this knowledge it is impossible ever to know anything perfectly.

For although I am of such a nature that as long as[20] I understand anything very clearly and distinctly, I am naturally impelled to believe it to be true, yet because I am also of such a nature that I cannot have my mind constantly fixed on the same object in order to perceive it clearly, and as I often recollect having formed a past judgment without at the same time properly recollecting the reasons that led me to make it, it may happen meanwhile that other reasons present themselves to me, which would easily cause me to change my opinion, if I were ignorant of the facts of the existence of God, and thus I should have no true and certain knowledge, but only vague and vacillating opinions. Thus, for example, when I consider the nature of a [rectilinear] triangle, I who have some little knowledge of the principles of geometry recognise quite clearly that the three angles are equal to two right angles, and it is not possible for me not to believe this so long as I apply my

19. 'In the idea of whom alone necessary or eternal existence is comprised.' French version.

20. 'From the moment that.' French version.

mind to its demonstration; but so soon as I abstain from attending to the proof, although I still recollect having clearly comprehended it, it may easily occur that I come to doubt its truth, if I am ignorant of there being a God. For I can persuade myself of having been so constituted by nature that I can easily deceive myself even in those matters which I believe myself to apprehend with the greatest evidence and certainty, especially when I recollect that I have frequently judged matters to be true and certain which other reasons have afterwards impelled me to judge to be altogether false.

But after I have recognised that there is a God – because at the same time I have also recognised that all things depend upon Him, and that He is not a deceiver, and from that have inferred that what I perceive clearly and distinctly cannot fail to be true – although I no longer pay attention to the reasons for which I have judged this to be true, provided that I recollect having clearly and distinctly perceived it no contrary reason can be brought forward which could ever cause me to doubt of its truth; and thus I have a true and certain knowledge of it. And this same knowledge extends likewise to all other things which I recollect having formerly demonstrated, such as the truths of geometry and the like; for what can be alleged against them to cause me to place them in doubt? Will it be said that my nature is such as to cause me to be frequently deceived? But I already know that I cannot be deceived in the judgment whose grounds I know clearly. Will it be said that I formerly held many things to be true and certain which I have afterwards recognised to be false? But I had not had any clear and distinct knowledge of these things, and not as yet knowing the rule whereby I assure myself of the truth, I had been impelled to give my assent from reasons which I have since recognised to be less strong than I had at the time imagined them to be. What further objection can then be raised? That possibly I am dreaming (an objection I myself made a little while ago), or that all the thoughts which I now have are no more true than the phantasies of my dreams? But even though I slept the case would be the same, for all that is clearly present to my mind is absolutely true.

And so I very clearly recognise that the certainty and truth of all knowledge depends alone on the knowledge of the true God, in so much that, before I knew Him, I could not have a perfect knowledge of any other thing. And now that I know Him I have the means of acquiring a perfect knowledge of an infinitude of things, not only of those which relate to God Himself and other intellectual matters, but also of those which pertain to corporeal nature in so far as it is the object of pure mathematics [which have no concern with whether it exists or not].

MEDITATION VI

Of the Existence of Material Things, and of the real distinction between the Soul and Body of Man.

Nothing further now remains but to inquire whether material things exist. And certainly I at least know that these may exist in so far as they are considered as the objects of pure mathematics, since in this aspect I perceive them clearly and distinctly. For there is no doubt that God possesses the power to produce everything that I am capable of perceiving with distinctness, and I have never deemed that anything was impossible for Him, unless I found a contradiction in attempting to conceive it clearly. Further, the faculty of imagination which I possess, and of which, experience tells me, I make use when I apply myself to the consideration of material things, is capable of persuading me of their existence; for when I attentively consider what imagination is, I find that it is nothing but a certain application of the faculty of knowledge to the body which is immediately present to it, and which therefore exists.

And to render this quite clear, I remark in the first place the difference that exists between the imagination and pure intellection [or conception[21]]. For example, when I imagine a triangle, I do not conceive it only as a figure comprehended by three lines, but I also apprehend[22] these three lines as present by the power and inward vision of my mind,[23] and this is what I call imagining. But if I desire to think of a chiliagon, I certainly conceive truly that it is a figure composed of a thousand sides, just as easily as I conceive of a triangle that it is a figure of three sides only; but I cannot in any way imagine the thousand sides of a chiliagon [as I do the three sides of a triangle], nor do I, so to speak, regard them as present [with the eyes of my mind]. And although in accordance with the habit I have formed of always employing the aid of my imagination when I think of corporeal things, it may happen that in imagining a chiliagon I confusedly represent to myself some figure, yet it is very evident that this figure is not a chiliagon, since it in no way differs from that which I represent to myself when I think of a myriagon or any other many-sided figure; nor does it serve my purpose in discovering the properties which go to form the distinction between a chiliagon and other polygons. But if the question turns upon a pentagon, it is quite true that I can conceive its figure as well as that of a chiliagon without

21. 'Conception,' French version; 'intellectionem,' Latin version.

22. intueor.

23. acie mentis.

the help of my imagination; but I can also imagine it by applying the attention of my mind to each of its five sides, and at the same time to the space which they enclose. And thus I clearly recognise that I have need of a particular effort of mind in order to effect the act of imagination, such as I do not require in order to understand, and this particular effort of mind clearly manifests the difference which exists between imagination and pure intellection.[24]

I remark besides that this power of imagination which is in one, inasmuch as it differs from the power of understanding, is in no wise a necessary element in my nature, or in [my essence, that is to say, in] the essence of my mind; for although I did not possess it I should doubtless ever remain the same as I now am, from which it appears that we might conclude that it depends on something which differs from me. And I easily conceive that if some body exists with which my mind is conjoined and united in such a way that it can apply itself to consider it when it pleases, it may be that by this means it can imagine corporeal objects; so that this mode of thinking differs from pure intellection only inasmuch as mind in its intellectual activity in some manner turns on itself, and considers some of the ideas which it possesses in itself; while in imagining it turns towards the body, and there beholds in it something conformable to the idea which it has either conceived of itself or perceived by the senses. I easily understand, I say, that the imagination could be thus constituted if it is true that body exists; and because I can discover no other convenient mode of explaining it, I conjecture with probability that body does exist; but this is only with probability, and although I examine all things with care, I nevertheless do not find that from this distinct idea of corporeal nature, which I have in my imagination, I can derive any argument from which there will necessarily be deduced the existence of body.

But I am in the habit of imagining many other things besides this corporeal nature which is the object of pure mathematics, to wit, the colours, sounds, scents, pain, and other such things, although less distinctly. And inasmuch as I perceive these things much better through the senses, by the medium of which, and by the memory, they seem to have reached my imagination, I believe that, in order to examine them more conveniently, it is right that I should at the same time investigate the nature of sense perception, and that I should see if from the ideas which I apprehend by this mode of thought, which I call feeling, I cannot derive some certain proof of the existence of corporeal objects.

24. intellectionem.

And first of all I shall recall to my memory those matters which I hitherto held to be true, as having perceived them through the senses, and the foundations on which my belief has rested; in the next place I shall examine the reasons which have since obliged me to place them in doubt; in the last place I shall consider which of them I must now believe.

First of all, then, I perceived that I had a head, hands, feet, and all other members of which this body – which I considered as a part, or possibly even as the whole, of myself – is composed. Further I was sensible that this body was placed amidst many others, from which it was capable of being affected in many different ways, beneficial and hurtful, and I remarked that a certain feeling of pleasure accompanied those that were beneficial, and pain those which were harmful. And in addition to this pleasure and pain, I also experienced hunger, thirst, and other similar appetites, as also certain corporeal inclinations towards joy, sadness, anger, and other similar passions. And outside myself, in addition to extension, figure, and motions of bodies, I remarked in them hardness, heat, and all other tactile qualities, and, further, light and colour, and scents and sounds, the variety of which gave me the means of distinguishing the sky, the earth, the sea, and generally all the other bodies, one from the other. And certainly, considering the ideas of all these qualities which presented themselves to my mind, and which alone I perceived properly or immediately, it was not without reason that I believed myself to perceive objects quite different from my thought, to wit, bodies from which those ideas proceeded; for I found by experience that these ideas presented themselves to me without my consent being requisite, so that I could not perceive any object, however desirous I might be, unless it were present to the organs of sense; and it was not in my power not to perceive it, when it was present. And because the ideas which I received through the senses were much more lively, more clear, and even, in their own way, more distinct than any of those which I could of myself frame in meditation, or than those I found impressed on my memory, it appeared as though they could not have proceeded from my mind, so that they must necessarily have been produced in me by some other things. And having no knowledge of those objects excepting the knowledge which the ideas themselves gave me, nothing was more likely to occur to my mind than that the objects were similar to the ideas which were caused. And because I likewise remembered that I had formerly made use of my senses rather than my reason, and recognised that the ideas which I formed of myself were not so distinct as those which I perceived through the senses, and that they were most frequently even composed of portions of these last, I persuaded myself easily that I had no idea in my mind which had not formerly come to me through the senses. Nor was it without some reason that I believed that this body (which by a certain special right I call my own) belonged to me more properly and more strictly than any other; for in fact I could never be separated from it as from other bodies; I experienced in it and on account of it all my appetites and affections, and finally I was touched by the feeling of pain and the titillation of pleasure in its parts, and not in the parts of other bodies which were separated from it. But when I inquired, why, from some, I know not what, painful sensation, there follows sadness of mind, and from the pleasurable sensation there arises joy, or why this mysterious pinching of the stomach which I call hunger causes me to desire to eat, and dryness of throat causes a desire to drink, and so on, I could give no reason excepting that nature taught me so; for there is certainly no affinity (that I at least can understand) between the craving of the stomach and the desire to eat, any more than between the perception of whatever causes pain and the thought of sadness which arises from this perception. And in the same way it appeared to me that I had learned from nature all the other judgments which I formed regarding the objects of my senses, since I remarked that these judgments were formed in me before I had the leisure to weigh and consider any reasons which might oblige me to make them.

But afterwards many experiences little by little destroyed all the faith which I had rested in my senses; for I from time to time observed that those towers which from afar appeared to me to be round, more closely observed seemed square, and that colossal statues raised on the summit of these towers, appeared as quite tiny statues when viewed from the bottom; and so in an infinitude of other cases I found error in judgments founded on the external senses. And not only in those founded on the external senses, but even in those founded on the internal as well; for is there anything more intimate or more internal than pain? And yet I have learned from some persons whose arms or legs have been cut off, that they sometimes seemed to feel pain in the part which had been amputated, which made me think that I could not be quite certain that it was a certain member which pained me, even although I felt pain in it. And to those grounds of doubt I have lately added two others, which are very general; the first is that I never have believed myself to feel anything in waking moments which I cannot also sometimes believe myself to feel when I sleep, and as I do not think that these things which I seem to feel in sleep, proceed from objects outside of me, I do not see any reason why I should have this belief regarding objects which I seem to perceive while awake. The other was that being still ignorant, or rather supposing myself to be ignorant, of the author of my being, I saw nothing to prevent me from having been so constituted by nature that I might be deceived even in matters which seemed to me to be most certain. And as to the grounds on which I was formerly persuaded of the truth of sensible objects, I had not much trouble in replying to them. For since nature seemed to cause me to lean towards many things from which reason repelled me, I did not believe that I should trust much to the teachings of nature. And although the ideas which I receive by the senses do not depend on my will, I did not think that one should for that reason conclude that they proceeded from things different from myself, since possibly some faculty might be discovered in me – though hitherto unknown to me – which produced them.

But now that I begin to know myself better, and to discover more clearly the author of my being, I do not in truth think that I should rashly admit all the matters which the senses seem to teach us, but, on the other hand, I do not think that I should doubt them all universally.

And first of all, because I know that all things which I apprehend clearly and distinctly can be created by God as I apprehend them, it suffices that I am able to apprehend one thing apart from another clearly and distinctly in order to be certain that the one is different from the other, since they may be made to exist in separation at least by the omnipotence of God; and it does not signify by what power this separation is made in order to compel me to judge them to be different: and, therefore, just because I know certainly that I exist, and that meanwhile I do not remark that any other thing necessarily pertains to my nature or essence, excepting that I am a thinking thing, I rightly conclude that my essence consists solely in the fact that I am a thinking thing [or a substance whose whole essence or nature is to think]. And although possibly (or rather certainly, as I shall say in a moment) I possess a body with which I am very intimately conjoined, yet because, on the one side, I have a clear and distinct idea of myself inasmuch as I am only a thinking and unextended thing, and as, on the other, I possess a distinct idea of body, inasmuch as it is only an extended and unthinking thing, it is certain that this I [that is to say, my soul by which I am what I am], is entirely and absolutely distinct from my body, and can exist without it.

I further find in myself faculties employing modes of thinking peculiar to themselves, to wit, the faculties of imagination and feeling, without which I can easily conceive myself clearly and distinctly as a complete being; while, on the other hand, they cannot be so conceived apart from me, that is without an intelligent substance in which they reside, for [in the notion we have of these faculties, or, to use the language of the Schools] in their formal concept, some kind of intellection is comprised, from which I infer that they are distinct from me as its modes are from a thing. I observe also in me some other faculties such as that of change of position, the assumption of different figures and such like, which cannot be conceived, any more than can the preceding, apart from some substance to which they are attached, and consequently cannot exist without it; but it is very clear that these faculties, if it be true that they exist, must be attached to some corporeal or extended substance, and not to an intelligent substance, since in the clear and distinct conception of these there is some sort of extension found to be present, but no intellection at all. There is certainly further in me a certain passive faculty of perception, that is, of receiving and recognising the ideas of sensible things, but this would be useless to me [and I could in no way avail myself of it], if there were not either in me or in some other thing another active faculty capable of forming and producing these ideas. But this active faculty cannot exist in me [inasmuch as I am a thing that thinks] seeing that it does not presuppose thought, and also that those ideas are often produced in me without my contributing in any way to the same, and often even against my will; it is thus necessarily the case that the faculty resides in some substance different from me in which all the reality which is objectively in the ideas that are produced by this faculty is formally or eminently contained, as I remarked before. And this substance is either a body, that is, a corporeal nature in which there is contained formally [and really] all that which is objectively [and by representation] in those ideas, or it is God Himself, or some other creature more noble than body in which that same is contained eminently. But, since God is no deceiver, it is very manifest that He does not communicate to me these ideas immediately and by Himself, nor yet by the intervention of some creature in which their reality is not formally, but only eminently, contained. For since He has given me no faculty to recognise that this is the case, but, on the other hand, a very great inclination to believe [that they are sent to me or] that they are conveyed to me by corporeal objects, I do not see how He could be defended from the accusation of deceit if these ideas were produced by causes other than corporeal objects. Hence we must allow that corporeal things exist. However, they are perhaps not exactly what we perceive by the senses, since this comprehension by the senses is in many instances very obscure and confused; but we must at least admit that all things which I conceive in them clearly and distinctly, that is to say, all things which, speaking generally, are comprehended in the object of pure mathematics, are truly to be recognised as external objects.

As to other things, however, which are either particular only, as, for example, that the sun is of such and such a figure, etc., or which are less clearly and distinctly conceived, such as light, sound, pain and the like, it is certain that although they are very dubious and uncertain, yet on the sole ground that God is not a deceiver, and that consequently He has not permitted any falsity to exist in my opinion which He has not likewise given me the faculty of correcting, I may assuredly hope to conclude that I have within me the means of arriving at the truth even here. And first of all there is no doubt that in all things which nature teaches me there is some truth contained; for by nature, considered in general, I now understand no other thing than either God Himself or else the order and disposition which God has established in created things; and by my nature in particular I understand no other thing than the complexus of all the things which God has given me.

But there is nothing which this nature teaches me more expressly [nor more sensibly] than that I have a body which is adversely affected when I feel pain, which has need of food or drink when I experience the feelings of hunger and thirst, and so on; nor can I doubt there being some truth in all this.

Nature also teaches me by these sensations of pain, hunger, thirst, etc., that I am not only lodged in my body as a pilot in a vessel, but that I am very closely united to it, and so to speak so intermingled with it that I seem to compose with it one whole. For if that were not the case, when my body is hurt, I, who am merely a thinking thing, should not feel pain, for I should perceive this wound by the understanding only, just as the sailor perceives by sight when something is damaged in his vessel; and when my body has need of drink or food, I should clearly understand the fact without being warned of it by confused feelings of hunger and thirst. For all these sensations of hunger, thirst, pain, etc. are in truth none other than certain confused modes of thought which are produced by the union and apparent intermingling of mind and body.

Moreover, nature teaches me that many other bodies exist around mine, of which some are to be avoided, and others sought after. And certainly from the fact that I am sensible of different sorts of colours, sounds, scents, tastes, heat, hardness, etc., I very easily conclude that there are in the bodies from which all these diverse sense-perceptions proceed certain variations which answer to them, although possibly these are not really at all similar to them. And also from the fact that amongst these different sense-perceptions some are very agreeable to me and others disagreeable, it is quite certain that my body (or rather myself in my entirety, inasmuch as I am formed of body and soul) may receive different impressions agreeable and disagreeable from the other bodies which surround it.

But there are many other things which nature seems to have taught me, but which at the same time I have never really received from her, but which have been brought about in my mind by a certain habit which I have of forming inconsiderate judgments on things; and thus it may easily happen that these judgments contain some error. Take, for example, the opinion which I hold that all space in which there is nothing that affects [or makes an impression on] my senses is void; that in a body which is warm there is something entirely similar to the idea of heat which is in me; that in a white or green body there is the same whiteness or greenness that I perceive; that in a bitter or sweet body there is the same taste, and so on in other instances; that the stars, the towers, and all other distant bodies are of the same figure and size as they appear from far off to our eyes, etc. But in order that in this there should be nothing which I do not conceive distinctly, I should define exactly what I really understand when I say that I am taught somewhat by nature. For here I take nature in a more limited signification than when I term it the sum of all the things given me by God, since in this sum many things are comprehended which only pertain to mind (and to these I do not refer in speaking of nature) such as the notion which I have of the fact that what has once been done cannot ever be undone and an infinitude of such things which I know by the light of nature [without the help of the body]; and seeing that it comprehends many other matters besides which only pertain to body, and are no longer here contained under the name of nature, such as the quality of weight which it possesses and the like, with which I also do not deal; for in talking of nature I only treat of those things given by God to me as a being composed of mind and body. But the nature here described truly teaches me to flee from things which cause the sensation of pain, and seek after the things which communicate to me the sentiment of pleasure and so forth; but I do not see that beyond this it teaches me that from those diverse sense-perceptions we should ever form any conclusion regarding things outside of us, without having [carefully and maturely] mentally examined them beforehand. For it seems to me that it is mind alone, and not mind and body in conjunction, that is requisite to a knowledge of the truth in regard to such things. Thus, although a star makes no larger an impression on my eye than the flame of a little candle there is yet in me no real or positive propensity impelling me to believe that it is not greater than that flame; but I have judged it to be so from my earliest years, without any rational foundation. And although in approaching fire I feel heat, and in approaching it a little too near I even feel pain, there is at the same time no reason in this which could persuade me that there is in the fire something resembling this heat any more than there is in it something resembling the pain; all that I have any reason to believe from this is, that there is something in it, whatever it may be, which excites in me these sensations of heat or of pain. So also, although there are spaces in which I find nothing which excites my senses, I must not from that conclude that these spaces contain no body; for I see in this, as in other similar things, that I have been in the habit of perverting the order of nature, because these perceptions of sense having been placed within me by nature merely for the purpose of signifying to my mind what things are beneficial or hurtful to the composite whole of which it forms a part, and being up to that point sufficiently clear and distinct, I yet avail myself of them as though they were absolute rules by which I might immediately determine the essence of the bodies which are outside me, as to which, in fact, they can teach me nothing but what is most obscure and confused.

But I have already sufficiently considered how, notwithstanding the supreme goodness of God, falsity enters into the judgments I make. Only here a new difficulty is presented – one respecting those things the pursuit or avoidance of which is taught me by nature, and also respecting the internal sensations which I possess, and in which I seem to have sometimes detected error [and thus to be directly deceived by my own nature]. To take an example, the agreeable taste of some food in which poison has been intermingled may induce me to partake of the poison, and thus deceive me. It is true, at the same time, that in this case nature may be excused, for it only induces me to desire food in which I find a pleasant taste, and not to desire the poison which is unknown to it; and thus I can infer nothing from this fact, except that my nature is not omniscient, at which there is certainly no reason to be astonished, since man, being finite in nature, can only have knowledge the perfectness of which is limited.

But we not unfrequently deceive ourselves even in those things to which we are directly impelled by nature, as happens with those who when they are sick desire to drink or eat things hurtful to them. It will perhaps be said here that the cause of their deceptiveness is that their nature is corrupt, but that does not remove the difficulty because a sick man is none the less truly God's creature than he who is in health; and it is therefore as repugnant to God's goodness for the one to have a deceitful nature as it is for the other. And as a clock composed of wheels and counter-weights no less exactly observes the laws of nature when it is badly made, and does not show the time properly, than when it entirely satisfies the wishes of its maker, and as, if I consider the body of a man as being a sort of machine so built up and composed of nerves, muscles, veins, blood and skin, that though there were no mind in it at all, it would not cease to have the same motions as at present, exception being made of those movements which are due to the direction of the will, and in consequence depend upon the mind [as opposed to those which operate by the disposition of its organs], I easily recognise that it would be as natural to this body, supposing it to be, for example, dropsical, to suffer the parchedness of the throat which usually signifies to the mind the feeling of thirst, and to be disposed by this parched feeling to move the nerves and other parts in the way requisite for drinking, and thus to augment its malady and do harm to itself, as it is natural to it, when it has no indisposition, to be impelled to drink for its good by a similar cause. And although, considering the use to which the clock has been destined by its maker, I may say that it deflects from the order of its nature when it does not indicate the hours correctly; and as, in the same way, considering the machine of the human body as having been formed by God in order to have in itself all the movements usually manifested there, I have reason for thinking that it does not follow the order of nature when, if the throat is dry, drinking does harm to the conservation of health, nevertheless I recognise at the same time that this last mode of explaining nature is very different from the other. For this is but a purely verbal characterisation depending entirely on my thought, which compares a sick man and a badly constructed clock with the idea which I have of a healthy man and a well made clock, and it is hence extrinsic to the things to which it is applied; but according to the other interpretation of the term nature I understand something which is truly found in things and which is therefore not without some truth.

But certainly although in regard to the dropsical body it is only so to speak to apply an extrinsic term when we say that its nature is corrupted, inasmuch as apart from the need to drink, the throat is parched; yet in regard to the composite whole, that is to say, to the mind or soul united to this body, it is not a purely verbal predicate, but a real error of nature, for it to have thirst when drinking would be hurtful to it. And thus it still remains to inquire how the goodness of God does not prevent the nature of man so regarded from being fallacious.

In order to begin this examination, then, I here say, in the first place, that there is a great difference between mind and body, inasmuch as body is by nature always divisible, and the mind is entirely indivisible. For, as a matter of fact, when I consider the mind, that is to say, myself inasmuch as I am only a thinking thing, I cannot distinguish in myself any parts, but apprehend myself to be clearly one and entire; and although the whole mind seems to be united to the whole body, yet if a foot, or an arm, or some other part, is separated from my body, I am aware that nothing has been taken away from my mind. And the faculties of willing, feeling, conceiving, etc. cannot be properly speaking said to be its parts, for it is one and the same mind which employs itself in willing and in feeling and understanding. But it is quite otherwise with corporeal or extended objects, for there is not one of these imaginable by me which my mind cannot easily divide into parts, and which consequently I do not recognise as being divisible; this would be sufficient to teach me that the mind or soul of man is entirely different from the body, if I had not already learned it from other sources.

I further notice that the mind does not receive the impressions from all parts of the body immediately, but only from the brain, or perhaps even from one of its smallest parts, to wit, from that in which the common sense[25] is said to reside, which, whenever it is disposed in the same particular way, conveys the same thing to the mind, although meanwhile the other portions of the body may be differently disposed, as is testified by innumerable experiments which it is unnecessary here to recount.

I notice, also, that the nature of body is such that none of its parts can be moved by another part a little way off which cannot also be moved in the same way by each one of the parts which are between the two, although this more remote part does not act at all. As, for example, in the cord *ABCD* [which is in tension] if we pull the last part *D*, the first part *A* will not be moved in any way differently from what would be the case if one of the intervening parts *B* or *C* were pulled, and the last part *D* were to remain unmoved. And in the same way, when I feel pain in my foot, my knowledge of physics teaches me that this sensation is communicated by means of nerves dispersed through the foot, which, being extended like cords from there to the brain, when they are contracted in the foot, at the same time contract the inmost portions of the brain which is their extremity and place of origin, and then excite a certain movement which nature has established in order to cause the mind to be affected by a sensation of pain represented as existing in the foot. But because these nerves must pass through the tibia, the thigh, the loins, the back and the neck, in order to reach from the leg to the brain, it may happen that although their extremities which are in the foot are not affected, but only certain ones of their intervening parts [which pass by the loins or the neck], this action will excite the same movement in the brain that might have been excited there by a hurt received in the foot, in consequence of which the mind will necessarily feel in the foot the same pain as if it had received a hurt. And the same holds good of all the other perceptions of our senses.

I notice finally that since each of the movements which are in the portion of the brain by which the mind is immediately affected brings about one particular sensation only, we cannot under the circumstances imagine anything more likely than that this movement, amongst all the sensations which

25. sensus communis.

it is capable of impressing on it, causes mind to be affected by that one which is best fitted and most generally useful for the conservation of the human body when it is in health. But experience makes us aware that all the feelings with which nature inspires us are such as I have just spoken of; and there is therefore nothing in them which does not give testimony to the power and goodness of the God [who has produced them[26]]. Thus, for example, when the nerves which are in the feet are violently or more than usually moved, their movement, passing through the medulla of the spine[27] to the inmost parts of the brain, gives a sign to the mind which makes it feel somewhat, to wit, pain, as though in the foot, by which the mind is excited to do its utmost to remove the cause of the evil as dangerous and hurtful to the foot. It is true that God could have constituted the nature of man in such a way that this same movement in the brain would have conveyed something quite different to the mind; for example, it might have produced consciousness of itself either in so far as it is in the brain, or as it is in the foot, or as it is in some other place between the foot and the brain, or it might finally have produced consciousness of anything else whatsoever; but none of all this would have contributed so well to the conservation of the body. Similarly, when we desire to drink, a certain dryness of the throat is produced which moves its nerves, and by their means the internal portions of the brain; and this movement causes in the mind the sensation of thirst, because in this case there is nothing more useful to us than to become aware that we have need to drink for the conservation of our health; and the same holds good in other instances.

From this it is quite clear that, notwithstanding the supreme goodness of God, the nature of man, inasmuch as it is composed of mind and body, cannot be otherwise than sometimes a source of deception. For if there is any cause which excites, not in the foot but in some part of the nerves which are extended between the foot and the brain, or even in the brain itself, the same movement which usually is produced when the foot is detrimentally affected, pain will be experienced as though it were in the foot, and the sense will thus naturally be deceived; for since the same movement in the brain is capable of causing but one sensation in the mind, and this sensation is much more frequently excited by a cause which hurts the foot than by another existing in some other quarter, it is reasonable that it should convey to the mind pain in the foot rather than in any other part of the body. And although the parchedness of the throat does not always proceed, as it usu-

26. Latin version only.
27. spini dorsae medullam.

ally does, from the fact that drinking is necessary for the health of the body, but sometimes comes from quite a different cause, as is the case with dropsical patients, it is yet much better that it should mislead on this occasion than if, on the other hand, it were always to deceive us when the body is in good health; and so on in similar cases.

And certainly this consideration is of great service to me, not only in enabling me to recognise all the errors to which my nature is subject, but also in enabling me to avoid them or to correct them more easily. For knowing that all my senses more frequently indicate to me truth than falsehood respecting the things which concern that which is beneficial to the body, and being able almost always to avail myself of many of them in order to examine one particular thing, and, besides that, being able to make use of my memory in order to connect the present with the past, and of my understanding which already has discovered all the causes of my errors, I ought no longer to fear that falsity may be found in matters every day presented to me by my senses. And I ought to set aside all the doubts of these past days as hyperbolical and ridiculous, particularly that very common uncertainty respecting sleep, which I could not distinguish from the waking state; for at present I find a very notable difference between the two, inasmuch as our memory can never connect our dreams one with the other, or with the whole course of our lives, as it unites events which happen to us while we are awake. And, as a matter of fact, if someone, while I was awake, quite suddenly appeared to me and disappeared as fast as do the images which I see in sleep, so that I could not know from whence the form came nor whither it went, it would not be without reason that I should deem it a spectre or a phantom formed by my brain [and similar to those which I form in sleep], rather than a real man. But when I perceive things as to which I know distinctly both the place from which they proceed, and that in which they are, and the time at which they appeared to me; and when, without any interruption, I can connect the perceptions which I have of them with the whole course of my life, I am perfectly assured that these perceptions occur while I am waking and not during sleep. And I ought in no wise to doubt the truth of such matters, if, after having called up all my senses, my memory, and my understanding, to examine them, nothing is brought to evidence by any one of them which is repugnant to what is set forth by the others. For because God is in no wise a deceiver, it follows that I am not deceived in this. But because the exigencies of action often oblige us to make up our minds before having leisure to examine matters carefully, we must confess that the life of man is very frequently subject to error in respect to individual objects, and we must in the end acknowledge the infirmity of our nature.

Essays

Essay 1
Introduction

DAVID WEISSMAN

The contributors to this volume are persuaded that our intellectual inheritance is cogent and vital. We differ from writers who suppose that current thinking should pass out of time and context into an eternal present. Such writers relegate the history of ideas to footnotes, where it serves merely as backdrop and contrast to established truths. We emphasize questions about our intellectual debts and origins, because we believe that we shall not understand ourselves unless we can answer them. We ask: From whom do our ideas come? How have they been transformed? What are the conceptual paraphernalia of our beliefs and assumptions? What are we trying to say? Locating ourselves within a tradition that we have not made but do inherit, we discover the historical depth, contingency, and irresolution in our thinking about the world. We clarify our tasks and assumptions all the better to see the vector and motive for the changes we shall make in these ideas.

Many notions that shape our thinking originated in or passed through René Descartes. We are forever saying that he is the step beyond late medieval times into the modern era; but this estimate minimizes the range and impact of his views. This book seeks to recover his ideas and illustrate them in contexts ranging from contemporary physics and mathematics to politics, psychology and literature, epistemology and metaphysics. Most books about Descartes emphasize the intractable puzzles in his work. They ask: Is "Cogito, ergo sum" an inference or a report of self-inspection? Is self-knowledge conditional upon our knowledge of God, or vice versa? With so many analyses of these questions available elsewhere, we give little consideration to them here. What *we* do is describe Descartes' views and then their restatement, amendment, or transformation by his successors.

There are lineages that carry Descartes' ideas into the present. *Lineage* is a term borrowed from biology. It signifies successive generations of replicating species or reproducing individuals. It implies that successor generations either duplicate or modify the genetic material of their ancestors. The analogy to intellectual history is problematic but clear: ideas as much as DNA are inherited (Hull 1989, pp. 181–204). Transmission, alteration, and dispersion occur in both cases, though nothing in the character or transmission of ideas corresponds exactly to the mechanical integrity and interaction of DNA molecules. For there are some disanalogies.

Biological evolution generates and assimilates differences without being the dialectical play of opposites. This compares with successive episodes of discord and accommodation between ideas that may be compatible or opposed as they are reworked and applied. Think of all that is unresolved in our ideas about the relation of individual freedom to community, or in the ideas of freedom *from* and freedom *to*. Differences such as these may remain unreconciled over centuries of dialectical conversation. Biological lineages never skip a generation, but the paths of evolving ideas are frequently broken, as when a book is neglected for decades or centuries until discovered by a prepared reader. Shall we say that its transmission was interrupted between the book's publication and its rediscovery, or that continuity obtains because of its presence on some library shelf? Both interpretations are acceptable, because neither supposes that every intellectual lineage is a succession of regularly punctuated, generational acts of reproduction. We have a better analogy for some intellectual histories in the grain found in Egyptian tombs and made to germinate in a modern laboratory.

These sample histories – dialectical or episodic – illustrate a question about flow: How continuous must a train of ideas be in order to count as a lineage? The lineages in which Descartes figures vary between these extremes: from literal restatement, with no change of content, through steady modification, to saltant transformation (i.e., they jump).

Saltant lineages are dramatic. Consider Descartes' conservative political views (his respect for secular and religious authority) then compare the political thinkers who succeeded him. They ignored his prudence in favor of the revolutionary idea he suggests. For there is this flagrant, albeit undeclared, implication in the *Meditations* and the *Discourse*: that I am free of all external constraint if I exist, though all the rest of the world does not. What legitimate principles limit my freedom? Only the rules I make for myself. This is not an idea that Descartes formulates, but one that can be inferred from his skepticism. Who infers it? Rousseau makes this leap when he asserts at the beginning of his *Social Contract* (1749), that "Man is born free but is everywhere in chains." Each of us is "born free" in the moment that we confirm two things: that we exist when thinking, and that thinking discovers no sanction but power for the laws or rules that constrain us. Why are we in chains? Because we lack an offsetting power, and because, as Descartes argued in the sixth *Meditation*, we live in a material world which operates mechanically, without exemption for us humans.

Rousseau has exposed a paradox that challenges our self-esteem: How can we tolerate slavery when freedom is our birthright? The contrariety of these ideas seems irresolvable, until Kant rethinks them in his *Critique of Practical Reason* (1788). He liberates the thinking subject from the claims of mechanical necessity by elevating it to transcendental status: thinkers are said to exist outside space and time, hence independently of law-governed, material circumstances. Freed of those constraints, a thinker observes only such laws as are consistent with its rational nature. These are rules – maxims – the thinker makes for itself. Descartes, on this telling, is the unintended sponsor of liberal political theory, and goad to the American and French revolutions. The lineage he provoked is radically discontinuous, but consequential.

Intellectual lineages are, nevertheless, problematic. We want answers to these three questions about them: (i) Is it ideas or beliefs that evolve? (ii) Why is it that lineages are ignored in favor of current formulations of ideas? (iii) What is a lineage?

(i) *Is it beliefs or ideas that evolve?* Beliefs and ideas are often entwined in ways that make it difficult to separate them. But always there is this difference in principle. Lineages of belief entail a history centered upon the individual or individuals who believe them. What they believe and why they believe it provides information about these thinkers. Compare lineages of ideas: these are histories of repetition, amendment, or transformation of the contents believed. One may specify ideas, or their altered versions, without assigning names of believers to each successive formulation. A comprehensive history of ideas does both things, though either may be done without the other. We shall sometimes describe the evolution of an idea without mentioning all the intermediate steps and without assigning credit to all those who contributed to its lineage.

(ii) *Why is it that lineages are ignored in favor of current formulations of ideas?* No one resists believing that his hands resemble those of his grandfather. Why are we annoyed when told that our ideas are derivative? Partly out of vanity. *I did it*, we say; the fact that others have done the same thing, or something similar, is incidental to my achievement. Suppose, too, that my formulation seems cogent and complete. Surely, the history of past amendments is incidental to whatever content and form are exhibited in this complete idea. For the idea is true or false; and truth – not history – is my concern.

This persuasion explains contemporary hostility to the history of ideas. I am responsible for having coherent, complete, correct ideas. Let historians occupy themselves with earlier, less integrated, or merely different notions from which my ideas evolved. Consider a tune: it is complete merely by virtue of its notes. It may quote an earlier song, one that has been altered repeatedly; but no one need know this lineage in order to hum the tune.

Why should we care about the lineages of ideas? Because ideas betray their development. In content or emphasis or style, an idea expresses something of its origins, hence its contingency. It could have been, would have been, different but for considerations now buried and forgotten. Such factors may be incidental to an idea's content, as happens in the refinement of mathematical ideas. But more often, ideas are not so independent of their history: mathematical notation is radically contingent; philosophical claims may be quixotic or shallow apart from their dialectical context. We cannot recapitulate the entire dialectic as we affirm an idea; but the idea has evolved in time, so it has this history as its context.

(iii) *What is a lineage?* The plausible answer is that a lineage is a repetition or transformation of an idea or theory. Like a story, the idea or theory is retold or reinterpreted, criticized or amended. A lineage is the sequence of these formulations, whatever their direction and whatever the rhythm or cycle of the changes. A lineage may include interpretations of antecedent ideas, but the accuracy of these readings is incidental. For repetitions are only one – static – kind of lineage. Lineages that include misreadings, extrapolations, or reinterpretations are usually more fruitful.

This account, though not mistaken, is simplistic. It neglects a vital question: namely, what sort of continuant could a lineage be? One thinks of knot theory and its assumption that every twist and loop is permitted so long as the rope is not cut. Or we image a plastic structure (i.e., the idea or theory), which may be deformed in many ways so long as it is not broken or torn. These metaphors are useful only insofar as we are careful to reject the figures of speech they support.

Continuity, *development*, and *transformation* are terms implying that identity is preserved through change. But what are the identities preserved when the words expressing our conceptualizations are successively altered through the course of a lineage? If one thinker proposes that happiness is the good and a successor describes it as pleasure, we have substitution and discontinuity, not an identity-preserving development.

Discontinuity is confirmed when ideas are identified with the words and sentences used to express them. Different words usually convey different thoughts. Indeed, every occurrence of a word or a sentence may express a different notion if the idea is subtly altered by the idiosyncrasies of context and use. Our original assumption – that an idea is a plastic, deformable structure – has dissolved. There is a sequence, but the sequence is not a process. There is change, but not development or transformation. Perhaps no idea is constrained by the character of its antecedents.

We avert this conclusion by remarking that ideas have two elements: mental representations – thoughts or words – and their contents or referents. My mental representation for *bathos* may be nothing apart from this word, but its referent is a complex property, not the word. This property may or may not be instantiated: it may be possible but not actual. Accordingly, thought and language are not like wordless song. We would not care so much about the lineages of thoughts and words if they did not affirm successive claims about possibilities that exceed thought and language.

Granted the separability of words and the ideas they express (i.e., the properties or states of affairs signified), is there development or transformation in the referents? Let circularity be our example, and suppose that thoughts, words, and sentences express ideas by signifying possible states of affairs, as *circle* does. Imagine a logical space in which each possible state of affairs (e.g., the possibility of a property or complex of properties) is a point. There is, we suppose, an infinity of points, hence an infinity of contents for our ideas, or senses for our words. Some points are clustered together, thereby representing the fact that the possible states of affairs they signify are similar with regard to one or more properties (e.g., they are possibilities for figures of similar shapes). Other points are mutually remote: they have fewer properties in common.

Where every possible property or complex of properties is a point in logical space, we say that the words or thoughts signifying these points may be connected by paths. It is these paths that represent the possible evolutionary developments of ideas. Development is a path connecting ideas that do not change (e.g., as we create Orion by drawing imaginary lines between selected stars). We no longer say – for the purposes of this literal model – that an idea develops: the words or thoughts may often change (from language to language, over time, and from referent to referent within a language); their referents (i.e., possibles in logical space) do not. Paths, by contrast, are altogether of our making. Points in logical space are connectible, and we sometimes connect them by the sequence of our formulations. One of us claims that the moon is made of green cheese (that is a possibility), then others, intrigued, repeat or modify the idea. We create these sequences against the static background of referents – the possibilities in logical space – that do not change.

Is there a possible path between any two points? This is true even of contraries, as the idea of democracy may evolve into the idea of fascism and back again. The universal connectability of points, hence the infinity of possible paths, entails that most paths are of no historical interest (e.g., it is unlikely that ideas about Roman coinage evolved from ideas about quadratic equations). Does each, or any, path develop? Think of a reel of film where each frame is dramatically different from neighboring frames. Playing the reel as a motion picture, we see arbitrary shifts in the images. Equally, we lose coherence among successive ideas if paths are established among points so mutually remote that they support no relation. This threat is more abstract than real, because most thinkers know very little about the resources – the infinite array of referents – in logical space. Most lineages develop as thinkers struggle to understand a particular idea before replacing it with another that resembles it in most respects.

Some lineages hardly move beyond their initial starting point. These are repetitions. Others are generated because successive thinkers use the same idea for different purposes. The wheel is alternatively a religious symbol, a decoration, or a means of transport; the idea of God is used to extol, threaten, promise, or explain. Lineages of this sort may have no integrating principle. Paths that we call "developmental" connect points that satisfy Mill's method of difference: the possible states of affairs signified are alike in most salient respects, though deviations from the starting point accumulate as the path is extended. We say that these ideas are revised.

Dialectically interesting paths are of three sorts. *First* are paths connecting points that represent contrary expressions of a generic feature: ideas about the evolution of species are Lamarckian at some moments, Darwinian at others. Could ideas evolve as this path represents them? They could and did. *Second* are paths that never connect contraries. Let Descartes supply our example. His apriorism (about mind and geometry) was opposed to his taste for speculation: given unexplained phenomena, he hypothesized about their causes (as in his vortex theory). Newton was annoyed: "I do not make hypotheses" was his response to theorizing that was more inventive (or reckless) than precise and confirmed. He would have been surprised that Descartes' principal heirs are apriorists. Their motive was complex: they rejected speculation when Descartes' argument for the *cogito* established a ground for knowledge. This ground has two benefits: it stopped the regress of arguments that need a prior justifier for any last one proposed; and it promised an infallible intuition of the matters to be known. Descartes moved from one contrary to the other as circumstances required (see essays 4 and 5): perhaps their opposition was not apparent to him. It was evident to his principal philosophic successors. Intuition was their guarantee of truth. Abductive hypotheses (i.e., inferences from effects to their conditions) were shunned, because they risk error. Lineages of this sort evolve from one contrary or the other. They never return to incorporate the one abandoned. It may disappear, as the apriorist line almost obliterated evidence that Descartes was a speculator and an experimentalist. Dialectical paths of this sort resemble biological lineages: both contraries are subject to selection; only one or the other survives. *Third* are the paths generated when the structure – the "logic" – of a foundational idea invites elaboration or collapses provocatively. Descartes' realism is an instance. It implodes – in the direction of subjective idealism – if there is no God to guarantee the truth of clear and distinct ideas. But idealism is feeble if mind cannot make for itself what an extra-mental world would supply (e.g., objects for knowledge and a context for life-sustaining action). Cartesians respond by embellishing the *cogito*, making it self-sufficient. No instance of these three sorts of dialectical lineage is generated merely by drawing lines between arbitrarily chosen points. Paths are extended when the choice of contrary successors is determined by the character of the antecedents.

Paths are *interesting* or *useful* as they serve our purposes. Paths are *coherent*, *dialectical*, or *eclectic* because of mutually constraining relations that do or do not obtain among the ideas related by them. Eclecticism is the practice of connecting anomalous ideas, either by passing from one to another or by joining them as a single idea or theory. One eclectic theory familiar in our time joins Kantianism – the idea that "objects" are constructed when a conceptual system is used to project differences and relations onto sensory data – to naturalism or physicalism – the view that these same things exist independently of our thinking yet have properties that may be discovered by experimental scientists. We avert inconsistency by saying that sciences, too, are merely effective conceptualizations, not windows into an extra-theoretic reality. But now our realism is compromised. For anyone who forgets this qualification – anyone who affirms an extra-conceptual naturalism – while espousing the relativized ontology of conceptual systems commits the eclectic fallacy: his view is incoherent because inconsistent. Paths, too, may be eclectic, though the result is incoherence, rather than inconsistency, because the contrary views are affirmed in sequence, not all at once.

Tolerance for paths of every sort is therefore circumscribed. *Logic* speaks to our instinct that there are principles of integration intrinsic to the order of ideas. The distinction between semantics and syntax is often used to oppose this instinct (e.g., by those who say that order is imposed externally on ideas or sentences that have no mutually limiting relations to one another). The essays of this book suppose that the ideas of a lineage are themselves mutually constraining, as ontological naturalism and conceptual relativity are mutually exclusive.

Recall the motive for these claims about ideas and their relations: everyone who works with ideas is tempted by the assumption that they are plastic, deformable structures, and that thought alters an idea or tracks its changes through a succession of thinkers or circumstances. Think of clowns twisting balloons into raffish shapes. Can ideas be altered? Are they deformable, too? No, we replace the notion that ideas are protean with the model just proposed. What do such words as *development, evolution,* and *transformation* signify when used to describe lineages? They represent paths connecting points that are more or less closely arrayed in logical space. Do ideas evolve? Yes and no. The content or referent of an idea has an integrity of its own; it does not change. Yet sequences of complex ideas are generated when successive thinkers reorganize or amend the words or thoughts of their predecessors. Ideas are replaced, so that different properties construed as possibles are signified; or they are amalgamated in new ways, signifying an altered integration of possibles. And always, the sequence of ideas expresses, more or less obscurely, those constraints on integration founded in the properties themselves. Think again of the balloons: they retain a certain identity while being twisted and pinched. Ideas also have an identity, such that their integration is limited by their character. Disregard this character, and we create monsters with anomalous parts. Escher's drawings fascinate us, because he finds ways to represent impossible objects. Contradictory ideas are discouraged. Their lineages are mostly ignored, except for those (e.g., political or religious ideologies) having practical consequences.

These formal remarks are a backdrop for considerations that are more familiar. Suppose that we discern strong parallels to Cartesian notions in contemporary ideas, though the writers concerned have never read Descartes. What is more, their teachers never read him. Are we observing the late development of a Cartesian lineage or a parallel development having no historical basis in Descartes' texts? This is an empirical question; either answer is plausible. It would be premature, however, to discount the possibility of a lineage merely because proponents of an idea have no information about its origins. They could have learned it in many ways, just as many of us know something of the Bible without having read it. Where did we get the information? We may not know. Is it "in the air"? Not in any mysterious way, when so much of literature and ordinary life is informed by Bible stories and values. We would be suspicious of anyone who claimed originality for a story with strong biblical themes. We may be equally dubious about the alleged independence of any notion having strong affinities with ideas that have shaped curricula and practice for nearly four hundred years.

This characterization of lineages has a consciously realist bias: internally consistent ideas represent possible states of affairs; they signify properties and relations that may obtain, though many do not, as Plato's ideal state has no application. A lineage of ideas is the representation of successive possibilities. We do not invent the possibles; we only represent them. Realism of this sort will likely jar those readers who deny that lineages are repetitions or evolutions, discovered and described. These critics say that lineages are normative stories that we project onto the vague traditions we inherit. Is American history a record of successive liberations? Not on this view: it has whatever character we ascribe to it. Is this true because history is like the glass that is half full but also half empty, so that we correctly say either one? No, this is the claim that history, like everything else, has no decided character. It acquires a determinate form only as the bare framework of events assumed (invented?) is decorated with the properties and values projected by our interpretations.

Many contemporary thinkers believe that realities of every sort are the products of interpretation. They are created, according to this view, when we differentiate and organize experience in the ways prescribed by our purposes and the conceptual systems used to satisfy them. Lineages and natural laws – even physical objects and behaviors – are said to have this derivative reality, though it is usually supposed that we world-makers discover ourselves among the things we have made, oblivious to having made them.

Some things are constructed, as gender is in part an invented dance, one that prescribes meanings and behaviors to men and women in circumstances where anatomy alone would not require them. Should we generalize and say that all reality is a construct? Is it true that dogs, cats, and lineages too are made, not discovered? This relativizing, self-forgetting, Kantian view is pervasive in late twentieth-century thinking. The writers of this book demur. Cats and weevils evolve. Ideas do too, in the limited way specified above.

Readers may approach our book in either of two ways: they may look backward to Descartes' texts or forward through the lineages we describe. Students unfamiliar with Descartes may start with his works in translation. They may want the resonance of his ideas before considering their evolution. More seasoned readers – those who have views of their own about the lineages he nourished – may prefer to go directly to the essays. Readers of both sorts may be surprised by the variety of lineages, hence by the range of effects that Descartes continues to have within our thought and practice.[1] How odd that so much of our history is instigated by someone whose demand for certainty eliminated history as a candidate for knowledge.

The diversity of these lineages is offset by reflections that are lateral rather than historical. The first essay, "Descartes in His Time," describes the context in which Descartes wrote. It argues that certain ideas and particular events directed and shaped the texts reprinted here. The last essay, "Descartes in Our Time," argues that tensions in our thinking are promoted by differences between Descartes and Kant and by our uncertainty about the character of mind. Because the history of ideas will not end with us, we may want to alter the balance of these philosophical notions as they pass through us. This last essay makes some recommendations.

NOTE

1. Not all the lineages that begin with or pass through Descartes are considered here. One that we neglect – education – is critical. Descartes has carried the aristocratic preference for theory over practice into modern curricula. Some anomalies result: we prefer music to music theory and novels to literary criticism, though theory more than practice is rewarded with doctorates and professorial appointments. We deplore education that is merely vocational, though theory without application is often vapid. The Cartesian emphasis on theory makes thought self-sufficient, thereby removing thinkers from their context (i.e., we can ponder universals anywhere). Schools – universities especially – once neglected practical thinking (i.e., thought informed by local details and the thinker's interests). That has changed, because technologically driven economies require schools (including American land-grant universities and German technical schools) that match theory to practice. This lineage is vulnerable to the partiality of its dialectical extremes: on one side are abstracted truths; on the other, truth is reduced to interest and value. Descartes' preference for theory is balanced by Dewey's emphasis on practice (Dewey [1899] 1966).

REFERENCES

Dewey, John. [1899] 1966. *Lectures in the Philosophy of Education* (New York: Random House).

Hull, David. 1989. *The Metaphysics of Evolution* (Albany: State University of New York Press).

Essay 2
Descartes in His Time

STEPHEN TOULMIN

The Seventeenth-Century Crisis

It was the best of times, it was the worst of times, it was the age of wisdom, it was the age of foolishness, it was the epoch of belief, it was the epoch of incredulity, it was the season of Light, it was the season of Darkness, it was the spring of hope, it was the winter of despair, we had everything before us, we had nothing before us.

Charles Dickens's story *A Tale of Two Cities* opens with a famous passage that recalls the contradictory reactions of onlookers to the French Revolution. This passage could equally serve to introduce an account of European life and thought from 1610 to 1650: the forty years in which René Descartes played a distinguished part in cultural history and wrote the essays and books for which he is remembered today.

For many people, these years saw the birth of the crucial ideas of the modern era – in physics with Galileo Galilei, in philosophy with René Descartes, in political theory with Thomas Hobbes. To such readers, the first half of the seventeenth century was a time of intellectual glory unparalleled in the history of human thought. For others, the self-confidence of the Renaissance ran out of steam in the sixteenth century, giving way to a time of dogmatism, bigotry, and bloodshed that culminated, from 1618 to 1648, in the last, most destructive phase of the religious wars between Protestants and Catholics, what historians call the Thirty Years' War. (This covered all but the last two years of Descartes' career.) To them, the early seventeenth century is a period not of progress, but of retreat: an abandonment of the spirit of toleration and mutual understanding that was growing up during the Renaissance.

Either way, René Descartes was born at a turbulent time in European history. For four hundred years, starting with Pope Gregory VII's reforms in the eleventh century, Western Europe had made remarkable progress. In the year 1100, it is estimated, two cities in Europe – Venice and London – had more than 10,000 inhabitants: most people lived on farms or in towns of a few hundred. By the onset of the Black Death – the bubonic plague in the late 1340s that killed one-third of Europe's urban population – half a dozen cities had 100,000 inhabitants or more, and the urban society of the Middle Ages was well established. Meanwhile, economic expansion went on at a rate at least equal to that of the nineteenth-century Industrial Revolution, and new methods of trade and finance were being invented to support long-distance commerce. So, by the year 1300, Europe had entered the world of craft guilds and apprentices familiar to us from Richard Wagner's opera *Die Meistersinger von Nürnberg.*[1]

Throughout this time, most legal and administrative work in Europe, along with the institutions of higher education, were in the hands of the literate class called "clerics" – both because their clerical work accustomed them to handling written texts and because they were monks or ordained priests: they also acted as custodians of much of the intellectual tradition. Many lay people (not just Protestants) later came to see this ecclesiastical monopoly of learning as conservative, even oppressive. But at the outset, it had one remarkable result. It created a Europe-wide cadre of trained scholars, with a common language, literary inheritance, and body of questions. A young man born in Scotland or Sicily, Portugal or Poland, was trained to work in a community of professionals with colleagues across Europe, in a way that is barely possible even today, when European universities remain strictly "national" institutions.[2]

In a couple of hundred years, this society and culture built up a system of law and justice and a scientific world view that were directly challenged only after 1500. They did so by assembling the surviving texts of Greek and Roman antiquity (where necessary, translating them from Arabic, Hebrew, and other languages) and recreating a body of scholarly and legal thought that had been largely lost in Western Europe after A.D. 400. Far from being shaped by religious, let alone explicitly Christian, doctrines, this corpus introduced European scholars to a conversation that involved participants not just in Athens and Rome, but in Syria and Persia, Alexandria and Constantinople, Fez and Granada. From time to time, pre-Christian texts were challenged as heretical: during the thirteenth century, even Aristotle was under suspicion for his doubts about the beginning of time. But for the most part, the views of Aristotle the Greek, Cicero the Roman, and Maimonides the Jew met with the same respect among legal and moral philosophers as those of Augustine or Thomas Aquinas. In the last resort, ethics was, for moral theologians, the concern of a *ratio naturalis* ("natural reason") or shared human understanding.

This medieval consensus began to fall apart at the end of the fifteenth century, as the availability of printed books put both the Bible and other learned works into the hands of lay readers. Instead of being congregations of mere listeners, who turned to clerics to interpret Scripture, literate laymen read Scripture for themselves and judged rival interpretations by what they found in the texts. Meanwhile, a new infusion of classical literature was available for translation: the secular poetry, dramas, and biographies of the ancients. Medievals had debated human nature and the requirements for salvation as general issues: after the Renaissance, readers enjoyed books and poems that depicted individual human beings in all their follies and frailties, joys and frustrations, regardless of whether they were sinners or among the saved. (This novel focus on the varieties of human temperament and personality is evident, equally, in the works of Cervantes, Shakespeare, and Rabelais.)

The conclusive breakdown came in the late sixteenth century, when the findings of the Council of Trent led the Roman Catholic Church to oppose Luther's program of ecclesiastical reforms at all cost. Earlier in the century, Erasmus in Holland and Thomas More in England had resisted all moves to break with the Church, whether in the Protestant interest, as with Luther, or for personal and political reasons, as with King Henry VIII. But Luther and Henry were obstinate men, who insisted on bringing matters to a head, thereby giving conservatives the argument they needed to rouse opposition. What followed was a loss of authority on every side. All doctrines were put in doubt and became bones of contention, not just between Protestants and Catholics, but between Lutherans and Calvinists on the Protestant side, Jansenists and Jesuits among Catholics.

In turn, religious conflict encouraged political opportunism. Claiming the right to dictate the religious observance of their subjects, secular kings and princes strengthened their autonomy and built up alliances whose aims were merely political. In the most cynical of these alliances, Cardinal Richelieu arranged for the Catholic king Louis XIII of France to finance the mercenary army of the Protestant king Gustavus Adolphus of Sweden to stop the Catholic Habsburgs in Austria from seizing the lands of Protestant princes in Bohemia, Germany, and elsewhere, so helping the Habsburgs in Spain to cut France off from the rest of Europe. After an early Catholic victory in 1620 at the White Mountain near Prague, the Thirty Years' War hit a deadlock and dragged on interminably, while Richelieu's diplomacy prevented a speedy settlement.[3]

A similar deadlock developed in the world of ideas. Theologians of rival schools could give no unanswerable arguments in favor of their own doctrines or against those of their opponents; and this drew many sixteenth-century intellectuals toward some kind of skepticism. They lived as members of a church but did not accept its religion on the basis of doctrinal theories: for them, church affiliation was a cultural practice. Michel de Montaigne, for instance, saw that intellectual modesty required of him religious toleration: if he had been born in a Muslim country (he allowed), his own religion would presumably have been Islam.

In the 1590s the new king of France, Henry of Navarre – a Protestant from Béarn, but a friend of the Catholic Montaigne – raised toleration to the level of policy, by his Edict of Nantes. This called on loyal Catholic subjects to respect the rights of loyal Protestant subjects; and, in the hope of making this policy more acceptable to Catholic traditionalists, he became a Catholic himself. Yet toleration was less and less a popular cause. From the 1590s to the 1620s, economic conditions worsened all over Europe, with a loss of power by Spain, which was unable to protect the South American gold and silver fleets that had been bankrolling international trade.

To make matters worse, agriculture was hurt by a string of bad summers, which made it impossible to harvest saleable crops and depopulated large areas of marginal land: at this time, many formerly prosperous villages simply disappeared from the map. This bad weather was part of a larger climatic shift, which also produced the unusual winters depicted in Virginia Woolf's story *Orlando*: the river Thames in London was frozen over, and whole oxen were roasted on the ice. Deprived of a normal livelihood, farmworkers joined the pools of unemployed ("masterless") men available for service as mercenaries in the armies of the Thirty Years' War. As so often, economic bad times only sharpened the religious hatreds used to rationalize that terrible war.

Taking all these catastrophes together – intellectual, religious, economic, and social – many historians of early modern Europe have seen early seventeenth-century Europe as being in a state of general crisis. Over much of the Continent, nothing constructive could be done to restore its prosperity or stability until after 1648, when the Peace of Westphalia imposed inescapable compromises on the exhausted parties. Defined by the treaties of Osnabruck and Münster, this peace established the new political system in Europe so definitively that, to this day, political theorists speak of it as the "Westphalian" system of sovereign nation-states.

The closer we look at this crisis, the more strikingly do the political and economic disasters of the early seventeeth century contrast with the intellectual triumphs we trace back to those years. How, then, can we "place" Galileo and Descartes, who set their stamp on European physics and philosophy for three hundred years, against this background of tragedy and misery, folly and obstinacy? Were these men so indifferent to, and ignorant of what was going on around them, as to be oblivious to the horrors of their time: one-third of the German population slaughtered, one-half of its cities destroyed? Or was their passion for novel, more rational methods of intellectual inquiry one kind of intelligible response to the world into which they were born?

Many writers on the history of philosophy and science simply evade this question. Of the essays on this period in the *New Cambridge Modern History*, that entitled "The Scientific Movement and its Influence, 1610–50" is the only one to ignore the Thirty Years' War. Moreover, Cardinal Bellarmine's attack on Galileo's astronomy is too often presented as a clash between outdated medieval superstition and rational modern science; and, in a similar spirit, the twentieth-century *Grande Encyclopédie*'s entry on Descartes invites us to ignore all the events of his time except the place and date of his birth and his death: "His life is above all that of an *ésprit* [intellect]; his true life story is the history of his thoughts; the outward events of his existence have interest only for the light they can throw on the inner events of his genius." We are asked to think of a solitary Descartes thinking his own thoughts in his ivory tower, free from all outside influences – above all, wars and rumors of wars.[4]

It is easy to see why this view of Descartes' situation attracted later philosophers. His recipe for a *rational* method of thought was to dismiss from the mind all inherited ideas, which depend on birthplace and background, and start again from scratch with ideas open to people of all cultures, religions, and traditions. The philosopher's task was to identify basic ideas whose merits are transparent ("clear and distinct") to all reflective thinkers: these ideas will be the common possession of every human being. Such a program was attractive in two different ways: to those who were ready to set aside the world's practical problems in favor of purely abstract, universal questions and as an intellectual basis for a counterattack aimed at overcoming the confusion created by the breakdown of intellectual and religious authority. Instead of viewing Descartes as a solitary who ignored the political and theological problems of his world, therefore, we might do better to ask whether his philosophical agenda was not intended, rather, to rise above those problems.

Certainly, Descartes did not live in any ivory tower. Born in Touraine in 1596, he lost his mother before the age of two and was physically frail throughout childhood. His father got him a place in the leading Jesuit college, at La Flèche, where he studied with the most talented young men in the French world of administrators and scholars. As one of the Fathers' favorite students, he remained a devoted member of the college: however far his ideas might seem to stray from current Catholic orthodoxy, he kept up a correspondence with his teachers and tried (not always successfully) to present his own scientific and philosophical conclusions in terms that did not offend them.

Early on, Descartes' college experience taught him the relation of ideas to politics in France. When Henri IV (Henry of Navarre) was murdered in May 1610, Descartes was fourteen years old. By prior agreement, the dead king's heart was carried to La Flèche and enshrined at a solemn service before the college community: annual ceremonies in his memory, called *Henriades*, were inaugurated at La Flèche in 1611. In 1618, Descartes went to study in Holland, at Prince Maurits of Nassau's Academy of Military Science; and two years later he joined the Duke of Bavaria's staff, serving with the Catholic forces in Bohemia. Returning to France in the mid-1620s, he was already a man of the world, familiar with current events and able to read the signs of the times.

The France to which Descartes returned was very different from that of Henri IV. Under Henri's successor, Louis XIII, guided by Cardinal Riche-lieu, toleration was progressively eroded. Urged on by Catholic radicals, Richelieu assaulted the last Huguenot stronghold, at La Rochelle on the west coast, in October 1628. Soon after, Descartes came to the attention of Cardinal Bérulle, leader of the radicals who hoped to eliminate Protestant-ism from France entirely and were ready to censor and punish anyone whose ideas they found heretical. Worried by the growing power of these extremists, Descartes left France at short notice and spent the next sixteen years – the most creative years of his life – in the more tolerant atmosphere of the Netherlands.

All in all, then, we can scarcely view Descartes as untouched by the European crisis of the early seventeenth century: rather, his life and career serve as a counterpoint to the events of his time. His intellectual "method," guided by impartial reason, served as a weapon against dogmatism and superstition. His Jesuit training protected him from the fanaticism of the more violent Catholic factions and at the same time reinforced his own life-long demand for rationally defensible positions. His new lines of thought were presented so powerfully, and fitted together with such elegance, that they marked his system out as the prototype of what was to become (rightly or wrongly) the very model of modern philosophy.

Historically, Descartes took up current discussions and made original contributions to several fields: notably, the creation of a mathematical phys-ics and the debates about knowledge, skepticism, and the relation of reason to causality. Rather than introduce new themes for debate out of an entirely clear blue sky, Descartes in each case gave these discussions a new slant, which helped to define the distinctive agenda of philosophy in the modern era. Let us now turn to see how his personal background and interests enabled him to redirect these traditional debates.

The Physics of Galileo

In January 1611, not long before Descartes's fifteenth birthday, a little book appeared in Italy which left a permanent mark on his career and his style of thought. The book reached La Flèche in early spring, in time to catch the attention of students at the college: it was alluded to in the exercises for the first *Henriade* in summer 1611. The name of the book was *The Starry Messenger*, and it was written by Galileo Galilei, court mathematician to the Grand Duke of Florence. In this book, Galileo recorded the unexpected things he had seen in the heavens through his newly invented telescope: not least, the rugged texture of the moon's surface and four "circumjovial" satellites going round the planet Jupiter, as the planets in the solar system go round the sun. To readers educated in orthodox views of astronomy, Galileo's observations came as a bombshell. The book was read all over Europe, and within five years a copy reached Matteo Ricci, head of the Jesuit mission to China.[5]

Looking back on his years at La Flèche, Descartes never concealed his enthusiasm for Galileo's physics and astronomy. It was the prime starting point for his own work. Right up to his late book *Principes de la philosophie*, he saw himself not only as a general philosopher, but as a physicist – "natural philosopher" was the phrase at the time. (In the 1600s, our distinction between philosophy and natural science was unknown: the word *scientist* was invented only in 1840, in William Whewell's presidential address to the British Association.) Looking at the historical background to Descartes' philosophy, then, we must begin with his interest in the philosophy of nature. Many of his central problems about knowledge and certainty become clearer, once we look and see how they arose out of his concern with the structure and workings of nature.

This initial contact with Galileo's book put the fifteen-year-old Descartes squarely in a tradition that had been continuous since classical Greece. From the start, two main issues preoccupied philosophers: *cosmos* and *polis* – the constitution of the world of nature and the functioning of human society. From the start, philosophers also speculated about possible "harmonies" between nature and society. At best, these speculations underlay Plato's argument in the *Republic* that the principles of politics are best known to people who have mastered such mathematical sciences as geometry and astronomy. At worst, they led rulers to rely on methods of political forecasting – or "judicial astrology" – like those set out in Ptolemy's *Tetrabiblos*, which were still used to make a living, even in Galileo's time, by Johannes Kepler.

In late antiquity, two main groups of problems remained unresolved: the mathematics of bodily motions and the geometrical layout of the solar system. Galileo gave new vigor to both debates. In the centuries before the coming of the Arabs, scholars in Egypt – notably in Alexandria – tried to develop a consistent set of definitions for a theory of change and motion, taking Aristotle's scientific works as a starting point. The concepts that most perplexed them corresponded to our concepts of acceleration and momentum. Taken up again in the Middle Ages, these problems proved intractable, for two reasons. First, philosophers were still tempted to handle these issues too generally: a successful theory of change, they assumed, must cover changes of all kinds – not just bodily movements, but changing colors and sounds, ageing, and the rest. (Only in the seventeeth century did the mathematical philosophers of nature learn to study different kinds of changes separately.) Second, Aristotle's successors accepted too readily his commonsense conclusion that bodies will keep moving only for as long as they are pushed. As late as 1600, the converse idea, fundamental to the modern theory of bodily motion, that bodies move unchecked in a straight line for as long as nothing changes their motion, remained as counter-intuitive as it still is to beginners today.[6]

In the early fourteenth century, scholars in Paris and Oxford made real progress in the analysis of motion. Nicolas Oresme introduced the term *impetus* to record that bodies set in motion by an external "push" do not instantly stop moving when it is withdrawn – the push transmits an "impetus" to the body, which takes time to die. Meanwhile, new mathematical methods of representing bodily movements were devised, of a kind that later developed into the calculus. But, when Galileo entered the debate around 1600, some crucial points were unclear. In an early letter to his colleague Sarpi, he still found no conclusive reason to choose between two measures of "uniform change of motion" – that is, acceleration. Should one measure it by the change of speed in a given time (that is, in modern terms, by dv/dt) or by the change of speed in a given distance (dv/ds)?[7]

This was a matter of mathematical definition, not of physical fact, and the second measure led to paradoxical results. (On this definition, a body that starts moving from rest can get up speed at all only if its initial "acceleration" is infinite!) Before long, Galileo set this difficulty aside and went on to develop the concept of "inertia" that his mathematical theory of motion needed. On this theory, a body will change its speed or direction of motion only if acted on from outside. Quantity of motion ("impetus") does not die out of itself: it has to be destroyed by air resistance, friction, or the like.

Soon he ran into another obstacle, in the physics rather than the mathematics of motion. In the absence of any outside force, his account implied, a body continues to move at a steady speed in a straight line. But what counts, in real life, as "moving in a straight line"? All his experiments and observations pointed to the same conclusion. If a body ever moved in real life "at a steady speed in a straight line" – an abstraction from anything we ever observe in fact – it would move along a horizontal plane at a fixed height above the earth – that is, in a circle round the center of the earth.

From a modern point of view, this argument has something badly wrong with it: Galileo is plainly ignoring one outside force acting on the object – the force of gravity. In physical terms, gravity prevents any such body from moving off, along a Euclidean straight line tangential to the earth's surface, into the sky. Is this a serious error on Galileo's part? Not at all: the modern objection is anachronistic. As late as 1642, the year Galileo died and Newton was born, it was not yet generally agreed that gravity is a "force." Isaac Newton put the point beyond doubt for the time being only in 1687, in the theory of planetary motion that he set out in his masterpiece *The Mathematical Principles of Natural Philosophy.*

In addition to problems in the mathematics of bodily motion, there remained the second group of questions, about the geometrical layout of the solar system. In 1611, when *The Starry Messenger* reached La Flèche, these were topics of very active controversy. For more than sixty years, the choice between the two principal "world systems" – the traditional geostatic system of Ptolemy and Aristotle and the heliostatic system devised by Aristarchus and recently revived by Copernicus – had been a matter of public debate, though some sophisticated astronomers, seeking a middle way between radical novelty and conservative tradition, developed compromise systems using elements from both. Given the widespread inclination to see the order of nature as linked with the social order, this astronomical controversy was sensitive. Those who deplored the loss of the traditional consensus, like John Donne, denounced Copernicus as a troublemaker; and the outbreak of the Thirty Years' War only made these issues more delicate still. So, when Galileo published his famous *Dialogue* on the two world systems in 1632, a storm broke about his head.[8]

For Descartes, hearing that the Church had condemned Galileo's book was a bitter blow – as if his two parents had quarreled bitterly and gone opposite ways. He had written an account of his own world system, the *De Mundo*, which he at once withdrew from publication; but there is no doubt of the heartbreak that this decision involved. Unwilling to break with the Church openly, he did not dare to add his Copernican voice to that of Galileo; but no one who reads the physical theories in his *Principes de la philosophie* will find his views ambiguous. First, he works out a mechanical theory of the origin and structure of the physical world, and then he pauses to cover himself. As to such things, Descartes says, he *of course* accepts the account in Holy Scripture as being the truth: his own theory is meant to show *only* that the results of God's wisdom in the creation could have come about alternatively (though over a greater time) as a natural outcome of mechanical processes.[9]

In the discussions of the theory of motion and the layout of the solar system, Descartes begins at a point midway between Galileo and Newton. His vision of an overall system of natural philosophy – that is, a comprehensive theory of the workings of physical nature – is more ambitious than Galileo's. But he is in no position to carry it to completion with anything like the same accuracy and detail as Newton did forty years later. Yet, in one respect, Descartes' improvement on Galileo's position is clear. In applying the concept of inertia to actual physical cases, Galileo had never fully sorted out mathematical issues from observational ones: the abstract concept of a Euclidean straight line remained entangled with the physical idea of an orbit around the earth. Descartes went further. The status of Euclid's geometry was so central to his theory of knowledge and certainty that he could generalize it, raising it to the level of an abstract mathematical system, more readily than a practical physicist like Galileo – or, for that matter, Newton – could.

In Descartes' theory of motion, accordingly, the natural subjects of all motion are "extended geometrical figures." (The relevance of these shapes to the bulky objects of mechanics and astronomy will be shown separately, later.) At this point, physical theory ceased to be a digest of practical experience and became a general framework for the representation of nature. The foundations of this framework had been laid by Euclid long ago: the task for the new natural philosophy was to develop mechanical ideas that were natural extensions of Euclid's spatial ones. In this respect, Newton's work simply continued and completed the project that Descartes began.

It is a historical irony of physics that the only detailed presentation of Descartes' theory of the motion of the planets round the sun is in Book II of

Newton's *Principia*. By the 1680s, Descartes' theory had become "the one to beat"; so Newton, while clearly in the same business as Descartes, took care to demonstrate at length that this "vortex" theory can be kept in play only at the price of empirical assumptions for which no independent evidence exists – for example, regarding the "subtle fluid" that supposedly filled the space between the planets. (In due course, Cartesians made a parallel objection to Newton's theory. But Newton's assumption that interplanetary space is empty was less arbitrary than Descartes' assumption that it is full of an invisible material whose other properties we do not know.) More important, the mathematical consequences of Newton's theory checked out in concrete detail as explanations of Kepler's planetary observations, as well as of most everyday terrestrial motions, in ways that allowed physicists to dismantle the traditional barrier between terrestrial and celestial objects.[10]

In the last part of his *Principes de la philosophie*, Descartes himself emphasized that any system of natural philosophy is in the last resort a "decipherment" of nature, like, say, Ventris and Chadwick's reading of Linear Minoan B as a language very close to classical Greek. It continues to carry conviction only if it makes fresh sense of the new messages to which it is applied. If Francis Crick and James Watson "cracked the code" of molecular biology, René Descartes and Isaac Newton set out to "read" the motion of the planets in a language as close as possible to that of Euclid's geometry.

If Newton, rather than Descartes, gave modern physics its foundations, it is because, in the long run, Newton's interpretations, rather than Descartes', continued to make consistent and intelligible sense of the phenomena. All the same (we may note), as they figure in Newton's laws of motion, dynamical "ideas" like action and reaction, acceleration and momentum, were not accepted merely because they are "clear and distinct" – let alone, given by God to all reflective human beings. Increasingly, from 1687 on, the tests of a physical theory became pragmatic, rather than theological.

Freedom and Mechanism

Descartes found in Galileo not just unresolved problems in mechanics and planetary astronomy: more centrally, Galileo gave him a new intellectual vision of natural philosophy. The abstract systems of mathematical theory that are at the heart of modern physics played little part in medieval ideas of nature. Medieval writers were preoccupied with more pedestrian aspects of the natural world, and their concern with them was more edifying than accurate. A medieval bestiary, for example, described the beasts as topics for parables, sermons, or homilies, rather than as objects for close study or detailed observation. Medieval books of beasts or flowers were illuminated with elegance and artistry, but the painted illustrations in their margins contain accumulated errors, which show that they were copied not from life, but from earlier manuscripts.

The modern vision of nature, as an organized mechanism open to human study and mastery, took on clarity and definition only in the sixteenth century. This did not happen all at once. In fifteenth-century Italy, the philosophical debate among Renaissance humanists was dominated by Neoplatonist writers like Marsilio Ficino and Pico della Mirandola. These writers regarded human beings as free to shape their own destinies in more respects than conservative theologians would have allowed; but they aimed at practical, rather than intellectual, mastery, and saw an understanding of nature as embodied less in abstract mathematical concepts than in ideas drawn from alchemy, astrology, or the other kinds of natural magic. (These arts kept their charm well into the seventeenth century, alongside the new mathematical and experimental natural philosophy.) The first steps in what Dijksterhuis has called "the mechanization of the world picture" began with the recovery of classical atomism – notably, the tradition of Democritus and Epicurus – and the availability in translation of Lucretius's poem "On the Nature of Things" (*De rerum naturae*).[11]

Lucretius's purpose, like that of Epicurus before him, was emancipatory more than explanatory: he was fighting not *for* scientific understanding, but *against* superstitious anxiety. He took different kinds of natural phenomena used to arouse terror or guilt in onlookers and made it his concern to show how one may account for them in natural terms. There was no reason to be intimidated by, for example, an eclipse of the sun, for this might happen quite naturally in any of a number of ways, none of which is *ominous* – that is, none of which serves as a warning to human beings that they may expect some punishment, collectively or as individuals. Both Epicurus and Lucretius were ready to multiply the *possible* explanations of phenomena, without asking which is the *actual* explanation. If we can think up twice as many naturalistic accounts of the appearance of comets, say, this will halve our fear that they are portents or omens and double our opportunity to liberate ourselves from needless anxiety. If nature is a machine, its operations will grind on inexorably, regardless of human vices or virtues. So let the great gods be! They have more on their minds than human pleasures, pains, and peccadilloes.

Quite late in the seventeenth century, these assurances were still needed. The president of Harvard, Increase Mather (Cotton Mather's father), still took seriously the belief that comets are portents of human misfortunes. Even in 1687, in an introductory poem praising the achievements of Newton's *Principia*, Edmund Halley still thought it worth applauding Newton for liberating us from this belief:

Now we know the sharply veering ways of Comets, once a source of Dread; Nor longer need we quail beneath Appearances of Bearded Stars.

Yet the names of Epicurus or Epicureanism remained under a cloud for a long time yet: Newton, for instance, did not relish being attacked as an Epicurean and took care to speak of the ultimate material units in his theory not as atoms, but as particles.

Still, once the vision of the cosmos as a mechanism was recovered, it reawakened the interest of philosophers in naturalistic explanations. Galileo turned to classical literature and took up again questions raised by Democritus in the fifth century B.C. – for example, about the mechanisms of sense perception and their effect on our sensory inputs. This led him to restate the distinction between "primary" and "secondary" qualities of physical objects, which had been known to Democritus and was to be revived as a centerpiece of John Locke's theory of knowledge. In this way, Galileo could frame an agenda for epistemology, even before Descartes himself had written anything on the subject.

Mechanization of the world picture was further encouraged by a change in theological climate. Medieval metaphysicians spoke of the relations of God to nature in timeless terms – of God as the "ground" of all being. God sustained the world not just at the beginning, but at all times equally: what gives evidence of his presence is the fact that anything at all exists, anytime or anywhere. In the sixteenth century, however, theologians began to focus on creation. God was seen as an architect, whose wise design was embodied in the world of nature at the time of creation, and what provide evidence of his role in the world are the traces his wisdom and rationality left on the world that was so created. At the end of the *Principia*, for instance, Newton wrote with confidence that the success of his laws of motion and gravitation confirmed the rationality of God the Creator.

Before long, the standard trope was to compare God the Creator to a clock-maker. The phenomena of nature were seen as like the movements of the hands on an elaborate clock mechanism, and the unchanging precision with which this operated was evidence of the Creator's omnipotence. By 1714, this image was entrenched: it shaped the rhetoric of Leibniz's onslaught on Newton's *Principia* in the letter to Princess Caroline that opens his correspondence with Samuel Clarke. If Newton failed to give a mathematical proof of the laws of nature as rigorous as rationalist principles demanded, this, Leibniz said, was a sign that he had "a very mean notion of the wisdom and power of God." [12]

A rational God, in Leibniz's eyes, would do better than to create a planetary system whose stability was in doubt: that would mark him as a very imperfect clock-maker! Yet Newton's theory provided no formulae for calculating the future movements of the planets in the entire solar system, but only for the special case of the sun and one planet at a time. The same mathematical obstacle – the so-called n-body problem – left open the possibility that, in some situations, bodies may interact in complex ways, whose results are wholly unpredictable. But could a rational God tolerate a natural world in which things happen in radically unforeseen ways? Thus began a debate about the essential predictability of nature, which was taken up by Laplace, passed on by way of Henri Poincaré to Albert Einstein, and has culminated today in chaos theory and nonlinear mathematics. [13]

When Descartes arrived in the Netherlands from France at the age of thirty-two, just about New Year 1629, his first home, Richard Watson tells us, was a castle belonging to a Catholic family at Franeker in Friesland, whose university was itself "a haven for persecuted Protestants from all over Europe." By this time, Descartes was presumably well aware of Galileo's mechanistic world picture. Certainly, the town he chose to live in was hospitable to such intellectual novelties. Anyone who goes to Franeker today is exhorted to visit its "planetarium," a small seventeenth-century house on the main street whose interior was made over to this purpose by an enthusiastic astronomer. The ceilings of the living rooms hide meticulously handmade wooden axles and cogwheels, which control the motions of dozens of dials, hands, and miniature astronomical objects. The dinner table thus gave the family a front-seat view of the newly mechanized cosmos. [14]

Most significant for Descartes, the mechanization of the world picture gave people a new view of causality in nature. In particular, it introduced to French thought a kind of physical determinism that had been rare in the Middle Ages. In sixteenth-century France, most philosophers were drawn to a Stoic view of the relations between humanity and nature: that far from these realms operating in radically different ways, there are systematic harmonies between the kinds of reason at work in the inanimate, living, and intellectual worlds. In particular, sixteenth-century moralists argued, human conduct is to be governed in ways that respect the harmony of humanity and nature. In terms familiar from the 1960s and 1970s, they claimed:

"Morally right conduct is also Natural conduct" – that is, human conduct should conform to the same patterns as the world of nature.

For anyone who adopted a mechanistic approach to nature, a serious problem at once arose. If humans must behave in conformity with the natural world, and the natural world is a mechanistic, causally determined system, it follows that humans too are mechanistic, causally determined systems. This conclusion was difficult to accept: on the contrary, it was generally taken as damaging to any Stoic system of ethics. Nearly all the seventeenth-century natural philosophers who commited themselves to a mechanical theory of nature did so at a price: they had to contrast the causal mechanisms in the world of passive matter with the immaterial agencies that were responsible for spontaneity in the world of active beings. Animal behavior was intelligible within Galilean physics – as Giovanni Borelli was to find – only at the price of vitalism; and ethics and logic could escape from mechanical causality only at the price of dualism.[15]

With these arguments in the background, Descartes was as badly off as the other mechanical philosophers of nature when it came to finding a place for humanity in nature. He could be a conscientious advocate of Galileo's physics only if he set the world of reasoning and action aside, and viewed it – at least, as a working assumption – as forming a distinct, immaterial, nonmechanical realm. Only so could he protect human ability to think or act rightly, make mistakes, take credit for moral actions or intellectual achievements, or initiate thoughts and actions that go beyond the simple transfer of motion from one body to another.

The dualism of mind and body that was to play a crucial part in Descartes' general philosophy was thus not merely (as *La Grande Encyclopédie* implies) a spontaneous product of his own self-unfolding *ésprit*, or genius. It is helpful to see this dualism as a response to problems that had arisen in Descartes' time for all the natural philosophers ("scientists" if you will) who were attracted by the mixture of mechanical models and geometrical arguments that constituted Galileo's personal trademark.

To get the full flavor of the historical situation of Descartes' own thought, we must step back from the twentieth-century assumption that philosophical issues can be handled in isolation from problems in the natural sciences and put ourselves inside the heads of those who would find this assumption incomprehensible. For Galileo and Democritus, Newton and Descartes, natural philosophy embraced sensory psychology as much as the philosophy of perception, logical atomism as much as the study of material particles, and the philosophy of geometry as much as the infinitesimal calculus. In the academic world of today, we are accustomed to an intellectual specialization that in 1610 was still far in the future. A student entering the Jesuit college at La Flèche was free to try out his scholarly powers in any direction he pleased; and, from all we know about the young René Descartes, it is clear that he took full advantage of that freedom.

The Rebirth of Mathematics

If the line dividing the natural sciences from philosophy was harder to draw in the seventeenth century than it is now, the same is true of the line between the natural sciences and mathematics. In Descartes' time, indeed, all three of these intellectual activities were regarded as aspects of a single enterprise.

From the start, natural philosophy always involved *observations*, with or without actual experimentation. Astronomers, for example, recorded the positions and motions of the heavenly bodies, without having any chance to experiment on them, just as naturalists did for birds or plants, animals or insects. From the start, too, wherever the positions and motions of, say, the planets embodied regular patterns, *mathematical* analysis was used to confirm that these motions traced out well-known geometrical figures: circles to begin with, ellipses and other figures later. Finally, wherever these phenomena – that is, "things becoming visible" – were open to theoretical explanation, *philosophical* methods were invoked to arrive at systematic and consistent definitions of the terms used to account for those phenomena.

In Newton's *Principia*, for example, different parts of the book had different aims. The opening pages comprise definitions of the key terms used in Newton's theory of force and motion: not just formal, analytical definitions of the different variables appearing in the main body of his theory, but also empirical, operational definitions, indicating how, in practice, those terms are used to refer to measurable quantities and magnitudes. Next, the mathematical structure of the theory is set out, starting with axioms and proving a sequence of theorems, just as in Euclid's *Elements of Geometry*: the empirical content of this part is minimal, citing only the facts needed to specify the kinds of cases the theory is intended to cover. Finally, only after setting out this mathematical structure, does Newton turn and compare the resulting theorems with the available observations, to confirm that the theory can be used to explain the reported phenomena.

The order of the inquiries was not crucial: what mattered was that all three elements, well-defined terms ordering well-established phenomena in a formally coherent theory – that is, philosophical concepts, mathematical theorems, and empirical observations – were indispensable to the enterprise. That is why the founders of the modern physics called it a "mathematical and experimental philosophy" of nature.

This had not always been the central role of mathematics. The alliance of mathematics with natural philosophy from which modern physics began resulted from a historical convergence of several traditions. Historically, mathematics was independent of other fields early on: in classical Greece a tradition of mathematical investigations was born that was as autonomous in most respects as the "pure mathematics" of modern times. From Theaetetus to Euclid and on, geometers divorced their subject from its origins in the surveying of land for purposes of taxation; algebraists took the abstraction still further, by eliminating all references to specific subject matter; and, in time, a start was made on questions about the nature of mathematical knowledge and the requirements of mathematical proof.

This tradition of pure mathematics was still vigorous in the late fourth century A.D., when Pappus of Alexandria assembled his *Mathematical Collections*; but it was not an aspect of classical thought that had any immediate relevance for medieval churchmen. Up to the Renaissance, its survival depended more on Islamic scholars, from Iran to Morocco, than on anyone in Christian Europe. So the great names in the history of medieval mathematics are those of such people as the Persian scholar al-Khwarizmi, whose novel procedures are immortalized in the word *algorithm.*

Pure mathematics as we know it became a serious element in European intellectual life only with the second, Renaissance recovery and republication of Classical texts, along with much of Greek biography and literature and Lucretius's philosophical poem *De rerum naturae.* As late as 1618, when Descartes went to Breda in Holland to study at Prince Maurits of Nassau's military academy, the tradition of pure mathematics had scarcely impinged on the consciousness of most educated Europeans. Euclid's *Elements* had been available much earlier and was in the curriculum of the French Jesuit colleges, so there is no mystery about how Descartes came to love geometry and to be fascinated by the intellectual power of mathematical demonstrations. But the classical tradition of pure mathematics, revived in sixteenth-century Italy by Cardanus and Fibonacci, was fully reborn only in the mid-seventeenth century, with the analysis of infinitesimals by writers like Cavalieri in Italy, John Wallis and Isaac Barrow in England, and Pierre Fermat and Blaise Pascal in France.

So, as matters turned out, the new tradition of pure mathematics largely bypassed Descartes, coming to fruition in the late seventeenth century, after his death. Still, one thing about mathematics did catch Descartes' attention:

the significance of mathematical knowledge for general philosophy. At La Flèche, he mastered all the arguments familiar since antiquity about the limitations of sensory perception: that often, things turn out to be other than they first seem, if we just look at them, listen to them, smell, feel, or taste them. In a time of uncertainty like the early seventeenth century, with dogmatic theologians claiming a "certainty" far beyond the modest truths of everyday experience, any field of inquiry whose results could claim permanent, solid truth had its charm. Like Plato before him, Descartes found in geometrical theorems and proofs truths that had seemingly withstood the passage of time and outlasted everything else in human knowledge.

Descartes was not the only person in his time (or the first) to see such a value in mathematics. When Prince Maurits of Nassau set up his military academy, he put mathematics at the heart of the curriculum. No doubt he did so in part with its military applications in mind: in Italy, dukes and princes had long employed mathematicians to calculate, for example, the trajectory of cannon shots. But Maurits had something else in mind. He was a leading personality in the one European country that had made single-minded efforts to keep a balance between the ideological parties of the time. Calvinism was the established religion of the northern Netherlands, as Catholicism was in the southern Netherlands – modern Belgium – but the Protestant inhabitants of Amsterdam did not harass Catholic, Jewish, or other dissenting fellow citizens; nor did the Catholic loyalties of a painter like Jan Vermeer get him into serious difficulty at Delft.

As for Prince Maurits himself, he was determined to avoid the fanaticism that was destroying so much of Central Europe and accepted into his academy students from all sides of the current ideological divides: his love of mathematics thus expressed a personal commitment to rationality. Remarking that Maurits was "an excellent patron saint" for Descartes, Richard Watson tells a story about the Prince's last hours: "On his deathbed in 1625, a Minister asked [Prince Maurits] to state his beliefs. 'I believe,' Maurits said, 'that $2 + 2 = 4$ and that $4 + 4 = 8$. This gentleman here,' he said, referring to a mathematician at his side, 'will inform you of the details of the rest of our beliefs.' "[16] This was too serious a moment for him to abandon his reasonableness and tolerance: as a good Netherlander, he would do nothing to put his fellow Netherlanders at risk. Only beliefs that people of all religions can share were, in his eyes, clearly "rational"; so he refused to die with partisan dogmas on his lips.

By this time, the idea that Euclid's geometry was the prime exemplar of a rational discipline was taking hold widely. Thus the Dutch legal theorist

Hugo de Groot (Grotius) gave his treatise *On the Law of Peace and War* (1625) the axiomatic form of Euclidean geometry. So when Descartes addressed the problems of knowledge and certainty and pointed to geometry as a well-formed theory, he was in good company. The merit of geometry for Descartes, as an example of certain, timeless knowledge, was thus as much negative as positive. If Euclid is right, it is *not* the case that we know *nothing* permanently and for certain. A natural philosophy grounded in mathematics avoids the traditional objections to empirical or sensory knowledge: the sixteenth-century skeptics had been premature in despairing of any enduring systems of theoretical knowledge.

It is not that Descartes was unrealistic about the kinds of knowledge that human beings can achieve in practice. In the *Principes de la philosophie* (we noted), he claimed that the truth of his theory of nature was *certain* but remarked that this "certainty" was neither mathematical nor metaphysical: rather, it was the pragmatic certainty we have in the correctness of a successful decipherment. This analogy to decipherment skirted a crucial philosophical question. In cryptography, circumstantial reasons of many kinds, arising from our experience of human communication, give us confidence that a given message can be correctly deciphered in only one way. But in physics Galileo's belief that the book of nature was written in a symbolic language that only mathematicians can read was a matter of faith: and Descartes, who shared this belief, was left with an epistemological difficulty on his hands.

If natural philosophy is to be based on mathematical principles, what guarantee do we have that one, and only one, such set of principles is uniquely correct? May not the phenomena of nature lend themselves to explanation in terms of alternative systems of principles? This was one of the problems that Descartes addressed by his claim that all reflective human beings are endowed by God with "clear and distinct" ideas.

Descartes' successors did not find this theologically based position convincing. Thus began a discussion that shaped the philosophical debate for 150 years. On the one hand, philosophers took up unresolved questions about Euclidean geometry: Are Euclid's axioms uniquely self-consistent? Can it be proved, in particular, that the axiom of parallels – namely, the assumption that, through any point on a plane surface, one and only one line can be drawn parallel to a given line – follows mathematically from the other axioms taken together? Or is Euclid's system only one of several equally consistent systems of geometry? Only in the mid-eighteenth century did mathematicians come to recognize that, by formal standards, we cannot rule out alternative non-Euclidean systems which amend the axiom of parallels and generate alternative sequences of hypotheses and proofs, without running into inconsistencies.

On the other hand, philosophers and mathematicians asked similar questions about the seventeenth-century systems of natural philosophy. Leibniz would never concede that Newton's system of physics was theologically acceptable. If God is truly rational, he argued, one cannot say, as Newton does, that God could have created the world on whatever principles he pleased; instead, philosophers must *prove* that the principles embodied in the natural creation were the only rationally valid ones for him to adopt. By contrast, Leibniz's German successors, from Leonhard Euler to Immanuel Kant, took Newton's success for granted, and asked, rather, how the unique correctness of his theory could be guaranteed.

Euler still hoped for a mathematical proof of Newton's system like that which geometers had earlier sought in the case of Euclid's geometry. Kant, who knew from his friend Lambert, a pioneer of "non-Euclidean" geometry, that other kinds of geometry are formally possible, gave up trying to validate *analytically* the priority of Euclid in geometry and Newton in mechanics and began to look for more pragmatic ways of explaining the "*synthetic* but necessary truth" of Newton's theory. Either way, the philosophy of mathematics had come a long way since the revival of pure mathematics in the late sixteenth and seventeenth centuries, and the road was clear for the developments that the subject was to see after 1800, at the hands of Gauss and his successors.[17]

Varieties of Skepticism

At the time of the Thirty Years' War, when national loyalty and dynastic ambition found expression in the language of religious commitment and theological dogmatism, prudent men had few ways to go. Prince Maurits of Nassau could tweak the minister's nose by pretending that his knowledge of mathematics was the only creed he required; but this was easier for a prince than for commoners. The only other choice was between submitting to the authority of doctrines one could barely understand, let alone explain, and withholding intellectual commitment from all general doctrines equally. During the religious wars, many thinkers and writers preferred the second alternative; so, from the early sixteenth century on, as we have seen, they were attracted to one or another kind of skepticism.

Descartes was no exception. At a time when all reflective thinkers in

Western or Central Europe were tantalized by questions concerning the foundations of belief (not just religious belief, but belief of all kinds), he inherited a debate that had been vigorous for more than a century, ever since Erasmus's satirical essay *In Praise of Folly*. This had to do with the question of whether there are inescapable limits to all human knowledge. Is it not presumptuous for any human beings – philosophers, theologians, or anyone – to claim that they know the truth of their doctrines for certain? Should they not, rather, practise a decent intellectual modesty, setting their sights on less grandiose, more pedestrian targets? This suggestion had played a lively part in the philosophy of Greek antiquity, and the sixteenth-century humanists knew all the relevant classical authors: from Pyrrho, who traveled as far as India with Alexander the Great's army around 330 B.C., by way of Carneades in the second century B.C., to Sextus Empiricus, the physician and teacher who produced his definitive account of the skeptical philosophy in the years around A.D. 200.

In relation to Descartes, it is worth recalling the central theses of the tradition of classical skepticism which young René first met at La Flèche. This was not at all like the modern skepticism referred to in philosophical debate nowadays, whose exemplar is Descartes' maxim of systematic doubt; and systematic doubt is itself only one of a family of positions known as skepticism over the years from 300 B.C. to A.D. 1650. In classical terms, Descartes' own variety of skepticism was quite atypical. All beliefs that we cannot *prove*, he says, our respect for reason should require us to *deny*: this is a position that most classical authors would prefer to call "negative dogmatism."

An ambiguity here needs sorting out. In twentieth-century colloquial usage, "skeptical" means *not ready to believe*. Someone skeptical about religious beliefs is understood to *dis*believe them. So, when we hear that the sixteenth-century humanists were drawn to skepticism, we assume that they were some kind of atheists, who had concluded that the evidence for God's existence was not convincing. It then comes as a surprise to hear John Calvin called a humanist: how can a serious-minded theologian like Calvin afford to be "skeptical" about God's existence?

The classical meaning of "skeptical" was quite different, however. The hallmark of classical skeptics is that, confronted by general doctrines, they neither asserted nor denied them. As they saw matters, denying these doctrines is as much a mistake as asserting them, since it concedes that they make sense; and if nothing is achieved by either asserting or denying them, what sense do they have? The story is told of a student who, at high school, shocked the neighbors by being a vociferous atheist and denying their most respected religious beliefs. Returning home after his first term at Oxford, he was transformed. As he told his family, learning about skepticism from his philosophy tutor had opened his eyes. He no longer saw any point in denying the truth of religious beliefs: for he had come to see that they had no meaning. "The things that I previously *denied*, I now no longer *understand.*"

Classical skeptics did not question the *truth* of general beliefs – religious, scientific, metaphysical, or whatever. What they challenged was the basis on which people claim to know, as true, things that are not open to proof. Philosophers, in their view, were always trying to "prove" conclusions more grandiose than humans can hope to demonstrate. The value of recognizing the limits to human knowledge was not, of course, to devalue the skills or practices of, say, medicine or agriculture: practical knowledge is judged pragmatically and requires no formal proof. The skeptics recognized that much can be decided – provisionally, at least – by pragmatic tests, which save us from the temptation to jump to over-ambitious conclusions. Physicians, for instance, learn which of the things they come across in practice are comparatively stable, which more changeable. But they do not have any occasion to ask whether everything whatever is in flux: that is a thesis they neither agree with nor reject. Experience never puts such things beyond question, and grounds are not available for proving them either way. We are, of course, free to maintain religious or intellectual loyalties, but these loyalties need other foundations – tradition or faith, say, rather than experience or logic.

As the most influential skeptic of his time, we should recall Michel de Montaigne. In the 1570s or 1580s, fifty years before Descartes wrote his *Méditations* and *Discours*, Montaigne published three widely read books of *Essais* – he himself invented the essay as a genre – and the college at La Flèche possessed a fine copy of his collected *Essais*. The most philosophical, and longest, was the "Apologie de Raimond Sebond"; in effect, this presented to sixteenth-century French readers the views of Sextus Empiricus – not least, the need to avoid dogmatism about doctrines beyond human justification.

Having set out the case for classical skepticism in the "Apologie," Montaigne put philosophy aside and devoted the remaining essays to human issues of kinds that call for detailed, concrete, particular discussions. Aristotle had long ago argued that human affairs are so dependent on circumstances that they are kaleidoscopically varied and defeat all our attempts to generalize about them. Montaigne took the same position: the best we can do is to collect testimony from our own lives, from our friends, from histories and biographies, poetry and literature, and, given all this testimony, build up a picture of the kinds of ways in which human life tends to work out in actual practice. The result is less than a general theory and surely will not claim any kind of certainty. But it is all that the nature of the case admits, and it can give us a healthy feeling for human frailty and limitations.

In a word, Montaigne's *Essais* are a founding document of the modern humanities. They mix history, psychology, and autobiography with ethnography, poetry, and moral reflection. In the end, Montaigne is as skeptical about well-founded theories of nature as he is about well-founded theories of human affairs: the limits to human knowledge deny us certainty in either case. (The varied Greek pictures of nature, from Thales on, showed, in his view, the impossibility of reaching a consensus in natural philosophy.) The classical skeptic thus carried away from a reading of Sextus, or of Montaigne, the conviction that *nothing whatever* can be known for certain.

Montaigne died in September 1592, less than three years before Descartes' birth. His *Essais* were best-sellers until after the turn of the century; but after 1610, with Henry IV's assassination, matters took a turn for the worse. The toleration for which Montaigne and Henry both worked in different ways no longer had wide appeal: once ideological conflict developed into general war, the voices of the dogmatists shouted down those of more reasonable people. Montaigne's reasonableness kept its charm, but John Dewey's ill-fated "quest for certainty" was about to begin.[18]

However engaging Montaigne's *Essais* might be, Descartes was thus caught in a tug-of-war between skepticism toward the religious dogmatists on the one hand and Galileo's vision of the book of nature on the other. He saw the merits of skepticism in the humanities, but he could not easily abandon his dreams for natural philosophy. It might be right to adopt a healthy doubt toward local traditions and superstitions in the human realm, but Galileo had opened up the road to a mathematical decipherment of the world of nature, and Descartes was anxious to travel along it.

The skeptical issue was not so much the *truth or falsity* of our beliefs as their claim to *certainty*. For Descartes, as for Plato, all "knowledge" properly so-called must have a "certainty" that puts it beyond risk that we might later be forced to correct it. For Descartes, as for Plato, again, the examples that gave him confidence that certainty is, after all, achievable were those from Euclid's geometry. So Galileo's program for the philosophy of nature could resist Montaigne's critique only if its foundations had the certainty of geometry. Thus the *epistemological* challenge for Descartes was to hold the skeptics at bay, by doing what Sextus and Montaigne had dismissed as impossible: identifying one single truth, at least, that all reflective human beings can *know for certain.* At the same time, the *scientific* challenge facing him was to decipher the mathematical language of the book of nature in a way that carried *empirical* conviction.[19]

Planted in his mind by his readings at La Flèche during those final years before the Thirty Years' War and reinforced by his subsequent experience in the military, this dual challenge remained with him when he left Paris at the end of 1628 for the castle at Franeker. Settled in the Netherlands, he was free to put down in writing the theories he had been working out in his mind during the years since he had left the care of the Jesuits. It took him a dozen years to bring the task to effective completion. He began with a first draft of his *Méditations*, which served as his reply to Montaigne, and ended with the four-volume *Principes de la philosophie*, the comprehensive work that was his ultimate homage to Galileo, which gave his most detailed attempt to "crack the code" of the book of nature.

Twentieth-century readers see Descartes' work as making a clean break with earlier philosophy and creating a fresh starting point for debate. Yet he himself did not claim that his rational methods were wholly original: he was too well read to ignore all those earlier thinkers, from Plato on, who had argued along lines parallel to his own. Far from rejecting the opinions of earlier philosophers and mathematicians, Descartes built on their ideas in a dozen ways.

In calling for a clean break and a fresh start, he was not providing the community of philosophers with a new research program: rather, this "fresh start" was something he invited reflective thinkers to undertake, as individuals. Nor was this call an attempt to relocate philosophy, by framing its problems in terms that set them "outside History": rather, it was a challenge to the people of his time to rise above the *odium theologicum* – the doctrinal conflicts and hatreds – that for so long had been relied on to excuse brutality and destruction and to agree on novel methods of argument that could carry conviction for anyone, whether "heathen, Turk or Jew."

Whether or not Descartes succeeded in his project to find "clear and distinct" ideas available to all reflective human beings, this project addressed intellectual problems that were key problems for his time. Whether or not his philosophy of nature was a correct decipherment of the mathematical language in which Galileo's "Book of Nature" was written, it contributed, in ways that are not sufficiently recognized, to the development of a conception of "theoretical physics" that Isaac Newton took over almost unchanged.[20]

In the late twentieth century, many writers are unhappy with the view of rationality that was adopted by Descartes' successors. At the same time, concepts of reasonableness and rationality lay at the heart of the seventeenth-century crisis, and philosophers were right to take up Prince Maurits of Nassau's challenge to the dogmatists. An understanding of the basis of the consensus in mathematics was the first step along a road that might lead the peoples of Europe out of the shadow of the religious wars by clearing the ground for new, more constructive methods of inquiry and reasoning.

NOTES

1. Harold J. Berman, *Law and Revolution: The Formation of the Western Legal Tradition* (Cambridge, Mass.: Harvard University Press, 1983), pp. 102, 363–364.

2. See ibid., pp. 161–162, commenting on David Knowles, *The Evolution of Medieval Thought* (London: Longmans, 1962), pp. 80–81.

3. The Treaty of Augsburg (1555) gave the ruler of each territory the right to decide what religion was established in his territory, in accord with the maxim *cuius regio, eius religio* – "of whom the region, of him the religion." This rule was preserved in the new European order that followed the Peace of Westphalia (1648), which ended the Thirty Years' War.

4. See, e.g., Stephen Toulmin, *Cosmopolis* (New York: Free Press, 1990), pp. 45–62, 69ff.

5. For *The Starry Messenger*, see the anthology *Discoveries and Opinions of Galileo*, ed. Stillman Drake (New York: Doubleday, 1957). The authoritative English translation of this work is that by Albert van Helden (Chicago: University of Chicago Press, 1989).

6. On the intellectual background to Galileo's mechanics, see Marshall Clagett, *The Science of Mechanics in the Middle Ages* (Madison: University of Wisconsin Press, 1959).

7. For the letter to Sarpi, see Drake, ed., *Discoveries and Opinions of Galileo.*

8. Thomas Kuhn, *The Copernican Revolution* (Cambridge, Mass.: Harvard University Press, 1957). On John Donne's *Ignatius his Conclave*, see Toulmin, *Cosmopolis*, pp. 62–69.

9. On the authority of the biblical account of creation, see René Descartes, *Principes de la philosophie* (1644), pt. 3, articles 42–47: (*CSM*, I, esp. pp. 223–291; AT, VIII A, 40–329).

10. See Kuhn, *Copernican Revolution*.

11. See E. J. Dijksterhuis, *The Mechanization of the World Picture* (Oxford: Clarendon Press, 1961).

12. See Toulmin, *Cosmopolis*, pp. 121ff.

13. Stephen Kellert, *In the Wake of Chaos: Unpredictable Order in Dynamical Systems* (Chicago: University of Chicago Press, 1993).

14. Richard Watson, "On the Zeedijk," *Georgia Review* 43, no. 1 (Spring 1989): 19–32.

15. See, e.g., the introduction to Giovanni Borelli, *De motu animalium* (1680).

16. Watson, *On the Zeedijk,"* p. 24.

17. For the problem of mathematical knowledge in Kant and the relation between Lambert and Kant, see Gottfried Martin, *Kant's Metaphysics and Theory of Science*, trans. P. G. Lucas (Manchester: Manchester University Press, 1955).

18. John Dewey, *The Quest for Certainty* (1929); the standard edition is that edited by Jo Ann Boydston (Carbondale, Ill.: Southern Illinois University Press, 1984).

19. Léon Brunschvicg, *Descartes et Pascal, Lecteurs de Montaigne* (New York: Brentano's, 1944).

20. For Isaac Newton's methodological debt to Descartes, see (e.g.) Alexandre Koyré, *Newtonian Studies* (London: Chapman and Hall, and Cambridge: Harvard University Press, 1965).

Essay 3
Metaphysics

DAVID WEISSMAN

Descartes' Platonism

Metaphysics defines itself by the questions it asks: What are we? What is the world? What is our place in it? Answers vary with our choice of method. Aristotle supposed that we discover the categorial nature of things by reflecting on our observations of material particulars. We perceive or infer that things in space and time are discrete, that the properties qualifying them are essential or accidental (as dogs differ essentially from cats but accidentally from one another), that the growth of living things is propelled by an internal aim (a *telos*), and that things of an essential type behave in predictable ways. We humans, he thought, are (mostly) natural creatures subject to the laws of our kind. Plato, his teacher and opposite, remarked that sensory experience is unstable and confused. Knowledge is achieved as mind reflects upon its innate ideas, while remarking their imperfect, shifting expression in the material flux. These ideas are direct intuitions of paradigmatic differences and relations – the Forms. Metaphysics is autonomous, because a mind grasping the Forms sees the cosmic design. What we call empirical inquiry is merely an occasion for using the Forms to clarify differences in the flux.

Descartes was usually a Platonist. We start with his claims about mind, matter, and God, before describing the principal developments of these ideas. Descartes would have welcomed some of them; others he would have renounced.

Descartes' Ontology

MIND

Descartes introduces his account of reality with a claim about himself: "I am, I exist, is necessarily true each time that I pronounce it, or that I mentally conceive it" (64; *CSM*, II, 17; *AT*, VII, 26). What am I? "A thing which thinks" (66; *CSM*, II, 19; *AT*, VII, 28). *Thought* is Descartes' word for awareness, or consciousness. Doubting, conceiving, judging (affirming or denying), willing, perceiving, imagining, and feeling are some principal modes of awareness. Each one is *intentional*, meaning that awareness is directed to some content. Describing such contents as *intentional objects* (not a phrase Descartes used) signifies that they exist as entertained. That some intentional objects represent things that exist apart from awareness – Africa, but not Atlantis – is incidental here. Two modes of awareness are especially crucial, because their product is truth or error. Conception alone is merely the presentation of an idea. It is affirmation or denial – assertion or judgment – that achieves truth. We avert error by taking care not to affirm or deny ideas which do not satisfy Descartes' test for truth: clarity and distinctness (68; *CSM*, II, 21; *AT*, VII, 31). *Clarity* is the property of an idea distinguished from other ideas as it stands before the mind. *Distinctness* is the property of an idea that exhibits its structure or form – its essence.

Is this criterion logical or psychological? Descartes never resolved the issue. His intuitionism encourages a psychological reading: clarity and distinctness imply that the mind's eye is perfectly focused, and that truth is achieved when the matters to be known are presented, without mediation, to our inspecting minds. This is Plato's theory of knowledge. *Nous* is said to attain knowledge and truth by apprehending the Forms as qualifications of itself (Plato 1964, pp. 1589–1590): truth is the identity of knower and known. Descartes endorses this condition for knowledge, though mind's object is, he says, itself: mind discerns and truly reports its own existence and structure. Descartes sometimes implies that mind also has this intuitive, clear and distinct grasp of essences (e.g., of matter as extension). But he is more cautious about them, probably because he agrees that we are too easily deceived by our apparent grasp of concepts or propositions directly entertained. Confidence in their truth requires that clarity and distinctness should also be a logical test. We defend ourselves from error only as an idea or judgment is counted true because its negation is a contradiction. We apply this logical test first by negating an idea or judgment, then by deriving a contradiction from it; or by altering an idea within the imagination in order to produce – like an Escher drawing – a representation of an impossible object.

Descartes moves uncomfortably between these alternative tests for truth, because most of the ideas or judgments that concern him are neither intuitively confirmed truths about mind's existence and structure nor logically tested, mathematical truths. These other claims are true contingently, if at all. Not being able to demonstrate that their negations are contradictions, he settles for a less demanding application of the psychological – intuitionist – reading of his truth test: contingent claims are true if an exhaustive, undistorted perception of the matter at issue justifies belief that we know the thing as it is. That God is required to guarantee the truth even of clear and distinct ideas – whether they satisfy the intuitive or the logical test – is a point considered below.

Descartes is more explicit about mind's *reflexivity* and *will*. Reflexivity is implied throughout the first *Meditation*, as when Descartes considers his circumstances: "I have delivered my mind from every care" (59; *CSM*, II, 12; *AT*, VII, 17). It is implied again when he questions the frequency or duration of his existence: "I am, I exist, that is certain. But how often? Just when I think; for it might possibly be the case if I ceased entirely to think, that I should likewise cease altogether to exist" (65; *CSM*, II, 18; *AT*, VII, 27). Saying that I am is an existence claim waiting upon evidence sufficient to confirm it. The evidence is missing if I am unselfconsciously aware of a thing other than myself (Weissman 1987, pp. 30–32), for I am aware of it, but not of me. One may infer that I am from what I do, as thinking of Paris implicates me who thinks of it. But inference is fallible. Knowledge that I exist must be supported by direct perception of me as I exist. How do I locate myself, in what guise? I discern myself, reflexively, as I think of other things: I feel the rain and know that I do. Descartes supposes that one can never be aware in either way without being, or being able to be, conscious in the other. There is, however, this difference between them. The original awareness may be obscure, as when dreaming is confused. Self-perception is clear and distinct in both the senses considered above: I have an unmediated perception of myself thinking, and it is a contradiction that I do not exist when thinking.

Where self-perception is first compressed – me seeing red, here, now – mind exposes its structure by discerning the functions performed. First is the sensorium, where contents of every sort – percepts, thoughts, and desires, for example – are registered. This is mind's passive side. Next is the awareness of these contents, an awareness that takes the several intentional forms listed above, including perceiving, willing, feeling, and conceiving. We simplify our characterization of mind by saying that awareness is, at once, receptivity and some mode of intention. Separate from both is reflexive awareness, mind's consciousness of itself. Mind attends to the idea or datum qualifying it – *first-order awareness* – while discerning its own act and qualifications – *second-order awareness*. Notice the reciprocity of these two: each is a necessary condition for the other. An empty mind – one presenting no data for first-order intentions – supplies no content for self-reflection; conversely, first-order awareness exists only as it is certified by reflexive awareness. Cartesian mind is the eternal dyad, each side a condition for the other.

First-order thinking is provoked by whatever things are presented for inspection. Second-order thinking has two effects, neither occurring without the other: performance or control of some vital mental function and self-awareness. The control exercised by second-order awareness is, generically, *normative*: it prescribes that first-order thinking or its contents shall satisfy particular standards. Where truth is valued and the standard is clarity and distinctness, second-order awareness scrutinizes its contents to verify that they are clear and distinct. Sensory data never satisfy this standard, because there is always some obscurity or anomaly in them: body distorts their transmission to our minds. Ideas may be obscure before we reflect on them, but they are never irremediably garbled – as percepts are – because mind's access to its ideas is unmediated: they are innate. Second-order awareness dissolves obscurity by exposing these ideas. Descartes' example is sealing wax, which is altered by heat or touch (67–70; *CSM*, II, 20–22; *AT*, VII, 30–33). The idea of wax's geometrical essence is to be used regulatively as we organize and interpret the shifting data: second-order consciousness uses the idea to differentiate and organize otherwise muddled percepts. And all the while, it restrains first-order awareness from impulsively making judgments for which the evidence is uncertain. We may suppose that training and habit are enough to make us careful, but habit is typically a material state, one to which consciousness is irrelevant. Descartes locates mind's control within second-order awareness. It makes us self-correcting and self-controlled. For we decide, conscious of what we are doing, that judgment should be withheld. Control lapses only when an idea is clear and distinct, for then we cannot help but affirm it.

How can I be responsible for everything that occurs within me, when some things happen, unselfconsciously, out of second-order sight? Descartes replies that mind's acts and qualifications are never hidden; each one is – or can be – perceived: no matter that intense preoccupation distracts us from other content and even ourselves, we easily recover – we never entirely lose – our comprehensive self-awareness. Why say this? Because of the evidentiary condition marked above: *esse est percipi* – to be is to be perceived. There is neither content for, nor an act of, first-order thinking if mind does not confirm their occurrence by inspecting itself. This condition may be interpreted generously or narrowly: mind is comprehensively self-aware because everything within it is perceived; or anything not satisfying this condition is purged from existence. Does second-order awareness fall to this same requirement? Does it exist only when perceived by a still higher-order awareness, thereby entailing a regress of self-reflections? Descartes stops the regress at the second order by supposing that mind is altogether self-transparent at the moment of its initial reflection: perception of first-order awareness and its content is also self-perception.

The mind so described is a theater bounded by the limits of its phosphorescent space. Nothing mediates between awareness and its content; the two orders of awareness and their contents are perceived as they are. It is this characterization of mind that justifies the intuitionist reading of clarity and distinctness: clear and distinct ideas are true because there is no gap, hence no need for a mediator, between the thing and our awareness of it. A judgment is true because it correctly affirms that something is as we perceive it. Where the things to be known are the mind's own qualifications, we have truth as identity: a mind reporting truths reports on these aspects of itself (Weissman 1993, pp. 160–169).

Each mind is a *substance*, self-sufficient and free-standing. This is critical for political and social theory, because it entails that a community of minds is never more than an aggregate: no mind depends on other minds for its innate ideas or, ideally, for its judgments. Distrust of authority, aversion or suspicion of every will but one's own, is the assured result.

MATTER

Descartes supposes that the created world has substances of two kinds, minds being one of them. The substance of the other sort is material. Materiality is extension, which implies that we misspeak when we say that matter *has* geometrical properties. Matter *is* extension: the geometrical properties characteristic of space are intrinsic to it. Descartes concedes that there are separate matters – sheep and goats – but these are modes of extension (as desire and perception are modes of awareness), not distinct substances. Each body, however self-sufficient, is only temporarily set apart from other modes (i.e., bodies), for matter, like Plato's flux, is protean and self-diversifying, but unitary. Modes that have consolidated as separable "entities" will dissolve some time into the material one. Aristotle explained the diversity of modes by inferring that things of a class or kind embody a distinctive form or essence. Descartes had this simpler explanation: that the variety of material things results from variations in three variables: magnitude, figure (including the configuration of parts), and motion. Bodies are numerically distinct, because each is a different region of space, and qualitatively distinct, because each has specific values for the three variables.

Nothing more is required to explain the difference between cats and dogs, or dead cats and live ones.

Every material thing, whether living or inert, is to be understood mechanically, by way of those geometrical laws that determine the relations of bodies in motion. Matter's relation to motion is, nevertheless, problematic in three respects. First, because motion is not implied by extension, its addition seems ad hoc. Second, because Descartes dismisses energy as an occult quality, he has no explanation for the plausible claim that motion – or a power for it – is stored. Third, he has no way of explaining the transfer of motion. These difficulties entail that matter, as extension, is passive and incapable of initiating, storing, or transferring motion. But notice that Descartes identified matter with extension so that geometry could supply an exhaustive representation of the configurations that change. A satisfactory kinematics was less exigent. Nor was Descartes obliged to supply one if all three considerations are finessed by saying that God is everywhere the creator and sustainer of motion (*CSM*, I, 240; *AT*, VIIIA, 61–62).

The relation of mind to matter is also problematic, in that neither has access to the other, because they share no common ground. Even the correlation of their states is puzzling for want of a measure applicable to both, since Descartes never establishes a correlation between subjective temporality and the temporal order of extended things. He must choose: explain the appearances – that mind and body interact – or concede that experience is systematically misleading. He uses two arguments, of unequal strength, in defense of the appearances.

First is the claim that a perfect God would not deceive us: perceptual experience – seeing the sun – is evidence that the categorial difference between mind and matter is bridged, somehow, by God. This is a weak argument, because Descartes has said that we cannot appeal to God's guarantee in the absence of clarity and distinctness. But there is no clarity and distinctness in perception, so God's guarantee is not properly invoked in cases where allegedly true judgments identify extra-mental causes of our percepts. Descartes relaxes the demand for clarity and distinctness in the sixth *Meditation* (102; *CSM*, II, 56; *AT*, VIII, 80–81), where inference to an extra-mental material world seems founded only on the claim that God would not deceive us so globally as to let us believe in a world apart from our perceptions if there were none. Or, we read the text differently. Rather than say that the standard for clarity and distinctness is relaxed, we say that Descartes compromises his earlier claim that mind has entire control of its will, hence of its powers of judgment. For, as Descartes remarks, God has given us a strong inclination to believe that sensory data are caused by external things, and no means to correct that inclination. Still, Descartes at his most rigorous does not sanction arguments from appearances to the conclusion that material things are as they appear. Add that the categorial difference between mind and matter provides no common ground for dynamic or static relations between them, and we concede that the appearance of their interaction is, or may be, deceiving.

The more compelling argument for mind–body interaction requires a shift in perspective. Before, it was supposed that mind surveys things arrayed before it in space, as one sees cups and plates on a dinner table. Now, we suppose that mind's relation to matter is more intimate, as when a mind inhabits a body. Before, bodies were seen or heard, as from a distance. Now, one's own body is best known kinesthetically. We say, without regard for the miracle implied if mind and matter are categorially distinct, that there is overwhelming evidence of mind's interaction with its personal body – as when a tooth aches. Descartes was so impressed by this evidence that he identified the pineal gland as the crossover point, on the side of body, for their relation. He then explained the reciprocity of mind and body by describing the activity of "animal spirits" in this gland (*CSM*, I, 328–332; *AT*, XI, 327–335): mind feels changes in its body and often directs body's behavior. The kinesthesis of bodily states also extends to bodies other than one's own. For my body is not separate from others (as Aristotelian substances are self-sufficient and mutually separable) when every body is a mode of one material substance. Matter is an elastic medium such that impulses – motions – are propagated in every direction within it; my body resonates with alterations in other modes. Sensory perception is mind's way of registering alterations initiated within its linked body or in other bodies remote from it.

These two ways of characterizing matter – as categorially distinct from mind or as coupled to it – express an irresolution at the heart of Descartes' metaphysics. One implies mind's separability from matter, its exemption from mechanical laws, hence its autonomy. The other acknowledges the reciprocity of mind and body and the unity of persons.

GOD

God is the third item in Descartes' ontology, a God known to reason, not faith, a God who is all the more worthy of reverence when we understand his nature and role. Descartes' claims about him have several motivations:

(i) Where God's existence is the issue, Descartes proposes his version of the ontological argument. (ii) Descartes' "new" argument for God's existence infers from our idea of an infinite being to its infinite cause, and from mind's finitude to its infinite ground. (iii) We rely on God to supply a condition, cause, or link that is otherwise missing in a variety of contexts in which Descartes is otherwise unable to justify some claim he makes. This is God in the role of *deus ex machina* as he is introduced to save some part of Descartes' theory. (iv) Reflecting on our imperfections, we extrapolate to the grandeur and perfection of God, then measure ourselves against our idea of him. (v) Striving to learn more of God, though his infinity and perfection are incomprehensible, we look for something in ourselves that may be a clue to his nature. Affirming that we are made in God's image and that our minds are the point of affinity, we reflect upon and characterize them, before inferring that God too thinks and wills, though in ways that are different from, because infinitely greater than, our own.

Consider these five ways of characterizing God:

(i) The idea of God is the idea of a being than which none greater can be conceived; or, in Descartes' preferred formulation, the idea of a perfect being. Existence is one of God's perfections, so God's essence – the sum of these compossible perfections – entails his existence. The idea of such a being is possible; it contains no contradiction. Yet God must be more than possible: this possibility must be actualized because it would be a contradiction, given his essence, if God did not exist (93; *CSM*, II, 46–47; *AT*, VII, 66–69).

(ii) The idea of a perfect being present within us is one that we could not have invented ourselves. Why? Because there must be as much reality in the cause as there is in the effect, though we who are finite cannot create the idea of an infinite being. Only God could have been this idea's cause. (Thought is assimilated to perception, as the idea of God, like percepts, is alleged to have a cause independent of mind.) This is Descartes' "new" argument for God's existence (74–78; *CSM*, II, 26–31; *AT*, VII, 38–45). Our idea of God is a complex: it includes ideas of our human imperfections and the idea of an operation for extrapolating from these finite properties to God's infinitely greater ones.

Descartes emphasizes this formulation, though it is insignificant compared with one he merely intimates:

> [T]he whole strength of the argument which I have made use of to prove the existence of God consists in this, that I recognise that it is not

possible that my nature should be what it is, and indeed that I should have in myself the idea of a God, if God did not veritably exist. (82; *CSM*, II, 35; *AT*, VII, 51–52)

The idea of God within me is subsidiary to my own nature, hence this question: How is God's existence presupposed by my own? Descartes answers that my finitude presupposes God's infinite being (78–79; *CSM*, II, 31; *AT*, VII, 45–46). The question and reply seem empty and formulaic, because we are misled by the particle *in* of the word *infinite*. It implies a privation – the want of finitude or specificity: the infinite seems derived from the finite, hence no cause of it. This is false to the assumption that Descartes shares with Augustine, Plotinus, Philo, Plato, and Parmenides. Infinity, for them, is the condition of an unbounded whole having no internal, contingent partitions. Infinity is the positive state. The partitions are finite, sundered, privative, and incomplete. None of them exists or is understood apart from the infinite One. Yet, Descartes agrees – as all Neoplatonists do – that infinity is incomprehensible to our finite minds. We never do grasp the One or comprehend ourselves as its parts. The idea of it is more a trajectory than a content.

Resolution of the "Cartesian circle" is here. Descartes is charged with having argued that mind discovers itself before it discovers the idea of God, but also that mind cannot know itself until it is established that God is guarantor of clear and distinct ideas, including the idea of oneself. Where knowledge of each presupposes knowledge of the other, how can God or mind be known? We break the circle by distinguishing mind's existence from its essence, then by distinguishing that which is prior in knowledge from that which is prior in being.

Discovering my own existence when everything else has been doubted, I do not yet know what I am. I quickly ascertain my nature when I discover that I am a being that thinks. Having a direct perception, a self-perception, of my thinking, I know it necessarily (65; *CSM*, II, 18; *AT*, VII, 26). Still, the clarity and distinctness with which I perceive that I am are different in quality from the perception of what I am. The first is categorical; the other is qualified, as when Descartes writes: "From this time I begin to know what I am with a little more clearness and distinction than before" (67; *CSM*, II, 20; *AT*, VII, 29). This difference between perceptions that are categorical or qualified expresses an ontological difference. Existence is an all-or-nothing affair: existing or not, I do or do not perceive that I exist. The perception of what I am is nuanced, because finite things are thinkable only derivatively as partitions of an infinite being. (As Hegel will later say, "as if philosophy were anything else but the positing of the finite in the infinite" (Hegel [1801] 1977, p. 178).)

The infinite – God – is prior in being, though my own existence and the incomplete perception of my nature are prior in knowledge. I may struggle to supersede my finitude in order to know myself as God knows me, or even to know God, the unlimited; but doing so requires that I pass out of finitude into infinitude – that I become God. The "Cartesian circle" is therefore these two things: trivially, it is a logical puzzle; irenically, it is the impossible quest of finite thinkers who struggle for a footing, amidst partition and alienation, in the infinite One.

Consider again the details of the assumption that generates the circle: I know that I exist before knowing that God exists, although it is only God's guarantee which credits the truth of my claim to exist. This, the generating statement of the puzzle, is mistaken. My self-intuition does not require God's guarantee. God could have determined that I not exist; but he cannot deny me existence at the moment when I discover – by self-inspection – that I am. Indeed, this is the moment when I am closest in nature to God, for it is existence, not merely one or another of its many forms, that is the primordial, creative fact.

Now, having discovered myself, I realize that the conditions for knowledge of other beings are different from the conditions for knowing myself (i.e., that I am and have an unmediated grasp that I am). Indeed, I am forever confounded as I strive to join these two, seeking in the perception of my existence the ground for more ample knowledge of myself and other things. I directly perceive my own existence and, less comprehensively, my thinking, but I have nothing better than clear and distinct representations of things existing apart from me. It is here that I need God's guarantee, though, paradoxically, my knowledge of him derives from a clear and distinct idea. The passion for knowing my nature and other things is thwarted, because judgments about them can never be confirmed beyond doubt by my self-inspection (as happens when I know that I am). I can only intend these other things, never being sure that my judgments of them are not mistaken.

Hope is not lost, because Descartes, the Neoplatonist, solves in being a problem that is intractable from the standpoint of a knower who has a merely partial self-perception, one who stands apart from other things to be known. This thinker perceives that his existence is feeble and conditioned: "I know clearly that I depend on some being different from myself" (81; *CSM*, II, 34; *AT*, VII, 49). This self-perception includes the recognition of my limits, hence, by intimation, the perception of that which is unlimited.

For I perceive God, the One, as that being in whom I dwell as one of its partitions. Whereas other knowledge claims are circular – I know God, my nature as a thinker, and other things insofar as he guarantees my ideas – reflection on my own existence is a veridical perception both of me and, more obscurely, of God. This is plausible only if we assume that truth is identity, that I truly affirm that I am (because I am and perceive that I am), and that I also perceive, however dimly, that I, in my limitations and contingency, am a qualification of the unpartitioned One. We are to believe that God's existence is no more remote from me than I am from myself. Grasping my own existence, I discern that God is.

(iii) There are four occasions on which Descartes relies on God to save some feature of his argument. He makes these four claims: (*a*) God is the necessary being who creates and sustains beings whose existence is precarious because contingent. (*b*) God is the cause of motion. (*c*) God establishes the otherwise mysterious link between mind and matter. (*d*) Clear and distinct ideas or judgments are trustworthy because God guarantees their application.

(*a*) God cannot fail to exist. Every other thing, whether a particular mind or body or essence, exists contingently. How is their existence initiated and sustained? Descartes' answer is that of Aquinas:

> (A)ll the course of my life may be divided into an infinite number of parts, none of which is in any way dependent on the other; and thus from the fact that I was in existence a short time ago it does not follow that I must be in existence now, unless some cause at this instant, so to speak, produces me anew, that is to say, conserves me. (80; *CSM*, II, 33; *AT*, VII, 48–49)

A contingent being may have been created by an antecedent like itself, but all contingent beings would lose existence – would be annihilated – were they not sustained in existence by a being, God, whose existence is necessary.

The success of this argument depends on our reading of *contingent*. The argument is more plausible if contingency is taken as a deficiency, thus implying that contingent existence is incomplete, provisional, or conditioned. Contingent existents can then be said to require the support of a thing or things whose existence is not impaired. This argument is not compelling, because the contrariety of contingency and necessity has no implications for the character of existence. Suppose that a necessary existent is one that cannot not be, whereas a contingent existent may not be. Nothing in this distinction entails that the existence of something contingent is provisional or incomplete *qua* existence. Existence may be all-or-nothing: one has it or not. Still wanting a site for necessity, we may locate it within essences, as some configurations of properties (e.g., right triangles) entail other properties (e.g., the Pythagorean theorem). We may even allow that God's essence entails his existence without inferring that God's existence, qua existence, is different in kind from the existence of contingent things. Descartes would surely disagree: God's existence, like his every other property, differs from ours to a degree that is incomprehensible. Because our very being is deficient, we would surely lose it without God's support.

(*b*) Matter – meaning extension – is passive, hence incapable of initiating motion. Needing a cause for motion, Descartes postulates that God is its cause. God creates matter, recreates it at every moment, and is active everywhere in space as the only source of motion: "*God is the primary cause of motion; and he always preserves the same quantity of motion in the universe*" (principle 36, *Principles of Philosophy* [*CSM*, I, 240; *AT*, VIII, 61]).

(*c*) Mind's relation to body is perplexing, because the categorial difference between them leaves no ground for their interaction or correlation. God is their liaison. It is his meditation – not the pineal gland – that explains the effect of desire on bodily motion or the pain of stubbing a toe.

(*d*) Clarity and distinctness are sufficient signs of truth only if there is a guarantor who creates referents – in the form of essences or particulars – for clear and distinct ideas. Why do we need a guarantor for necessary truths – those whose negations are contradictory? Because God is responsible for the laws of geometry and logic (*CSM*, II, 291; *AT*, VII, 432): he could alter them, even to the point of suspending the principle of noncontradiction, thereby prefiguring worlds that satisfy (or fail to satisfy?) this new condition.

It is sometimes said that Descartes' remarks about God had no purpose but that of saving him from the Inquisition. This is a plausible reading if we consider only his claim that all the phenomena of physics and physiology have constituents, causes, and laws that are exclusively material and mechanical. There are, however, the contrary implications of the four points just cited: the idea of God is a conceptual convenience, one that Descartes invokes whenever his theory would otherwise founder; or Descartes' metaphysics is contrived so that God is required to bridge or brace every part of it.

(iii) Descartes supposes that his "new" argument does more than prove God's existence. It also supplies the objective for an infinite quest: the idea of our creator is an intimation of him and a beacon for our intellectual devotion. Where God's existence is the ground of our own, we elevate ourselves by thinking of him (82–83; *CSM*, II, 35–36; *AT*, VII, 51–52). Exalting God is our telos. Eliminating final cause from matter and motion, Descartes reserves it for this, our moral and intellectual trajectory.

(iv) The most consequential of these arguments tells us *what* God is, not merely *that* he is. It prescribes that we should understand God by reflecting upon ourselves. For God is the cogito writ large. He too is a mind, one with a structure which is analogous at least to our minds: we have a "clear and distinct idea of uncreated and thinking substance, that is to say, of God" (*CSM*, I, 211; *AT*, VIIIA, 26). Though now we do more than extrapolate from our finite existence to God's necessary and infinite being. We also generalize from mind's self-perceived powers and structure: "I bear the image and similitude of God" (86; *CSM*, II, 40; *AT*, VII, 57).

Four powers ascribed to God have been discovered within ourselves. *First*, we suppose that he knows everything in an immediate self-inspection, because our self-knowledge is unmediated. This want of mediation – there is no gap between knower and known – makes us certain that we correctly report our own existence and character. Equally, we suppose that God's self-perceptions are error-free. *Second*, all God's ideas are clear and distinct, never conjectural or obscure. Each one captures the essence of whatever quantity, quality, or relation he considers. (Even the accidents of created things have an essence for him.) Each of his ideas is normative: it prescribes a character for any contingent event that satisfies the idea. *Third*, volition in us requires effort. Volition in God is effortless. Our will has limited effect, whereas God's will is unconstrained, even by the principle of contradiction. He could remake the world in ways that violate this principle merely by thinking, then willing, an alternative (*CSMK*, 235; *AT*, IV, 188). Why would he do this? The only condition required is God's conviction that the effect would be good. Our world, this implies, with all the truths about it, is a function of God's will and values (*CSM*, II, 117; *AT*, VII, 166). Descartes refuses to speculate about them.

Fourth, we dimly understand God's unity, including the unity of his creation, because we discover the basis for our mind's unity in its self-consciousness. Whereas first-order awareness illuminates individual things, as in thought or perception, self-reflection joins the diversity of things perceived or conceived, first to one another, then to things remembered or anticipated. Is this also God's way? The infinitude of God's mind makes the other term of the analogy incomprehensible. Still, this is the vector for extrapolations from our nature to God's. He is infinite thought, thinking itself. He sees everything and knows himself to be seeing it. He knows it at once, for God is fully realized at every moment; anything less would be an imperfection. The temporality characteristic of our self-awareness has no application to him who has neither beginning nor end nor duration. Nor is there temporality in the things he thinks, since all of them – the created world – are perceived at once. They are unified, logically and atemporally, by this world's ordering principles (what we conceive as laws of nature) and by the unifying force of God's self-awareness.

The "new" argument proving God's existence – the argument requiring that we infer to God's existence from our innate idea of him – is relevant again. That idea was said to be clear and distinct but also, paradoxically, incomprehensible; we know how to extrapolate from our imperfections to God's infinite perfections, though we have no idea of an infinite being. Now we supply content for our idea of God by arguing analogically from our character as self-conscious thinkers to God's character. It is God's mind – especially his unifying self-consciousness – that is the One. We suppose that God, like us, discovers and affirms his existence in an act of self-reflection, though he never doubts that he is and must be.

Assembling these claims about mind, matter, and God, we get this result. Mind discovers itself, including the two-layered structure of first- and second-order awareness. Mind is studded with innate ideas, some of them satisfied by events occurring in the space that is categorially distinct from mind. Matter is a single, protean substance, one diversified by motion into myriad changing shapes. Each mode, whatever its complexity, is a mechanism all of whose properties and behaviors are explicable by way of magnitude, figure, and motion. Mind determines which of its ideas have application to extended things by relying, first, on sensory evidence, then on the clarity and distinctness of the ideas used to differentiate and organize the data. Geometry supplies comprehensive representations for everything that does or could happen in space. Yet, mind is unable to confirm directly that extended things have the properties indicated by its clear and distinct ideas. Never having direct evidence of matter, mind relies on the divine guarantee. A perfect God does not deceive us; ideas or judgments which are clear and distinct – they stand undistorted before the mind's eye or their negations are contradictions – are true. Finite mind, ever sensitive to its imperfections, struggles to organize its practical affairs so that it may devote itself to thinking about that perfect being in whose image it is made.

Questions Addressed by Descartes

Descartes proposed these views about mind, matter, and God in a context that we may represent by a series of questions. His solutions tell a coherent, metaphysical story, though individual questions may seem odd until we have the succession of dovetailing answers.

First are six, linked questions about being. (i) Is existence homogeneous, or does it vary intensively, as Plato (1964, p. 753) distinguished Being from Becoming? (ii) Is reality a collection of autonomous substances, a community of things that are reciprocally related rather than self-sufficient, or a single substance, a self-diversifying One? (iii) What are the categorial features – the essential generic properties – of substances? Should we revise or replace the Aristotelian scheme of matter and form and the four causes? (iv) What is the status of activity? Is it distinct from and incidental to the character of substances, or essential to them? Could activity alone supply the essence for a substance? (v) Is matter distinguishable from space and time? Aristotle thought that it is, but Pythagoras argued, and Plato agreed in the *Timaeus*, that matter is essentially spatial, hence geometrical. Physics was of two minds. Are the various kinds of enmattered things distinguished from one another by the essential forms intrinsic to each kind, as goats are different from sheep? Or do their many disparate features express the smaller set of properties – including shape, magnitude, and motion – that exhaust the possibilities for variability in space? (vi) Scholastic philosophers distinguished essence from existence and argued about their relative priority. Can there be uninstantiated essences? Or do essences exist by virtue of their instances?

Next are four questions about being that emphasize some principal consequences: for knowledge, for the task facing us humans, or for God. (vii) The separability of discrete bits of matter implies that relations among substances are external and accidental. This subverts the possibility for knowledge, because it entails that the connection between knower and known is brittle and uncertain. Error, hence ignorance, may forever sabotage the claim that something external to the mind is known. Plato's solution averts the problem. He believed that the innateness of ideas – the Forms – assures the internal relatedness of knower and known: the knower apprehending a Form is connected to it by virtue of discovering the Form within itself. We have, therefore, this question: Are the relations among substances internal or external? The answer is critical whenever knowledge relations are vital to a metaphysical theory. (viii) Aristotle and the Scholastics supposed that teleology is an active force in nature, whereas Descartes, like Galileo, eliminated final cause from his physics. But was it purged altogether from his thinking about the world? (ix) Anthropology – meaning reflection on the place and character of man in the world – is the shared focus of philosophy and religion. What am I? What is the world? What is my place in it? What is it good to do or to be? We would like a single, if complex, answer to these four questions. Anthropology, as the study of diverse cultures, describes the several contexts in which this answer would apply. But a single, multiply applicable answer (even one that is inflexible but coherent, or separate answers to each of the four questions) is not assured. *Man-in-the-world* names our dilemma: Which part is material, which remotely divine? (x) How is God separated by his works from himself, then reunified within himself? Descartes' answers to all these questions are somewhat as follows:

(i) *Reality*, *being*, and *existence* are equivocal, because God's reality is different in kind from our own. His existence is necessary, whereas ours is contingent. We exist because he created and now recreates us each moment.

(ii and iii) Whereas Aristotle spoke for the diversity of primary substances, and Plotinus located everything within the One, Descartes promotes an intricate compromise. His distinction between mental and extended substances splits the Plotinian One in ways that look irreparable. This categorial difference in quality is matched by diversity in quantity: no limit is specified to the number of self-discovering minds or to the number of spatial regions organized as bodies. The One seems shattered. Yet, Descartes has resources to fix it. Material substances are not as separate as they seem if they are only regions of a single space in which a small number of variables – magnitude, shape, and motion – are subject to mechanical laws that apply universally. Indeed, space is a single machine, wherein motion is conserved because each of the parts is reciprocally connected to every other. The diversity of minds is also reduced if each finite mind is an image of the divine mind, for then each one has the same structure, the same innate ideas, and the same cause. The differences among them reduce to the accidental difference that each one has a distinguishing perceptual content, perhaps because it has a different perspective on the whole. Nor could this be a perspective removed or remote from God if each finite mind is a mode of his mind.

Only the categorial difference between matter and mind divides the One into incommensurable parts. But even this breach is reparable if we remark that time (essential to the life histories of minds) and space (essential to matter) are ways of perceiving the created world from within it. They are phenomenal, not real. God himself perceives the world as an order, with all its parts contemporaneous with one another. Creation of this finite world seems to fracture the One, but that is only an appearance. The One, undivided, retains its integrity.

This is a Plotinian reading that Descartes might have given, if pressed. It is more inferred than explicit. Emphasizing the One is useful, because it underscores the tension in Descartes' views: there are the disparate minds and myriad regions of space, but also the community they form. If all their differences are perspectival or phenomenal, considerations having no currency for God as he thinks the many as qualifications of himself, their community is the One.

(iv) The Scholastics assumed that every substance of any kind is a discrete, usually autonomous agent qualified by its attributes, and that every agent is susceptible to change. Living things initiate changes within themselves, whereas other things would be inert if they were not altered by their neighbors. There is a state of rest appropriate to things of every kind, living ones included, such that motion ceases when a thing has achieved its natural state (i.e., equilibrium) or place. Descartes demurs. Nothing, he believed, is naturally inert. Minds are perpetually active (in the manner of Plato's nous or Aristotle's active intellect). Their essence is their act, as I am by virtue of my thinking. Matter is more problematic, because it is no contradiction to imagine extension without motion. Descartes nevertheless believed that motion is intrinsic to matter, not a state imposed on it. Each bit of matter would move eternally in a rectilinear trajectory if its motion were not opposed by other things (*CSM*, I, 93; *AT*, XI, 37).

There is, however, this uncertainty about motion. Descartes is at times emphatic that matter is essentially active. At other times he recoils from this idea, for either or both of two reasons. He has described matter as extension, saying nothing that would qualify it for anything but passivity – it can be moved, but it has no power to move itself. There is also the question of how motion is transferred. Again, Descartes is confounded by his definition of matter: nothing in the character of extension supplies an answer. Descartes responds by qualifying his Galilean defense of active matter. Before, he supposed, matter, once moving, continues in a straight line until opposed. Now, he infers that God supplies and sustains the motion of otherwise passive matter (*CSM*, I, 240; *AT*, VIIIA, 61–62). The quantity of motion does not change, because God perpetually adjusts the accounts: taking a little here, he gives a little there.

(v) Descartes rejected the Aristotelian–Scholastic notion that material substances are diversified by essential forms, as there are fish and frogs. These essences, each with its distinguishing powers, serve no purpose if all the differences among material things are explained by different values for magnitude, figure, and motion. Descartes rarely supplied these values for even the simplest natural phenomena. Still, his foresight reminds us of Pythagoras, for it is astonishing how much of nature is explained by theories that invoke these variables and few others.

(vi) "(A)ccording to the laws of true logic," says Descartes, "we must never ask about the existence of anything until we first understand its essence" (*CSM*, II, 78; *AT*, VII, 107–108). Essence, this implies, is distinguishable and may be separable from existence, just as we may have the formula for circularity without knowing that any actual figure satisfies it. It was usually the separability, not the distinguishability, of essence and existence that agitated the Scholastics. For what is the status of an essence when no actual particulars instantiate it? The question embarrassed Aristotle, because he supposed that universals (e.g., red considered as a kind or type) exist *in rebus*, not *ante rem*. An essence having no instances is saved from annihilation, on his "conceptualist" telling, only as we have an idea of it. "Realist" accounts say that an essence, a universal, does not risk annihilation because of being uninstantiated: it exists as a Platonic Form, as an idea in the mind of God, or as an eternal possibility (Weissman 1977, pp. 72–107).

The distinguishability of essence and existence was uncontroversial in every case but that of God. Why are they indistinguishable in him? Because necessary existence is a feature of God's essence, not a consideration distinguishable from it: his nonexistence, given his essence, would be a contradiction. Descartes' version of the ontological argument amplifies this point by saying that existence is essential to God as one of his perfections. But now, more provocatively, Descartes elicits the veneration accorded to God for us finite beings. He does this by implying that essence and existence are more than incidentally linked in us: "I am, I exist," he says, "is necessarily true each time that I pronounce it, or that I mentally conceive it" (64; *CSM*, II, 17; *AT*, VII, 25). When do I exist? "Just when I think" (65; *CSM*, II, 18; *AT*, VII, 27).

Does this coupling imply that essence and existence are indistinguishable in finite, thinking beings? No, Descartes' argument merely expresses the point that existence is never unqualified, as it is always something of a particular nature which exists: given that I exist, it remains to determine what I am. Thinking fills this role, so that Descartes specifies an essence for the existent without conflating essence and existence. He could not plausibly join them to the point of indistinguishability, because my nonexistence is not a contradiction; my essence does not entail my existence.

Descartes has, nevertheless, reduced the difference between God and me by saying that my existence, like God's, is invoked by my essence. I can think and know that I think only as I exist. My essence does not *entail* my existence. Yet the one does *require* the other, because my essence, unlike geometrical essences, is thinkable only by the one who instantiates it and by God. My essence would be unknown and unknowable to everyone but God did I not exist while perceiving myself.

Is this mistaken in supposing that each individual thinker has an essence peculiar to itself? Scholastics typically believed that every angel is the single instance of an essence, though other creatures of a kind share an essence that has, or may have, multiple instantiations. It is signate matter, not essence, that differentiates us lesser individuals (Aquinas 1965, p. 44). Descartes never considers the relation between essence and existence in these Scholastic terms: he does not say, for example, that we finite thinkers have a status closer to that of angels than to that of artifacts or animals. He implies the uniqueness of every thinker in the moment of its self-discovery. For my essence is not some general formula, but rather the product created when the essence for thinking beings is expressed, on this occasion, by the act of my being. I have the essence only as I perceive and declare that I do.

I speculate that Descartes may have thought about essence in the following way. The essence of circularity is determinable with respect to the magnitude of possible circles: they may be large or small. Suppose, however, that this determinable has a specific value, as it does if the radius of a possible circle is 1 centimeter. Supplying this value creates an essence that is qualitatively determinate. It may have one, many, or no instantiations. Compare an essence which is determinable *not in regard to some property, but rather as regards existence*. It is a particular act of existence that supplies the missing determination for essences of this sort: they are made determinate by virtue of their instantiation. Consider now these fully determinate essences, meaning every self-reflecting I. Essence and existence are indistinguishable in them, because, repeating the formulation, existence is intrinsic to the essence instantiated: the essence achieves determination as it is instantiated.

The previous paragraph is a surmise. It would explain why the difference between essence and existence dissolves, *in this special case,* at each moment of a thinker's self-discovery. Never mind that God expresses the union of essence and existence more perfectly than we do. For we are set apart from other contingent things in expressing this less exalted version of it: our existence is inseparable and indistinguishable from our thinking in the moment of reflection and self-assertion. Why does this formulation not apply universally to all created things? Perhaps its limited application, extending the surmise, is evidence of God's desire that we be set apart from them.

(vii) Scholasticism endorsed Aristotle's belief that primary substances are autonomous, so that relations among substances, whether spatial, temporal, or causal, are incidental to the essential character of things. This is consequential for knowledge, because it entails that the knower is only loosely connected to the known: rather than grasp the known as a qualification of oneself, we use signs to represent it. This loose connection allows for misrepresentation and error, as when seeing something as red tells me little or nothing about its cause. Why? Because the distinction of primary from secondary properties entails that sensory data constitute an uncertain basis for judgments about their causes.

An alternative hypothesis about relations supports knowledge claims by precluding error. This other hypothesis supposes that relations are sometimes internal to the things related. *Internality* signifies that there is coordination between two things such that a condition in one is unequivocal evidence of a condition in the other. Internality in the knowing relation may be expressed in either of several ways. Two thinkers may be linked, each one having intuitive, unmediated knowledge of the other's thoughts, as spouses, friends, and parents often believe that their feelings are an unmediated reading of the internal states of people important to them. Or events in the world may be prefigured within each thinker's mind by innate ideas, ideas which are excited – brought to awareness – as the events occur. Philosophers persuaded by the notion of internal relations have usually preferred the latter of these views: they secure knowledge claims by supposing that innate ideas, representations rather than intuitions, establish the internality of relations between knower and known.

Apriorism is a direct consequence of this assumption, though the sense of a priori needs explaining. A priori knowing is currently understood as the apprehension of one's own constructions or the innate rules used to make them. This Kantian interpretation has displaced and obscured the meaning of Plato and Descartes, who supposed that innate ideas are the intra-psychic expression of internal relations. Reflection upon them was thought to supply information about matters of fact which exceed our finite minds – as Plato's Forms, essences, and other minds exceed them. Innate ideas promise that we shall have access to these things in one of three ways. Suppose we have sensory data: we remark the data but make little sense of them until they have aroused the innate idea which provides a deeper understanding of the thing observed; or we scan the data, seeing in them the differentiating, organizing lineaments of an innate idea; or we turn away from the data after the idea is aroused – even to the point of ignoring them – so that we are not distracted as we clarify the idea.

Descartes favored the third alternative when he applied the logical test for clarity and distinctness to mathematical ideas and propositions. Sensory data never satisfy this criterion: they are discounted when we test mathematical ideas to confirm that their negations are contradictory. Recall now that geometrical ideas are said to prefigure the relations of material bodies. It follows that physics as much as geometry is a priori (or that physics *is* geometry, so that the one is a priori because the other is).

What is the basis for the internal relation of knower and known, as it obtains in physics? It is not, for Descartes, the result of bombarding the mind with sensory data loaded with clues about the character of their extramental causes. An empirical basis would reduce knowledge to a surmise. Knowledge would be external, fragile, and unreliable. Descartes never supposes that the material world imposes ideas of itself upon our minds. Knowledge of it derives, he thinks, from God's agency: the ideas innate in our minds represent the essences used by God to create the modes that differentiate the material world.

The idea of God resembles those of material things insofar as it is a priori, not empirical, but this idea is distinctive in two respects: first, because there is no hope that our idea of God may be complete, despite its being innate; second, because it is God himself who has placed the idea within us, so this idea connects us directly to its cause (unlike geometrical ideas, which represent, but are not caused by material things). Our noetic relation to God is, therefore, also consequential metaphysically. For this is the relation that saves minds from isolation, given the categorial distinction between mind and body and the separation of self-sufficient minds from one another. Indeed, individual minds are monads, with no relations to anything except God and themselves. Our knowledge of other things seems to belie this isolation. But mind's relations to the things it knows are equivocal: we know them intimately, as from within, because we have innate ideas of them; yet we know them only because God has furnished these ideas, not because of any more direct relation between us and them.

Internality, innateness, intuition, and the a priori: these are the resources for securing our knowledge; but equally, they are the flavors of a poisoned grail. Accepting them guarantees our alienation from the things to be known.

(viii) Descartes, like Galileo, banished teleological explanations from physics. Every difference and change in nature was to be explained by a difference in magnitude, size, or motion. Aristotelians believed, to the contrary, that nature is replete with final causes, every kind having aims appropriate to itself. Does Descartes argue that *nothing* is moved by a final cause, neither matter nor mind? No, there is one final cause to which I am subject: namely, God. We may never discover the idea of God within us; or, remarking the idea, we may ignore its content. But no one who reflects upon the idea can forget the flash of self-understanding. Perceiving the idea of God, however flawed my grasp, I better understand what I am and should be. For God is perfection, hence the standard for appraising beings made in his image. Thinking of his infinity, I understand that any virtue of mine is an imperfection. Better than before, I know what and where I am and what I need to do.

(Talk of God's "image" exposes this irresolution in Descartes' Christian Neoplatonism: on the one hand, God is perfection and a paradigm we should imitate; on the other, he is the unlimited, the infinite, the One, purged of all the properties that would divide him from his infinite self by making him comprehensible and finite. Descartes, like every Christian Neoplatonist, affirms both sides.)

(ix) What am I? What is the world? What is my place in it? What would it be good to do or be? Some answers are forthcoming. I am an imperfect creature who is partly material, partly conscious, one whose character intimates, as in the power of my will, the divinity of the God who sustains me. This, the self-reflecting, self-sufficient God, is my lure. When appetites disrupt me, I regulate them. Liberated from desire, I contemplate God and his creation. Knowing myself, in part by knowing them, I fulfill my nature as a thinking being. There is no superior happiness.

Descartes has invoked the Neoplatonic conception of man-in-the-world.

Souls of necessity lead a double life, partly in the intelligible realm and partly in that of sense, the higher life dominant in those able to commune more continuously with The Intelligence, the lower dominant where character or circumstance are the less favorable. (Plotinus 1975, p. 66)

With God as apex and all the rest below, man is suspended in the middle: some of our faculties resemble those of God's mind; all the rest is material and base. We are half lost but half saved, separated from ourselves by our ignorance but wanting to return in knowledge – as our contingency is already linked in being – to this perfect parent, the ground of our existence, God.

(x) What is God? A thinker like myself, but different from me in that his will and thought create and sustain all the finite world. God's power is visible not only in the diversity of his creation, but also in the cascade of internal relations which bind minds to minds, matters to matters, minds to matters, and all to God. There is also the unity achieved by God's self-awareness as he contemplates the created world and his responsibility for having made it. The One is not divided from itself; it persists, whatever the many appearances of its self-alienation. Discovering the idea of God within ourselves, we find the signature of his unity. He, as Being, is identical with himself.

This voice is inflected by scruples learned from Plato, Philo, Plotinus, and Augustine. Sanitizing Descartes by ignoring them distorts his metaphysics.

Four Cartesian Lineages

The Descartes who survives among us is a set of shards: think of disputes about the Cartesian circle or the logic of "Cogito, ergo sum." We polish these bits and pieces with little thought of their place within the whole, for we do not believe most of the story that Descartes tells. Better to recount the details than endlessly repeat that his dualism, foundationalism, and theology are mistaken. Descartes seems antique: most of us prefer to speak in the style of Kant. But this perception of our origins, and even of our current selves, is shallow. Descartes is nearly everywhere in our thinking about knowledge and reality. This is apparent in the several views of reality which have evolved from his ideas. There are, principally, five of these lineages – in physics, psychophysical dualism, psychocentric ontology, theology, and phenomenology and existentialism. The transformation of Descartes' views about mechanism and matter are described in essay 4. The other four lineages are considered here.

PSYCHOPHYSICAL DUALISM

Descartes postulated two kinds of substances: matter and mind. Agree that substances of both sorts are self-sufficient, and you are obliged to explain their interaction or the correlation of their states. For how could body and mind interact or be correlated when Descartes failed to specify a common ground for their mutual access or correlation?

There are, principally, five dualist alternatives: interactionism, occasionalism, parallelism, epiphenomenalism, and emergence. There are also two more radical solutions: materialism and mentalism. These are dualism's limiting conditions. We mostly ignore them when considering its five variant forms.

Descartes supposed – perhaps thinking of toothaches – that mind and body interact. God connects them ("[T]here is . . . nothing in them which does not give testimony to the power and goodness of the God [who has produced them]" [107; *CSM*, II, 60; *AT*, VII, 87]), though Descartes says nothing to explain his way of linking mind and body. Malebranche clarified the issue by elaborating on Descartes' suggestion that God is the intermediary ([1688] 1980, pp. 39, 43–55, 147–153). God, he said, supports the truth of clear and distinct judgments by providing their referents: essences for mathematical ideas, material objects or laws for the truths of physics. God is also the sole cause of motion where extension is passive and incapable of moving itself. Why not suppose that God, like a switchboard operator, perpetually acts as intermediary whenever matter or mind seems to be directly affected by the other? Leibniz objected that this occasionalist assumption, "which gives all external actions to God alone, has recourse to miracles, and even to miracles that are unreasonable, hardly worthy of divine wisdom" (Leibniz [1675–1716] 1989, p. 265).

What are the other dualist alternatives? The preferred options were parallelism and epiphenomenalism. The first is an idea that Leibniz favored, though his use of it was independent of this issue. He remarked that two clocks keeping the same time seem to be correlated – perhaps by way of a third thing, their common cause – though they are mutually independent. Monads seem to communicate but do not, because each is a soul which has all its history and future inscribed in it by God at the moment of its creation. Thus they are "windowless." The apparent harmony among them is the product of God's original design (ibid., pp. 213–214). Interaction is superfluous.

Applying this notion to the relations of mind and body requires that we identify two lines of descent. Terms in one series are to be correlated with terms in the other, as pain is felt when a toe is stubbed. Notice the assumption that we have a common ground for correlating the two series – namely, the time they share – though this premise is spurious, because a mind that is in touch only with itself has no direct knowledge of temporality in the other series. By this I mean that the order of motions in material things is represented under the regulative force of mind's own style of presentation, so Cartesian mind never escapes its own temporality to establish some ground, independent of itself, on which to correlate the temporal order of thoughts with the order of physical motions. Parallelism fails because it never establishes this ground, short of postulating it as the sensorium of God.

There is this alternative: abstract from time, represent each series numerically or algebraically, then correlate them. Leibniz, who regarded time as an order subject to mathematical expression (ibid., p. 179) might have favored this alternative, even as a way of expressing the relation between his twin clocks. But this is costly: it works only as we abstract from the character of matter and mind to the order that each exhibits. Observing the apparent interaction of mind and body, willing to settle for correlation but not for abstraction, we want a solution that respects the distinguishing character of the two series.

Our first choices seem hopeless: interaction because of the categorial difference between mind and matter, parallelism because we have only the abstract, algebraic solution for correlating the two series. Epiphenomenalism reduces the difference between them by saying that mental activity is the irreducible, immaterial state generated within a physical system by certain of its activities. An analogy that errs for being too explicitly material compares awareness to the glow of a copper wire whose molecules are heated and agitated by a passing electric current. Awareness, this implies, is a secondary effect, an efflorescence which occurs in or around neurons as we think. Perversely, this analogy scuttles the dualist claim that mind has autonomy and powers peculiar to itself: mind, it says, is just a glow; action and power are elsewhere.

A different solution, still favoring matter over mind, preserves mind's powers but not its independence. This is the emergentist or supervenience view. It holds that mental activities are the result of configuring matter so that it has new properties. Think of line segments that acquire new relations and properties when they are configured as a right triangle, or of oxygen and hydrogen atoms assembled to create water and its properties. Perhaps mind is best identified with the powers and activities that originate in a complex neural network (e.g., the brain). A different strategy argues that there is nothing peculiarly mental in the body, though there are bodily behaviors that count as intelligent or moral, as we win games or save children from burning houses. This too is dualism at or beyond the limit where it becomes materialism: bodies, it says, are things capable of action, whereas mind is identified with some of a body's activities, or, as Gilbert Ryle suggested, its successes and failures (1966, pp. 149–153). These gestures save dualism by reducing mind to a slightly generous physicalism.

The offsetting strategy of diminishing matter for the benefit of mind has a moral purpose. Defending ourselves against a comprehensive mechanism, we dread the loss of free will. For if mind is only a set of bodily activities, we shall be carried along by our appetites or circumstances. This is a reason for regretting the materialist reduction; but it is no argument or evidence that mind is not material. Our moral anxiety will not keep engineers and physiologists from identifying necessary and sufficient material conditions for all mental activity. How shall we save free will? Perhaps by remarking that every stable system has an inside and an outside: internal complexity creates resistance to things outside the system and control over some of its internal activities. We satisfy the moral purpose – confirming phenomenological reports of our free will – within the context of an ample physicalism.

Movement among the five kinds of dualism is overshadowed by the competition between the two extremes: each side of the dualist coupling – mind or matter – tries to consume the other when cohabitation becomes insupportable. This is more apparent (below) when the topic is the claim of psychocentric ontologies that matter and all objectivity are mind's own product. Descartes is the inspiration for reductions which go the other way: animals are machines, he said, having exclusively material constituents and causes (*CSMK*, 99–100, 134; *AT*, II, 40–41, 525). Descartes was thinking of toys activated by mechanisms like those in clocks. We make his point with machines that calculate, recognize patterns, mimic intentionality (by using negative feedback), and learn (to the point of modifying their own rules). Even self-consciousness may be mimicked by hierarchically organized systems that take readings of themselves. These achievements, however primitive, confirm Locke's dictum that it would be no contradiction were matter to think ([1756] 1959, vol. 2, p. 193). Dualism survives because one feature of mental life is neither duplicated in physical systems nor explicable (yet) in terms appropriate to their description: we do not understand the physical basis for the presentation – the consciousness – of sensory data, including sights, sounds, smells, pleasures, and pains. "Attending" to these "phenomena," we are as little able as Descartes to explain that they are the effects (and qualifications) of material systems. Dualism has this much life in it.

How shall we avoid wholesale devaluation of ourselves if study confirms that mind is only material? Many of us approve of abortion and euthanasia, so we especially are responsible for an answer to this other question: Why should our value be uncompromisable between birth and death if it is diminished or uncertain at the beginning and end? Why not treat people badly if matter, in itself, has no worth? The burden of having to rework our moral assumptions is one reason for resisting the reduction of mind to matter. We prefer living in the middle, rooted in our animal nature but also free of it, because either reduction is unsatisfactory. Reductions to mind postulate that all matter is a qualification of mind, though mind – activity without an agent – floats in a void. Or we doubt the possibility of mind's reduction to matter because we believe that one or more of the states or activities cited by Descartes (e.g., conception, sensibility, or self-consciousness) may have no sufficient basis in matter. The incompleteness of one compares to the incoherence of the other: The idea of activity without an agent seems irretrievably flawed. The materialist program may be very close to fulfillment. Rethinking our moral lights is urgent business.

We avoid the issue because we are half-anesthetized by the cyclical, oddly static character of the dualist lineage. It starts with Descartes' claim that mind and matter are categorially different and then identifies plausible strategies for defending his dualism. The alternatives have hardly changed since their discovery. Each is proposed when another is faulted, then withdrawn because of its failures. This instability will likely persist until every mental activity is explained in physical terms. It would persist forever were someone to show that awareness cannot have a wholly physical basis.

PSYCHOCENTRIC ONTOLOGY

"I am, I exist," Descartes said, "each time that I pronounce it, or that I mentally conceive it" (64; *CSM*, II, 17; *AT*, VII, 25). But what am I, and what else is true necessarily? Descartes' successors were transfixed by these questions, but divided in their responses. Some (see sec. ii below) embellished the cogito: they made it self-sufficient, as substances are traditionally said to be, and reduced other things, including percepts of "extra-mental things," to mind's qualifications. Descartes had supposed that finite minds are the model for God, though God now becomes our model: we become world-makers in his place. Synthesizing mind, now credited with a normative force and principles that would once have been ascribed to nature itself, creates experience by projecting qualities and relations onto sensory data.

Other successors (see sec. iii below) seem modest and sober by comparison. They emphasize conceptual economy and logical rigor, while proposing a more ascetic ontology: ideas, judgments, or sentences are true as they are or can be perceived or demonstrated; things exist only as they are set before the mind's eye. This version seems flatter than the one above, because the cogito is increasingly de-emphasized by successive contributors to the lineage: in its place go impressions, ideas, or words. World-making is underplayed; rigor is emphasized. Indeed, the demand for presentation and rigor becomes the justification for a corrosive skepticism. It dissolves every speculation whose referent cannot be directly perceived or demonstrated, then confirmed by perception. Where the things eliminated are significant – as laws, dispositions, and causes are significant – these skeptics look for inspectable surrogates in percepts, words, or grammar. Anything for which there is no substitute on the side of mind – matter and God are examples – is eliminated. What is left of the world? Only the structured phenomena, which are set before the mind's eye, though, paradoxically, mind has often disappeared (Weissman 1987, pp. 133–139).

(i) Descartes' Ontology Implodes

Responses of both kinds evolved when Descartes' realism imploded because of his preference for knowledge over true belief. There is also his persuasion that necessary truths are the only ones that support our claims to knowledge: they alone are perceived clearly and distinctly, because their negations are contradictions. What happens if we turn the tables, applying this test to Descartes' ideas of mind, matter, and God? Do they satisfy his conditions for knowledge?

It is all-important for Descartes that God should exist, because God is the guarantor of clear and distinct ideas and the cause of both motion and mind–body interaction. But is the idea of God clear and distinct? Yes, says Descartes; it would be a contradiction that God not exist given that existence is one of his perfections. We do not have positive content for the idea that God is infinite; but we confirm his necessary existence by establishing that his essence entails his existence. There are some doubts, however. For what are the many perfections, and what is the evidence that each is consistent with the others? Why assume that existence is a perfection? These considerations were usually ignored, perhaps because they were thought scandalous. Other suspicions were expressed openly.

Principal among them is the objection that we do not have a clear and distinct idea of an infinite being: "*Are* you clearly and distinctly aware of an infinite being? What, in that case, is the meaning of that well-worn maxim which is common knowledge: *the infinite qua infinite is unknown?*" (*CSM*, II, 69; *AT*, VII, 96). This is the objection of "Caterus," Johan de Kater, a Dutch priest. Descartes replied:

> I apply the term 'infinite', in the strict sense, only to that in which no limits of any kind can be found; and in this sense God alone is infinite. But in cases like the extension of imaginary space or the set of numbers, or the divisibility of the parts of a quantity, there is merely some respect in which I do not recognize a limit; . . . these items are not limitless in every respect. (*CSM*, II, 81; *AT*, VII, 113)

This response is deficient, because Descartes has defined infinity, hence God, operationally and negatively – as that which has no limits. He supplies no additional, positive content to the idea, so the clarity and distinctness claimed for it apply only to the operation of extrapolating beyond a current limitation to the notion of a being who is more perfect or greater than any being that is or could be conceived. Adding universality of respects does nothing to turn the infinitely denumerable – Hegel's "bad infinite" ([1812–16] 1961, p. 152) – into the positive infinity appropriate to God. The word *God* is place-marker for an incomprehensible being and a negative – "limitless" – or empty idea.

Has Descartes confirmed God's existence and his role as guarantor of truths despite having no adequate idea of him? Influential successors would not concede that he had, some because they believed that God's existence and role are known to faith not argument, others because Descartes' arguments seemed flawed. There is, for example, the "new" argument that the idea of an infinite being must have been placed in us by God because it cannot have been produced by creatures having merely finite powers. This claim fails, because we can generate this idea, as we have the idea of an indefinitely extended series of numbers and also the idea that this operation may be applied to any perfection. Descartes' version of the ontological argument also fails: it proves that a necessary existent is possible, because the idea embodies no contradiction, but it does not prove that this possibility is instantiated, that a necessary being is actual. Descartes supposed that a possibility for necessary existence must move out of possibility into actuality as though empowered by the urgency of its necessity. But this is a view he nowhere justifies. Accordingly, he has not established – by reason, not faith – either that we have a comprehensible idea of God or that God exists.

This result is critical, because it deprives us of a guarantor for the applicability of clear and distinct ideas. Consider, for example, the idea of matter. Why should we believe that matter is more than an idea, if the clarity and distinctness of the idea are no evidence, in the absence of God's guarantee, that it has application beyond our minds? Leibniz answers by reconstruing matter as a phenomenon having no application apart from thought:

> I believe that primitive or derivative force which is conceived in extension or mass as outside of perceivers is not a thing but a phenomenon, as is extension itself, as well as mass and motion, which are things no more than an image in a mirror or rainbow in a cloud are. ([1675–1716] 1989, p. 184, n. 239)

We are stripped of two ideas fundamental to Descartes' metaphysics: we have no positive content for the idea of God and no certainty, hence no knowledge, as to his existence; nor is there evidence sufficient to confirm that matter exists outside the mind.[1] The ascertainable truths about existing things reduce to the claim that I exist, for there is no gap between me and the phenomena I inspect:

> [N]o one can be certain that he is thinking or that he exists unless he knows what thought is and what existence is. But this does not require reflective knowledge, or the kind of knowledge that is acquired by means of demonstration. . . . It is quite sufficient that we should know it by that internal awareness which always precedes reflective knowledge. This inner awareness of one's thought and existence is so innate in all men . . . that we cannot in fact fail to have it. (*CSM*, II, 285; *AT*, VII, 422)

Certain about my own character and existence, I may be skeptical about the extra-mental existence of everything else.

Descartes' metaphysics has collapsed onto its core: his three-part ontology – of matter, mind, and God – is reduced to mind alone. But who can advocate a theory having this single resource when Descartes has emphasized mind's inability to produce its ideas or assure their applicability? *Where the standard for knowledge is certainty, and where effects previously ascribed to matter and God cannot be referred to either of them, we are obliged to choose: establish mind's self-sufficiency, hence its power for creating these effects within itself; or use logic to assure the coherence of thought or experience while ignoring or denying the conditions for experience, whether these conditions are extra-mental or the mind's own faculties.* Descartes' idealist successors emphasize one or the other of these alternatives. German philosophers credit mind with powers for doing the things that were previously ascribed to God or the material world. Thinkers who were English, Scottish, or Irish suppose that mind has more limited powers. They say little or nothing of these faculties, while demanding that ideas be purged of their speculative excesses, then organized for clarity and rigor.

Thinkers of both sorts exploit the cogito. Mind, as Descartes described it, is an open door to its percepts. They appear uninvited, because of mind's link to the pineal gland and the body's sensory system. Mind is also passive to the natural light, ideas and a power for discerning them having been placed in us by God. Passivity extends even to self-reflecting mind as it observes itself. Yet, passivity is balanced by mind's activity: mind discovers itself, uses ideas to organize and elucidate percepts, analyzes obscure ideas, constructs or deduces complex from simple ideas (the *more geometrico*), then gives or withholds assent. The two elaborations diverge as each stresses some of these points but not others. With the emphasis on self-reflection, will, and the use of ideas to organize percepts, the cogito is transformed into Leibniz's monads, Kant's transcendental unity of apperception, Fichte's will-driven ego, and Hegel's Absolute. Descartes' modest thinker becomes a world-maker. Largely ignoring self-reflection and the mind's own structure, emphasizing the analysis of ideas and their logical organization, we get the phenomenalist views of Locke, Berkeley, Hume, Russell, and the positivists. Either way, Descartes' realism is superseded by a drastic idealism.

(ii) All Reality Is Mind or Its Qualifications

The drift to Leibniz and Kant is anticipated by this passage from the *Meditations*:

> I remember that, when looking from a window and saying I see men who pass in the street, I really do not see them, but infer that what I see is men. . . . And yet what do I see from the window but hats and coats which may cover automatic machines? Yet I judge these to be men. And similarly solely by the faculty of judgment which rests in my mind, I comprehend that which I believed I saw with my eyes. (69; *CSM*, II, 21; *AT*, VII, 32)

We infer that hats and coats are the garments of men passing our window when ideas and judgment supervene on percepts. What is implied about the relation of ideas to sensory data?

There are several options. Percepts are the obscure or cluttered expressions of essences which intellect discerns within them. Or clear and distinct ideas of these essences are present already within the mind, so the task of judgment is that of decoding percepts by using ideas as templates or paradigms. Or ideas in the mind are rules used to differentiate and organize percepts, thereby supplying an order that makes them thinkable.

Leibniz ([1675–1716] 1989, pp. 217–218) and Malebranche ([1688 1980, pp. 81–105) supposed that thought discerns essences through the perceptual veil of encumbering accidents. Spinoza agreed, though he also emphasized the use of ideas as paradigms: we use the idea of equality or circularity as a standard for making sense of relevant percepts (1677] 1955, pp. 7–14). Descartes may be construed in either way; but equally, we may understand him to be saying that the percepts of hats and coats are too obscure to be informative until the idea of man is invoked – *as a rule* – to differentiate and organize them.[2] Imagine that one of the men observed is walking quickly, that the streets are fogbound, and that we catch just a glimpse of him. It is more plausible now that the idea of man is used as a rule to differentiate this man's parts and the clothes he seems to be wearing.

Remember that Descartes regarded space and time as ideas, neither of which can be known to have application beyond our minds when confidence in God's guarantee is lost. Which of the three options cited above is appropriate to ideas of them? There are, again, three possibilities: hearing music from a distance on a windy day, we listen attentively for the tune; or we know the tune, so we hear the fractured melody by comparing it to the song we hum; or we hear the notes in the correct sequence because, knowing the song and using it as a rule, we assign every next sound its proper value.

These are not Leibniz's examples, but they cover the gamut of his concerns. For if it first seems that we listen for an order already present in things, we may quickly pass to believing that the idea of order is a rule for creating it. "Extension," Leibniz remarks, "is the order of coexisting possibles, and . . . time is the order of inconsistent possibilities" ([1675–1716] 1989, p. 178). He has also said that time and space are phenomenal, implying that these are orders that mind makes, not orders it discerns in extramental things. This is an important finding, because space and time have a unique status among organizing ideas: they are used to order and present every other thing perceived. Accordingly, we have this transitional result.

Space and time are the ordering principles for other phenomena: every datum within a monad's experience is subjected to these orders or to the temporal one only. Moreover, these orders are known intuitively, if obscurely, as modes of presentational immediacy, as one perceives an array of colors or sounds.

We explain the inception of these orders by recalling Descartes' remark that I exist only so long as I think. Temporality is the order in which mind represents itself to itself, hence the order of thought. Why should the mind be self-presented in this way? The answer is uncertain. If temporal development is real, then the experience of one's own temporality is a direct perception of mind's evolution. If time is only a phenomenal mode for representing atemporal things, mathematicals for example, then temporality is both a mode of presentation and a source of confusion. Leibniz speaks for both sides: temporality is the constitutive ordering principle and the mode of presentation for finite minds – monads – though it has no role in the presentation of God's ideas. Why is space also a form of presentation? One answer is that space differs from time as the order of coexistence differs from that of succession. But this is not reason enough, because time tolerates both coexistence and succession, just as there are single notes and chords. The better explanation is that space was previously assumed to be the mode for representing extra-mental, extended things. The representational form remains when skeptics and idealists have supposed that nothing exists in an extra-mental space. This result is either embarrassing or unexpectedly useful: we have the artifact of a delusion or the means for giving the appearance of extra-mental, material things, though there are none. Either way, time has priority over space because of being mind's way of representing itself to itself.

Kant emphasizes what Leibniz passed over more lightly: space and time are modes of presentation and ordering principles with universal application – to "outer" and "inner" phenomena respectively (Kant [1781] 1965, pp. 65–91). The use of ideas is hereby deflated. Their domain, so far as we can think it, is only that of human experience: they are rules used to schematize sensory experience, as the name of a friend may organize one's impressions of him or her. Supposing that ideas have application in an extra-mental world, be it material or divine, has become a vulgar fantasy.

The world, so far as we can think or know it, is the set of phenomena differentiated and organized in space and time. "Objectivity" is the orderliness, hence the predictability, of these phenomena, given whatever additional rules limit or determine associations of sensory data. What does *truth* mean when truths do not have extra-mental referents? It signifies their consistency and coherence under rules of three kinds: rules for consistency, including noncontradiction and excluded middle; rules for coherence, including rules that apply throughout the domain of phenomena ordered temporally or spatially (e.g., harmonic or geometrical rules); and rules for organizing things of a specific kind or domain (e.g., for schematizing bats or birds). Think of the idea of man as Descartes supposed that we use it to organize and identify our percepts of hats and coats, then imagine telling a coherent story about a particular man, one that jibes with one's own memories of the man and other thinkers' stories about him. Now discount the intimation that these are events occurring independently of our minds. Where the coherence of our story is all that truth could be, we have Kant's transformation of Descartes' views about the use of ideas, including those of space and time.

Consider now the cogito itself. Descartes emphasized the mind's imperfections: our ideas are too often obscure; we are liable to err when inferring one idea from another. Only patience, the ideal of clarity and distinctness, and our power to withhold assent are defenses against these weaknesses. Leibniz too stressed our imperfections, especially our merely perspectival view of things and our obscuring, phenomenal perception of intelligibles (i.e., we discern them through the mask of sensory experience). But Leibniz, following Descartes, supposed that we effectively perceive (conceive) the character of the environing, extra-experiential world. Kant replies that we are self-deceived: reason mistakenly wants to apply its ideas beyond the forms of intuition, space and time. Why should we not apply ideas, such as cause and effect, beyond the array of schematized phenomena to identify, if only speculatively, the extra-mental conditions for experience? Because we have no way to confirm that the rules used to create experiences apply to the relation of mind to the extra-mental world, if there be such. The world as we know it is only the world we ourselves make. It exists, "within" us, as mind's qualification. The world-in-itself exercises a limiting effect upon our minds as it supplies the raw sensory data from which mind creates experience, but this limiting condition is noumenal: there is *nothing* we can say about it. We exceed this restriction even in speculating that it supplies sensory data for schematization, because *supplies* is a causal word, though cause and effect is a relation among phenomena within sensible experience, not an idea properly applied beyond it. Thought violates its own proper constraints merely by speculating that an extra-experiential world exists, for existence too is a notion that has no content – with one exception – apart from the forms of sensibility (space and time) where data appear as existing. Thought's ambit is reduced to the domain of the experiences it makes, then inspects, although thought also affirms – the one exception – its own existence. This affirmation is indirect in the first *Critique*, where we infer from the existence of experience to the existence of its condition, the transcendental ego, but is direct in the second *Critique*, where Kant describes thought as it shapes the will (Kant [1788] 1963, pp. 216–218, 232).

Kant supposes that a mind reflecting upon its experiences perceives them without mediation: its grasp is an *intuition*. This was Descartes' reason for saying that mind is certain when reflecting upon itself: there is no gap between the subject and object of this relation if the object is just the subject turned on itself. Kant also accepts Descartes' assumption about mind's structure, though he elaborates on the notions of first- and second-order awareness in ways that vastly empower reflexive awareness while making it less available to self-inspection.

How is Descartes' modestly endowed thinker transformed into a world-maker? Consider the two orders of awareness as the balance between them is adjusted in either direction. All the power for apprehending the objects of awareness (e.g., things conceived or perceived) might reside in first-order thinking, reducing self-consciousness to the role of passive witness. Or first-order awareness might be impulsive and careless: judgments made there might go awry without the direction of higher-order awareness. Descartes favored this second alternative. Clarity and distinctness are achieved only as first-order awareness is superseded by the analyses undertaken by second-order reflection. For what is the power that exposes ideas that are innate within us? What suppresses the first-order impulse to make premature judgments? Only second-order reflection. Descartes supposed that all mind's powers for deliberation and self-discovery are located there, and, furthermore, that reflexivity discovers the horizon, the limit of my being: "The author lays it down as certain that there can be nothing in him, in so far as he is a thinking thing, of which he is not aware" (*CSM*, II, 150; *AT*, VII, 214). Consciousness is the bounded efflorescence in which I perceive myself.

Leibniz had agreed that mind is a structure comprising first- and second-orders of awareness: "The passing state which involves and represents a multitude in the unity or in the simple substance is nothing other than what one calls perception, which should be distinguished from apperception" ([1675–1716] 1989, p. 214). This identification of apperception with consciousness does not imply that perception is not also a kind of awareness: rather, perception is awareness of content, without self-awareness. Leibniz would have us believe that every substance is an entelechy, a monad, having perception and appetite, and that some monads also have apperception –

self-awareness. Apperceiving monads discover themselves when they "rise to *reflective acts* . . . through the knowledge of necessary truths and through their abstractions" (ibid., p. 217).

This passage is more strikingly Platonic than Cartesian. Nous for Plato is the depersonalized act of knowing the Forms, though it is personification and self-reflection – a self discovered in doubt – that distinguish mind as Descartes describes it. Why does Leibniz emphasize necessary truths as the basis for mind's knowledge of itself? Probably because these are the proper domain for God's reflection, and because finite minds are most like God when they rise beyond their distinguishing perspectives to reflect upon truths known to God. Where perception is perspectival, hence particularizing (as in monads), apperception reflects upon its distorted, individuating perspective or rises – beyond perspective – to the intellectual perception of necessary truths.

Kant's transformation of the cogito couples particularity to a different sort of necessity. His "transcendental ego" is a thinker marooned in a skeptical void, a thinker that saves itself from emptiness – Hegel's "nothingness" ([1812–16] 1961, pp. 95–100) – by creating a thinkable experience. This thinker is each of us. Having no extra-mental, yet thinkable, supporting order in which to find our place and no divinity to guide and guarantee our progress, we provide those things for ourselves. What resources do we have? Here the balance between first- and second-order awareness shifts – more radically than Descartes conceived – to the side of self-reflection: all the support once assigned to God and the world is translated into powers for making a thinkable experience. Leibniz wrote that

> God alone is the primitive unity or the first simple substance; all created or derivative monads are products, and are generated, so to speak by continual fulgurations of the divinity from moment to moment, limited by the receptivity of the creature, to which it is essential to be limited. ([1675–1716] 1989, p. 219)

Kant supposes that each thinker does God's work for itself. Rather than live within and struggle to understand the world God has made, each thinker is obliged to make something sustained and coherent from nothing richer than sensory data. Kant assumes, without proving, that the data are atomic, so that all the relations among them are supplied when the data are schematized. The resources required to organize them include mind's receptivity to sensory data, its concepts (meaning, rules), and apperception – second-order awareness. Apperception unifies the data in two ways: by ordering and re-presenting all of them in space and time, the forms of intuition, and, concurrently, by using particular concepts to schematize individual sets of data. Imagine a photograph in which the black and white dots are organized to create the faces of family members, each one standing in some determinate relation to the others. Second-order awareness, the "transcendental unity of apperception" (see Kant [1781] 1965, pp. 135–161), has these same effects within experience: everything is related spatially or temporally to everything else, while particular sets of data are set apart by the relations which connect them to one another (e.g., the uncle standing to the left of an aunt). The result is a unitary but differentiated view of "things perceived."

We are quick to recognize these ways of unifying experience because Descartes anticipated both of them. (*a*) Kant affirms that phenomena are unified in time – they occur successively – whereas time is unified by the transcendental unity of apperception. Descartes also supposed that all phenomena are joined to one another – as concurrent or successive – within a temporalized self-awareness. (*b*) The judgments said to unify subjects and their qualities, or subject terms and their predicates, recall Descartes' remark about our perception of the sun. Is it large or small? Second-order consciousness corrects the impression that the sun is a small, flat disk by judging that the body perceived is much larger than the Earth. The subject term, 'sun', and the predicate, 'large' or 'small', are unified by this act of judgment. Kant's transcendental unity of apperception is, in these two ways, an articulation of the cogito, one that distinguishes and separates first- and second-order consciousness more severely than Descartes ever did.

How should we explain the fact that judgments, hence experiences, differ among thinkers? The commonsense answer is that our perspectives and histories differ: you see things from a different angle than I do; things that have bitten me may not have bitten you. We expect that Kant must have some other explanation, for he does not concede that experiences are representations of things existing apart from our synthesizing minds: all objectivity insofar as we can think or know it is, he says, re-presented – presented after synthesis – for mind's inspection. This is puzzling, for how shall we explain differences among the experiences of disparate thinkers if there is no common world to control what each perceives?

Kant's answer is uncertain because he sometimes retreats from the extremity of his skepticism to agree that the extra-mental world is a "limit" on experience, one that obtains though we cannot specify it in any positive way. But then he adds, on the side of subjectivity, another explanation for differences among experiences: we choose the empirical rules – what he calls *empirical schemas* – used to schematize sensory data. Why choose one rule rather than another? In order to satisfy our aims. Having different interests, we make different experiences after choosing different empirical schemas (Kant [1790] 1987, p. 16, n. 18). How extraordinary that the power to create a thinkable world, a power once reserved to God, is now claimed for individual, finite, *practical* egos. Fichte makes the point exactly:

> *In relation to a possible object*, the pure self-referring activity of the self is a *striving*; and as shown earlier, an infinite *striving* at that. This boundless striving, carried to infinity, is the *condition of the possibility of any object whatsoever*: no striving, no object. ([1794–95] 1982, p. 231)

Descartes' characterization of the will has been transformed. Critics thought that his description of the will as a power for giving or withholding assent was excessively intellectual. Other conceptions of it, Spinoza's for example, are more robust:

> [E]ffort when . . . related to the mind alone, is called "will," but when it is related at the same time both to the mind and the body is called "appetite," which is therefore nothing but the very essence of man, from the nature of which necessarily follow those things which promote his preservation. ([1677] 1955, p. 137)

Leibniz made the similar point that "[a] monad's natural changes come from an internal principle" ([1675–1716] 1989, p. 214]; "[it] brings about the change or passage from one perception to another (that) can be called *appetition*" (ibid., p. 21).

Kant demurs. He invokes the intellectualized, Cartesian will – not brute, animal will – when he explains the balance of necessity and choice as mind uses rules to schematize experience. The categories of understanding are used involuntarily to create a thinkable experience, hence experience cannot fail to have properties of all three kinds: we cannot think a world that lacks quantity, quality, or relation. Yet we experience people and things as having specific features, not a generic quantity, quality, and relation. Mind must also choose and apply – assent or not to the use of – the particular empirical schemas (e.g., rules for schematizing dogs or cats) that give expression to the categories, thereby creating the experience of particular things (e.g., dogs or cats). Choosing particular rules, we create some one of the infinitely many possible experiences. Declining to use a rule, we refuse to think of the world as having objects of the sort that would be schematized thereby.

This is Cartesian will fulfilling its power for deciding the shape and details of the experience that understanding makes. Consider this evolution. Descartes supposed that mind is passive to sensory data and even to the innate ideas that they arouse in us. Will, by comparison, is one of mind's active powers, as we give assent to clear and distinct ideas but withhold it from ideas that are confused. Kant, too, supposed that mind, as will, must choose: it surveys the empirical schemas, some of them contraries, selecting those it will use to make a thinkable experience. The result is a particular experience, hence a specific world, one that is differentiated and organized in the style prefigured by the empirical schemas used to make it.

Descartes anticipated this result. For he supposed that God's will decides both the logical form and the specific character of the world. Kant extended this claim, giving our finite minds a power for world-making that is somewhat less grand than the one that Descartes ascribed to God: we choose among schemas for making alternative experiences, though we – unlike Descartes' God – cannot revise the principles of general logic, including noncontradiction, identity, and excluded middle (*CSMK*, 235; *AT*, IV, 118). Descartes insisted that we achieve clarity and distinctness in our ideas before we give or withhold assent: will is free to assent or dissent; but it is to be moved, one way or the other, by the quality – the truth – of ideas. Kant implies that will's determinants – like those Descartes ascribes to God,[3] are utilitarian, not intellectual: "All the soul's powers or capacities can be reduced to three that cannot be derived further from a common basis: the *cognitive power*, the *feeling of pleasure and displeasure*, and the *power of desire*" (Kant [1790] 1987, p. 16). Will chooses such instruments as give us pleasure and avoid pain. Descartes expressed an apparently similar view when he remarked that "(N)ature . . . truly teaches me to flee from things which cause the sensation of pain, and seek after the things which communicate to me the sentiment of pleasure" (103; *CSM*, II, 57; *AT*, VII, 82). This last affinity is shallow, because Descartes believed, as Kant's critical idealism denies, that we live as bodies within a nature we have not made.

Kant's reinterpretation of these Cartesian themes is the watershed for his successors, especially in continental Europe and the Americas. Seven of the notions that he embroidered are critical: (1) Mind is the ample arena within which objects of knowledge are presented to our inspecting minds. (2) Things known exist within our minds, rather than being merely represented there, by thoughts, words, or sensory data. (3) Things known are created by the judgments which differentiate and organize sensory data or, as Kant expresses this point, when mind uses rules to schematize the sensory manifold. (4) The two kinds of rules pertinent to schematization are universal categories – quantity, quality, and relation – and empirical schemas which express those categories in more specific ways. The categories are innate; empirical schemas are improvised or learned. (5) Use of the categories is involuntary, hence necessary and universal; the choice of empirical schemas is determined by our values.

(6) Each of us strives to make a world congenial to him or herself. Doing this has the effect, noted above, that will is the final arbiter of the world we live in or know, because will decides the rules to be used for creating any particular thinkable world. Why create one world rather than another? So that a particular desire may be satisfied. Descartes ascribed this power only to God. Kant confers it on each of us. The result is explosive in Kant's successors when world-making coalesces with Descartes' claim that God's will supersedes even the elementary principles of logic (*CSMK*, 235; *AT*, IV, 118). World-makers can do anything, even remake the conditions for rationality. Is doing this irrational, because arbitrary and disruptive? Think of it as freedom: our will, like God's, is unconstrained by any higher power as it alters rules and principles.

Kant hopes to limit the will by restricting its choice of maxims (i.e., rules of action) to those which are universalizable without contradiction: could everyone do as we propose to do without producing conflict of a sort that would subvert the proposed activity (e.g., asking for a loan but willing that creditors should not be paid, so that eventually no loan is given) (Kant [1788] 1963, pp. 31–33)? The demand that we use this principle (the "categorical imperative") is, however, no more than the *recommendation* that we act in accord with our rational nature. Kant does not establish that there is some generally effective procedure (e.g., punishment), faculty (e.g., empathy), or value (e.g., prudence) that deters us from changing empirical schemas or maxims if whim or appetite impels us. Will sets the agenda. Thought can struggle to establish reason's mastery over will; or thought can go along, accommodating itself to whatever values and rules will supplies – all this because Kant ascribes to finite minds what Descartes ascribes to God. Will chooses the rules and empirical schemas to be applied as intellect schematizes the experience – and world – whereby desire is satisfied. This is a theme embellished by Fichte and Nietzsche, one exploited to terrible effect in our century.

(7) This other consideration is more perplexing. The activity directing our synthesis of experience is second-order awareness, as happens when the awareness of my desires prompts me to choose and apply one or another set of rules. Paradoxically, Kant and his successors often suppose that mind's self-awareness has disappeared. This is best explained by a difference between Descartes and Kant. For the one, second-order awareness is always

immediately accessible to itself: "I am, I exist" was Descartes' startled exclamation. For the other, second-order awareness is transcendental, hence known inferentially, if at all. Leibniz said that every monad perceives, but that only some monads apperceive – perceive themselves. He credited apperception to every monad capable of thought, for he supposed that thought requires self-regulation (i.e., self-correction). Leibniz would have been surprised that self-reflection is denied to thinkers who make worlds. Why do many Kantians believe otherwise? Why do they suppose that mind is inaccessible to itself at the moment of making experience?

Hegel's explanation ([1807] 1967, pp. 218–227) is compelling. Thought alone supplies no content for awareness. We are aware of ourselves thinking only as we are aware of something else; second-order consciousness presupposes an object for first-order awareness. Thought turned upon itself discovers some content or object, but never itself. This was Kant's assumption when he supposed that the transcendental unity of apperception is known inferentially, not by inspection: second-order awareness discovers the experience it has made, but not itself. This belief is common to Kant's principal heirs in our time. There are, for example, Rudolf Carnap's (1969) views about the reconstructed empirical theories used to create thinkable worlds. We reasonably infer that minds using these theories stand apart from – are prior to – the worlds they create. Carnap, however, says nothing about the thinkers who make and use conceptual systems. Minds are made thinkable, he argues, only as they are characterized in empirical psychology, a reconstructed theory like every other one used for knowing things separate from us. We have this paradox: the minds that formulate and apply psychological theories have disappeared, only to reemerge as the schematized empirical phenomena created by their own theories. We would expect the thinkers who make and use theories sometimes to notice themselves. But there is no trace of reflexivity in Carnap's writings apart from his Fichtean remarks about the pragmatic uses of theories (viz., that they are useful, given the self-acknowledged interests of their users). Second-order awareness, self-awareness, has otherwise disappeared.

Perhaps this self-oblivion is our embarrassed response to Hegel. For if the thinkable world has the Absolute – God – as its schematizer, then any finite thinker who admits to being a world-maker is claiming God's role for himself. This is more grandiose than we usually care to be. Hence our problem: how to claim the enlarged powers that Kant ascribed to the cogito while averting megalomania? We do it by modestly disclaiming a conscious responsibility: we certainly do not know ourselves to be making thinkable worlds. Our activity is more routine: we are reconstructing scientific theories – though now we add, with a certain Kantian righteousness, that the only thinkable worlds are those presented by way of these reconstructions. Which of the two are we doing: rigorous housekeeping or world-making? We emphasize the one with a diffidence that obscures mind's role as it does the other. Why are we compelled to make worlds? Because we cannot do otherwise, given our skepticism about extra-mental things and our need of a thinkable world.

Recall that Descartes credited second-order thinking with two powers: one for self-awareness, the other for normative thinking (e.g., applying ideas as templates or rules). He supposed that these two are distinguishable but not separable. Carnap, after Kant, has ignored the one while exploiting the other. This is morally dangerous, because it implies that mind acts – even to the point of making thinkable worlds – while unaware of, hence disclaiming responsibility for, what it does. Kant wanted to avert this result wherever our thinking is practical: mind should always be self-aware, he said, when the choice of rules and aims has moral consequences, as happens when other thinkers are affected by what we do.[4] But then it should follow for Kant that mind is always duty-bound to act subject to the brake of conscious self-control. For he believed that every mind's choice of schemas is driven by desire, and that the unregulated opposition of desires, as exhibited in their contending worlds and behaviors, creates a turmoil wherein few or no desires are satisfied. Self-conscious moral control would be dispensable only if the task at issue were not practical, as the aim of science is knowledge and truth, not some personal advantage. Someone writing in the shadow of Kant – Carnap, for example – could reasonably use this pretext to excuse himself from responsibility for self-conscious control of his schematizing. He could explain that second-order awareness innocently loses sight of itself when truth is the only interest motivating us. The danger recurs, because thinkers oblivious to themselves, hence to their world-making, will schematize experiences and worlds "for science," out of sight of motives (e.g., power and efficiency) which are not disinterested. Better that mind know its responsibility for what it does. Better Descartes than the self-forgetfulness learned from Kant (and Hume).

Passivity (as perceptual data are presented) or activity (as thought schematizes a thinkable world), self-awareness or self-oblivion: these are two of the oppositions that form the dialectical spine of this lineage. Each pair prescribes alternative postures for second-order awareness, and each starts out on a Cartesian footing before shifting to one that is emphatically Kantian. On one side, we discover ourselves within a world we have not made. On the other, we are self-forgetting world-makers. Join the two sides, as Hegel does in the *Phenomenology*, and we get the story of an Absolute that discovers itself in the course of its dialectical reflections on the world it has made.

World-making is also energized by a third pair of contraries: privacy and sociality. Cartesian privacy – I am, I exist each time I think it – is a reflection upon one's particular existence, and the universals available to every thinker. Most of Leibniz's monads are ignorant of universals, though each has a singular view of the world. Indeed, there is no common world for Leibniz, but only the set of perspectives integrated when God thinks them as one. Each monad's experience is, in this respect, a private world, one that risks isolation when none can speak to others about a world they share. Successive thinkers have argued that we breach our isolation by creating a common world. Kant described a community of lawmakers, each one legislating for himself and every other. Where Descartes' cogito is private, Rousseau's "general will" ([1749] 1988, p. 129), Marx's subjective conditions for class loyalty ([1843–44] 1992, pp. 348–350), Dewey's "Great Community" ([1927] 1954, pp. 143–184), and Wittgenstein's linguistic tribes, distinguished by the languages they speak and the language-games they play (1966, pp. 1–10) are the agents or expressions of our world-making: we create settled meanings, habits, and behaviors. We establish, thereby, the milieus of people called "civilized," because each one embodies the expectations, values, and skills that make us recognizable to our fellows. What principle explains the evolution from Cartesian privacy to a Kantian or Hegelian social self, from monadic, private worlds to a common world?

Self-reflection, as Descartes described it, is the paradigm for privacy, whether the contents are particular and contingent or universal and necessary. For no matter that I enjoy an ephemeral pleasure or a geometrical theorem, the presentation is mine. Democracy, meaning each one's right to the choice and pleasure of his or her experience, has its justification in this notion of privacy: witness John Stuart Mill's "three regions of liberty," especially freedom of consciousness and conscience ([1859] 1987, p. 16). There is, however, the opposing claim that consciousness leavens particularity and idiosyncrasy – in thought, impulse, or action – with universality and sociality. How is socialization achieved?

One may suppose that Kant's moral theory was the principal step: that rational agents are socialized by willing the categorical imperative (Kant [1788] 1963, p. 119). But this is not so: his theory cannot generate the socialization we want to establish or explain. His categorical imperative creates a formal sociality only, one mediated by each thinker's determination to do nothing that every other thinker could not also do. This is a sociality so formal that moral agents are not obliged to universalize the same maxims: it is enough that each confirms the universalizability of his own projected rule of behavior (everyone could do it without contradiction, though no one but me may want to do it). The Kantian emphasis on moral rules and rule-making evolved into a pragmatic, almost tactile sensibility (e.g., Wittgenstein's language-games) for the warp and detail of community-making rules. Yet rules alone do not create the sociality favored by Kant's successors. For there are these four distinct bases for an ample sociality: rules, the common will of the agents socialized, their internal relations, and their unification in the mind of God. Descartes embellished all these notions, except that of internal relations.

His contributions are focused by the cogito, though this is an odd point of reference for sociality when mind's self-sufficiency implies an aggregate of thinkers, not a society of reciprocally dependent members. How can the many privacies be linked so that each depends on the others or communicates with them by way of a ground they share? Is privacy superseded when thinkers use the same language to exchange information and work together for common aims? These considerations, stressed by Kant and Mill, surely establish a weave of viable relations among us. Still, the socialization they describe hardly touches the inner core of our Cartesian isolation, with the result that these communities are always at risk of dissolving into their parts. Their participatory democracies never exceed a moderate atomism.

The cogito is, nevertheless, a baseline for theories which argue that individual identity derives from each thinker's place within a society that is more and other than the sum of its parts. Consider those three of the four ideas cited above that derive from Descartes: ideas as rules, will, and the community of finite thinkers joined in God. (*a*) Descartes supposed that ideas (e.g., of man and the sun) function as rules, hence that thought is regulative, not only representational. Ideas are joined in such a way that the ideas used to interpret sensory experience constitute a system of rules. (*b*) No idea is to be affirmed or denied if it is not clear and distinct, but the restraining force on judgment is will, not intellect. Where clarity and distinctness are achieved, the inhibition dissolves so that all of us will the same thing: think of Rousseau's general will. (*c*) We are joined to one another not only because we use the same ideas – this only makes us similar – but also because we finite thinkers are partitions of God's infinite mind.

The fourth point, internal relations, is inspired by the third one, though it derives more explicitly from Leibniz. He supposed that each monad is a perspective, from within, of the whole. Monads are calibrated to one another, so that the whole is comprised of their many perspectives and would be incomplete were any of them missing. This is the internal relatedness of the parts: the character of each is a function of all the others in their mutual relatedness (e.g., as the shape of any one piece in a jigsaw puzzle is a function of the space left empty when all the other pieces are assembled). There is also this odd corollary: that monads are windowless – none communicates with any other – though the perfect adaptation of each to every other should make for easy communication among them, given the common medium and mutual access supplied by God.

Internal relations are not required to establish socialization. Moral rules will do that. Internal relations are required for a unification deeper than that provided by such rules. We have an analogy when Kant dispenses with the internal relations of the sensory manifold, thereby atomizing it, so that all its unity derives from the spatial and temporal relations imposed when the transcendental ego thinks them as one. This externally imposed socialization, a socialization created by rules, creates an aggregate, not something internally unified (e.g., as traffic laws impose a kind of socialization, which lacks the inner, mutual determination that distinguishes life in families). Leibniz would not have agreed that monads have only this shallow connection with one another. They are related, he supposed, by an intrinsic ordering principle, the character of each being a function of the place left open for it within the structured complex established by the character and relations of the others.

Hegel collects the views of Descartes, Leibniz, and Kant. As each self-perceiving monad strives to complete itself by discovering its place within the whole, so the *Phenomenology of Mind* (Hegel [1807] 1967) describes the progress of finite thinkers as each rises from the obscurity of his or her particularity and contingency. Each one does or can discover his or her place in a world made to coalesce by internal relations *and* necessary laws, a world unified by the thinking of the Absolute. Each one also finds contingent, fellow creatures. The principal condition for their unity is not formal and abstract, like Kant's transcendental unity of apperception, for Hegel recovers at the limit, in the experience of the Absolute, the spontaneity and interplay that Descartes ascribed to first- and second-order awareness. Kant drastically separated these orders in the first *Critique*, reducing second-order awareness (the unifying transcendental ego) to an abstraction by requiring that it be known inferentially. Reconnecting the two orders of awareness in the Absolute – emphasizing immediacy and concreteness in the one, normativity and universality in the other – energizes self-reflection by making each accessible to the other. The demands of law acknowledge the claims of feeling. The effect on community is dramatic, because the formality and externality of necessary laws are tempered when the thinkers they organize cultivate sensibility, in themselves and one another. We express our mutual feelings in the self-conscious persuasion that this too is good and right. Atomism is superseded, sociality is confirmed: we are a rigorously organized community, not a mere aggregate.

We now profess to do as a society what individual minds were previously left to do by themselves: we claim to make worlds by making the rules and organizations which give meaning and purpose to our corporate lives. Marx is a test case for this claim about world-making, because his materialism is so plainly contrary to the idealism of this Cartesian lineage. Marx describes our submission to the organizing economic relations in our lives; but he also affirms that the domain of economic forces is a world structured by human behaviors, narratives, and attitudes. This world is deepened by self-reflection. For its objective pole, that of competing interests and coordinated activity, has its complement in the many centers of deliberation and self-regard. First conscious of him or herself, each thinker may become aware of and loyal to – almost without prejudice or preference – anyone in circumstances like his or her own (Marx and Engels [1848] 1967, pp. 105 and 121). For if the considerations distinguishing us from these others are real, they are ephemeral when compared to the facts – of class, duty, and opportunity – that join us. Marx demands that reflection go deeper: that it expose the fact that our social world, in all its complexity and advantages, is organized to create wealth. We are obliged to extend the comprehension of ourselves and our circumstances until we discern the structure, history, and trajectory of the system in which we participate. Then, discovering that our work creates this social world, we take control of this, our product.

Does Marx suppose that the social world is made or discovered? It is both at once. Its wealth and all the details of its social organization result from the adversarial relations of those who work or invest and from the work done. World-making is a complex act, one that engages the many people who think or perform in ways prescribed by their economic interests. Discovery comes later, as we discern our place within the system. This reflection transforms us, as though our previous thought and behavior were acts of a mind on automatic pilot, a mind driven by interests that it had not acknowledged in itself. Now discovering our role and power, we (laborers) claim ownership of the wealth and leadership of the social system. What was previously the mutual hostility of workers (or capitalists) becomes the empathic union of loyalty to one's class, its members realizing that they are interchangeable for the purposes of this class's economic role. This is the solidarity of people who have discovered a shared identity, not merely a shared interest. The world to which they formerly submitted is now perceived as the world they have made.

Nietzsche discounts the idea that social structures are fixed essentially by a single determinant (e.g., economics), though he concedes to Marx that everyone but the exceptional strong man is the creature of social circumstances (Nietzsche [1887] 1956, pp. 158–188). This is a world made in stops and starts. For we of the herd do nothing that has vitality or worth. Only the sporadic infusions of genius or tricks from hated conquerors revitalize and save us from boredom, enervation, and self-loathing. Envying these creators, we are careful to make ourselves uniform, predictable, and safe. Every social order is a record of these makings, near extinctions, and reanimations. Nietzsche describes the dissension that moves the process along.

Wittgenstein's strictures against private languages in the *Philosophical Investigations* (1966, pp. 119–129) reaffirm the Kantian emphasis on rules. (There is also a tacit allusion to the common pool of awareness or intelligibility in which people of the law participate. This is the whiff of Hegel's Absolute in the "metaphysical subject" of the *Tractatus* [Wittgenstein 1963, p. 117].) But now, contrary to Nietzsche's hopes for salvation at the hands of the inventive few, there is no outlet, no access, to a world different from the one of everyday, routinized practice. Having somehow made this world, we are obliged to live in it, as certainly we shall become pariahs or invisible if we do not learn its ways. Society's rhetoric and rituals – its language-games – are as palpable as factories and mines and more abiding. Shared meanings keep the games, our world, from coming unstuck, though Wittgenstein is never far from the thought that these repetitions may drive us mad. We would not want these doubts to be too clear and distinct. They are suppressed: we do as the rules prescribe.

Hegel supposed that social mind is distinguishable from its successive, historical expressions because it has its inception in the Absolute. Marx believed, to the contrary, that a social class exists only by way of its members, for there are no language-games without people trained to play them. Dewey is closer to Marx and Wittgenstein than to Hegel when he writes of the "public" and the "Great Community." These two are attitudes as much as entities. They come into existence as individual thinkers discover their interest in neutral authority and mutual sympathy. Both the public and the Great Community are intended to have normative force on independent thinkers. Yet this obligation is feeble. It is hardly more than an appeal for unity when Dewey cannot found it on anything superior to the hope that we shall discover the advantages of foresight, neutrality, cooperation, sympathy, and mutual respect ([1927] 1954, pp. 35 and 151–161). Dewey's views regarding cooperative inquiry and action recall Peirce's ideas about the self-regulating scientific community. Its members yearn to discover their place in the world. Their socialization is founded in their shared commitment to experimental inquiry and to the belief that scientific learning is cooperative and cumulative. But more, scientific inquiry has a discipline and a history, so its members live within a world shaped by their beliefs and practices (Peirce 1934, vol. 5, pp. 186–187). This line of knowers, grounded in spirit, becomes ever more attenuated, without quite expiring. Carnap does not tell us that semantic frameworks are made by committees. He believes that it is a scientific community, not isolated thinkers, that use conceptual systems to create the thinkable worlds that are accessible to all the community's members.

Each of these views exploits, without resolving, the ambiguity left in place since Hegel: Is there a social mind independent of finite, socialized thinkers? The answer was *yes* for those who identified mind with the Absolute's unitary, normative perception of the whole. It is *no* for every one who rejects this notion of God. These atheists or agnostics merely turn nostalgic when they can find no alternative basis for the normative character of social reality. Dispensing with God the unifier and legislator, they describe the nuanced lives of small children on their way to becoming socialized adults. An a priori story about self-discovery and self-transformation becomes an empirical theory about social learning and moral development. The results are imperfect: learning, guilt, and sympathy do not bind as effectively as a common will and rules, the internal relations of moral agents, and God's unifying consciousness. Atomism – mutually opaque individualism – is the awful contrary.

What happens when we combine the several strands of this psychocentric lineage? Sometimes the effect is benign, as when the emphasis on self-reflection amplifies and articulates our self-perception and responsibility. Other times, when world-making turns social and rules change with every spasm of the members' will, we have a social problem. For then no one is in charge. The thinker, the rule-maker, has disappeared. In its place is the unifying idea of the nation-state or the people, but no one who is accountable for either the rules or the things done in their name. The state has its "higher" purposes, its "spirit" and "will," but no one to speak for it. Where the mob has a will of its own, there is no one who can be held responsible for what mobs do. Actions are performed, rules are obeyed or broken, there is experience and the intensification of experience, worlds are made; but here – in the very space defined by the dimensions and powers of the cogito – reflexive, controlling mind has disappeared. Philosophers extolled our self-reflection before losing track of mind, then – more perniciously – of our responsibility for the things minds do.

(iii) Phenomenalism and Logical Atomism

Remember that psychocentric ontology has two variants. One elaborates on the powers of the cogito as it creates a thinkable experience and emphasizes mind's structure, faculties, and autonomy. It supposes that experience – hence the world so far as we can know it – is differentiated, ordered, and unified as mind uses ideas or rules to schematize sensory data or organize behavior. This is the line from Descartes to Leibniz, Kant, Fichte, Hegel, Schopenhauer, and Nietzsche. The other variant, with its coupling of truth and enjoyment, is more introspective and analytic. Its origins are in Plato: nous achieves aesthetic pleasure and truth when it grasps the Forms, distinguishing and comparing them. Descartes skewed the balance, favoring knowledge over enjoyment. Knowledge emerges as the product of analysis and synthesis, somewhat in the style of the *Theaetetus* (Plato 1964, pp. 908–916). Descartes' principal formulation is the *Rules for the Direction of the Mind*: "There are," he argued, "no paths to certain knowledge of the truth accessible to men save manifest intuition and necessary deduction" (*CSM*, I, 48; *AT*, X, 425). The *Discourse* offers a précis:

> The first of these [rules] was to accept nothing as true which I did not clearly recognize to be so: that is to say, carefully to avoid precipitation and prejudice in judgments, and to accept in them nothing more than what was presented to my mind so clearly and distinctly that I could have no occasion to doubt it.
> The second was to divide up each of the difficulties which I examined into as many parts as possible, and as seemed requisite in order that it might be resolved in the best manner possible.
> The third was to carry on my reflections in due order, commencing with objects that are the most simple and easy to understand, in order to rise little by little, or by degrees, to knowledge of the most complex, assuming an order, even if a fictitious one, among those which do not follow a natural sequence relatively to one another.
> The last was in all cases to make enumerations so complete and reviews so general that I should be certain of having omitted nothing. (13; *CSM*, I, 120; *AT*, VI, 18–19)

This line passes from Descartes to Arnauld and Nicole (their *Port-Royal Logic*), then to Locke, Berkeley, Hume, and Russell. One of Kant's ideas is also decisive. The lineage is prominent in current thinking because of Frege and Moore, though they substitute intuitionist realism for the phenomenalism (a different intuitionism) of their predecessors (Weissman 1987, pp. 53–108). Realists and phenomenalists agree that mind has only such powers as it requires for entertaining percepts and ideas, then analyzing and presenting them economically. Their ontological views are antithetic. Phenomenalists are successively less confident about the existence of an external world, with the result that reality shrinks as this variant evolves. In the beginning, with Descartes and Locke, it included the material world and God. Later, the extra-mental world and mind too are stripped away, as reality is identified with the configuration of percepts, ideas, words, or sentences. Intuitionist realists are Platonists. They recover Descartes' claim that clear and distinct ideas express or represent essences whose existence is independent of our thinking: Frege's "thoughts" (1956, pp. 289–311) are an example. This reversion to a Cartesian ontology is a saltant lineage: there are few intermediaries (e.g., Lotze) between Descartes' realism and theirs. Only the phenomenalists are considered here. Their logical atomism turns upon two values that dominate the *Rules*: rigor and the self-sufficiency of whatever logically ordered phenomena are set before the mind's eye, whether sense-data or sentences.

Six considerations distinguish this variant:

(*a*) Mind is alternately passive and active. Passively, mind is a sensorium qualified by its sensory impressions and ideas; actively, it attends to or manipulates its contents. Thinking is both these things: a way of entertaining and discriminating – sometimes enjoying – content set before our inspecting minds and the activity of organizing mental content, including sensory data, ideas, and sentences, so that these reconstructed ideas may be presented perspicuously and seen. Which is more critical: enjoyment or the analysis that culminates in knowledge? One can have either or both, though usually the latter is emphasized by thinkers of this lineage.

(*b*) Unreconstructed percepts and ideas may be confused, their meaning and truth uncertain. Thought fulfills itself in knowledge, but knowledge requires certainty, so confused ideas and inferences must be replaced by judgments secured against error. Analysis extracts the salvageable core from unreconstructed percepts and confused ideas. It identifies simples that satisfy the criteria for meaning and truth, then the truth-preserving complexes created from the simples. These two – simples and complexes – are the only suitable vehicles for truth. They replace our commonplace beliefs and percepts as the content of knowledge.

(*c*) Simples are said to be distinguishable and separable from one another, where completeness – hence self-sufficiency – is the condition for separability. Descartes is allusive but vague when he characterizes simplicity: "[T]here are very few pure and simple natures which we can intuit straight off and *per se* (independently of any others) either in our sensory experience or by means of a light innate within us" (*CSM*, I, 22; *AT*, X, 383). A candidate simple is distinguished from other things, then imagined alone (as one can imagine the separate notes of a tune); or linguistic analysis is used to show that the truth condition for the sentence representing or expressing a simple is independent of truth conditions for other sentences coupled to this one (as the truth of "This is red" is independent of "This is round"). Simples are combined – in imagination or as words or atomic sentences combined by grammatical rules – to produce complexes.

(*d*) There is a persistent ambiguity about the relations used to construct complex ideas: are they founded in the properties of the constituent simples (e.g., similarity and difference) or imposed (e.g., as spatial and temporal or grammatical relations are imposed)? This question is not critical if our principal concern is that of inspecting phenomena, for then the array of data is seen and enjoyed without regard for this question about relations. The question is obligatory if we are devoted to the project of reconstruction, for then we want to know if relations within a complex are essential or accidental to the simples compounded.

(*e*) The character of existence, as claimed for mind's contents or referents, is modified successively as this version of psychocentrism moves from naive representationalism to a severe idealism. First, extra-mental, material existence is credited to whatever things are represented by percepts and ideas. Then skepticism about an extra-mental world restricts existence to minds and their qualifications, God's mind included. Later, inability to discover a mind distinct from its qualifications further reduces the ambit of existence to these contents – their force and vivacity are the marks of their existence. Last, existence becomes the function of a grammatical or theoretical commitment: there "are" as many kinds of things in one's universe as there are predicate terms in one's language for signifying these differences; or existence is construed syntactically as the value of a bound variable (e.g., "There is an x, such that x is a whale, and x is described by Melville"), thereby requiring the assertion of a proposition prefiguring the existent; or existents are posited by a well-formed, empirically confirmed theory (e.g., as physical theory testifies that leptons and hadrons exist). These successive changes have a result familiar to Descartes: something *is* because we perceive it – as I, myself, am known by acquaintance – or, like God, it exists because there is a theory, consistent with other theories, which affirms its existence. Existence as Descartes understood it implies self-sufficiency. Now, in the maturity of this lineage, existence is derivative: even God's existence is nothing apart from the language or theory that postulates it.

(*f*) Mind is absorbed by sensory data and ideas to the point of giving little or no thought to itself: the self-reflection conspicuous in the *Meditations*, Leibniz, Fichte, and Hegel – though not in Kant's first *Critique* – is suppressed or absent. Some participants in this lineage say that an introspecting mind discovers nothing but its qualifications, meaning sensory data or ideas.

Suppose that knowledge is achieved, as in the example of wax in the second *Meditation*, when obscure ideas are replaced by complex ideas constructed from clear and distinct simples (e.g., the ideas of self and extension). Starting from the idea of matter – as extension – then adding whatever specificities are appropriate to the geometry of the matter known as wax, we construct an idea that replaces the confused percepts and ideas from which we started. Before, we could only compare the shifting appearances of wax's superficial qualities – its color and feel, for example. Now, we regard these qualities as expressions of wax's essence, qualities that appear as wax is subjected to particular, mechanical conditions (e.g., heat or pressure). Regularities that were inexplicable in our confused perceptions are now explained. Let us assume that simple ideas, as of mind or matter, are to be the elements of reconstructed ideas. What is required of simples, after their separability and self-sufficiency have been established? Are they homogeneous? One may think so, given Descartes' supposition that the idea of matter is a simple: "[E]xtension is something absolute, but among the varieties of extension length is absolute" (*CSM*, I, 22; *AT*, X, 382–383). The idea of mind is simple if we identify mind with awareness; but it is considerably more complex if mind includes first- and second-order awareness and perceptual or other content. We infer that simplicity does not preclude complexity if each of the constituent parts is "inseparable" from the others (*CSM*, I, 46; *AT*, X, 421). This means that each of two features in a complex is a necessary condition for the other, or that each feature of an idea having three or more features is necessarily conditioned by one or more of the others. Eliminate one or more such feature, and the idea is incomplete or incoherent (e.g., in the style of one hand clapping).

What is the basis in simples for the relations that bind them, hence for the rules that prescribe their combinations? The *Rules* says too little about either. The rules of the title are procedures for analyzing obscure ideas. They are described in detail; but little is said about the rules or relations binding simples. Descartes does mention "links which connect other simple natures together, and whose self-evidence is the basis for all the rational inferences we make" (*CSM*, I, 45; *AT*, X, 419). He lists some pertinent rules, including "Things that are the same as a third thing are the same as each other" and "Things that cannot be related in the same way to a third thing are different in some respect" (*CSM*, I, 45; *AT*, X, 419). These sample rules are founded in the principle of identity: everything is identical with itself and distinct from anything that differs numerically or qualitatively from it (e.g., as identical twins differ numerically from one other and qualitatively from other things). Identity and difference are a firm basis for relatedness, because both apply universally: everything is identical with itself and different from other things. But here, as in Plato's *Sophist*, from which this idea derives (Plato 1964, p. 1000), identity and difference are too general. They are the categories of a comparative logic, not relations sufficient for coupling particular simples to make this or that complex idea.

The issue is clarified only a little by Descartes' remark that the union of simple natures is "either necessary or contingent" (*CSM*, I, 45; *AT*, X, 421). For where is the basis for the necessity of these relations? Is it in the terms related, in the relationship of terms, or in the structure of the medium in which the relationship is accomplished?

Consider a right triangle: is the necessity of the Pythagorean theorem in the character of the line segments, in the figure itself, or in the structure of the space in which the triangle is embedded? The character of the line segments is critical but not sufficient, as the Pythagorean theorem does not apply to them in any configuration but that of a right triangle. Is the necessity founded only in the figure? This seems right, though it may not be. For imagine that the triangle is embedded in an irregularly rutted space. The rutted – three-dimensional – area of the square on the hypothesis is likely to be greater or smaller than – but rarely equal to – the rutted area of the squares on the sides. Accordingly, the necessity of the relations within a figure is a function of the figure itself and the space in which it is embedded. We normally ignore the medium by supposing, as in the case of the Pythagorean theorem, that space is flat. But this only obscures the match between a figure and its embedding medium, or the constraining effect of one on the other. Either way, the figure exhibits a structural feature of the space. This point is worth emphasizing because it justifies saying that the character and necessity of relations between or among some simples – the extended ones – are founded in the character of both the simples and the medium in which they are joined. The process of construction, this implies, is a way of surveying the medium to discover its intrinsic form: which relations it tolerates and which it bars.

Now consider Descartes' programmatic answer to the question about the relations of simples within complexes: Are they founded in the character of the simples or in the medium in which they are embedded? Descartes never answered this question in a comprehensive way, though he did prescribe the character of a solution acceptable to himself: "Deduction . . . remains as our sole means of compounding things in a way that enables us to be certain of their truth" (*CSM*, I, 48; *AT*, X, 424; see also *CSM*, I, 70–71; *AT*, X, 459–461). This formalist solution abandons altogether the idea that we may find a basis for relations in either the things related or their medium (e.g., space). Instead, it authorizes mind to impose relations that satisfy the standards of demonstrative proof.

Knowledge hereby loses its implication that true sentences or ideas are the re-presentation of the realities known. The ordinary reading of this word requires each substantive term or relation to signify a difference in the things represented. Compare Descartes' formalist solution: it implies that nothing in our complex ideas represents the relations of their constituent simples or a foundation for these relations in either the simples or their embedding medium. Knowledge is reconstrued as the state of mind achieved when simple ideas or complexes of simple ideas – all their relations clearly and distinctly perceived (as they are in deduction) – are inspected.

This is a very restricted conception of knowledge. Descartes himself does not affirm it, as he could have done by elaborating on his remark about deduction. He does require that our simple and complex ideas should represent the essences that God may instantiate. And he does consider some of their relations, as when he – after Plato – emphasizes their mutual similarities and differences. Still, his treatment of relations – his failure to ground them in simples and his inclination to treat them syntactically, as forms of deduction – invites the formalism that evolved among logical atomists.

This question about the ground of relations is often disguised by a renewed emphasis on the sensuousness of experience: enjoyment of the whole displaces concern for justifying the rules used to bind the parts. The example of the *Discourse* and the *Rules* is, nevertheless, plain: we are to achieve knowledge by replacing obscure data and concepts by simples and complexes that satisfy rigorous standards for meaning and truth. Successors in this lineage sometimes relish experience; more often, they are dedicated to the rigorous explication – the reconstruction – of obscure ideas.

Locke is pivotal. A realist, like Descartes, he nevertheless emphasized that knowledge of the world is limited to knowledge of the mind's own states:

> This, therefore, being my purpose – to inquire into the original, certainty, and extent of *human knowledge*, together with the grounds and degrees of *belief*, *opinion*, and *assent*. . . . It is therefore worth while to search out the bounds between opinion and knowledge; and examine by what measures, in things whereof we have no certain knowledge, we ought to regulate our assent and moderate our persuasion. (Locke [1756] 1959, vol. I, pp. 26–27)

Locke's familiarity with Descartes' *Rules* is apparent but puzzling. The *Rules* was first published in 1701, the first edition of Locke's *An Essay Concerning Human Understanding* in 1690. The link is probably Locke's reading of both Descartes' already published work and Arnauld and Nicole's *Port-Royal Logic*. The authors of the *Logic* used Descartes' *Rules* when preparing the second edition of the *Logic*, published in 1664 (Arnauld and Nicole [1662] 1851). This is the probable source for Locke's use of doctrines that were not otherwise available until the *Rules* came out in 1701. Why emphasize the *Rules* when Descartes' *Discourse* was unproblematically available to Locke? Because his "historical plain method" (Locke [1756] 1959, vol. 1, p. 27) is the application of a procedure that is sketched in the *Discourse* but detailed in the *Rules*. Where ideas are obscure, we are to use this method to reconstruct them: we analyze obscure ideas in search of phenomenal simples – not, as in Descartes, rational simples, ideas – from which to construct, in imagination, a surrogate for the obscure idea.[5]

What does Locke say about the relations used to reconstruct ideas? Are they imposed on simples, or found within them? He answers that "The nature . . . of relation consists in the referring or comparing two things one to another" (ibid., vol. 1, p. 428). (Compare Descartes: "[I]t will be to the reader's advantage . . . to think of all knowledge whatever – save knowledge obtained through simple and pure intuition of a single, solitary thing – as resulting from a comparison between two or more things" [*CSM*, I, 57; *AT*, X, 440].) Relations derive, this implies, from the similarity or difference of the simples compared. This response is disconcerting, because the reformulated idea of, say, rabbit is not compounded of simples chosen only for their mutual likeness or difference. Some things are missing, including salience. Complexes are generated when phenomenal simples are significantly like or unlike one another, as when it is the number of a rabbit's ears, not their color, that is salient. Locke says as much when he insists that "respect" ([1756] 1959, vol. 1, p. 427) is significant for these comparisons: we ignore incidental similarities when only some particular one concerns us.

Now this question: Is it sufficient for the relatedness of simples that the percepts awaiting composition are saliently like or unlike? Could we assemble clarified, complex ideas suited to replacing all familiar but obscure ones merely by requiring that the simples be like or unlike in a pertinent respect? Consider an example: Locke supposes that the relatedness of cause and effect is founded on a structure or power in the cause. The cause is different from the effect, but we say nothing about this relation if we merely repeat that it exploits a specific difference.

Why does Locke believe that sameness and difference are a sufficient basis for the relations of simples, when examples such as cause and effect are so badly served by them? Because of his persuasion that complex ideas are the product of association, as my idea of a rabbit is assembled from elements that are like (e.g., percepts or memories of ears) and unlike (e.g., percepts or memories of ears and feet). Mind receives sensory data, then parses them as same or different as it constructs a diversity of complex ideas. Locke assumes that mind has no resources for importing relations of a more substantive sort, and that it has no need for them: sameness and difference in specific respects are all that mind requires to construct ideas naively or to reconstruct them precisely. Nor (he believes) should we assume relations that would strangle imagination, preventing it from combining sensory data in almost any order (e.g., golden mountains). For nothing in the data restricts association, though certain exclusions mark the categorial differences among sensory modalities, such that there are no yellow pains or loud tastes.

What of cause and effect, our counterexample? How can Locke provide within complex ideas for relations based in things themselves, relations for which sameness and difference in some respect are too feeble a support? He responds that such relations are unknowable (and by implication unthinkable) by us whose knowledge of other things is always mediated by representations. Causal relations founded in causal powers exceed our knowledge, for we have only percepts of causes, with nothing in them that would reveal the causal powers. Locke credits things with having real essences – relation-supporting essences – but then supposes that knowledge of essences is never available. We make do with formulas better described as "nominal essences" (ibid., vol. 2, p. 253), given that all the content of these ideas is provided by sensory data and the ideas derived from them. Relations among percepts are always extrinsic to the percepts (e.g., spatial and temporal relations) save those founded in similarity and difference.

Locke, like Descartes, would have us produce ideas in which complexity is transparent. Deduction is the guarantee of that transparency for Descartes; music, painting, or the plastic arts are a better paradigm for Locke. Where nothing is obscure or inferred (because hidden), all aspects of a complex stand unequivocally before our inspecting minds. Too bad that Locke's account of knowledge is insufficient to support the ontological realism that particular knowledge claims are intended to confirm. For there is a conspicuous shortfall between our persuasion that sensory data are the effects of extra-mental causes and our certainty about the composition of simple and complex ideas or our certainty that our minds exist. Remarking the difference, we agree that our belief in extra-mental, material causes is baseless. *Matter* seems to be a word without sense or reference. Locke never said this, but Berkeley inferred it. "Esse est percipi" was his dictum: to be is to be perceived (Berkeley 1964, vol. 2, p. 79). Presence before the mind, he says, is a necessary condition for existence, implying that our knowledge of a thing's existence is guaranteed for whatever time it is present. Locke's uncertainty that our ideas are adequate to things in themselves gives way to the categorical assertion that there is no extra-mental material world to which ideas conform. God and his ideas apart, there is nothing to know but percepts or ideas, their configurations, and mind itself.

Descartes' realism has imploded again, with this effect: Descartes' *Rules*, Locke, and now Berkeley restrict the domain of human knowledge to the phenomena set before our minds. Yet knowledge requires more than presentation. Ideas must be purged of their obscurity, as happens when mind produces substitutes for obscure ideas by constructing complex ideas from clear and distinct simples. There are, however, the questions unresolved in the *Rules* and Locke: what is the basis for the relatedness of simples? Do simples support these relations by way of features intrinsic to themselves, or are they joined externally, as formal or spatial and temporal relations are external?

Hume's answers are explicit and well considered. He identifies simples with sensory impressions and the ideas that copy them. Simples are created by the atomizing principle that he inherits from Descartes: everything distinguishable is separable (Hume [1739–40] 1978, p. 79; *CSM*, II, 86; *AT*, VII, 120). This has the effect of making complexes problematic, for what are the relations that bind the simples? Hume distinguishes two kinds: natural and philosophical. The natural relations are "RESEMBLANCE, CONTIGUITY in time or place, and CAUSE and EFFECT" (Hume [1739–40] 1978, pp. 10–11). Resemblance is founded in the things themselves, while cause and effect and contiguity in space and time are accidental to the character of the things joined: imagination can join impressions of any sort in either way. Describing these relations as "natural" makes the point that ideas or impressions are associated mechanically, without reflection.

Philosophical relations are introduced as we reflect upon and compare our impressions and ideas. They are rubrics used to construct complex ideas from their simple (or simpler) constituents. There are seven of these relations: resemblance, identity (over time), space and time, degrees of quantity, degrees of quality, contrariety as regards existence and nonexistence, and cause and effect. The character of the things related is critical for the relations of resemblance, identity, and degrees of quantity and quality, though here, as in Descartes and Locke, the foundation achieved is meager support for the relations of ideas, because each of these philosophical rubrics is an application of resemblance, hence similarity. How many complex ideas – as represented in dictionaries, for example – have similarity and difference as their generating principles? Very few. The other rubrics apply without regard to the character of the terms related: changes of relative position in space or time do not, by themselves, change the things moved; existence and nonexistence are mutually exclusive whatever the character of the impression or idea compared. We infer, with Hume's encouragement, that every complex includes one or more relations to which the character of the terms – hence similarity and difference – is incidental: some of the relations in many complexes are spatial or temporal; everything exists or not.

The previous paragraph is liable to confuse, because it implies that philosophical relations are used to bind things rather than ideas, as when we speak of cause and effect or the spatial relations of things. Every such locution is to be understood as shorthand for a claim about ideas, though these may be ideas of things related causally or spatially. Hume was especially attentive to the possibility of this confusion: we ascribe dubious features to the character or relations of things, first, because we misconstrue them, then because we project our confusions onto the things themselves. This error is especially prominent, he thought, when we suppose that the relations of things are founded in their character, as we speak of fire-extinguishers, thereby inferring from the term to an internal power for action and relation in the things named.

Aristotle, most Scholastics, and common sense hold that the idea of an effect presupposes that of a cause as surely as the idea of a valley presupposes that of hills or mountains. Hume never doubts that we construe ideas in this way, but Cartesian-style analysis shows that nothing in the sensory content of the ideas – their only content – supports the relations implied. Seeing cause and effect together, we learn to expect one when seeing the other, though contiguity is the whole content of this relation: nothing in it depends on the character – the similarity or difference – of the things related (ibid., pp. 77 and 97).

Hume was less committed than Descartes to purging obscurity from all our knowledge claims; but this was not so much laziness as the result of his assumption that ideas are copies of impressions. No skull-cracking analysis is required for these clarifications if careful inspection of one's ideas already supplies them to someone enjoying the sensuousness of experience. Is "enjoyment" paradoxical, given that Hume has inferred that mind is nothing apart from the aggregate of its contents? Think of Plato's claim that nous, meaning depersonalized intellectual intuition, is suffused with pleasure as it grasps the Forms, losing thereby its separate identity (Plato 1964, pp. 53 and 1589–1591). Hume's impressions, like Plato's Ideas, are present and perceived, though nothing – no mind – exists to perceive them. Humeans ignore the paradox that presentation requires no witness to whom the data are presented. Their difficulty can also be formulated with this other emphasis. Berkeley's "Esse est percipi" has reduced the things known to mind's qualifications, but how can these qualifications exist if their sustaining medium – mind itself – has no existence apart from them? Is every impression and idea an autonomous substance? Hume's answer recalls Plato's comment about the existence of the Forms (1964, p. 891):

> The idea of existence . . . is the very same with the idea of what we conceive to be existent. To reflect on any thing simply, and to reflect on it as existent, are nothing different from each other. That idea, when conjoin'd with the idea of any object, makes no addition to it. Whatever we conceive, we conceive to be existent. Any idea we please to form is the idea of a being; and the idea of a being is any idea we please to form. (Hume [1739–40] 1978, pp. 66–67)

Ignore the illegitimate phrase "we conceive" – illegitimate on Hume's terms – and the intimation that conception is the intentional act of a thinker distinct from the phenomena conceived. What is it that exists? Only impressions and the ideas that copy them.

What is left of reality? Just these impressions and ideas. How well integrated are they? Poorly, because everything distinguishable is separable. The seven philosophical relations have reduced to resemblance, contiguity in space and time, and the contrariety of existence and nonexistence. The one of cause and effect is an instance of contiguity in space and time;

identity over time is the similarity, hence resemblance, of a thing's properties from moment to moment. The relations binding things to one another, whether simples in complexes or complexes to one another, are slack. Only resemblance is founded in the character of impressions and ideas; and resemblance is too feeble a binder. Reality is loosely packed.

We have this new uncertainty: if the relations used to construct complexes from simples do not derive from the simples themselves, the rules introducing these relations must be justified in some other way. What could that justification be? Kant is neither a phenomenalist nor a logical atomist, but he supplies an answer: atomic data are assembled by rules founded in the understanding. Descartes anticipated this claim when he supposed that innate ideas are presented and perceived *or* used as rules to interpret sensory phenomena (e.g., as the various appearances of wax would be ordered and explained if we had the innate idea of wax's geometrical essence).

Kant assumed that sensory data are content, whereas rules are form ([1781] 1965, p. 280). The latter are schemas – bare frames – for organizing the data. Synthesis – schematization – connects each percept to every other as all are presented for inspection within the forms of intuition, space and time. Kant described these rules as synthetic a priori truths (ibid., pp. 48–55). They are synthetic, because they establish relations between or among notions which are not interdefinable (e.g., the numbers of the equation, $7 + 5 = 12$). They are a priori with respect to their origin: mind does not extract these truths from sensory data; it brings them to the data, as ordering principles innate within the understanding. This is the reason for their necessary and universal application, for mind is structured so that it cannot entertain the data without applying the rules. We add that these innate a priori rules, the pure categories of understanding, are determinable: they require that every experience have some quantity, quality, and relation, without prescribing more specific values for them. Sensory data and empirical schemas are required to supplement these a priori rules if experience is to have detail, as when we perceive cats or dogs.

The previous question is answered. Rules that bind atomic data are either intrinsic to the understanding, requiring that every thinkable experience have quantity, quality, and relation; or they are empirical rules contrived to satisfy the thinker's practical interests while introducing specificity into rules that are innate but more abstract. Hume's solution was psychological, but vague: data, he said, are associated by custom or habit. Kant's solution tells what rules must do, while it specifies their content and foundation.

Kant's psychology is, nevertheless, problematic. His rules are known by way of their effects in experience, as we infer from quantity, quality, and relation in the sensory manifold to their transcendental conditions. This makes phenomenalists unhappy, because they despise every alleged entity whose existence and character are not directly inspectable. Kant's faculty of rules and the rules themselves are inferred entities. Why give credence to them when other noninspectables, including the material world and a mind distinct from its contents, have been eliminated? Phenomenalists require that the rules used to organize sensory data themselves be inspectable. Let them be rules that are available to, or apparent within, every experience.

These are not impossible demands. Kant himself satisfied them when he inferred the identity of the transcendental categories from the table of judgments (ibid., pp. 106–110). This table has four corners, each marked by a linguistic form, a sentence, expressing a judgment: the judgments are universal and positive (e.g., "All men are mortal"), universal and negative (e.g., "No men are mortal"), particular and positive (e.g., "Some man is mortal"), or particular and negative (e.g., "Some man is not mortal"). These judgments exemplify rules in being their applications. We are saved from having to infer the rules because we have the thoughts, even the sentences, that exhibit them. Only the judgments themselves are problematic, because transcendental. We eliminate them, satisfying empiricist scruples, by affirming that words and sentences, thought's perceived vehicles, are all of its content. Judgment may be nothing more than the act of formulating sentences. The rules of thought may be grammatical rules for joining words or sentences. This is the step beyond Kant's own psychologism into our time.

Progress is quick and efficient. Some words – observation terms – are defined ostensively: they signify specific, sensory differences. The rules coupling words to these referents are semantic: we learn the rules by learning to signify data of distinct kinds by using particular words. There are also syntactic rules, some for combining words to make sentences (e.g., the requirement that a sentence have a subject and a predicate or a dominant relation such as "A gave B to C"), others for combining sentences. Sentences reporting the observation of a single property, whatever the number of their terms, are *atomic*. Other rules control relations among *molecular* sentences. They prescribe the use of logical connectives, including 'and', 'or', 'not', and 'if . . . then . . .'. We use these terms to create rubrics for joining sentences (e.g., ". . . and . . ."). Such terms are said to have no empirical import, just as *and* has none in the sentence "Squeeze an orange, and fish fly."

Atomic sentences are meaningful if they satisfy grammatical formation rules and if their descriptive terms are defined ostensively. They are true if matters stand as the sentences affirm they do. A sentence (whether atomic or molecular) is valid if it is derived (i.e., deduced) by a succession of combinations and detachments, sanctioned by rules of inference, from the previous sentences of an argument. Such a succession of sentences – a proof – constitutes a molecular sentence. It is valid if true for every consistent substitution of truth-values for its sentential variables (i.e., the individual atomic sentences). The validity (i.e., logical truth) of molecular sentences or of their last lines (in relation to the lines preceding) compares to the truth of atomic sentences. Truth is material but contingent; validity is necessary but syntactic: it has no empirical import. One more of these logical points is relevant. Where the sentence at issue is molecular but neither a tautology nor a contradiction (neither valid nor false for every consistent substitution of truth-values for its sentential variables), its corporate truth-value is a function of these two things: the truth-values of its constituent atomic sentences and the organization of its logical constants (e.g., a sentence of the form p *and* q is false if atomic sentence p is true while q is false, but true if p and q are true).

The answer to our question about relations – Are they founded in, or imposed on, the terms related? – is implicit in the difference between empirical and logical truths. Kant supposed that the rules of understanding connect data which are essentially autonomous. This assumption is retained when Kant's rules of understanding are superseded by syntactic rules of language: the truth of any one atomic sentence has no implications for the truth of any other, though we do construct complexes of simple sentences. Material truth and validity are, in principle, easily distinguished and determined in both.

These are some rudiments of Bertrand Russell's logical atomism (Russell [1901–50] 1964, pp. 177–281). Both motives impelling this lineage are apparent in him. First is the phenomenalist concern, which requires that every knowledge claim be stripped of references to inferred entities and reduced to whatever matters are directly inspectable. Just as "I am, I exist" is confirmed each time we think or pronounce it, so shall we confirm every other candidate for truth. Second is the project of Descartes' *Rules*. We are to achieve knowledge in two steps: by isolating simple ideas, then combining these simples into complexes having evident constituents and relations. Russell satisfies both conditions in terms that are sensitive to the issue left unresolved by Descartes and Locke but clarified by Hume and Kant: he distinguishes observation terms from the rules used to compound them. As in Hume, every simple – every atomic sentence – is associable with any other; as in Kant, it is rules or schemas, not anything intrinsic to the simples, that configure them.

Logical atomism faltered because universal, intentional, and normative statements could not be analyzed in this way (e.g., "I want it" does not seem to report a connection of sensory atoms). Russell's suggestion is, nevertheless, a plausible resolution for the project that began in Descartes' *Rules*: we get simples and complexes, atomic and molecular sentences, each of which points to, or shows, the conditions for its meaning and truth.

What is reality for logical atomists? Just the montage of sensory data overlaid by the grid of atomic and molecular sentences. Where is mind in this story? It disappears, or, more accurately, it is the assembly and presentation of the montage. What motive drives this proposal? Russell tells us: "Wherever possible, substitute constructions out of known entities for inferences to unknown entities" (ibid., p. 326). Recall Rule V of the *Rules*:

> The whole method consists entirely in the ordering and arranging of the objects on which we must concentrate our mind's eye if we are to discover some truth. We shall be following this method exactly if we first reduce complicated and obscure propositions step by step to simple ones, and then, starting with the intuition of the simplest ones of all, try to ascend through the same steps to a knowledge of all the rest. (*CSM*, I, 20; *AT*, X, 379)

In Russell, as in Descartes, the emphasis on reconstruction is paired with the demand that there be a validating inspection.

(iv) Mixing Lineages

These two ways of elaborating Descartes' psychocentric views differ principally in their claims about mind and its role. The variant that evolves from the *Rules* assumes, in Locke and Berkeley, that mind is the ample place where data and ideas are entertained, analyzed, and reconfigured. Later, Hume and Russell deny that mind is anything additional to these luminous phenomena. The data are self-sufficient. But more, there is nothing represented by either sentences or the percepts that confirm them. Reality is exhausted by free-standing impressions and the sentences that signify them.

This result is a paradox to anyone who believes that data are perceived because they qualify a reflexive consciousness. Still, there is nothing to preclude the assimilation of these variant lineages – the one that passes through Leibniz, Kant, and Hegel, the other that passes through Locke, Hume, and Russell – when their differences are suppressed. The neutral monism proposed by William James (1968, pp. 194–214) and supported for a time by Russell ([1901–50] 1964, pp. 177–281) is a case in point. It couples phenomenalism without reflexivity to the view that objects are generated when the sensory manifold is schematized. Altering relations among the data creates the subjective and objective "poles" of experience – the "experiencing subject" and the "things" construed as existing "out there." What agent applies the rules? What is the source of the data schematized? How is experience sustained? James does not tell us.

More influential in our time is a view – Carnap's – that joins Kantian themes to those of Descartes' *Rules*. First are some comments that echo the *Rules* and the phenomenalist, logical atomist side: "All objects can be constructed from my elementary experiences" (Carnap 1969, p. 255). "We shall construct the 'world of physics' with the aid of the 'world of perception' " (ibid., p. 150). The aim of construction theory consists in formulating a "constructional system, i.e., a stepwise ordered system of objects (or concepts). . . . To begin with, a basis must be chosen, a lowest level upon which all others are founded" (ibid.). Consider, too, a comment more appropriate to the Kantian line of psychocentric ontologies:

> By categories are meant the forms of synthesis of the manifold of intuition to the unity of the object. . . . Since the concepts in our constructional system are clearer than those of the traditional systems, we ask what is there in the constructional system as a system of the synthesis of objects which corresponds to the categories? In construction theory, the manifold of intuition is called "the given," "the basic elements." The synthesis of this manifold to the unity of an object is here called the construction of this object from the given. (ibid., pp. 134–135)

The reality of anything, Carnap said, "is nothing else than the possibility of its being placed in a certain system" (1934, p. 20). "Actually . . . I already went beyond the limits of explicit definitions in the construction of the physical world" (Carnap 1969, p. viii).

Is it paradoxical that conceptual frameworks should be used to reconstruct empirical theories, hence thinkable worlds, although there are no minds to make and use these systems? It does not seem so to Carnap: he would reformulate all scientific claims about mind within a conceptual system designed for empirical psychology (ibid., pp. 175–190). Mind, insofar as we can think or know it, is to be rendered – schematized, objectified – by this system. Why is Carnap exempt from having to specify the mind

whose existence and character must be independent of this or any conceptual system if mind is to make and use these systems? Because he takes
Hume and Kant as his examples. After Hume, he is unwilling to admit the
inconsistency of emphasizing presence when there is no thinker to whom
the data are present. After Kant, he writes of mind's labor – that of creating
thinkable worlds – while assuming that mind has no direct access to itself.

Second-order consciousness, as Descartes describes it, is both a comprehensive inspection of everything occurring within the mind and the
agent performing certain regulative tasks – it clarifies ideas or uses them to
interpret sensory data. Descartes supposes that these functions are distinguishable but not separable. Carnap, like Kant in the first *Critique*, ignores
self-awareness while emphasizing the work that mind does. He is the watershed for positivist thinking in our century and the foil for positivists newly
described as pragmatists. We should not be surprised if the variant forms of
psychocentrism merged in him are also present in them.

Theology

Descartes' arguments concerning God evolved in disparate ways. Some
barely survived criticism (e.g., the ontological argument). Others lapsed
because they were ad hoc hypotheses introduced to support claims that
were themselves abandoned (e.g., the occasionalism encouraged by Descartes' dualism). Still others, especially the ideas that God is an infinite One
or a mind analogous to our own, were more fruitful. What follows is a
sketch of these developments, one that ignores most of the contributors in
favor of the evolving ideas.

(i) The Ontological Argument

Arguments that Descartes inherited include the idea that God is first
cause of created things, that the created world exhibits God's rational design, that its contingency requires God's continuous support or re-creation
(Aquinas [1266–68] 1964, vol. 2, pp. 13–17), and (from Anselm) that
God's essence entails his existence. The first three arguments are reinterpreted by Descartes and his successors in terms appropriate to the notion
that God is a mind. Comments about them are deferred to section iv. It is
only Descartes' use of the ontological argument that concerns us here.

Descartes supposed that existence is a property insofar as an essence
may have it or not. Flying is characteristic of birds but not of fish; and, by
rough parity, humans exist for a time, but griffins never do. God exists

necessarily and eternally, because the perfection of his essence entails his existence. Compare Plato's contrary assumption that existence, as the state or mode of an instantiated particular, is not one of the properties constitutive of Forms or essences. Only the Good is an exception. It exists as a lure for other Forms, but this is an odd feature of Plato's cosmology. He never revises the claim – one more implied than formulated exactly – that an essence does not entail its own instantiation.

It is said that Kant exposed the fallacy of the ontological argument when he distinguished having money from the *idea* of having it. The character of money is the same in the two cases, though it is not the addition of a property that makes the difference. This is moot, because *property* has two senses: it signifies differences of quality, quantity, or relation and also the different modalities of existence. Yellow and square are properties of the first sort; possibility and actuality of the second (it matters considerably that the Tooth Fairy is merely possible). Kant's example assumes that the only properties are those of the first sort. His argument proves that existence is not one of them: existence adds no quantity, quality, or relation to the determinations constitutive of money. Kant's argument is nevertheless deficient because it ignores properties of the second sort. He discusses the "modalities" ([1781] 1965, p. 113), including contingent existence, but only in the context of describing the relation of sensory data to mind's schematizing faculties. He does not consider them – actuality and possibility, especially – as modal properties.

Kant's objection to the ontological argument – that existence is not a predicate or a property – is therefore less than decisive. The original question stands: Does God's perfection entail his existence? Notice that "perfection" is too impressionistic and rhetorical to be helpful: someone may believe that humility is a perfection, and that nonexistence is the zenith of humility. Ignoring this, we suppose that God's perfection includes necessary existence, and that his essence embodies no contradiction. What does this prove? Only that a necessary being is possible. Descartes may have supposed that possibilities have an energy which seeks actualization, so that God, the necessary being, passes immediately from possibility to actuality. But this is a question-begging metaphor. Wanting a formulation that is more literal and specific, we say that possibility and actuality are two modes of being, where anything actual is possible (Weissman 1977, pp. 57–107). It does not follow that everything, or anything, possible is also actual. God is possible if he embodies no contradiction; but some additional factor is required if he is to pass into actuality from possibility. What that factor might be is nowhere specified in the ontological argument. This lack justifies a conclusion like Plato's: that an essence or Form may exist as a possibility, with no implications for its instantiation.

Critics of the ontological argument are usually nominalists or conceptualists. Philosophers of these persuasions would say that my recasting of Descartes' argument, especially my assumption that possibility is a mode of being, is no less odious than his argument. Their objections to his views are expressed in this simpler way: words and ideas do not entail the existence of their referents, whatever the properties of the referent. This point, urged by Descartes' critics (*CSM*, II, 69–70, 91, 135–136; *AT*, VII, 95–97, 127, 193–194), explains the near universal persuasion that no a priori argument can prove the existence of God or any other extra-conceptual thing.

(ii) Ad hoc Arguments for God's Existence

Descartes' ad hoc arguments for God's existence were no more successful. There are five to consider: (*a*) his claim that the contingency of finite things requires the support of a being whose existence is unconditioned; (*b*) his claim that God must be the cause and sustainer of motion, because impotent matter cannot be its source, and because nothing in matter explains the transfer of motion; (*c*) his claim that the categorial difference between mind and matter requires God's intervention to connect them; (*d*) his claim that God guarantees the truth of clear and distinct ideas by creating their referents; (*e*) his "new" argument for God's existence, treated separately above, which we now consider in its more simplistic formulation as one of the ad hoc inferences used to confirm his existence. Each of these arguments was superseded when critics reformulated the assumptions that underlay it.

(*a*) We infer from contingency to its sustaining, necessary ground if we suppose that existence is incomplete and crippled because it is not necessary. But nothing may be lacking in the existence of contingent things. Contingency may imply only that an existent has not existed, and will not exist, forever. This may entail nothing faulty in the manner of its existence, but rather a fact about its character: it did not exist until there were circumstances to create it; it ceases to exist because of exhaustion or because another thing destroys it. This is a failure of character or an accident of circumstance, not a deficiency in the style of its existence.

(*b*) Descartes supposed that matter, as extension, is passive. Leibniz agreed that this characterization of matter implies its impotence: "[M]atter includes only what is passive. . . . [C]onsequently action cannot originate from a modification of matter. Therefore, both motion and thought must come from something else" ([1675–1716] 1989, p. 263). That "something else" is God: he creates each monad so that it has a principle of action – an entelechy – within it. Remember that Descartes, too, made God the source and sustainer of all existence:

> For all the course of my life may be divided into an infinite number of parts, none of which is in any way dependent on the other; and thus from the fact that I was in existence a short time ago it does not follow that I must be in existence now, unless some cause at this instant, so to speak, produces me anew, that is to say, conserves me. . . . [I]n order to be conserved in each moment in which it endures, a substance has need of the same power and action as would be necessary to produce and create it anew, supposing it did not yet exist. (80; *CSM*, II, 33; *AT*, VII, 48–49)

Descartes is frequently described as a deist, meaning one who believes that God supplies the world's material and plan before setting it in motion, and that this initial push is sufficient to sustain motion through what could be an unending history, given laws which prevent its dissipation. A deism (such as Voltaire's) seems anticipated by passages such as this from the *Principles of Philosophy*: "Admittedly motion is simply a mode of the matter which is moved. But nevertheless it has a certain determinate quantity; and this, we easily understand, may be constant in the universe as a whole while varying in any given part" (*CSM*, I, 240; *AT*, VIIIA, 61). But this is not deism, because God is more than an observer of the world he has made. God, says Descartes, is perpetually interfering: each moment is a re-creation.

This conclusion is vastly consequential, if augmented by four assumptions: first, that matter is passive; second, that matter is phenomenal; third, that states of matter or, equivalently, sensory data are distinguishable and separable over time; fourth, that there is no God to support this string of contingencies. The result is Hume's dictum about causality: "[T]here is no absolute nor metaphysical necessity, that every beginning of existence should be attended with a [cause]" ([1739–40] 1978, p. 172). Anything may follow from anything else, because there is never an antecedent event which determines, necessarily or contingently, either the existence or the character of its successor. Causality, induction, and the identity of individuals over time are, instantly, the despair of metaphysicians.

There is also this other way to avert God's intervention as source and sustainer of motion. We deny that matter is impotent because of being extension and nothing more; we say and confirm that matter also has mass (convertible to energy) and velocity, hence force. Matter does not need God to move it if it can move itself. Reconsider Hume's conclusion. His notion of causality duplicates Descartes' assumptions about the passivity of matter (the impressions that are surrogates for matter are also inert) and the separability of its successive states. Hume's causal theory survives because he has translated questions about successive states of matter into questions about successive states of sensory data. Skepticism about induction survives, because this is a consequence of Hume's phenomenalism, not only the result of misdescribing matter.

(c) Descartes supposed that the pineal gland is the point of transition, on the bodily side, between mind and matter. He conceded that communication between these two categorially distinct substances is a mystery. Malebranche ([1688] 1980, pp. 27–28) accepted the dualism of mind and body but denied their interaction; there is, he said, only the appearance of interaction. The appearance is explained if God perpetually intervenes between the two, simultaneously causing one to be in action when the other suffers an effect of which the first seems to be the cause. Malebranche also admitted this other, more Platonic solution (ibid., pp. 43–45). God may have created physical things to establish symmetry between our finite ideas and their apparent referents. But he need not have done so: all the appearances would be as they are if our ideas had no contents or referents but the ideas in God's mind.

Occasionalism did not survive the skeptical assault on Descartes' realism, for there is no need to secure the reciprocal access of mind and body if body is an idea or phenomenon having no extra-mental referent. Nor would occasionalism survive if mind were the activity of a physical system, for then minds would be affected as bodies interact.

(d) Descartes supposed that the clarity and distinctness of our ideas is a test of their truth, because God guarantees that such ideas have referents. God supplies the essences that are objects of our geometrical ideas and the individuals that would be their referents were there clear and distinct ideas of material particulars. The burden is lighter when Descartes' successors aver that space and matter are phenomenal, for this frees God from having to guarantee the extra-mental application of existence claims about individual things or events. Descartes' successors were typically nominalists or conceptualists. Believing that essences are either nothing at all or inventions, they did not require that God guarantee our claims about essences by creating them.

What truths were left to guarantee? Just two: that I exist – qualified by my experiences – and that God exists. But I do not need God to guarantee the truth of the claim that I exist. This is true necessarily, each time I think or pronounce it, for there is no gap between the idea and its object, hence no place for error. I need God's guarantee only to confirm that he exists. But now the very demand for a guarantee risks perpetrating a theological error (perhaps a sin of vanity). This is the heresy of inverted priorities: God is diminished if we assume that he causes himself to exist merely to validate our idea of him. Accordingly, there is nothing for God to do as guarantor, or nothing we could respectfully ask him to do.

Descartes' successors were left to choose between these alternatives: no idea can be known to be true, because the clarity and distinctness of our ideas are no guarantee that they have application in an extra-mental domain; or the truth of our ideas does not require that they have application to extra-mental things. Skeptics and idealists – many of Descartes' successors were both – preferred the second alternative. Truth as correspondence was superseded by the notion that truth is the coherence of sentences or ideas. This notion was anticipated by Descartes himself, for remember his frequent assumption that clarity and distinctness constitute a logical requirement, sentences or ideas being true if they are necessary. Sometimes individual thoughts or sentences – tautologies – satisfy this standard. More often, it is the last sentence in a string of sentences – Descartes' deductive arguments – that is valid. Validity is welcomed by every skeptic who, having repudiated correspondence, fears that truth may degenerate into being a mere impression of truth.

Leibniz espoused this logical standard when he argued that God's truths have the form of identity – $A = A$ ([1675–1716] 1989, pp. 30–31). This is also Hegel's view: the progressive inquiry that seems to be a dialectical, albeit loose-jointed, ladder to a finite consciousness is, from God's point of view, a necessary deduction ([1807] 1967, p. 808). Still, the stability of truth claims is unresolved, because Descartes believed that the principle of non-contradiction is itself a contingency that God could alter: it too requires a guarantee that he will not tinker with it. These successors typically deny that this principle is alterable. Consequently, every truth or string of truths shown to be necessary because its negation is contradictory surpasses contingency. It requires no guarantee.

What guarantees contingent truths, given that snow might have been blue, not white? Logical validity is too strong, but no divine guarantee is required if we say, with Descartes' idealist successors, that contingent truths are supported by inductive rules: "Snow is white" is true because it coheres with claims that have already been made and established, including sentences about natural light and the consensus of perceivers. Why are these inductive rules exempt from the requirement that their applicability be guaranteed? Because these successors believe that nothing extra-mental is signified by contingent truths, and because the principal guarantee for the rules that generate them is our determination to use them. We make the rules, and we could change them if our interests were to dictate that we make a different world, hence different truths and rules. Why describe partisans of this view as Cartesians? Because they paddle in a skeptical void. Adrift in a boat that is a shell of the cogito, they use as a rudder the inductive rules that derive from Descartes' a priori ideas and Kant's empirical schemas.

(e) Descartes' "new" proof for God's existence starts with the discovery that there is an idea of God within us. Insisting that we are incapable of producing the idea of an infinite being, he argues that God must have put it there. Critics were unimpressed, because the only positive content to our idea of God is the idea of ourselves, the idea of God being an extrapolation from ideas of our finite powers. This is perverse, because it requires that God's powers be modeled on our imperfect abilities. The argument is also deflated in this other way: everything finite – not only this idea – is God's effect, but nothing of God's infinite nature is learned by inspecting finite things. Spinoza expresses this objection in the terms of his metaphysical views: "*The actual being of ideas owns God as its cause, only in so far as he is considered as a thinking thing, not in so far as he is unfolded in any other attribute*" (Spinoza [1677] 1955, p. 85). Nothing in our idea of God is more than an intimation of him. Objections like this one were intended as a caution: our idea of God is not a direct illumination revealing God's nature or existence. The effect is evidence of a cause, but not its direct apprehension.

This "new" argument is more powerful if its emphasis is shifted. God's existence is confirmed by my finite existence, not merely by the idea of God within me: my finitude is a partition that presupposes God, the unrestricted infinite. As Descartes expressed this point in the context of his "new" argument: "I see that there is manifestly more reality in infinite substance than in finite, and therefore that in some way I have in me the notion of the infinite earlier than the finite – to wit, the notion of God before that of myself" (78; *CSM*, II, 31; *AT*, VII, 45). This (old) argument is the high road from Parmenides and Plato through Plotinus and Augustine to Spinoza and Hegel. There would be no richer idea of God if someone were to make sense of the true infinite.

(iii) Pantheism

"The unit," Descartes observed, is "in every sense an extended object and one susceptible of countless dimensions" (*CSM*, I, 66; *AT*, X, 453). Add that Descartes' God is both infinite and One, and we have all but formulated Spinoza's idea of God. It is said sometimes that *God* is Spinoza's prudent euphemism for nature. But this cannot be right, because nature, as he describes it, is comprised of the modes expressed in just one of God's infinite attributes: namely, extension. Where attributes are "that which intellect perceives of substance, as constituting its essence" (Spinoza [1677] 1955, p. 50), nature can be only one of the infinity of perspectives for comprehending God.

What is God's relation to the things he creates? Are such things qualifications of God or separate from him? Spinoza's pantheism entails that all modes – all finite things – are "in" or "of" God as partitions of his infinite being. The categorial difference between God and finite things is vast, but our distance from God is less, for we finite things are drawn into his very being. This is intimated in the often delirious confirmation of our individual existence, for existence in us is the intimation of being in God. Religious authorities have often demanded that there be a respectful distance between God and ourselves. But it makes no difference what they prefer: if God is the One, then everything that is, is in him. Malebranche, Leibniz (fitfully and inconsistently), and Whitehead say as much. Their God, like Hegel's Absolute, is Spinoza's One made self-conscious (Hegel [1807] 1967, p. 802). They all agree that created things, whatever their relative autonomy, exist in God.

Spinoza's notion of God is grander than theirs, because the self-consciousness they stress is, like extension, just one of God's many attributes. We emphasize it because we know consciousness in ourselves, but there is nothing privileged or exalted about our human standpoint: any mode construed from the perspective of any attribute is as good – and as feeble – a basis for speculating about the character of the infinite One. Why, if this is so, should we believe that God cares for created things, or that his care consoles us because it is recognizably like human care? Spinoza's God falls in and out of favor as we are more or less willing to postulate an unthinkable God who has no special concern for us.

(iv) God as a Mind

The most exploited of Descartes' notions of God is his speculation, affirmed but not argued, that God is a mind somewhat like our finite minds (*CSMK*, 309; *AT*, IV, 608). This is the notion opposed by Spinoza but embellished by Malebranche, Leibniz, Berkeley, Kant, Hegel, Kierkegaard, and Whitehead. They disagree about the exact point of the analogy, but each affirms that God is consciousness, nous, or spirit. Notice too the inclination to think of God as having personality. The cogito is always some particular *I*, and we infer that God, too, as in Christ, is a particular, self-conscious I. What are the detailed respects in which a thinking, self-thinking God resembles our finite minds? There are five emphases to consider.

(*a*) One elaboration reverts to Plato's belief that nous is both world soul and an innate power for understanding the Forms (Plato 1964, p. 64). Where God is identified with nous, in the way of Malebranche ([1688] 1980, pp. 39 and 179) and Berkeley (especially in his *Siris* [1964, vol. 5, p. 57]), the objects of our finite thinking are in God, and we participate in him – to the limit of our finite abilities – as we perceive the cosmological order founded and displayed in God's ideas. This theological view has secular expressions, as when Edmund Husserl calls for an "all embracing a priori phenomenology," one that surveys "the systematic unfolding of the *Universal logos of all conceivable being*" ([1950] 1960, p. 155). An alternative view despairs of direct access to God's ideas and settles for understanding him by way of nature, his product. This is the hope of natural philosophers – physicists – including Newton ([1704] 1952, p. 405–406): knowing the mathematized product of God's thinking, we partly understand his mind.

(*b*) God may be identified, primarily, with his will. For remember Descartes' remark that our minds are most like God's mind in respect to will. This is plausible, because will is an either-or affair: an idea or judgment is affirmed or denied. God could do no more. This is problematic, because God never withholds assent because of being uncertain about his ideas: they are always clear and distinct, hence true. Nor should desire be credited to God's mind as Leibniz ascribes appetition to monads, because desire implies a deficiency, though nothing can be lacking in God if he is pure act, all his perfections realized.

Still, God may have a will like our own if he could have done something he has chosen not to do. Suppose, for example, that there are contraries, so that choosing one entails rejecting others. We have the intimation that God chooses among contraries when Descartes credits him with deciding which laws shall be the baseline for order in our world: God could have willed that our world should violate the principle of noncontradiction, but he chose a contrary course (*CSMK*, 363; *AT*, V, 372). Similarly, Leibniz argued that there is an infinity of possible worlds, some better than others, so God needs a will in order to actualize the best of them.

These versions of will are notably intellectualized, whereas human will is often driven by impulse or appetite: think of urge and desire as sources of power. Will of this sort is also ascribed to God, perhaps on the assumption that Descartes rightly identified the critical faculty but then misdescribed it. The evolution of this idea is apparent when Spinoza's God is naturalized so that will, as unconscious striving, is everywhere the mark of this plastic, self-transforming One. Recall Schopenhauer's characterization of nature:

> Every glance at the world . . . confirms and establishes that the *will-to-live*, far from being an arbitrary hypothesis or even an empty expression, is the only true description of the world's innermost nature. Everything presses and pushes toward *existence*, if possible toward *organic existence*, i.e., *life*, and then to the highest possible degree thereof. (Schopenhauer [1844] 1969, vol. 2, p. 350)

This is will as the ground of being, and in that respect it is will as divine power. Schopenhauer's Cartesian (and Plotinian) sources are explicit:

> From the most ancient times, man has been called the microcosm. I have reversed the proposition, and have shown the world as the macranthropos, in so far as will and representation exhaust the true nature of the world as well as that of man. (ibid., p. 642)

(*c*) Crediting ourselves with free will, we suppose that God must have it too. This freedom, his and ours, is apparent in the use of ideas and logical rules. Descartes supposed that we are born with these ideas, though we are free to use them poorly or well. Only when ideas are clear and distinct does mind lose its indifference and affirm their truth as if it could not do otherwise. God's freedom is superior in this respect. He is never coerced, for he has unconditional freedom in the choice of his ideas and logic, even to the point of being able to create worlds that violate the principle of contradiction.

Leibniz protested that God is as much constrained as we are by such principles as noncontradiction, excluded middle, and identity. Nor is God free to create or disestablish the eternal possibles – meaning every difference and relation that embodies no contradiction. Leibniz credits God with the freedom to choose among possible worlds; but then he supposes that God instantiates the best one ([1675–1716] 1989, p. 220). Could God refuse to actualize the best world, or should we save God's freedom of choice by saying that this world is best because God chose it? Either way, by acknowledging goodness or deciding what shall count as good, God's freedom is the power to see the good realized within our world. Kant agreed, but with this difference: Leibniz's God chooses a world in which the mix of goods and evils is determined in advance; Kant's God oversees a world in which the choice of good or evil is left to individual wills. God does not tell us what to do; he may not even foresee what we will do. What he promises is that moral souls will be rewarded, in death, for their virtuous choices (Kant [1788] 1963, pp. 220–229).

Kant also exploits God's freedom in another way. Like Descartes, he supposes that phenomena in space and time constitute a closed mechanical system such that every change has sufficient, material conditions. Unlike Descartes, Kant believes that this system of mechanical agents is the phenomenal product of schematizing mind. Mind – Kant's transcendental ego – is free of these mechanical constraints, for space and time are merely the forms in which mind presents to itself the experiences it has schematized. Mind's transcendental synthesis is unconditioned, hence spontaneous. This freedom has two expressions. One is anticipated by Descartes' God, who invents logical rules that define the limits for order in our world. Likewise, the transcendental ego freely constructs the empirical schemas appropriate to its aims. The other expression of mind's freedom is its use of these rules to create experiences that satisfy its interests. Who will take the argument a step further and say that God too is a synthesizing ego, one that makes worlds?

Hegel says it, as he reflects on Spinoza's God:

> [S]pirit at once recoils in horror from this abstract unity, from this self-less substantiality, and maintains as against it the principle of Individuality. But after Spirit has externalized this principle in the process of its culture, has thereby made it an objective existence and established it throughout the whole of existence, has arrived at the idea of "Utility" and in the sphere of absolute freedom has grasped existence as its Individual Will, – after these stages, spirit then brings to light the thought that lies in its inmost depths, and expresses essential Reality in the form Ego = Ego. ([1807] 1967, p. 802)

God might have refused to create any world (that is his freedom). But then he would not have experienced the world while discovering himself as its author: he would have failed to realize his telos as a self. The exercise of freedom is a condition for selfhood, though freedom always requires that we do or make something, so that mind may discover itself in the otherness it has made. God is our example of freedom and selfhood, as the cogito is an intimation of him.

(d) If God is a mind, hence conscious, then we finite minds are connected to one another merely by dwelling together in his awareness. For no matter that we are autonomous monads or pointlike regions in God's own awareness, his consciousness unifies us. We are a community in him.

We have the paradox that Descartes' narcissistic individualism – I exist only when I perceive myself as existing – has supplied the basis for socializing an aggregate. The emphasis on community is explicit in Spinoza ([1677] 1955, p. 211), Malebranche ([1688] 1980, pp. 175 and 177), and Leibniz ([1675–1716] 1989, p. 220). It is emphatic in the Platonism of Berkeley's later work (1964, vol. 8, pp. 136–137), in Kant's "kingdom of ends" ([1788] 1963, p. 51), and in Hegel's account of culture as the objectification of the Absolute ([1807] 1967, pp. 455–679). The idea of community turns secular, while retaining a normative force that derives from its origin as a claim about God's consciousness, when Marx stresses the subjective – conscious – basis for group loyalty. Marx was invoking Rousseau's "general will," the notion that communities are unified by a normative desire supervening on the self-interested desires of particular members. This is consciousness inflated beyond individual thinkers so as to engage disparate minds within the community thereby created. Leibniz almost said this of monads as they are organized within God, but his monads are incapable of solidarity because, being windowless, they are mutually oblivious. Rousseau describes this conscious unity while saying little of God. Dewey believed that a "Great Community" is to be founded on the mutual sympathy of its members, each one discovering something of him or herself in the others of the community. But Dewey makes the point without reference to God – which is costly, because these secular notions of community lack the normative force imposed when God thinks us as one. They merely encourage a unity that he commands and creates.

Whitehead's notion of community is more traditionally theistic and nearly Leibniz's own. The Cartesian root is explicit. Whitehead "fully accepts Descartes' discovery that subjective experiencing is the primary metaphysical situation which is presented to metaphysics for analysis" ([1929] 1978, p. 160). Whereas Descartes described the cogito, Whitehead writes of "actual entities." They are

> the final real things of which the world is made up. There is no going behind actual entities to find anything more real. . . . The final facts are, all alike, actual entities: and these actual entities are drops of experience, complex and interdependent. (ibid., p. 18)

Every actual entity "prehends" some others by differentiating, grading, then organizing their effects upon it. The entities prehended are always the prehenders' antecedents: contemporaneous entities never affect one another. Each would be isolated from its contemporaries but for God's unifying awareness. For God too is an actual entity, which implies that other actual entities exist as they are prehended – experienced – by God. There are two recurring moments in God's eternal life. First – his primordial nature – is the moment when God's thought is pure receptivity. This moment is unstable, because thought without an object or content is a kind of nonbeing, as space may be reduced to nonspace by the absence of extended things. God is filled and fulfilled – his consequent nature – by prehending finite actual entities: he turns luminous and self-aware only as these contents reflect his light. This effect on God is coordinate with an effect on the actual entities prehended: entities that are contemporaneous and otherwise isolated from one another are prehended together as the organized manifold – the content of God's awareness. He grades and unifies them, providing – in his consciousness – a medium or matrix in which they are joined. There is, however, this limitation on community: actual occasions, like Leibniz's monads, remain distinct and alien from one another. For this is not the solidarity of mutually solicitous class members or the sympathy and respect of free men who have joined to regulate and repair the unexpected consequences of their associated behaviors. Think of Kant's transcendental unity of apperception: it can only join things externally. This – and nothing more – is the effect when Whitehead's actual entities are joined in God's consciousness.

(f) We are strangely endowed. Finite in ourselves, we have within us the infinite effect of an infinite cause: namely, the idea of God. Blind as we first struggle to understand ourselves, we come upon this idea, first as an ember, then as a shaft of light. Glimpsing this intimation of God within us, we may rise to contemplate him, the cosmos, and our place there. Or we may engage him in conversation. The relation of the interlocutors is unequal, the means of communication uncertain. The very possibility of rapport between God and oneself may be a delusion. Still, there is the record, from biblical times to the present, of the many believers who suppose that this dialogue is sustained in prayerful discourse and reflection.

Kierkegaard ([1843, 1849] 1974) turned upon himself when he hoped to make God accessible after Hegel had described him in ways that were abstract and remote. Buber, too, assumes that God, like human minds, has a personality, and that the conversation between God and ourselves, however unequal and cryptic, requires individuality – perhaps wit and idiosyncrasy – on both sides (1965, pp. 14–15). Lévinas supposes that God's transcendence precludes any chattiness between him and us, but he too emphasizes

God's accessibility through disciplined reflection and prayer ([1987] 1994, p. 83). These preoccupations are not unique to Descartes and his heirs: Abraham, Moses, Jesus, and Muhammad conversed with God. Still, Descartes' emphasis on God as mind encourages the belief that we commune with him in ways that resemble our discourse with one another.

These five ways of construing God as a mind share the vulnerability of Descartes' argument for the divisibility of mind and matter: Can there be a mind, divine or finite, without a body? The separability of mind and body is proved, Descartes said, because we may have an idea of either without the other (100; *CSM*, II, 54; *AT*, VII, 78). Still to answer is this question: Is the idea of mind complete: Does it represent a possibility that is instantiable as considered? Descartes argued that the idea of mind is complete. Hobbes objected: "I who am thinking am distinct from my thought; but my thought, though not separate from me, is distinct from me in the same way in which . . . jumping is distinct from the jumper" (*CSM*, II, 125; *AT*, VII, 177). Descartes' reply – "I do not deny that I, who am thinking, am distinct from my thought" (*CSM*, II, 125; *AT*, VII, 177) – is unsatisfactory, because he does not specify or even suggest what characteristics would distinguish him from his thought. Indeed, Descartes missed, or reinterpreted, Hobbes's question. Hobbes insisted that activity presupposes an agent. Descartes replied by distinguishing thought, as a genus, from the various activities which give it specific expression (e.g., conceiving or perceiving). He never speaks to the direct question: What is the thinker in addition to his thinking?

Descartes has failed to distinguish activity from the agent it presupposes. Mind, as he describes, it, is pure activity: it is awareness in one of its modes, often or always with self-awareness. But can there be activity without an agent? There is no physical activity without a body, as there is no spinning in the absence of the wheel that spins. Is mind exempt from this condition? Descartes answered that mind may be described and *essentially defined* by reference to its activities. This is the dubious assumption concealed in his response to Hobbes. For there seems to be no activity that is free-floating, no activity that is not distinguishable from something that acts. Descartes could have replied that thinking is the exception: here, he might have said, is an activity that requires no agent distinct from itself. But this is a claim to be explained and argued, not assumed. Thinking, like jumping, may require a body. God's thinking may require that God have an identity distinct from his thinking. A divine body – one that is "pure act" because all its potencies are realized – prompts questions that are nowhere considered by Descartes or his successors.

Phenomenology and Existentialism

All the lineages mentioned so far pass through Descartes without having originated in him. In each of them, Descartes is a Platonist, one who has personalized nous, thereby fracturing the world soul into a myriad contingent thinkers. Descartes' place among the phenomenologists is different: his appropriation of Augustine's remark that assurance about one's own existence is the starting point for knowledge (1962, pp. 236–237) provokes reflections which have few antecedents. (Plotinus is one of the few: "Thus is it true to say that 'to be and to think are the same thing' " [1975, p. 51].)

Hegel's *Phenomenology of Spirit* is the monumental realization of Descartes' passion for self-discovery. Hegel has assumed what Brentano would later declare:

> Every mental phenomenon is characterized by . . . reference to a content, direction toward an objection (which is not to be understood here as meaning a thing), or immanent objectivity. Every mental phenomenon includes something as object within itself, although they do not all do so in the same way. In presentation something is presented, in judgment something is affirmed or denied. . . . We can, therefore, define mental phenomena by saying that they are those phenomena which contain an object intentionally within themselves. (1973, pp. 88–89)

Intentional attitudes are familiar from Husserl's suggestion that we suspend judgment in the extra-mental reality of the phenomena perceived or thought – "bracketing" or "parenthesizing" experience – so as to consider "everything meant in them *purely* as meant in them" ([1950] 1960, p. 20). Notice the articulation of a point left implicit in Descartes' *Meditations*. There, second-order awareness is emphatically intentional, as when ideas are inspected and judgment is withheld for want of clarity and distinctness. First-order consciousness is more a luminous effusion, a passive awareness. All that is changed in these passages from Brentano and Husserl, for they emphasize the intentional character of *first*-order awareness. It is these first-order activities and their (intentional) objects that second-order awareness is to investigate.

Examples may be culled from Kierkegaard, Nietzsche, Husserl, James, Heidegger, and Proust. Bergson is our paradigm:

> When, with the inner regard of my consciousness, I examine my person in its passivity, like some superficial encrustment, first I perceive all the perceptions which come to it from the material world. These perceptions are clear-cut, distinct, juxtaposed or mutually juxtaposable; they seek to

group themselves into objects. Next I perceive memories more or less adherent to these perceptions and which serve to interpret them; these memories are, so to speak, as if detached from the depth of my person and drawn to the periphery by perceptions resembling them: they are fastened on me without being absolutely myself. And finally, I become aware of tendencies, motor habits, a crowd of virtual actions more or less solidly bound to those perceptions and these memories. All these elements with their well-defined forms appear to me to be all the more distinct from myself the more they are distinct from one another. Turned outwards from within, together they constitute the surface of a sphere which tends to expand and loose itself in the external world . . . What I find beneath these clear-cut crystals and this superficial congelation is a continuity of flow comparable to no other flowing I have ever seen. (1992, p. 163)

There are four domains in which reflections like this are appropriate. One comprises the ideas or rules that articulate or organize sensory data or the percepts themselves. Another is mind's investigation of itself, including its acts, attitudes, and structure. Next is mind's inspection of the body it inhabits. Last is each thinker's perception of the world as it is mediated and shaped by specific ideas, interests, and moral values and by having a particular body. Notice that a self-affirmation – I am, I exist – is the energizing perception that grounds each of these phenomenological inquiries (though the individuality of the thinker may be suppressed or absent in the domain of ideas). Ideally, mind's perception of its existence, along with its ruminations in these four domains, would be folded into a single characterization of man-in-the-world, as in Hegel's *Phenomenology*. More often, phenomenologists disagree among themselves about the details and balance of the four. Only a few reconcile their introspectionist starting point with the likelihood that the self-observant thinker is a material body.

Phenomenology is also the site for a fifth topic: whether metaphysics is defunct. Aversion to theory is a natural prejudice in philosophers who suppose that philosophical thinking should abjure conceptual distortions in favor of informed perception. Descartes' likely response is a final point.

(i) *Phenomenology as the reflection upon and description of percepts, ideas, or rules.* This is a development that Plato foresaw: perception of the Forms was to be mind's highest achievement. Their specification in language was to be the outcome of this inspection, though language distorts the matters it reports, so descriptions of the Forms are less reliable than their perception

(Plato 1964, p. 1590). Descartes invokes this reflection when he proposes, in the *Rules*, that knowledge requires the intuition of simple ideas, then the construction before the mind's eye of more complex ideas. This Platonic emphasis is apparent in many of Descartes' successors, Husserl included: "[*E*]*idetic intuition is the fundamental form of all particular transcendental method*" ([1950] 1960, p. 72). Perceiving essences – the counterpart to Plato's Forms – supplies "the all-embracing science (which is) grounded with absolute strictness" (ibid.).

Plato's emphasis on rational intuition and the Forms somewhat obscures the fact that sensory data may also satisfy the demand for inspectable content. Hume is paradigmatic:

> All the perceptions of the human mind resolve themselves into two distinct kinds which I shall call Impressions and Ideas. The difference betwixt these consists in the degrees of force and liveliness, with which they strike upon the mind, and make their way into our thought or consciousness. ([1739–40] 1978, p. 1)

Mind "is flooded with light" as it contemplates the Forms (Plato 1964, p. 1591). But so are Hume's impressions and ideas, as well as Husserl's ideas, illuminated and grasped, not inferred or described. This is also the point of Russell's distinction between knowledge by acquaintance and knowledge by description ([1901–50] 1964, pp. 127–174), though he stands with Hume, against Husserl, in disputes about the contents of this founding knowledge: are they concepts (Forms) or impressions?

Some phenomenologists of both persuasions agree that a mind preoccupied with its content loses sight of itself. Plato's nous and Aristotle's "active intellect" are identified only by way of their content; similarly, mind as described by Hume in the *Treatise* ([1739–40] 1978, pp. 232–233) or Wittgenstein in the *Tractatus* (1963, p. 117) has no identity apart from the percepts and ideas that are its content. Does mind have no power for self-inspection because it has no content or structure apart from the matters it perceives? Or is mind forgetful of itself only when it concentrates on other things?

Neither answer satisfies the existentialist concern. For no matter whether the objects of awareness are universals (with Plato) or particulars (with Hume), existentialists – including Descartes, Locke, Leibniz, Berkeley, Kant (in some contexts), and Sartre – require that a concurrent self-inspection confirm, in the moment of qualification, that the mind's own act – its thinking – is the necessary condition for the existence of the content perceived. Esse est percipi: Plato and Descartes believed this as surely as did Berkeley. The Forms exist because nous perceives them, as, presumably, there are no Humean impressions if they are not perceived. It is equally critical for the existentialism that Descartes encouraged that the mind inspecting content is, and discovers itself to be, a particular thinker. For it is not just any one thinking just now: the ambiguity of the contrary would reduce or confuse responsibility for the act and its affirmations. I who think am responsible both for thinking and for what I think. Existentialists insist that mind recognize itself whenever it serves as the subject of qualification for whatever things it inspects. Neglecting this self-intuition and the responsibility it carries is "bad faith" (Sartre [1943] 1969, pp. 86–116). Phenomenologists of this first sort, including Hume and Russell but also Plato, resist this demand. They ignore our self-impression, or deny that we have it.

(ii) *Phenomenology as reflection upon the mind's own structure.* Granted that I exist, what am I? A thing that thinks was Descartes' answer, though *thinks* is too simple a word for the complexity of mind's two orders. Can mind discover its complexity by self-inspection alone? Or is inference required for information that is otherwise unavailable? Descartes affirmed that mind is, or always can be, exhaustively self-aware, where nothing that is uninspectable in principle can be one of mind's structural features or qualifications (*CSM*, II, 171; *AT*, VII, 247). His successors say many different things.

Leibniz objected that Descartes made reflexive awareness a required feature of every mind – none could exist if it did not know itself to exist. Leibniz himself argued that every monad has perception, whereas only some monads have apperception. Kant provides for both emphases. Second-order activity, now called "transcendental apperception," is inferred as the condition for a unitary, schematized manifold; only as reason shapes the will does mind attend to itself. Fichte, Schelling, Hegel, Schopenhauer, Peirce, James, Dewey, Husserl, and Sartre dwell on the back-and-forth movement between these orders, though mind's telos always requires a progression from unselfconscious engagement with things – as in perception or desire – to the second-order awareness wherein mind is intellectually controlling and morally responsible. This is the evolution from naiveté, savagery, or dumb habit to civilized self-control.

Freud implies that the traditional question is incorrectly formed: self-access is not an all-or-nothing affair. Much intentional activity – including perception, conception, or desire – is unconscious, because learned standards of moral behavior, hence guilt, impel us to disguise these intentions from ourselves. (Freud 1966–74, vol. 19, 45–47). Sartre responds for Descartes: mind is comprised of first- and second-order thinking; there cannot be one without the other, so no intentional activity can be imputed to mind yet described as unconscious. If intentional, it is conscious, hence perceivable – whatever the bad faith that makes us prefer that it not be observed. Or it is not intentional, and is no part of mind (Sartre [1943] 1969, pp. 712–734).

This is a dispute about borders. Descartes implies that mind has rigid limits, established by self-awareness. Something that is nowhere to be found within this arena is no part of mind. Freud supposes that the borders of consciousness are permeable and not well defined (i.e., repression is sometimes breached). Bringing matters to consciousness is like fishing: one lands fish from deep water, but the fish are there and make a difference, whether or not we catch them. Where do these fish swim? Freud requires that we locate mind's structure within its material context. This includes the body, whose brain is organized for first- and second-order consciousness, and the circumstances, both current and historical, in which the body is variously affected. Phenomenology of a Freudian kind, as in psychotherapy, is a search and description, sometimes a confrontation. One draws into consciousness material that would not otherwise be there.

(iii) *Phenomenology of the body.* Descartes' analysis of bodies reduces them to extension, each body having some distinguishing size and configuration. He supposed that animal bodies, human ones included, are machines, all their parts, functions, and actions characterizable in mechanical terms. Each thinker's body is nevertheless its own, so there is a special intimacy and unity between them. Descartes' abstract characterization of body as extension is alien here where mind is asked to explain its experience as inhabitant or pilot of a particular body. What is it like to blink an eye or raise a hand? The geometry appropriate to representing the mechanical relations of bodily parts is hard to apply or irrelevant to these experiences. Indeed, there seems to be no way of integrating these geometrical descriptions with the thinker's perceptions of his or her body. Nor is fascination with one's body superseded when Descartes' idealist successors remark that space and time, therefore body, are phenomenal, implying that what we call body is a set of phenomena that qualify our minds: now, as before, we have the experience of embodiment.

Descartes was convinced that mind and body are unified, however mysteriously (*CSM*, II, 50–62; *AT*, VII, 71–90). Their relation is explored when awareness illumines the body's architecture, acts, and powers from within, as we use the body – we walk, taste, and talk – to know better what sort of machine it is. Merleau-Ponty (1962) after sketches in Hegel's *Phenomenology*, describes these experiments and interprets the results. His descriptions are phenomenological, but their subject is existential: a thinking body engaged with other things discovers itself.

(iv) *Phenomenology as reflection on the place of embodied mind in the social and material world.* Descartes proposed that we establish comity with others while satisfying our needs in prudent, simple ways (*CSM*, I, 356–357; *AT*, XI, 388–389). We should also reflect upon the God who created us, thereby locating ourselves in the fixed order of things. The *life-world* is this vast universe, but especially the neighborhood consisting of people and things having effective relations with one's embodied mind.

Hegel's *Phenomenology of Mind* is the orienting text. Descartes set existential concerns – I am, I exist – against essentialist ones – knowledge requires certainty about the universal truths of geometry. Hegel reconciles the two as he describes the progression of awareness from particularity and contingency to universality and necessity. Phenomenologists of the life-world write in the shadow of this achievement, each altering Hegel's format or perspective in ways determined by the writer's moral viewpoint or situation. Two quite different attitudes are prominent. On the one side are phenomenologists of a strongly Platonic tendency, for whom intelligibility is the principal value. They – Husserl is an example – see the life-world statically, from the perspective of its differentiating, organizing forms. The other standpoint is more plastic and accommodating: Heidegger (1975) emphasizes that we are "thrown" into a world we have not made, one in which we shall surely die, though we have skills with which to survive for a while. Compare William James, remembered as much for his enthusiasm about our prospects as for his irony (1968, pp. 717–740).

Descartes' self-discovered thinker discovers a life-world, one whose parts are valorized and ranked by its valuing center (see Scheler [1913–16] 1973). This thinker should also be a democrat, for he or she (because thinkers are embodied) observes or surmises that there are many others like him or herself, each one an end in itself because each is qualified, as Kant said, to make laws for all mankind (Kant [1788] 1963, pp. 49 and 105). John Dewey is often credited or blamed for encouraging our pragmatic, populist culture, though Descartes is its more remote sponsor: every thinker empowers himself, saying I am, I exist, while doubting every other thing. Power and content derive, for each of us, from this reflecting, valuing center. Descartes would have us cultivate thought and sensibility as we locate ourselves in a world of other things. But humility should never exceed self-concern. For we know the world only as we engage other things in order to satisfy ourselves. Each of us, as a mind embodied, is the measure of all that is or is not. Yet Kant was mistaken: we are not so much world-makers as lion-tamers. We hold the complex that encircles us in a tension that stretches us while it manages our engagement with these other things. We struggle so that the ambient world will neither spread beyond our ability to control it nor implode, stripping us of both content and the center that would perceive and appraise it. This is Descartes' legacy to us and the reason that James, Dewey, Heidegger, and Nietzsche are some principal phenomenologists of the life-world since Hegel.

(v) *Is metaphysics defunct?* Some people say it is or wish it would be, because they are bored by metaphysical questions. Descartes had a better answer. Suppose that philosophy is mostly talk. Why look there for truths, when they stand already before the mind's eye? Reality is here and inspectable in the efflorescence of conscious mind. Forget the talk. See things as they are. Plato had said this already.

Heidegger says it again. His *The End of Philosophy* (1975) is a memorial to the world lost when *logos* intruded into the place where presence was once the only authority. This last is a perspective to which Heidegger would have us return: Dasein should explore itself and its context ([1927] 1962, pp. 85–87). But did that standpoint ever exist? Could it be that the transparency claimed for self-reflecting mind (and Plato's Forms) is a myth, a fable that sentimentalizes the desire for incontrovertible truths – exposed and seen – while demonizing the languages and theories that make us critical but inform us better? (Peirce 1934, vol. 5, pp. 121–127; Weissman 1989, pp. 73–137).

Descartes is not an innocent bystander. He celebrated presence as the foundation of knowledge and being: mind itself and the essences of some other things stand before the mind with a clarity that defeats doubt. Perceiving ourselves and these ideas, we are the prisoner who struggles out of Plato's cave into the light of the sun. No one who sees this world could be impressed by the shadows and icons left behind. Heidegger exploits the comparison: the metaphysical dialectic of cave-bound argument is to be superseded.

Descartes' likely response is useful, though inferred. He would be flattered that Dasein is so conspicuously a rendering of the embodied cogito. He would probably remind us that the report of his reflections was only a first, if decisive, step. Having written the *Meditations*, he solicited replies.

Upon receiving them, he responded, often in fury, always in detail. Did he think metaphysics was finished? Or did he suppose that philosophical views, his own included, require justification? The hundreds of pages written in self-defense are an answer. Are the pages irrelevant, because they prove only that Descartes suffered an obsessive tic? Critics despised his vanity but never doubted his conviction that probing arguments, seriously intended, are a test of truth.

Philosophy would be over if truths were so many neon signs, blinking pink, green, and yellow in a black sky, or shining, ready-to-hand, in the cogito's self-reflection. There may be such truths, but which ones are they? Could truth be something else? There is room for dispute.

NOTES

1. Leibniz would not have coupled his doubts about the extra-mental status of matter to doubts about God. He, like Berkeley, shared the view of Malebranche (Malebranche [1688] 1980, p. 133): that God could give us the idea or illusion of matter without creating any thing to which the idea corresponds. Skepticism was extended to God's existence or efficacy when Hume and Kant proposed that mind contrives the idea or appearance of matter.

2. That Descartes favored using ideas as rules seems plain from such passages as the one above. That he would have formulated the point this way – saying that ideas function as rules – is moot. *We* might not express it this way, but for Kant.

3. God "necessarily willed what was best" (*CSMK*, 348; *AT*, V, 166). "God's purposes are hidden from us" (*CSMK*, 349; *AT*, V, 166).

4. How transcendental egos affect one another is a point that Kant never explains. That human bodies are affected is less mysterious: they are schematized by the ways we think them, hence by the schemas chosen to create a thinkable world. But then it also follows that you, known to me only by way of the body and behaviors I schematize, do not have a value that is equal, for me, to my own: I know my own desires; yours have no reality for me apart from the way that I think about you. How I identify your transcendental ego, the source of your moral worth, with the body I schematize and why I believe that the kingdom of ends has any members other than myself are questions that Kant does not answer.

5. Readers may object that Descartes intended his *Rules* as a set of procedures for solving complex questions. But this is only one of its two aims and

not the dominant one. Locke emphasized the other (i.e., to show that obscure ideas can be replaced by clear and distinct simples and their complexes). Nor is it decisive that Descartes' simples are abstract ideas, such as duration, extension, and volition, whereas Locke prefers empirical simples. It is Descartes' program for replacing obscure ideas with simples and complexes, not the character of the simples, that is decisive for this lineage.

REFERENCES

Aquinas, Thomas. [1266–68] 1964. *Summa Theologiae*, trans. Timothy McDermott. New York: McGraw-Hill.

———. 1965. *Selected Writings of St. Thomas Aquinas*, trans. Robert P. Goodwin. New York: Bobbs-Merrill.

Arnauld, Antoine, and Nicole, Pierre. [1662] 1851. *The Port-Royal Logic*, trans. Thomas Spencer Baynes. Edinburgh: Sutherland and Knox.

Augustine. 1962. *City of God*, trans. Gerald G. Walsh, Demetrius B. Zeana, and Grace Monahan. Garden City, N.Y.: Doubleday.

Bergson, Henri. 1992. *The Creative Mind*, trans. Mabelle L. Andison. New York: Citadel Press.

Berkeley, George. 1964. *The Works of George Berkeley, Bishop of Cloyne*, 9 vols. London: Nelson.

Brentano, Franz. 1973. *Psychology from an Empirical Standpoint*, trans. Anton C. Rancurello, D. B. Terrell, and Linda L. McAllister. New York: Humanities Press.

Buber, Martin. 1965. *Between Man and Man*, trans. Ronald Gregor Smith. New York: Macmillan.

Carnap, Rudolf. 1934. *Philosophy and Logical Syntax*, trans. Max Black. London: Kegan Paul, Trench, Trubner.

———. 1969. *The Logical Structure of the World*, trans. Rolf A. George. Berkeley: University of California Press.

Dewey, John. [1927] 1954. *The Public and Its Problems*. Chicago: Swallow.

Fichte, Johann. [1794–95] 1982. *Science of Knowledge*, trans. Peter Heath and John Lachs. Cambridge: Cambridge University Press.

Frege, Gottlob. [1968] 1984. "The Thought: A Logical Inquiry," trans. A. M. and Marcelle Quinton, *Mind*, vol. 65, no. 259, 1956, pp. 289–311.

Freud, Sigmund. 1966–74. *The Standard Edition of the Complete Psychological Works of Sigmund Freud*, 24 vols. London: Hogarth Press.

Hegel, G. W. F. [1812–16] 1961. *Science of Logic*, trans. W. H. Johnstone and L. G. Struthers. London: Allen and Unwin.

——. [1807] 1967. *The Phenomenology of Mind*, trans. J. B. Baillie. New York: Harper.

——. [1801] 1977. *The Difference between Fichte's and Schelling's System of Philosophy*, trans. H. S. Harris and Walter Cerf. Albany: State University of New York Press.

Heidegger, Martin. [1927] 1962. *Being and Time*, trans. John Macquarrie and Edward Robinson. New York: Harper and Row.

——. 1975. *The End of Philosophy*, trans. Joan Stambaugh. London: Souvenir.

Hume, David. [1739–40] 1978. *A Treatise of Human Nature*, ed. L. A. Selby-Bigge and P. H. Nidditch. Oxford: Clarendon Press.

Husserl, Edmund. [1950] 1960. *Cartesian Meditations*, trans. Dorian Cairns. The Hague: Martinus Nijhoff.

James, William. 1968. *The Writings of William James*, ed. John J. McDermott. New York: Random House.

Kant, Immanuel. [1788] 1963. *Critique of Practical Reason and Other Works*, trans. Thomas Kingsmill Abbott. London: Longmans.

——. [1781] 1965. *Critique of Pure Reason*, trans. Norman Kemp Smith. New York: St. Martin's Press.

——. [1790] 1987. *Critique of Judgment*, trans. Werner S. Pluhar. Indianapolis: Hackett.

Kierkegaard, Søren. [1843, 1849] 1974. *Fear and Trembling and The Sickness unto Death*, trans. Walter Lowrie. Princeton: Princeton University Press.

Leibniz, G. W. [1675–1716] 1989. *G. W. Leibniz: Philosophical Essays*, ed. and trans. Roger Ariew and Daniel Garber. Indianapolis: Hackett.

Lévinas, Emmanuel. [1987] 1994. *Outside the Subject*, trans. Michael B. Smith. Stanford, Calif.: Stanford University Press.

Locke, John. [1756] 1959. *An Essay Concerning Human Understanding*, 2 vols. New York: Dover.

Malebranche, Nicholas. [1688] 1980. *Dialogues on Metaphysics*, trans. Willis Doney. New York: Abaris.

Marx, Karl. [1843–44] 1992. *Early Writings*, trans. Rodney Livingstone and Gregor Benton. London: Penguin.

Marx, Karl, and Engels, Frederich. [1848] 1967. *Communist Manifesto*. Harmondsworth: Penguin.

Merleau-Ponty, Maurice. 1962. *Phenomenology of Perception*, trans. Colin Smith. London: Routledge and Kegan Paul.

Mill, John Stuart. [1859] 1987. *On Liberty.* New York: Macmillan.

Newton, Isaac. [1704] 1952. *Opticks.* New York: Dover.

Nietzsche, Friedrich. [1870–71, 1887] 1956. *The Birth of Tragedy and the*

Genealogy of Morals, trans. Francis Golffing. Garden City, N.Y.: Doubleday.

Peirce, Charles Sanders. 1931–35. *Collected Papers*, ed. Charles Hartshorne and Paul Weiss, 6 vols. Cambridge, Mass.: Harvard University Press.

Plato. 1964. *Collected Dialogues*, ed. Edith Hamilton and Huntington Cairns. New York: Pantheon.

Plotinus. 1975. *The Essential Plotinus*, trans. Elmer O'Brien. Indianapolis: Hackett.

Rousseau, Jean Jacques. [1749] 1988. *Rousseau.* New York: Macmillan.

Russell, Bertrand. [1901–50] 1964. *Logic and Knowledge*, ed. Robert Marsh. London: Macmillan.

Ryle, Gilbert. 1966. *The Concept of Mind.* New York: Barnes and Noble.

Sartre, Jean-Paul. [1943] 1969. *Being and Nothingness*, trans. Hazel E. Barnes. New York: Washington Square.

Scheler, Max. [1913–16] 1973. *Formalism in Ethics and Non-Formal Ethics of Values*, trans. Manfred S. Frings and Roger L. Funk. Evanston, Ill.: Northwestern University Press.

Schopenhauer, Arthur. [1819, 1844] 1969. *The World as Will and Representation*, 2 vols. New York: Dover.

Spinoza, Benedict. [1677] 1955. *On the Improvement of the Understanding, The Ethics, Correspondence.* New York: Dover.

Weissman, David. 1977. *Eternal Possibilities.* Carbondale, Ill.: Southern Illinois University Press.

——. 1987. *Intuition and Ideality.* Albany: State University of New York.

——. 1989. *Hypothesis and the Spiral of Reflection.* Albany: State University of New York.

——. 1993. *Truth's Debt to Value.* New Haven: Yale University Press.

Whitehead, Alfred North. [1929] 1978. *Process and Reality.* New York: Free Press.

Wittgenstein, Ludwig. 1963. *Tractatus Logico-Philosophicus*, trans. D. F. Pears and B. F. McGuinness. London: Routledge and Kegan Paul.

——. 1966. *Philosophical Investigations*, trans. G. E. M. Anscombe, 3d edn. New York: Macmillan.

Essay 4
Epistemology

JOHN F. POST

§1. Introduction

Nothing can be more easily or more evidently perceived by me than my mind. So says Descartes (69–70; *CSM*, II, 22–23; *AT*, VII, 34). Indeed, I can know the nature of my mind more distinctly than anything material, and "there can be nothing in me, that is to say in my mind, of which I am not aware" (*CSMK*, III, 165; *AT*, III, 237). Material things like wine have an internal substance or hidden chemical constitution (*CSM*, II, 193; *AT*, VII, 276–277), which can be investigated by natural philosophy, but mind has no hidden constitution, chemical or otherwise. When unclouded and attentive, not distracted by the senses or the imagination, mind is immediately known to itself, epistemically transparent.

This belief in the self-transparency of mind could be Descartes' most fundamental belief. It shapes his whole philosophy, and it continues to shape the philosophies of many who congratulate themselves on having overcome his insidious influence. To be sure, few today accept the self-transparency thesis with the sweeping generality that Descartes intended. We are heirs after all not only to Descartes but to Freud; there is much more to mind than meets the mind's eye. Yet many suppose that however wrong Descartes may have been about some aspects of mind, he was right about others; there remain essential features of mind that have no "hidden constitution" and are epistemically diaphanous.

One such feature, according to many, is what we mean by what we say, and what our ideas are ideas of; matters of meaning and aboutness, or intentionality, are more readily known to us than are material things. Descartes too believed that this feature of mind is essential; our capacity for reason, which necessarily involves language, is what distinguishes us from animals, and this capacity includes an a priori understanding of meaning. In his *Replies* to objections to the *Meditations*, Descartes exempts our understanding of the meanings of words from the scope of general doubt; we know pre-reflexively, via internal awareness, what we mean (*CSM*, II, 278, 285; *AT*, VII, 422). Hence doubt cannot extend to the terms of the premises that Descartes needs for his argument that he is not being deceived by an evil demon or a malign god and can therefore trust whatever he clearly and distinctly perceives. I cannot be wrong about the meaning of the words I use, including *true*, *false*, and *God*; nor can I be mistaken about sameness and difference of meaning, or about sameness and difference of the contents of my beliefs. "When understanding what I say, I can express nothing in words, without that very fact making it certain that I possess the idea of that which these words signify" (*CSM*, II, 113; *AT*, VII, 160). Further, every idea is without fail an idea of something, and even if I can be mistaken as to whether the something exists, I cannot be mistaken as to what the idea is an idea of. As Husserl would say three centuries later, "In the very essence of an experience lies determined not only *that*, but also whereof it is a consciousness" (Husserl [1913] 1962, p. 108).

What goes for meanings goes, too, near enough, not only for their sameness and difference but also for certain other relations among them, including logical consistency/inconsistency. Given the meanings of the terms 'round' and 'square', it is transparent to the attentive mind that the predicate "is round and square" is an inconsistent predicate and cannot possibly apply to anything. So too do we have a priori knowledge of the kind of possibility/impossibility involved, and of the principle of noncontradiction also involved (to the effect that nothing can have both a property and one of its contraries, or fall under both an idea and its negation). Knowledge of meaning, of possibility, of logic, and of sameness and difference of meaning is a priori knowledge, or at least knowledge from our armchairs, as is knowledge of the deductive relations among our concepts. The very idea that these matters could have a "hidden constitution," or that we could thereby be fundamentally mistaken about them, makes no sense.

I shall be tracing some of the persistent subterranean effects of these largely internalist, Cartesian ideas about language and our knowledge of meaning, possibility, and logic. One of the defining features of twentieth-century philosophy is the widespread belief that language is where the mind meets the world, and that language mediates whatever access to the world we may have. Philosophy of language is therefore the ground on which today's battles are fought over whether to view the world as something beyond the text or as text; whether truth is correspondence or anything but; whether the world is ready-made or we are world-makers; and in general, whether to believe realism or one of the many irrealisms.[1] Suitably lin-guisticized, these are today's versions of traditional philosophical struggles over who we are, what is the world, and what is our place in it.

Descartes' epistemology continues to make itself felt in our attempts to answer these questions, and many others, by way of its unsuspected influ-ence on received philosophies of language and theories of meaning. There persists a kind of unwitting Cartesian rationalism about meaning. This "meaning rationalism," as it is called,[2] is a cluster of views centered on the idea that the meaning of a term, and its aboutness, and the sameness and difference of meaning of terms, together with the nature of meaning itself, are things we can know, if not exactly a priori, then from our armchairs. The way they seem to the attentive mind, "internally," is the way they are; nothing is hidden ultimately from a sufficiently supple, diligent phenome-nology or conceptual analysis.

The meaning-rationalist cluster includes variations on Descartes' inter-nalism, his individualism, his method of analysis, and what counts for him as an inference that we can rely on to justify its conclusion. One or another of these elements of meaning rationalism lurks undetected, often repressed, in the thought of many philosophers widely admired as our most resolute anti-Cartesians – indeed, lionized for having led the way in overcoming Descartes' influence. Among them, I argue, are Wittgenstein (who coined the dictum, "Nothing is hidden"), Carnap, Heidegger, Derrida, Quine, Put-nam, and Rorty. These may be the leading irrealist philosophers of our time, and their irrealism is enabled, if not driven, by elements of meaning ra-tionalism, as we shall see.

Why is meaning rationalism so seductive and so tenacious? One reason is the seeming lack of a plausible alternative. Where, after all, is the philos-ophy of language that makes adequate sense of meaning in a way that is not internalist, individualist, or committed to armchair knowledge of meaning and its nature? We encounter just such an "externalist" alternative in §§6–7. But first we need to consider another reason why meaning rationalism, together with the irrealism it enables, is so seductive and tenacious. This is a centuries-old fundamental objection to any attempt to "justify our factual language" – any attempt to show that it somehow conforms to a preexisting world in which sameness and difference are not made but found. The objec-tion is well known and is widely seen as not only insurmountable but equally effective against related metaphysical pretensions. What is less well known, if it is known at all, is how much the objection owes to Descartes, and how foundationalist it is even while it rejects foundationalism.

§2. Cartesian Inference and Grounding Language

According to Wittgenstein, we cannot possibly justify our factual language – say, on the ground that it conforms to reality – by appealing to facts which can only be stated in it; we cannot use language to get outside language. Wittgenstein was by no means alone in raising this form of objection to realism, and by no means the first. Anticipations may be found in Nietzsche, among others, and the groundwork lies unintentionally in Kant, who in turn is indebted to Descartes, as we shall see. Under Wittgenstein's influence, Rorty likewise insists that there can be "no noncircular argumentative recourse" for justifying (or rejecting) a "final vocabulary," including the factual, on pain of vicious regress (Rorty 1989, pp. 73ff., 80). We cannot look on reality bare and compare it with our final vocabulary, or with our language, our concepts or ideas of reality, in order to see whether they somehow conform to reality, track it, carve it at the joints, or whatever. There can be no such God's-eye view, and "the demand for an adequate mode of expression," as Nietzsche says, "is senseless"; so our metaphysical views are only the product of the grammatical structure of our language, and "The world appears logical to us because we have made it logical" (Nietzsche [1901] 1968, pp. 625, 484, 521). Putnam likewise condemns any God's-eye view: "The notion of comparing our system of beliefs with unconceptualized reality to see if they match makes no sense. . . . [T]he notion of a transcendent match between our representation and the world is nonsense" (Putnam 1981, pp. 130, 134). For we cannot justify belief in such a match by using language which presupposes it, any more than we could justify – or criticize – belief in a match between categories of the understanding and uncategorized things in themselves.

This hoary line of thought reflects, and is largely driven by, a form of argument that originated in Aristotle, impressed the sixteenth century, and powerfully shaped the thinking of both Descartes and his opponents. As we shall see, the argument turns out to presuppose, quite uncritically, something that Descartes himself characteristically presupposed: namely, that the inferences we can rely on to justify their conclusions, at least in philosophy, are all *transitive*, in the sense that if *x* justifies *y*, and *y* justifies *z*, then *x* justifies *z*. Further, it turns out not only that this transitivity presupposition is an important element in meaning rationalism, driving its internalism, among other things, but that it is deeply flawed, as we see in some detail in §5.

Granted, *deductive* inferential justification (in which, under certain conditions, *x* justifies *y* if *x* is justified and *y* is deducible from *x*) is transitive; and deductive justification is essential not only to Descartes' philosophy but to logic and mathematics. Yet several important *non*deductive forms of inferential justification are *not* transitive, as we shall see, including probabilistic inference, inference to the best explanatory story – roughly what Peirce called abduction – and inference from the track records of competing theories, paradigms, or research programs. This undermines the transitivity presupposition and with it the hoary line that our factual language cannot be justified, that there must be final vocabularies beyond which there is no noncircular argumentative recourse, and that " 'objects' do not exist independently of conceptual schemes" (Putnam 1981, p. 52).

The transitivity presupposition may seem a mere technicality, remote from Descartes and his influence, but it proves to underlie much of his thought, and indeed much of modern and postmodern philosophy. Let's begin to see why.

Epistemology in the sixteenth and seventeenth centuries was preoccupied with the problem of the criterion: Are there criteria whose presence to the aspiring knower would guarantee the truth, or at least the probable truth, of any beliefs that satisfy them? If so, the beliefs they guarantee could serve as the bedrock on which to construct the rest of our knowledge; we could start with what is close to us, hence better known, then build outward. Descartes argued that he had found such a criterion in clarity and distinctness; anything I perceive with the same clarity and distinctness with which I perceive my own existence must be true. By pushing skeptical doubt to its extreme, beyond what even the Pyrrhonian skeptics had dared, and nevertheless finding something immune to such doubt – something in the cogito – Descartes aimed to silence the skeptics and solve the problem they had done so much to elevate to crisis proportions.[3] He aimed also, through his radical method, to overcome Scholastic tradition and dogma, much of it theological; and theologians to this day value Descartes for making them suspend judgments that have no backing save tradition and authority.

But there were other responses to the Pyrrhonian crisis. Fideists – Protestant or Catholic, dogmatic or not – rejected not only skepticism but also Descartes' rationalism, arguing that ultimately everyone must take certain basic matters on faith. Nothing in the cogito suffices as a criterion or ultimate ground for belief; even reason is subject to doubt if not backed by faith (as Kierkegaard would repeat two centuries later [Popkin 1951, 1959]). It is faith that supplies the needed criterion, where faith is some (divinely inspired) self-certifying act, state, or faculty that yields nonrational yet warranted trust in the otherwise unjustified beliefs. Relativists, by contrast, agreed with the skeptics in seeing little to choose between such fideism and Cartesian or other foundationalism. Talk of faith, of clarity and distinctness – or of any other would-be immediate or noninferential justification or intuition or given – merely obscures the lack of any justification properly so-called. Our beliefs can only be justified relative to the arbitrary starting assumptions of an individual or a community.

Thus there were basically four parties to these disputes: foundationalists, skeptics, fideists, and relativists. These same four continue in various guises to dominate much of the philosophical landscape, in that many philosophers tend to be one or another (often relativists of some sort).

What the four parties shared is far more significant than what divided them. They shared the presupposition that the *structure* of epistemic justification is foundational, despite the fact that many of them rejected foundational*ism* – the view that the starting assumptions *can* be rationally justified, noninferentially. Even the anti-foundationalists remained *structural* foundationalists. After all, they thought, rational method is a matter of inferring propositions from further and better-known propositions. Since this cannot go on to infinity, there must be some starting point, some "foundation," beyond which there is no noncircular inferential justification, no noncircular argumentative recourse. This is the characteristic view of the *structural* foundationalist, who in our day is typically a relativist or a skeptic.

What divides structural foundationalists is what to say about the starting point. According to Descartes and other foundationalists, then and now, there exist criteria that enable us to start with beliefs whose truth, or at least whose probable truth, is known noninferentially – that is, immediately – or is at least believed justifiably, in light not of tradition or authority but of some sort of rational intuition (which for many foundationalists can be quite fallible, but which Descartes construes as "the conception of a clear and attentive mind, which is so easy and distinct that there can be no room for doubt about what we are understanding" [*CSM*, I, 14; *AT*, X, 368]). Not so, say the fideists; the starting point cannot be justified by so-called rational intuition – what Descartes sometimes calls "the light of reason," sometimes "the light of nature" – but only by a nonrational condition of faith. Skeptics and relativists reject both fideism and foundationalism. No starting point is known or even justified, whether by means of faith or the light of reason or anything else; the lack of any noncircular *argumentative* recourse is but the lack of any rational justification properly so-called.

Why have the parties all presupposed, from at least the sixteenth century on, that there must inevitably be starting points beyond which there can be no noncircular argumentative recourse? That is, why have they presupposed that the structure of epistemic justification must be foundational? The reason, in large part, is that they have been influenced, often unwittingly, by a classical argument (from Aristotle's *Posterior Analytics*, bk. I, chap. 3) known today as the regress argument. The regress argument is supposed to show that the structure of epistemic justification must be foundational. Aristotle recognized that if we are to have knowledge of the conclusion of an argument on the basis of its premises, we must know the premises. But if knowledge of a premise always required knowledge of some further proposition, then, in order to know the premise, we would have to know each proposition in an infinite regress of propositions. Since this is impossible, there must be some propositions that are known, but not known by demonstration from further propositions; there must be some basic, nondemonstrable knowledge which grounds the rest of our knowledge. The criterion problem was driven largely by the need to identify basic, nondemonstrable grounds – starting points – and to see whether they can be justified, even though not by inference from anything further. Descartes' internalism, in the form of an appeal to the cogito and to clarity and distinctness, was meant to provide a criterion that would stop the regress of reason-giving with something known immediately and infallibly.

Today most philosophers reject foundationalism – not only Descartes', but the moderate versions as well. *Yet even devout anti-foundationalists tend unwittingly to accept the regress argument, or at least a crucial presupposition of it*, a presupposition that Descartes characteristically adopts as well. As a result, they are *committed to the inevitability of starting points beyond which there is no noncircular argumentative recourse*, no further reason-giving. And this amounts to being committed to the foundational structure of epistemic justification. They reject foundationalism yet remain structural foundationalists – foundationalists despite themselves.

In order to see what the presupposition is – and why, even if it seems a mere technicality, so much flows from it – we must put the regress argument under a microscope (Post 1980, 1992). When we do, we find that it has the form of a reduction to absurdity of the conjunction of five propositions, each of which seems plausible in itself:

1. There are justified beliefs.
2. Every justified belief is justified by inferring it from some justified belief or beliefs.
3. No belief justifies itself.
4. If a belief x justifies a belief y, and y justifies z, then x justifies z.

5. There is no infinite sequence of beliefs each of which is justified by inferring it from its predecessor.

These five propositions jointly entail a contradiction. For (1)–(4) entail the contradictory of (5), namely:

6. There *is* an infinite sequence of beliefs each of which is justified by inferring it from its predecessor.[4]

To escape this absurdity, Aristotle rejects (2): Not every justified belief is justified by inferring it from justified beliefs; some are noninferentially, or immediately, justified. Among these noninferentially justified starting points are some that Aristotle counts further as known; there is nondemonstrable knowledge. Cartesian and other foundationalists likewise reject (2), as do fideists, who insist only that the starting points be certified not by rational intuition but by faith. Skeptics and relativists argue to the contrary that (2) is a necessary principle of any notion of rational justification properly so-called, and that the culprit is proposition (1) – there simply are no nonrelativistically justified beliefs.

None of the four parties rejects proposition (4) – not that they are aware of it – despite the fact that what (4) asserts, namely transitivity of inferential justification, is necessary to derive a contradiction; without the transitivity there is no absurdity (Post 1980, Black 1988). (To see why, assume that W is a possible world in which (a) there are just two beliefs, x and y; (b) x is justified by inferring it from y; and (c) y is justified by inferring it from x. Hence (1) and (2) are true of W. Assume further that (d) neither x nor y justifies itself, so that (3) is true of W. Assuming (d) in addition to (a)–(c) is consistent, because without (4) it does not follow from x's justifying y and y's justifying x that x justifies itself; so too for y. Hence (1)–(3) are true of W. But (6) is false: there are only two beliefs in W, not an infinite sequence of them. So (1)–(3) by themselves do not entail (6); (4) is required.) The regress argument for the inevitability of starting points beyond which there can be no noncircular argumentative recourse presupposes that all the relevant forms of inferential justification are transitive.

The relevant forms *are* all transitive *if* the only inferences we can count on to justify their conclusions are deductive, as Descartes and many others presuppose, at least when it comes to conclusions meant to have philosophical force. Even Descartes allows that outside philosophy some nondeductive forms of inference can be counted on to justify their conclusions, and we shall see that some of these prove to be nontransitive. Nevertheless, Descartes and many other philosophers allow only transitive inferences about the deepest or most basic affairs – the philosophical – thereby remaining structural foundationalists about such deep matters even when they grant nontransitive inference elsewhere. Let us call these philosophers *deep*-structural foundationalists.

Deep-structural foundationalists are not committed to the regress argument for the foundational structure of *all* justification, but only for justification concerning suitably deep matters (the philosophical). In particular, as we will see in detail in §4, the transitivity presupposition lives on in the conventional wisdom that if a categorial framework, conceptual scheme, final vocabulary, or language had a ground, it could only be, absurdly, a ground known noninferentially, or immediately, on pain of regress or circularity. The conventional wisdom is driven by deep-structural foundationalism even while it vilifies foundationalism.

Meanwhile, starting again with Descartes, let us trace some of the other effects of deep-structural foundationalism. The history illustrates how the transitivity presupposition is more fundamental and more tenacious than the presuppositions hitherto targeted so prominently by foundationalism's many critics. Descartes' foundationalism, like all foundationalism, aims to solve the regress problem by reference to starting points either in the cogito or in intuition, the given, sense impressions, ideas, what is presentable in some other epistemically efficacious way to the mind, or in the workings of a Kantian constructive understanding. Many philosophers reject any such foundationalism. But unless they also reject the transitivity presupposition, they will remain committed to the idea that at least with regard to suitably deep matters, the structure of reason-giving is foundational, in that no further noncircular reason-giving is possible. Furthermore, they will remain strongly inclined toward internalist philosophies of mind and language, as we begin to see next.

§3. Foundationalists Despite Themselves

The transitivity presupposition can predetermine one's philosophy by driving a kind of internalist stance, in which something counts as a philosophically relevant reason only if it is graspable by introspection, or at least by a sufficiently attentive phenomenology or analysis of concepts or experience. The transitivity presupposition confines us to the flat plane of how things appear to the attentive mind from its armchair of lived experience.

Why? Largely because of the kinds of reason-giving that the transitivity *excludes*. One of these, as we will see in §5, is abduction, or inference to the best explanatory story. Abductive inference is involved when we say that the fossil record is best explained by, hence supports, the story or theory that later species evolved from simpler ones over aeons. As Darwin said of his own theory, "It can hardly be supposed that a false theory would explain, in so satisfactory a manner as does the theory of natural selection, the several large classes of facts above specified."[5] This form of inference is quite common, not only in the sciences but also in philosophy and ordinary life, as when we explain footprints in the garden, a broken window, a rifled safe, and an empty beer can on the kitchen table by positing an unhurried burglar. In these kinds of cases, x inferentially justifies y in virtue of y's being the best explanation of x (or of the affairs described by x); y provides a better explanatory story – a better understanding – than any competing account. In §5 we will see in detail just why abductive inference is not transitive.

Meanwhile, we may begin to appreciate the philosophical significance of excluding abductive inference by considering Descartes' assumption that we cannot, on pain of circularity, justify our factual belief in an external world by appealing to facts which themselves are objects of such external-world belief. His idea is that our most basic external-world beliefs x – say, the belief that there is a lump of wax in front of me – are what ultimately justify our somewhat less basic external-world beliefs y; these in turn justify our still less basic external-world beliefs z; so if we appealed in turn to these beliefs z to justify our most basic external-world beliefs x, it would follow that our most basic external-world beliefs x justify themselves – a tight little closed circle prohibited by the principle that no beliefs justify themselves (recall proposition (3) in §2). But this follows only if the inferential justification involved is transitive (in order to conclude from "x justifies y," "y justifies z," and "z justifies x" that "x justifies x").

Since it never occurred to Descartes to question this transitivity presupposition, he was forced to break out of the threatened circle, or to try. To this end he argued from his very idea of God to the conclusion that the light of reason or "faculty of knowledge which God has given us can never encompass any object which is not true . . . in so far as it is clearly and distinctly perceived" (*CSM*, I, 203; *AT*, VIII, 16). This latter move landed Descartes in a *further* circle – what we call the Cartesian circle, pointed out by Arnaud and Gassendi – which arises when Descartes relies on clear and distinct ideas to prove the existence of God, and on the existence of God to validate clear and distinct ideas.

But what if Descartes had allowed the use of abductive inference to justify belief in the external world? Then he could have gone "externalist," positing a not directly graspable external world as (part of) the best explanation of certain of our experiences – such as seeming to see a lump of wax here and now – *without landing in circularity*, since circularity would follow only if abductive inference were transitive. True, Descartes is often said to have had a severe problem in justifying belief in an external world only because he required *deductive* inferential justification at this deep philosophical level. *But even if he had allowed some nondeductive inference, the problem would have remained if he had required that such inference be transitive*, as we see next in connection with Hume.

Hume's starting points consist of impressions and relations of ideas; what cannot be justified by admissible inference from these we must "commit . . . to the flames, for it can contain nothing but sophistry and illusion." The admissible kinds of inference, for Hume, are not only deduction, but a simple kind of induction: given that a certain pattern of impressions or experiences (or their putative objects) has occurred under certain conditions in the past, we may infer that this pattern will occur under those conditions in the future. The future, we assume, will resemble the past, and what we may infer from our impressions and ideas, or from the patterns in them, is more of the same (or further patterns in it). For Hume, reason operates only to compare impressions or ideas and make simple inferences from them, leading us to more impressions or ideas. Furthermore, his well-known argument that there is no noncircular justification of induction presupposes that such inference is transitive. Abductive inference to an external explanation or hidden cause or constitution of the uniformity – hidden in the sense that it is not restricted to the flat plane of patterns or structures in more of the same – is excluded, or at least not considered as possibly affording a noncircular justification of simple inductive inference from past patterns to future ones (Lipton 1991, pp. 10–14). Even though Hume allows some nondeductive inference, he too has a severe problem justifying belief in an external world, because the forms of inferential justification he allows are transitive.

Hume's empiricism, like Berkeley's and indeed all traditional empiricism, has trouble transcending the flat plane of experience and ideas to find a world beyond, a world that does not amount just to different patterns in more of the same. This is part of what is involved in Berkeley's claim that nothing but an idea is like an idea. Yet a parallel dilemma confronts any philosophy – phenomenological, linguistic, analytic, or whatever – that requires transitivity of the inferences used to argue for or against the starting points. Such a philosophy may find it impossible to transcend the plane of how things appear from the philosopher's armchair of lived experience or concepts. The reason is that the transitivity requirement blocks any abductive or related inference to what might lie beyond more of the same.

Granted, it is perhaps logically possible that there exists some form of transitive inference which, starting from the flat plane of lived experience and concepts, yields justified belief in something beyond. But until some such form of transitive inference turns up, the transitivity requirement blocks the one familiar, plausible way of transcending the more of the same: namely, abductive inference to the best explanatory story. Thus, in practice, the transitivity requirement leaves no alternative to a phenomenology or analysis of what lies close to us, the flat plane of how things appear to the attentive mind, language included. It constrains the philosopher to concentrate on internal matters about which, supposedly, nothing is hidden – matters of mind, meaning, logic, and value.

It should come as no surprise, then, that Descartes and many of his descendants, under the unwitting, yet self-imposed, restriction of philosophically relevant inference to the transitive, tend to concentrate on the cogito and its structures. For the cogito is accessible to the attentive thinker without abductive or other nontransitive inference to something not more of the same, something that might explain the characteristic structures of the cogito or Cartesian theater.[6] Of course, Descartes invoked what is clearly and distinctly perceived or intuited by the cogito mainly in order to stop the threatened regress of justifications, and thereby to defeat skepticism. But even if such intuition had not been deemed necessary to solve the criterion problem and stop the regress, philosophers deprived of abductive and other nontransitive inference would have had a hard time transcending what lies close to mind, including mind's most vivid intuitions and their seeming self-transparency.

These internalist tendencies, driven by the transitivity requirement, tend to discourage any search for external constraints on the mind's activity; indeed, they may discourage the very idea. External constraints are likely to be found, and belief in them justified, only or largely by means of abductive or related nontransitive inference, since any attempt to justify belief in them by means of transitive inference will be circular. For example, one such external constraint would be a mind-independent world about which some of our beliefs are true; another would be a world in which there are mind-independent samenesses or kinds or universals which our concepts might track. Yet, as we saw in connection with the Cartesian attempt to justify belief in an external world, if the only forms of inferential justification allowed are transitive, any justification of the belief which is not based ultimately on immediately justified or given starting points must be circular. And as we will see in §4, the same is true of belief in real samenesses, kinds, or universals – samenesses, kinds, or universals outside the mind – which could act as constraints on the mind's conceptualizing activities.

Once doubt is cast on external constraints, the obvious place to look for constraints is in the mind itself. Leibniz claimed to find them, or some of them, in rules for constructing experience of space and time, as subsequently in his own way did Kant (though both seem to have been anticipated by Descartes, for whom ideas may function as rules). Under Kant's influence, many later philosophers regard concepts as but rules for organizing experience or for constructing sameness and difference in a world that would not otherwise have them. Leibniz and Kant regarded such rules as necessary, unchanging, and innate, while many of their descendants regard them as contingent, easily changeable, and cultural or historical. We can make them up, and we can decide which ones to adopt. Rules as changeable internal constraints figure importantly in the philosophies of Carnap, the later Wittgenstein, and J. L. Austin and in several philosophies of mathematics (especially formalism and intuitionism). Carnap explicitly required transitivity of reducibility for the purposes of a constructional system, and regarded external questions about the system or framework not as questions of fact, but as practical questions, "a matter of a practical decision concerning the structure of our language" (Carnap 1967, p. 8; Carnap 1952, p. 210). In all these philosophies, the supposed internal constraints are among the starting points.

Other starting points, in various subject matters, have included principles of logic and mathematics, semantic rules, moral rules or imperatives (categorical, hypothetical, prima facie, or whatever), principles of justice and law, fundamental political axioms or ideals ("We hold these truths to be self-evident . . ."), and so on. In each case the dialectic is the same, under structural foundationalism. In each case there must be starting points beyond which there is no further argumentative recourse, no further reason-giving, on pain of circularity.

So too for reason itself: "We cannot so much as *raise the question* of the reliability of reason, or any other of our faculties, without taking the reliability of reason for granted. . . . [O]ne cannot sensibly try to determine whether reason is trustworthy, before relying on it, since one has no recourse but to rely on it in trying to make that determination" (Plantinga 1993, p. 103). This is a foundationalist speaking, but any of the deep-structural foundationalists would say much the same. Like Plantinga, they presuppose that the inferences which we could plausibly use to justify reason, or to warrant its reliability, must be transitive. They differ only on whether the starting point that is reason has some noninferential or immediate justification – as most foundationalists believe – or instead must be taken either on faith or not at all except relative to some language-game or practice of reasoning. Nietzsche saw this, as had Kierkegaard, and concluded not only that "The world appears logical to us because we have made it logical," but that (as William Bluhm puts it in the present volume, p. 327), "On Descartes' assumptions, to embrace reason – as an objective, universal order beyond the self – is an act of faith."

As Bluhm also remarks (p. 327), rightly, "This line of thought opens up the possibility that it is our fiat that creates the world." But of course this possibility opens up earlier, as soon as one concludes that there must be starting points beyond which there is no noncircular argumentative recourse, no further reason-giving. For the conclusion is driven by the transitivity presupposition, and the transitivity presupposition also drives the internalism that leads philosophers to look for the starting points in the cogito, in our understanding or language, or in their structures; and all these appear unconstrained by anything external, hence could be the result of our fiat. Bluhm says in connection with Nietzsche that "The 'Overman' would . . . know that no objective order of the world is given; she would have to create order from her own will." Yes, but it needs to be added that the Overman would "know" this only if the relevant forms of inference by which one might find an objective order, or justify belief in it, are all transitive.

By the same token, order would have to be created from the Overman's own will only if the transitivity presupposition is valid. The reason is that requiring transitivity excludes the one obvious way of going external: namely, abductive inference to the best explanatory story. (Indeed, toward the end of §7 we will see how an abductive inferential justification can be given for the element of reason we call the law of noncontradiction.) Otherwise, deprived of such nontransitive means of reason-giving, the self is left to brood on itself and on what is accessible to a supple phenomenology or analysis of the world-as-seen-from-within. In such a mood – and stimulated further perhaps by Descartes' claim that there is nothing which truly belongs to me except the control of my volitions (*CSM*, I, 384; *AT*, XI 445) – one may be struck by a kind of primacy of the will, according to which it is the will's self-sufficient, self-confident freedom to doubt received theories, concepts, rules, and vocabularies that creates a space, breathing room, in which the will can replace them with something else. The only constraints are genealogical; shatter them, and transvaluation can follow, whereby the new values, like the old, correspond to nothing external, nothing independent of the valuing self. Then there is Rorty: "the only thing we can be certain about is . . . our own desires. . . . The only cosmology we can affirm . . . is our own world picture, our own way of setting things up for manipulation, the way dictated by our desires" (1991, p. 29). We are not to be pushed around by any so-called transcendental universals, truths, or values.

Most of the philosophers mentioned in this section reject Cartesian and other foundationalism, whether by way of rejecting clarity and distinctness, a priori knowledge, certainty, truth-conducive rational justification, essentialism, intuition, ahistorical canons of logic and evidence, philosophy as the mirror of nature, or any metaphysics of presence. Despite these manifold differences, they remain foundationalists – deep-structural foundationalists. For they assume that with regard to philosophically deep matters, there can be no further inferential justification – or critique – on pain of circularity. There must be starting points beyond which there is no further reason-giving. Strip away all the differences of tradition, style, method, language, and emphasis – from Continental to pragmatic to the most obtuse analytic empiricism – and there still remains the shared presupposition that there must be such philosophical starting points. This deep-structural foundationalism is driven by the presupposition that the only philosophically relevant forms of inference are transitive. Moreover, the transitivity presupposition also drives the broadly internalist stance of much modern and postmodern philosophy, according to which nothing is hidden, and the metaphysician's "craving for depth" or theory or explanation is impossible, pointless, or pernicious. There is also a link here with postmodernist painting and architecture, which are distinguished by their "depthlessness" and emphasis on the façade (Jameson 1984). There is a link too with political theories that focus on the surface of political life, not some underlying social contract or other founding principle (Cooper 1993, p. 57). All these are related as well to an irrealism likewise enabled by the transitivity presupposition, as we see next.

§4. Circularity, Transitivity, and God's-Eye Views

Recall the Cartesian argument, presented near the beginning of §3, that we cannot, on pain of circularity, justify our factual belief in an external world by appealing to facts which themselves are objects of such external-world belief. Essentially the same form of argument appears in Wittgenstein, who holds that there can be no noncircular justification or grounding of our factual language. The idea is that the very use of factual language is presupposed by, hence part of what justifies, our most basic factual beliefs; they in turn justify more complex factual beliefs, including any about the relations between language and the world; therefore, if we appealed to the more complex beliefs to justify the very use of factual language (say, on the ground that it conforms to the world), it would follow that the very use of factual language justifies itself – a tight little closed circle. The transitivity presupposed here has the form, "x is part of what justifies y, y justifies x, therefore x is part of what justifies x." Because it never occurred to Wittgenstein to question this presupposition, he reasoned further that because we have no God's-eye view or other immediate justification of factual language, there can be no noncircular justification of it at all.

Rorty merely generalizes this hackneyed form of argument, wittingly or not, in order to conclude that there must be final vocabularies, the factual included, beyond which there is no noncircular argumentative recourse, "only helpless passivity or a resort to force" (Rorty 1989, p. 73). The same dialectic is at work when Kant posits categories of the understanding which can be neither justified nor criticized by appealing to matters themselves understood only through those very categories. Historicize the categories, as do many of Kant's successors, relativize them to forms of life or to methods of warrant or verification, or think of them as grammatical or as Derridian infrastructural matters of difference, and you have the recipe for today's typical irrealist.

All these irrealist philosophers presuppose transitivity of the philosophically relevant forms of inferential justification, as did Descartes and his sixteenth-century predecessors, even when they allow nontransitive forms outside philosophy. For not only do most of them run arguments like the one gleaned above from Wittgenstein. *They all use variations on the "look–see" objection to realism:* Realists could justify their view only by stepping outside language to compare it with reality, looking to see that they fit, rather like comparing a picture with what is pictured by staring at them side by side. And it is indeed true that many traditional realists did imagine some such dubious intuitive vision or mental grasp of word–world fit, some such God's-eye view. But this only shows that they were victims of the same form of argument as lies behind the look–see objection leveled against them. The idea in both cases is as above: were there some inferential justification (or criticism) of word–world fit – some further argumentative recourse – it would give rise to a tight little closed circle; there can be no noncircular inferential justification or criticism at this level of fundamentality. Therefore, if there is to be any justification at all, it must be noninferential – that is to say, by way of some immediate insight into the relation of representation to represented. Look–see. Again, the key presupposition is that the relevant forms of inferential justification are transitive. Like Descartes, the look–see objectors are mired in the sixteenth-century dialectical background.

Thus the transitivity presupposition is intimately involved in arguments to the effect that word–world fit and related matters of representation and meaning could only be known by some look–see method or related non-inferential intuition. That is why I put the presupposition in the meaning-rationalist cluster of views (§1), even though the presupposition figures in a number of other syndromes as well, such as internalism and the suppressed belief that the structure of justification is foundational. Transitivity, by way of the look–see arguments it drives, makes irresistible the idea that there must always be some starting point which, if it can be known at all, can be known only by means of some immediate intuitive grasp, if not a God's-eye view, on pain of circularity. Language is just philosophy's latest candidate for the starting point.

The same dialectic underlies the widespread conviction that, on pain of circularity, "one cannot use a part of one's present theory to underwrite the rest of it" (Rorty 1979, p. 294), or that "our language cannot be divided up into two parts, a part that describes the world 'as it is anyway', and a part that describes our conceptual contribution" (Putnam 1992, p. 123). For suppose we used one part of our language to describe the world "as it is anyway" and another part to describe our conceptual contribution, in order to see whether they match. Since the part we use to describe the world "as it is anyway" must itself include or express at least some of our concepts, we cannot appeal to it in order to justify those concepts, or even to criticize them, on pain of circularity. We must acquiesce in the necessity of having a language or system of concepts that is neither justifiable nor criticizable by appeal to matters themselves understood, if at all, only by means of the self-same language or system. Derrida puts it this way, almost ruefully: "There is no sense in doing without the concepts of metaphysics in order to shake metaphysics. We have no language – no syntax and no lexicon – which is foreign to this history; we can pronounce not a single destructive proposition which has not already had to slip into the form, the logic, and the implicit postulation of precisely what it seeks to contest" (Derrida 1978, pp. 280–281).

To be sure, look–see is not the only objection to realism. There remain further objections, to the effect that realism must be unacceptably essentialist, privileging, totalizing, noumenal, scientistic, reductive, or inimical to freedom. But realism properly so-called entails none of these; irrealists have set up a scarecrow (Post 1987, 1991). Moreover, a number of these further objections to realism prove on examination to rest ultimately on a look–see objection, which rests in turn on the transitivity presupposition.

For example, as Wolterstorff rightly remarks, "Fundamental to contemporary anti-realism is the affirmation of nominalism – that is, of . . . anti-realism with respect to universals outside the mind." The radical, world-making variety of anti-realism "is the resolute spinning out of the implications of nominalism," which has its roots in the medieval view that "natures as grasped by the mind are fundamentally altered from how they are in things" (Wolterstorff 1990, pp. 55, 63). But when we inquire about why we must not think that there are natures or universals outside the mind (or the text), the typical modern – and postmodern – reply is that we could never know or verify that there are any. For in order to know, the reply goes, we would have to adopt the absurd method of taking in one hand some segment of reality and in the other the universals in the mind, and then look to see whether the universals in the mind match anything in reality.

When we inquire further why there is allegedly no alternative to this absurd method of look–see, we encounter the idea that any attempt at an *in*direct or *inferential* justification of belief in real universals must be circular. For suppose we try to describe some segment of reality "as it is in itself," in order to infer, from this description, something about whether reality processed by universals in the mind matches reality "as it is in itself." Obviously, we cannot describe anything at all (say, snow as white) without applying universals in the mind (whiteness-as-grasped-by-us and snow-as-grasped-by-us). So universals in the mind are presupposed by, hence part of what justifies, any description whatsoever, including any would-be description of some segment of reality. Therefore, if we appeal to the latter description to justify the universals in the mind (on the ground that they match real universals), we land in a tight little circle: Universals in the mind are part of what justifies the would-be description of a segment of reality "as it is in itself"; this would-be description justifies the universals in the mind; therefore, the universals in the mind are part of their own justification. (This argument, like Wittgenstein's, has the form "x is part of what justifies y; y justifies x; therefore, x is part of what justifies x".)

It follows, we are told, that no noncircular inferential or argumentative justification is possible here; there is no alternative to a noninferential, immediate, or look–see method of justification for belief in real universals. Since this method is absurd, we can never know or verify whether there are real universals, and it is otiose to suppose there are. "What is hidden is of no interest to us" (Wittgenstein 1958, §126). There is nothing beyond what a sufficiently attentive phenomenology can tell us, and nothing beyond the text; as Heidegger says, "Let things be."

Once more, the alleged circularity follows only if the relevant forms of inferential justification are transitive. It looks as though irrealists share the transitivity presupposition with Descartes, and indeed with all those who have been sold what amount to regress arguments for the inevitability of starting points beyond the pale of noncircular argumentative recourse, which is to be sold into slavery to structural foundationalism. We may be forgiven the impulse to wonder whether they have come to love their chains.

§5. Nontransitive Inference

And yet. . . . What exactly is supposed to be wrong with the principle that if x is part of what justifies y, and y justifies x, then x is part of what justifies x? Consider. By 1820 there was extensive observational and other evidence for Newton's theory of gravitation, T_N. As applied to the known solar system, including recently observed irregularities in the orbit of Uranus, T_N entailed that there is another, unobserved planet X beyond Uranus, and entailed also certain key properties of X's orbit, including its semi-major axis, eccentricity, longitude of perihelion, and such further specifics as

O′. Planet X appears at orbital position p' at clock time t'.

Indeed, in context, T_N justifies O′, and by the 1840s T_N was seriously offered as justification for O′. When astronomers subsequently turned their telescopes to look at p' at t', they observed a planet where it should be, called it Neptune, and thereafter offered O′ as a reason for, hence as part of what justifies T_N. In fact, they regarded O′ as a strong reason for T_N, hence as a strong part of its justification, since O′ involved a novel prediction. Nor did they withdraw their previous offer of T_N as justification for O′. To the contrary, they now regarded O′ as having dual justification, from T_N and from observation. O′ was part of what justified T_N, T_N justified O′, yet O′ did not justify itself even in part. Parallel examples can easily be multiplied, to include the case of the discovery of Pluto, the case of starlight bent by the sun in conformity with general relativity, the case of the positron, and the case of the precession of the perihelion of Mercury (which was already known, so not a novel prediction). All are legitimate cases of non-question-begging mutual support between theory and evidence, and there are parallel cases well outside the sciences. Further, all are cases in which x is part of what justifies y, y justifies x, yet x is not part of its own justification, contrary to the alleged transitivity.

Another form of nontransitive inferential justification involves mathematical probability, as do several varieties of inductive justification. Suppose that x inductively justifies y only if, relative to x, y is probable to a certain high threshold degree, say, to at least 0.8; that is, $P(y/x) \nless 0.8$. Suppose further that y justifies z in the same sense, so that $P(z/y) \nless 0.8$. If transitivity held, x would have to justify z in the same sense, so that $P(z/x) \nless 0.8$. But, given only that $P(y/x) \nless 0.8$ and $P(z/y) \nless 0.8$, it follows only that $P(z/x) \nless P(y/x) \times P(z/y) \nless 0.64$, well below the threshold. Transitivity fails.

Still another nontransitive form is inference to the best explanatory story. Descartes himself was no stranger to abductive inference, being quite willing to posit hidden mechanisms to explain animal or other bodily behaviors. Indeed, in his day he was widely regarded as far too profligate in hypothesizing hidden causes (vortices, for example). But I can find no evidence that he asked himself whether such abductive inference is transitive, and in any case he thought that however valuable abductive inference may be for investigating nature, when it comes to true philosophy, we must use deductive inferential justification. The method of hypothesis, of abduction, of inference to the best explanation, was allowed for the material world, where objects can have a hidden constitution, but not for the mind. This fateful double standard persists to this day, often in linguistic form, as noted in §§3–4.

The point of inference to *the* best explanation is not that we are to infer only *one* explanation of some phenomena, but that we are to infer only one from among the *competing* explanations. Nor is the point that the explanation must always be in terms of some hidden constitution. Typically the same matter can be explained in several different but compatible ways, some of them in terms of a hidden constitution, some not. When I notice that the water I just put on the stove is still not boiling, I may infer that I forgot to turn on the burner, or I may infer that the mean kinetic energy of the water molecules is too low. The latter explanation invokes hidden constitution, the former does not. The two explanations are compatible; neither can be said, in the relevant sense, to be a better explanation than the other of why the water is not boiling. By contrast, an explanation in terms of the burner's not working does compete with the explanation that I forgot to turn it on. Of course, there is no way to tell which is the better explanation given only that the water is not boiling. So I enlarge my data set – I check to see whether the burner is turned on – in order to narrow the field of potential explanations and decide whether to undertake repairs or lament my absent-mindedness. In general, "Given our data and our background beliefs, we infer what would, if true, provide the best of the competing explanations we can generate of those data (so long as the best is good enough for us to make any inference at all)" (Lipton 1991, p. 58).

Now suppose that x justifies y in virtue of y's being the best explanation of x, and y in turn justifies z in virtue of z's being the best explanation of y. If transitivity held, then x would have to justify z in virtue of z's being the best explanation of x, a better explanatory story than any competitor. Three facts block this would-be transitivity. The first is that inference to the best explanation y results at best in y's being probable, to some threshold degree, given what it explains. Those varieties of abductive inference that require some such threshold probability could not be transitive, for the reason given three paragraphs back. The second is that relations of explanation, unlike those not only of deduction but also of reduction and causal and other determination, are not in general transitive; if x explains y and y explains z, it does not follow that x explains z (except in cases of deductive explanations).[7]

The third is that even if explanation were transitive, *best* explanation could not be. Given that y is *the best* explanation of x, as by hypothesis it is, and that z is the best explanation of y, z cannot also be *the best* explanation of x; there can be only one *best* explanation, and y is it. In a little more detail: To say that y is the best explanation of x, in the relevant sense, is to say that of the competing explanations we can generate of x, y is better than any other. Likewise, and again by hypothesis, z is the best explanation of y in the same sense. If transitivity held, z would have to be the best explanation of x in the same sense, meaning that of the competing explanations we can generate of x, z is better than any other. But by hypothesis y is better than any other explanation of x. So transitivity fails.

At this point, irrealists might agree that there are important forms of nontransitive inferential justification yet deny that they are philosophically significant. Where, after all, is the brave new abductive or other inferential justification of realism? Where is the needed inference to the best explanatory story, the needed positive externalist account, which would justify realism without begging any of the crucial questions? Until realists produce some such justification, we are entitled to be skeptical. The remaining sections consider in thumbnail outline how realists might supply the needed externalist account.

§6. Intentionality, Final Cause, and Cartesian Mechanism

It has been some time since philosophers dared to pit their intuitions and analyses against scientific accounts of matter, space, time, the origin of species, the functions of the brain, gender differences, and more. Not only have philosophers frequently proved to be spectacularly wrong about such matters – so have scientists – and not only have they frequently been wrongheaded, from Aristotle on the sexes to those brave souls who dismissed time travel as conceptually impossible, contrary to both the twins effect in special relativity and the possibility of closed, time-like curves in general relativity. In addition, in reaction to this history of lost territories, philosophers have tended to develop an image of themselves and their enterprise as largely independent of whatever the sciences might turn up. The philosopher's exclusive expertise is widely presumed to concern phenomenological and conceptual issues, including, perhaps above all, issues about language and its legitimate uses. The focus is on what can be ascertained by kinds of reflection that have no need to consult the sciences for guidance, let alone correction. Shades of Descartes. Indeed, the results of such reflection are deemed prior to scientific investigation, in a crucial sense – not exactly a priori, meaning prior to all experience, since it is often by a kind of phenomenology or analysis of experience or consciousness or perceived meanings that the philosopher is to proceed, but prior to whatever results the sciences might produce, and not falsifiable by them. It is in this spirit that Wittgenstein says, "Darwin's theory has no more to do with philosophy than any other hypothesis in natural science."[8] Within the exclusive province of philosophy, our intuitions and analyses reign supreme.

But suppose we consider concepts, language, meaning, and logic from the point of view not of how they seem to us on reflection from within, but of how they appear from without, in particular to biological science. By biological science I do *not* mean any of its possibly reductive subdisciplines, such as molecular biology, and certainly not any sociobiology. I mean the nonreductive, holistic biology of historically evolved living organisms in relation to their normal environments and to each other.

Such an approach stands in vivid contrast to the mechanism that Descartes did so much to advance. Indeed, he would have agreed that "Nothing happens in the world without . . . some redistribution of microphysical states" (Quine 1978, p. 25), meaning that all a material thing's traits are determined by the physical dispositions of its own micro-parts. But Quine, shockingly, nonetheless goes on to endorse talk of final causes (Quine 1992, pp. 74–76), whereas much of the point of Descartes' mechanism was to rid us forever of the very idea that material objects – animals and their organs included – could have in themselves any final cause, telos, purpose, or proper function. Variations on this mechanistic theme remain very much alive, not least among physicalists like Quine.

How, then, does Quine reconcile talk of final causes with his physicalism? He says: "Darwin at length settled that matter, reducing final cause in biology to efficient cause through his theory of natural selection" (Quine 1992, p. 75). Alas, Quine does not say how Darwin did this. But Quine probably has something like the following in mind. Consider the heart, if only because Descartes admired Harvey so much for having discovered that the heart is a mechanism that circulates blood, by pumping. Taking Harvey to heart, let us further assume, but this time with the vulgar, that pumping blood is the *proper function* of the heart. To be a heart is to be supposed to pump blood. Why?

According to a leading theory of the matter, the proper function of your heart is to pump blood, because it was by pumping blood that *past* hearts (or enough of them) enabled organisms containing them to survive and reproduce at rates higher than organisms without hearts, this prior successful performance thereby enabling the production of today's hearts, yours included. The trait selected for was one responsible for a mechanism or muscle that pumps, and your own heart has the proper function of pumping blood – what it is supposed to do, but may fail to do – in virtue of being a descendant in a "reproductively established family" of items in which a critical proportion of ancestors performed that function, your heart having been produced in significant part because often enough they did. The proportion of ancestor devices that performed successfully can sometimes be tiny; in this sense, the devices can be quite *un*reliable yet contribute just enough to enhance survival and reproduction. Hardly any of the myriad seeds of the wild fig in its jungle habitat manage to start new trees; the seeds are nearly all consumed by animals or insects or other mishap. Still, wild fig seeds have the function of starting new trees.[9]

This account of proper function is not an *analysis* of a concept; nor is it a bit of phenomenology. It is an abductive biological theory of what proper function is, to the effect that it is an affair in the world, not a projection of our ways of valuing and classifying things, an affair that can be defined in natural-selective terms; the best explanation of proper function is natural-selective.[10] Nor should we be perturbed if the abductive account goes beyond what a careful phenomenology might yield. According to Heidegger, "equipment" is constituted teleologically or functionally, in terms of what it is for, and this "for-the-sake-of-which," or functionality, is incapable of further analysis, hence primary, a starting point. All we can say of functionality is that it is based on "a possibility of Dasein's Being." Even though there are equipmental contexts in nature, the functionality involved is still based on a possibility of the user (where even the user in nature looks like a projection of an aspect of Dasein's being). For Heidegger, then, the functionality, or at least the possibility on which it is based, is a starting point; beyond it there is no further noncircular analysis, not even for a hermeneutic phenomenology. Nothing is hidden here; we should just "let things be." Heidegger is a deep-structural foundationalist, even while he condemns the foundationalist's dream of some look–see or other immediate justification of the starting points.

By contrast, natural-selective abductive accounts do not treat functionality as inexplicable in further terms. Without equating the functionality of a thing either with a possibility of a user or with the thing's causal powers or dispositions or mechanism, such accounts nevertheless place proper function firmly in the efficient causal order, enabling biologists and others to use the notion in their work, as they have all along, but with a clear conscience. Such accounts are congenial even to physicalism, since the matter of what traits are selected for, and which of their effects represent proper functions, is determined ultimately by affairs at the physical level (Sober 1984, pp. 48ff.; Post 1991, pp. 128–129).

Unfortunately, many physicalists believe further that an individual's traits are all determined by the states of *its own* physical parts. For example, "one's understanding of language, one's dispositions to respond, indeed one's very thoughts, cannot differ from one moment to another without some difference, however undetectable, in the states of one's physical organism" (Quine 1986, p. 75). This is why, in translation, "all the objective data [the field linguist] has to go on are the forces that he sees impinging on the native's surfaces and the observable behavior, vocal and otherwise, of the native" (Quine 1960, p. 28). Quine's physicalism is therefore individualist, in the sense that all a thing's higher-level properties are supposed to be determined without remainder by its own lower-level properties (or by those of its parts). And individualism, by §1, is an element of meaning rationalism.

Quine shares this individualist element of meaning rationalism with Descartes and with mechanists generally. For mechanism presupposes individualism. It asserts that given the forces impinging on a thing, purely kinematic dispositions of its parts determine its behavior and dispositions to behave. As Descartes puts it, "machines . . . act . . . only from the disposition of their organs" (35; *CSM*, I, 140; *AT*, VI, 57), and "it is nature which acts in [animals] according to the disposition of their organs" (36; *CSM*, I, 141; *AT*, VI, 59). This focus on kinematic properties of the "organs" or parts of the thing reflects a general principle of Descartes' method, expressed in the *Regulae*, to the effect that we should analyze complex motions into simple ones and reduce the obscure ideas of the senses to the perspicuous ideas of kinematics, the implication being that those not thus reducible, such as the idea of proper function, are to be eliminated.

Individualism was present at the creation of modern science and philosophy and shapes them still. But despite remaining the best approach to many kinds of phenomena, individualism faces severe problems. One is this. Natural-selective theories of proper function have the consequence that an object x's proper function not only is not determined by a mechanism internal to x; it is not determined by the totality of x's physical properties or dispositions or those of its parts. To see why, suppose, for the sake of vividness, that by some cosmic accident a collection of molecules hitherto in random motion were to collide and coalesce into an exact physical duplicate of your heart, down to the last micro-particle.[11] Because the history of the duplicate is wrong – it is not a descendant, not in the family – it would not *be* a heart (it would not be a member of the biological kind 'heart'), even though it would have all the physical powers and dispositions of your heart. What determines whether an object is a member of the biological kind 'heart' is the natural-selective matter of whether the object is a descendant in a reproductively established family of objects in which a critical proportion of ancestors pumped blood. It is not determined by the microphysical states of the object alone, or by the physical structure or dispositions of the particles that compose it, or by any disposition, mechanism, or morphology it may enjoy, but by the relevant natural-selective history.

It follows that if either mechanism or individualism is true, there are no hearts, since to be a heart is to have the proper function of pumping blood, which is determined not by a mechanism or by any individual properties, but by a natural-selective history. So too would there be no eyes, no brains, nor indeed any other natural kinds defined by their function. Mechanism and individualism have some explaining to do.

Now consider the honeybee, and suppose we want to understand the role of bee dances in the life of the hive, which role, biologists theorize, contributed to the evolutionary success of the bees. Careful observation and experiment reveal that the dance is a complex that consists not only of wing beats, steps, and waggles having specific frequencies and orientations, but also of bits of nectar and pollen that adhere to the dancing forager bees and tell the waiting bees about the kind and quality of nectar to expect at a certain distance and direction. That is, dance-complex variations map onto specific combinations of direction, distance, kind, and quantity of nectar, the mapping being a necessary causal factor in the waiting bees' being enabled to find the nectar.[12] This in turn provides significant support for the hypothesis that past dance complexes which did so map were selected for (or rather, the mechanisms which produced them in appropriate conditions, often enough, were selected for, or at least the genotypes responsible for these mechanisms). Granted the hypothesis and given the natural-selective theory of proper function, one of the proper functions of the complexes is to map onto direction, distance, kind, and quantity of nectar.

Note that the bee dances involve a kind of *intentionality* – or proto-intentionality, if you like, but intentionality nonetheless. For traditionally, the intentional is what is *supposed* to stand in relation to something else – something which it *intends* or *means* or is *about* or is *meant* to do – even if that something else does not exist or never happens.[13] The bee dance complex displays intentionality in this sense. An aspect of the dance, in virtue of a natural-selective history, has the proper function of standing in relation to something else – say, peach-blossom nectar at a certain location; it is *supposed* to stand in this relation even if somehow the nectar happens not to be peach blossom or not to exist there. The same can be said of indefinitely many other signing behaviors – say, the call that vervet monkeys use for cobras, their call for eagles, and so on.

To be sure, animal signing behaviors, systematic and articulate though some may be, are a long way from language, and their intentionality is a long way from characteristically human intentionality. But it is hardly a new thought that human abilities all have ample anticipations in the pre-human. Why not intentionality and language, and in particular how certain aspects of language seem to be determinately about or map onto affairs in the world? Irrealists and internalists must stop this entering wedge from biology if they want to preserve their characteristic ideas about language and avoid another lost territory. This is not at all easy to do, as we will see next.

§7. Knowledge of Meaning, Universals, and Logic: Descartes of the Bees

Imagine a Descartes of the bees, reflecting on the meanings of bee dances. Descartes of the bees concludes: "When understanding what I dance, I can express nothing in bee dances without that very fact making it certain that I possess the idea of that which these dances signify." When we bees are adequately reflective, not distracted by the senses or the imagination, we cannot be fundamentally mistaken about what a bee dance signifies. A dance which on considered reflection we take to be about peach-blossom nectar just is about peach-blossom nectar. Peach-blossom nectar is what the dance is supposed to map onto, and we bees cannot be mistaken about this even if we can be mistaken as to whether peach-blossom nectar exists.

From a human vantage point – abductive, external, informed by biology – we can tell where Descartes of the bees goes wrong. We can tell that what a given bee dance means, in the sense of what it is supposed to map onto, is determined by affairs in a natural-selective history, which affairs lie well beyond anything present here and now to Descartes of the bees. Indeed, they lie beyond the present bee dance practices of the whole hive and explain them. Unless the relation between a given bee dance and the appropriate natural-selective history is itself internal to the bee mind, what determines the meaning is not knowable by reflection on what is given in present experience, and not knowable by reflection even on present practices or on the intuitions of competent bee dancers. Knowledge of what a given bee dance means, in the relevant sense, is knowledge of what it is supposed to map onto, which is knowledge of its proper function, which is a matter of a natural-selective history of relations to a wider environment. So too for sameness and difference of meaning. Such matters can be known only fallibly and by way of inference to the best explanatory story – in the case of the bees, by way of the abductive biological story just sketched. Meaning has a "hidden constitution" – not mechanistic, but natural-selective and ecological.

By contrast, note how "internalist" Descartes of the bees is, in the sense of believing that bee dance meanings and sameness and difference of meaning and the nature of meaning are all knowable ultimately on the basis of how things seem to philosopher bees reflecting from their armchairs on perceived meanings, intuitions, and phenomenologically accessible rules of usage. Such internalism is the characteristic stance of phenomenology, conceptual analysis, ordinary-language philosophy, and more. It is at the heart of Wittgenstein's remark that "we may not advance any kind of theory. There must not be anything hypothetical in our considerations. We must do away with all *explanation*, and description alone must take its place.... The problems are solved, not by giving new information, but by arranging what we have always known" (Wittgenstein 1958, §109). Nothing is hidden. Not only is there no need for explanation, hence of inference to the best explanation; invoking such inference betrays failure to understand the problems.

Is that so? Imagine a Wittgenstein of the bees, whose method is a bee dance linguistic phenomenology in which philosopher bees are to investigate *what it makes sense to dance*; phenomenology is grammar (cf. Noë 1994, p. 20; Pears 1988, p. 455). What it makes sense to dance is a matter of what we would dance in light of our intuitions as competent dancers. If we bees want to get clear about what can sensibly be danced, and why, we should investigate our bee dance practice, not the phenomena external to it. "Grammar is not indebted to reality. Grammatical rules first determine meaning (constitute it) and are therefore not responsible to any meaning and are to that extent arbitrary." [14] The grammar is not imposed on us bees by reality or by any superior necessity, but by ourselves in our freedom. We cannot use bee-dances to describe a preexisting situation and show that it forces us to adopt a particular rule, since to do so would require us to use bee dances to get outside bee dances.

Wittgenstein of the bees not only gets it wrong. Given his internalist stance, he is bound to do so. We humans, from our biology-informed viewpoint external to the bees, can understand that the bee dance grammar is indebted to reality, even imposed by reality, in the sense that the rules, including the mapping rules, are not only determined by external affairs in a history but are determined in such a way that the received mappings are what enabled the bees to adapt their activities to affairs in the world beyond the veil of bee dances. The grammatical rules are not arbitrary but designed for a world that has certain fundamental preexisting features, including distance and direction and the nectar's being peach blossom or apple but not both. We can also understand, from our biological viewpoint, that bee philosophers of meaning who reject theory, hidden constitution, and abductive inference are unlikely so much as to guess what their situation is. And thanks to our explorations in §§2–4 of the regress and look–see arguments, we understand how the transitivity presupposition lies behind the insistence by Wittgenstein of the bees that we cannot use bee dances to get outside bee dances.

Ah, says the irrealist, these alleged preexisting features you speak of and this so-called reality *are* such only according to the categorizations of the sign system or language *we humans* employ when we do biology. How do we humans get outside *our* sign system? However it may go with the bees, when it comes to *language*, there is no outside, *no higher viewpoint.* In order to apply to ourselves the moral of the bee dance case, we would have to use language to describe the so-called preexisting affairs to which our language allegedly evolved to adapt us. Yet we cannot possibly justify our descriptive or factual language by appealing to facts which can only be stated in it. It makes no sense to say that our concepts answer to a ready-made world. Categories and concepts are but rules for introducing sameness and difference into a world that would not otherwise have them.

No higher viewpoint? This move, like so much of Western philosophy, exalts human being over the rest of nature. *Other* animals' sign systems conform to rules imposed by natural-selective pressures to adapt to a pre-existing reality, a ready-made world. *Ours* does not. Other animals' categories and concepts track samenesses that exist independently of their sign systems. Ours do not. For it is only relative to language that it makes sense to say that these very samenesses are there for the animals' categories and concepts to track. Indeed, it is only relative to language that it makes sense to say that there are the samenesses we call the animals. If there is no ready-made world, then there are no ready-made spotted owls. Quine's indeterminacy theses imply much the same, and they shape the irrealisms of Davidson, Putnam, and Rorty. It seems that we are to replace the despised God's-eye view, so called, with a world-making demigod.

This irrealist privileging of human being follows from an internalist account applied to us, combined with an externalist account applied to animals. We are not so very far from Descartes on "thoughtless brutes." The resulting picture, modulated by historicist and linguistic transformations of Kantian themes, is one of a free play of sameness-creating categories and concepts for humans and sameness-imposed categories and concepts for all other creatures; conceptual relativism for us, realism for them; world-making for us, a ready-made world for them – indeed, for them a world made by us. Putnam lets the cat out of the bag when he says, "Kant's Copernican revolution means we are in charge." There may be no more revealing a remark in all of modern and postmodern philosophy.

Because the privileging is furthered by the internalism, one suspects that it is a big part of what motivates the internalism. It may also be a big part of what motivates meaning rationalism, as we learned to call it in §1. Virtually all the elements in the meaning-rationalist cluster figure in one or another of the arguments on behalf of the irrealism that privileges human being. Among the premises of these arguments, as we have seen, is the assumption that knowledge of meaning, or at least of the nature of meaning, is a kind of armchair knowledge, certainly not the result of abductive inference to a hidden biological constitution. Included also are individualism, internalism, and the transitivity of inferential justification. The latter enters with the claim that however it may go with the bees, for us there is no outside, no higher viewpoint, since we cannot possibly justify our factual language by appealing to facts which can only be stated in it. One suspects that the meaning-rationalist cluster, together with the irrealism it drives, amounts to special pleading for the point of view of our species. Irrealism means that we are in charge.

Of course, it is a long way from bee dances to human language, and the full story of how to get there is too long to tell here.[15] In outline, this is how it goes. For some time, evidence has been accumulating that "the ability to use a natural language belongs more to the study of human biology than human culture. It is a topic like echolocation in bats or stereopsis in monkeys, not like writing or the wheel. . . . Language has been shaped by natural selection."[16] Some of the evidence testifies to the now uncontroversial existence of substantive linguistic universals – the building blocks of grammar that all theories of universal grammar posit. These include major lexical and phrasal categories, phrase-structure rules, rules of linear order, anaphoric elements, and mechanisms of complementation. Further, every language employs sentences that at a deep level are subject–predicate in form and subject to negation. This is just one way in which the specific expressive abilities of a language turn out to form a well-defined set that persists through enormous surface diversity. There is, in addition, strong evidence for an extensive genetic component in one's grammatical ability, including documented genetically transmitted syndromes of grammatical defects.

Nor is it plausible any longer to believe that "Human language is an embarrassment for evolutionary theory because it is vastly more powerful than one can account for in terms of selective fitness" (Premack 1985, pp. 281–282). Our species has been characterized from its origins by toolmaking, by complex social relations essential for cooperation, and by a folk biology of stunning sophistication. The effectiveness of all these is enormously amplified by language. "Devices designed for communicating precise information about time, space, predicate–argument relations, restrictive modification, and modality . . . [plus] socially relevant abstract information such as . . . beliefs, desires, tendencies, obligations, truths . . . hypotheticals, and counterfactuals" are hardly wasted efforts for a hunter–gatherer organism so deeply dependent on complex social relations, tool-using, and more. Recursion is especially useful, allowing its user to "specify reference to an object to an arbitrarily fine level of precision" and to express beliefs about the intentional states of others (Pinker and Bloom 1992, pp. 482–483).

Furthermore, many organisms are designed to be highly plastic in their behaviors and their learning. They can acquire biological purposes – things they are supposed to do – "that are peculiar to them as individuals, tailored to their own peculiar circumstances and histories" (Millikan 1993, p. 226).

For example, upon becoming ill within a few hours of eating a specific substance, rats will thereafter shun anything that tastes the same.[17] In doing so, they conform to "the proximal rat rule": "Don't eat what tastes like the stuff you had when you got sick." Conforming to this rule is a means of conforming to a more distal rule, perhaps: "Don't eat poisonous substances." Now suppose a rat becomes ill after eating the children's silly putty, a substance rats have encountered nowhere in their evolutionary history. In order to conform to the proximal rat rule, the rat must now conform to a further proximal rule: "Don't eat what tastes like silly putty." This is a *derived* rule, in the sense that it follows logically from the conjunction of the rule "Don't eat what tastes like the stuff you had when you got sick" with "The stuff you had when you got sick tastes like silly putty." The rat conforms immediately to the new rule, with ease, in order to adapt to something new under the sun.

Thus it looks as though many of our sentences, like bee dances, have among their functions certain biological functions or purposes; and novel sentences – sentences never produced before – have derived functions. The sentences produced, say, by a Pleistocene hunter–gatherer scout on returning to the band, including sentences never produced before, have the purpose or function of "adapting" the listeners to certain world affairs or conditions, such as food or shelter over the horizon. This enables the listeners to pursue their purposes in line with just those conditions, thus enhancing their chances of success. The sentences perform this function by virtue of mapping onto certain affairs in conformity with certain mapping rules. The mapping rules, not unlike those for bee dances, are rules in conformity to which "a critical mass of sentences have mapped onto affairs in the world in the past, thus producing correlation patterns between certain kinds of configurations of sentence elements and certain kinds of configurations in the world" (Millikan 1984, p. 99). The correlation patterns enable the listeners to adapt their activity to the configuration or world affair thus mapped.

Granted all this, consider the deep-structure subject–predicate form of sentences whose function is to map affairs in the world. The form appears to track a structure of the world in which language evolved, much as the syntax of bee dances conforms to a structure of sameness and difference, found not made, in the environments in which they evolved. The subject–predicate form tracks substances instantiating universals from among ranges of naturally admissible universals, where the substances instantiate no two universals that are contrary to each other in this world as a matter of natural law (ibid., pp. 239–296). Further, assume that a sentence which contains a negation – say, "Snow is not green" – maps not the absence of a world affair but the presence of a contrary affair (snow's being some other color, say white). Then the law of noncontradiction "reflects a thoroughly natural structural principle rather than an a priori metaphysical or rational principle, or the workings of our language . . . or . . . of a constructive Kantian understanding" (ibid., p. 257; see also pp. 221–229, 297–310).

Thus, knowledge of the law of noncontradiction and of the kind of natural necessity and possibility involved is a posteriori natural knowledge enabled by abductive inference. So too is knowledge of logic, insofar as it is to be a science of the relations among concepts that track samenesses in the world, rather than an abstract a priori science (ibid., p. 273). The world appears logical to us not because we have made it logical, but because in the relevant sense it is. To insist on the contrary would be as ludicrously self-important as a Nietzsche of the bees insisting that the world appears logical because bee dance grammar has made it logical.

The considerations advanced here are unlikely to persuade the skeptical; nor is that my intent. The point, rather, is to bring to light the deep-structural foundationalism that owes so much to Descartes and to disturb the slumber of those in thrall to the internalism and irrealism driven by this unacknowledged foundationalism and by the fallacious transitivity presupposition that underlies it.

NOTES

1. Putnam 1983 uses the phrase "ready-made world" to put down what he thinks the world must look like to the realist. I use "irrealism" to cover the view that the dispute between realists and their opponents is senseless, as well as the view that realism is just plain false. Realism about a class of affairs is the view that such affairs exist and have various features independently of our evidence, theories, conceptual schemes, language, and the like.

2. Following Millikan 1984, though here I use the phrase more broadly than she does.

3. Cf. Popkin 1979 on the predominant role of skepticism in the sixteenth and seventeenth centuries and the impact of the revived texts of Sextus Empiricus in generating the *crise pyrrhonienne.*

4. Why (1)–(4) entail (6) may be left as an exercise for the reader, or one may consult Black 1988.

5. Darwin [1859] 1962, p. 476. See Lipton 1991 for an accessible account of abductive inference and a solid defense of it against recent criticism.

6. Dennett's *Consciousness Explained* (1991) is one long series of inferences to the best explanatory story of why the lived features of the Cartesian theater are as they are, in terms of a "hidden constitution" that is not just patterns or structures in more of the same.

7. Cf. Post, forthcoming *a*, §3, on the nontransitivity in particular of explanations mediated by inter-level theories (e.g., explanations of some biological affairs in terms of properties of large molecules, via the inter-level theory we call molecular biology).

8. Wittgenstein 1961, §4.1122. He retains the theme in the *Investigations* (Wittgenstein 1958, pt. II, §xii). Cf. Pears 1988, pp. 450–459.

9. The detailed theory of proper function underlying this sketch, as well as the definition of "reproductively established family," occurs in Millikan 1984, pp. 17–49, and Millikan 1993, *passim.* Millikan develops the theory independently of, and improves on, the account in Wright 1976 endorsed by Salmon 1990, pp. 32, 111–115. Millikan's account, like Wright's, differs significantly from the propensity theory of Bigelow and Pargetter (1987), hence escapes its difficulties; cf. Millikan 1993, p. 39. For some further replies to objections, see Post 1995, §3; Post 1996, §4; Post, forthcoming *b*.

10. Post 1996, §4.3. Plantinga 1993, pp. 201–204, badly misconstrues Millikan 1984 as an attempt at an *analysis* (and confuses proper function with *direct* proper functions, which are the topic of Millikan's chap. 1; he seems scarcely to have read chap. 2 about *adapted* and *derived* functions).

11. Millikan 1984, p. 93, who presses the example against Quine.

12. Kirchner and Towne 1994 provide an accessible introduction with references. None of this is to suggest that the bee dances form a *language.* See Millikan 1984, pp. 40ff., 96–97; Wenner 1990.

13. See Millikan 1984, p. 95, and *passim* for a comprehensive account of intentionality and of why it need not entail consciousness.

14. Quoted in translation by Noë 1994, p. 23, from Wittgenstein's "Big Typescript" and *Philosophical Grammar.*

15. See above all Millikan 1984, 1993, and the excellent critical survey by Pinker and Bloom 1992.

16. Pinker and Bloom 1992, pp. 451–452, from whom I draw much of this paragraph and the next.

17. The example is from Millikan 1993, pp. 224–228.

REFERENCES

Bigelow, John, and Pargetter, Robert. 1987. Functions. *Journal of Philosophy* 84: 181–196.

Black, O. 1988. Infinite Regresses of Justification. *International Philosophical Quarterly* 28: 421–437.

Carnap, Rudolf. 1952. Empiricism, Semantics, and Ontology. In *Semantics and the Philosophy of Language*, ed. Leonard Linsky, p. 208–228. Urbana: University of Illinois Press.

———. 1967. *The Logical Structure of the World*, trans. R. A. George. Berkeley: University of California Press.

Cooper, David E. 1993. Postmodernism and "The End of Philosophy." *International Journal of Philosophical Studies* 1: 49–59.

Darwin, Charles. [1859] 1962. *The Origin of Species.* New York: Collier.

Derrida, Jacques. 1978. Structure, Sign, and Play in the Discourse of the Human Sciences. In *Writing and Difference*, trans. Alan Bass, pp. 278–293. Chicago: University of Chicago Press.

Husserl, Edmund. [1913] 1962. *Ideas: General Introduction to Pure Phenomenology*, trans. W. R. Boyce Gibson. New York: Collier.

Jameson, Frederic. 1984. Postmodernism, or the Cultural Logic of Late Capitalism. *New Left Review* 146: 54–92.

Kenny, Anthony. 1970. *Descartes: Philosophical Letters*, trans. and ed. Anthony Kenny. Oxford: Clarendon Press.

Kirchner, Wolfgang H., and Towne, William F. 1994. The Sensory Basis of the Honeybee's Dance Language. *Scientific American* 270: 74–80.

Lipton, Peter. 1991. *Inference to the Best Explanation.* London: Routledge.

Millikan, Ruth Garrett. 1984. *Language, Thought and Other Biological Categories.* Cambridge, Mass.: MIT Press.

———. 1993. *White Queen Psychology and Other Essays for Alice.* Cambridge, Mass.: MIT Press.

Nietzsche, F. W. [1901] 1968. *The Will to Power*, trans. Walter Kaufmann and R. J. Hollingdale. New York: Vintage Press.

Noë, Robert A. 1994. Wittgenstein, Phenomenology and What It Makes Sense to Say. *Philosophy and Phenomenological Research* 54: 1–42.

Pears, David. 1988. *The False Prison: A Study of the Development of Wittgenstein's Philosophy.* Oxford: Clarendon Press.

Pinker, Steven, and Bloom, Paul. 1992. "Natural Language and Natural Selection. In *The Adapted Mind: Evolutionary Psychology and the Generation of Culture*, ed. Jerome H. Barker, Leda Cosmides, and John Tooby, pp. 451–493. Oxford: Oxford University Press.

Plantinga, Alvin. 1993. *Warrant: The Current Debate.* Oxford: Oxford University Press.

Popkin, Richard H. 1951. Hume and Kierkegaard. *Journal of Religion* 31: 274–281.

———. 1959. Kierkegaard and Scepticism. *Algemeen Nederlands Tijdschrift voor Wijsbegeerte en Psychologie* 51: 123–141.

———. 1979. *The History of Scepticism from Erasmus to Spinoza.* Berkeley: University of California Press.

Post, John F. 1980. Infinite Regresses of Justification and of Explanation. *Philosophical Studies* 38: 31–52.

———. 1987. *The Faces of Existence: An Essay in Nonreductive Metaphysics.* Ithaca: Cornell University Press.

———. 1991. *Metaphysics: A Contemporary Introduction.* New York: Paragon House.

———. 1992. The Infinite Regress Argument. In *A Companion to Epistemology*, ed. Jonathan Dancy and Ernest Sosa, pp. 209–212. Oxford: Blackwell.

———. 1995. "Global" Supervenient Determination: Too Permissive? In *Essays on Supervenience*, ed. A. Savellos and U. Yalcin, pp. 73–100. Cambridge: Cambridge University Press.

———. 1996. Post-Quinean Philosophical Investigations. In *Quine and Wittgenstein*, ed. Robert Arrington and Hans-Johann Glock. London: Routledge.

———. Forthcoming *a*. Versus Asymmetric Supervenient Determination.

———. Forthcoming *b*. Putnam, Counterfactuals and Proper Function.

Premack, David. 1985. "Gavagai!" or the Future History of the Animal Language Controversy. *Cognition* 19: 207–296.

Putnam, Hilary. 1981. *Reason, Truth and History.* Cambridge: Cambridge University Press.

———. 1983. Why There Isn't a Ready-Made World. In *Philosophical Papers*, vol. 3: *Realism and Reason*, pp. 205–228. Cambridge: Cambridge University Press.

———. 1992. *Renewing Philosophy.* Cambridge, Mass.: Harvard University Press.

Quine, W. V. 1960. *Word and Object.* Cambridge, Mass.: MIT Press.

———. 1978. Goodman's *Ways of Worldmaking. New York Review of Books* 25: 25.

———. 1986. Reply to William P. Alston. In *The Philosophy of W. V. Quine*, ed. L. E. Hahn and P. A. Schilpp, pp. 73–75. La Salle, Ill.: Open Court.

———. 1992. *Pursuit of Truth* rev. ed. Cambridge, Mass.: Harvard University Press.

Rorty, Richard. 1979. *Philosophy and the Mirror of Nature.* Princeton: Princeton University Press.

———. 1989. *Contingency, Irony, and Solidarity.* Cambridge: Cambridge University Press.

———. 1991. *Essays on Heidegger and Others*. Cambridge: Cambridge University Press.

Salmon, Wesley C. 1990. *Four Decades of Scientific Explanation*. Minneapolis: University of Minnesota Press.

Sober, Elliott. 1984. *The Nature of Selection: Evolutionary Theory in Philosophical Focus*. Cambridge, Mass.: MIT Press.

Wenner, Adrian. 1990. *Anatomy of a Controversy: The Question of "Language" among the Bees*. New York: Columbia University Press.

Wittgenstein, Ludwig. 1958. *Philosophical Investigations*, trans. G. E. M. Anscombe, 3d edn. New York: Macmillan.

———. 1961. *Tractatus Logico-Philosophicus*, trans. D. F. Pears and B. McGuinness. London: Routledge.

Wolterstorff, Nicholas. 1990. Realism vs. Anti-Realism. In *Reality in Focus: Contemporary Readings in Metaphysics*, ed. Paul K. Moser, pp. 50–64. Englewood Cliffs, N.J.: Prentice-Hall.

Wright, Larry. 1976. *Teleological Explanations*. Berkeley: University of California Press.

Essay 5
Physics and Mathematics

LOU MASSA

Aristotle explained the differences in the things he observed by inferring that things of a kind have distinctive causal powers. The system of these powers was called an *essence* or *substantial form*. Goats are different from sheep, air from water. Descartes acknowledged these differences but explained them differently. They are, he said, the diverse, local expressions of a single substance: namely, the extension that we call *matter*. Each particular – the things described by Aristotle as *primary substances* – is a region or mode of extension, and each differs from the others because of its size or shape or motion. The qualitative differences that we observe are the myriad expressions of these few variables.

Galileo was already experimenting with telescopes and inclined planes when Descartes' formulation raised the stakes. The physical universe, Descartes alleged, is a single, mechanical system having an intrinsic geometrical form. He proposed the use of an algebraicized geometry (his analytic geometry) to represent all its relations and trajectories. Physics is mechanics. A mathematical physics would be the ideal representation (ideal because perspicuous, concise, and accurate) of every configuration and change that may occur in nature.

The implications of this hypothesis have rumbled through science and the popular imagination for nearly four hundred years. Descartes would have us believe that everything in the material world – the evolution of the universe, as much as the design of hearts and eyes – can be studied and explained mechanically. This assumption transforms our ordinary lives. For we are practical people. Wanting to secure and satisfy ourselves, we do it better by understanding the mechanical, mathematical character of the place we occupy. Where something is broken, we fix it. Where nature defies our interests, we intervene, using mechanical principles like the ones that already apply within these systems (e.g., as vision is corrected by measuring its deficit and making lenses).

Descartes' ideas about universal mechanism, nature's mathematical form, and the hypothetical method organize his *Dioptrics*, *Geometry*, *Me-*

teors (published with the *Discourse on the Method*), and his treatises on physiology. These essays show Descartes practising science as we do today. Given some phenomenon, he infers to its conditions, including its structure, parts, causes, or laws. Tentatively identifying a condition, he predicts, then looks for, its effects. And always there is the idea that matter has a geometrical form, so explanations would be exhaustive and exact if there were mathematical representations for the relevant variables and their effects. This hypothetical method is plainly opposed to the emphasis on intuition and a priori truth in the *Rules*. Descartes demanded certainty of self-knowledge and geometrical proof. He settled for empirically confirmed hypotheses when the topic was nature.

Readers may object that I make too much of Descartes' affinities with the science of our time. The objection is not unreasonable. Both the generalities and details of his mechanics are different from ours in many respects. We have ample experience with the hypothetical method and numerous books describing it. Descartes was naive by comparison. Nevertheless, few working scientists would dispute his universal mechanics (everything is constituted of physical properties only, every change is explained by alterations in the properties or relations of things in motion), his use of mathematics (often more programmatic than real), and his commitment to hypothesis and experiment.

These were the postulates of Descartes' scientific program from the time he met Isaac Beekman in 1618 until he heard of Galileo's censure in 1633. Before, Descartes accepted Beekman's proposal that things move in straight lines unless or until they are stopped by opposition from other things. Before, nature was assumed to be a self-sufficient machine, at least from the time when God made it. Now, God becomes the centerpiece of Descartes' physics. God is said to be the cause and sustainer of all motion, so that no material thing has any efficacy of its own. Other natural philosophers – Newton is a principal example – also emphasized God's role in nature; but for them, God is a background condition (i.e., the sustainer of an order and processes that may be described without reference to him). Descartes' God is immanent in nature as its only efficient cause. This is not only a general claim about God's efficacy, but one that Descartes also makes specific: the laws of motion formulated in the *Principles of Philosophy* require God's active participation in nature.[1]

This new role is critical for understanding the theological aspect of Descartes' physics, but not for appraising the science that he conceived after his discussions with Beekman. Descartes' most fruitful ideas, from the perspective of his scientific successors, are those he formulated (though had not yet published) before he was frightened by the Inquisition. Those claims – about mathematics, matter, motion, and mechanics – are the ones that I shall be reviewing. My survey of Descartes' legacy comes after some remarks about his specific contributions to mathematics, optics, and mechanics.

Analytic Geometry

Analytic geometry is an essential mathematical tool for practically every physical scientist. Descartes invented it. The essence of his discovery is the one-to-one correspondence between a plane curve and an equation involving coordinates in the plane. The equation holds at every point on the curve and expresses its every property. A well-defined curve implies the existence of a well-defined equation, and, equally, a well-defined equation implies the existence of a well-defined curve. Curves constructible by straight edge and compass were the only ones acceptable to Greek mathematics and science, because they were the only ones whose existence was assured. This was a crippling deficiency, one that was not repaired until analytic geometry "filled the page" with an infinity of acceptable curves. These are the mathematical shapes and trajectories required to describe the material world.

Descartes' invention was anticipated in his early years when he built a mechanical compass that delivers mean proportions. The limbs of the compass prefigure the x and y axes of a Cartesian coordinate system. Figure 1 shows such a compass constructed of two straight lines hinged at their origin, Y. The upper limb of the compass has points B, D, F, . . . through which perpendicular lines pass down to the lower limb at points C, E, G. . . . The points D, B, F, . . . and C, E, G, . . . may slide along the limbs to which they are attached. They are mechanically interconnected so that, as the compass opens, C pushes D along, E pushes F along, and so forth. For any given opening, one has, by similar triangles,

$$\frac{B}{C} = \frac{C}{D} = \frac{D}{E} = \frac{E}{F}. \tag{1}$$

This defines the relationship of mean proportionals. The mean proportional is that value of C which satisfies the above equation, given B and D. It may be read quantitatively as a distance taken along the limbs of the compass.

Descartes' compass enabled him to solve the legendary problem of doubling the cube. This problem is said to have been suggested by an oracle at Delos who asked what dimensions a cubic altar would have if its volume

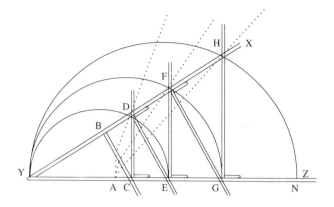

Figure 1. Descartes' mechanical compass. From Descartes [1637], 1954, p. 46.

were doubled. It was known to Hippocrates of Chios in the fourth century B.C. that the problem was solvable if two mean proportionals could be found between a, one side of the cube, and $2a$. This task may be expressed as an equation to solve:

$$\frac{a}{x} = \frac{x}{y} = \frac{y}{2a}. \tag{2}$$

It is assumed that a is known. We want to know the values of x and y. For in such a case,

$$\frac{a^3}{x^3} = \frac{a}{x} \cdot \frac{x}{y} \cdot \frac{y}{2a} = \frac{1}{2}. \tag{3}$$

It follows that

$$x^3 = 2a^3. \tag{4}$$

That is, a cube of side x doubles one of side a. Descartes determines values for x and y by sliding B to distance a and opening the compass until E is pushed along to distance $2a$. He then reads the value of x off the compass. This satisfies the oracle's command by delivering mechanically a side length x of a cube whose volume is exactly twice that of any given cube of side length a. An ancient problem was thus elegantly solved.

Descartes argued, correctly, that his mechanical compass assures the existence of more complicated curves, just as the compass of the Greeks supports the existence of circles. Suppose that pens are placed at positions B, D, F. . . . Then, as the compass is opened, the pens trace curves B, D,

F, . . . Curve B is a circle, but curves D, F, . . . correspond to algebraic equations of increasingly higher order. Accordingly, Descartes is able to construct both the circular curves of Greek mathematics and the more richly variegated curves of analytic geometry. Science could represent and explain the generation of curves more complicated than those constructed by a straight edge and a compass. Equally critical for science was the fact that algebraic equations came to be associated with the curves of the mechanical compass, so that in time *constructibility was replaced altogether as a criterion of existence*. Thereafter, *an algebraic equation was sufficient to ensure the existence of its companion curve*. Here is some confirming detail.

The algebraic equations that Descartes assigned to the pen points of his mechanical compass may be obtained as follows. First, consider pen point D, for which

$$x_D^2 + y_D^2 = R_D^2, \tag{5}$$

where the subscripts refer to a given pen point whose distance from the compass origin is R, with orthogonal Cartesian coordinates x and y. The mechanical compass is constructed to deliver the mean proportional relation

$$\frac{R_B}{x_D} = \frac{x_D}{R_D}, \tag{6}$$

which, solved for R_D, gives

$$R_D = \frac{x_D^2}{R_B}. \tag{7}$$

Substituting this value of R_D into equation 5 yields

$$x_D^4 = R_B^2(x_D^2 + y_D^2). \tag{8}$$

Or, dropping the subscripts, we have

$$x^4 = R^2(x^2 + y^2), \tag{9}$$

a fourth-order equation for the locus of points drawn by pen point D. By analogous reasoning, the curve drawn by pen point F is

$$x^8 = R^2(x^2 + y^2)^3. \tag{10}$$

By pen point H, it is

$$x^{12} = R^2(x^2 + y^2)^5, \tag{11}$$

and so forth.

These equations make the points argued above: that Descartes' mechanical compass was a machine for constructing mean proportionals and for drawing an infinity of curves, many of them more complex than those drawn by the Greeks. Each curve could be specified by an algebraic equation representing a mean proportional relation inherent in the compass. There is, conversely, a curve for every algebraic equation.

Descartes' mechanical compass could also be used for solving equations; for example,

$$x^3 - x = c. \tag{12}$$

Let point B in figure 1 be unit distance from the origin and C be distance x, so that

$$\frac{1}{x} = \frac{x}{x^2} = \frac{x^2}{x^3} \cdots \tag{13}$$

The Cartesian compass requires by construction,

$$\frac{1}{x} = \frac{x}{R_D}. \tag{14}$$

Thus, one has

$$R_D = x^2, \tag{15}$$

and similarly

$$R_F = x^3, \tag{16}$$

etc. Simply opening the compass until

$$x^3 - x = c \tag{17}$$

allows the solution x to be read off the compass as a distance.

Descartes' scholarly friends sometimes asked him to demonstrate his compass by drawing curves. These demonstrations were the high-tech graphics of their day, probably because the machinery of the compass added to the palpability of the lines drawn. It has less effect on us, because we believe so thoroughly in the power of equations.

Now put aside the compass to consider the modern Cartesian coordinate system which evolved from it. We start by drawing x and y coordinates, vertical and horizontal lines that intersect at right angles (see fig. 2). Their point of intersection is o. The lines are marked off at regular intervals using a scale of ascending numbers. Numbers on the vertical axis lying above the horizontal are positive, those below are negative. Points on the horizontal to the right of the vertical are positive, those to the left are negative. Points in

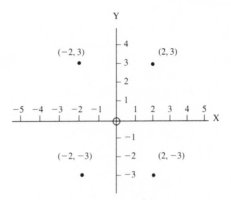

Figure 2. A modern orthogonal, Cartesian coordinate system in two dimensions. A typical point (e.g., +2, +3) is indicated in each of the four quadrants.

any of the four sectors established by the lines can now be located exactly by specifying their values on the x and y axes. Trajectories can be represented by equations: points in any of the four quadrants can be smoothly connected to form a line. ("Smoothly" implies that the function is well-behaved, having values and derivatives at every point.)

Descartes emphasized the use of analytic geometry for the solution of determinate construction problems – that is, problems whose solutions are a unique length (Descartes [1637] 1954, p. 12). His method involved assigning letters to all quantities, whether known or unknown, then expressing their relations as equations. For n unknowns, n equations are required for their solution. Descartes typically illustrated his algebraic solutions with geometric constructions. Suppose, by way of example, that an unknown line, x, satisfies the quadratic equation:

$$x^2 - ax - b^2 = 0. \tag{18}$$

One algebraic solution of this equation is:

$$x = \frac{a}{2} + \sqrt{\left(\frac{a^2}{4} + b^2\right)}, \tag{19}$$

as may be seen by direct substitution into the original quadratic equation. The second term on the right-hand side of this last equation is recognized, through use of the Pythagorean theorem, as the length of a hypotenuse of a right triangle whose other sides have length $a/2$ and b respectively. If this right triangle is constructed, as in figure 3, a circle may be drawn with

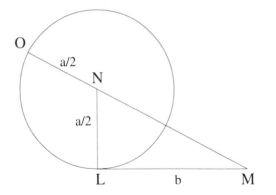

Figure 3. A geometric construction illustrating a solution of a quadratic equation. From Kline 1972, p. 309.

radius $a/2$ and its center at the apex where the hypotenuse meets the side. Now extend the radius that lies along the hypotenuse by $a/2$, thereby forming one continuous line of length x. This construction displays the algebraic solution expressed in equation 19.

Descartes also discovered indeterminate construction problems (ibid., p. 22). In these, solutions of algebraic equations permit many possible lengths, not, as in the example above, a unique length. The several lengths taken together form a locus (i.e., a set) of points, all of which are solutions of the problem. Such a locus is a curve having a companion algebraic equation that describes it completely. Descartes solved the ancient problem of Pappus (viz., finding a locus of points such that the product of their oblique distances from n given lines is proportional to the analogous product from n other given lines) by treating it as an indeterminate construction problem.

Figure 4 shows the case where the number of lines, $n = 4$. The derived locus must satisfy

$$\frac{CB}{CD} \cdot \frac{CF}{CH} = \text{constant},\qquad (20)$$

where the ratio is given, and the angles subtending the intersecting lines are given. Notice that AB and BC of figure 4 form a set of oblique Cartesian coordinates, x,y, with point B as origin. Using these variables and deferring to the geometry of the problem, we rewrite equation 20 thus:

$$y^2 = ay + bxy + cx + dx^2.\qquad (21)$$

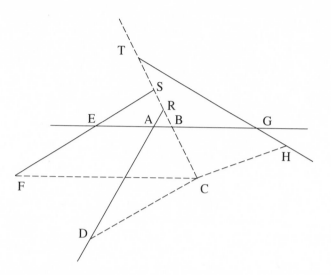

Figure 4. The problem of Pappus for the case of four lines. From Descartes [1637] 1954, p. 27.

This is a second-order equation whose coefficients a, b, c, and d are given by the known quantities of a problem. The equation becomes a quadratic equation for y, whatever the value of x. The equation can be solved, then confirmed by a construction, as discussed above. If this is done for various values of x, one can construct the values of y that trace out the locus of points solving the problem of Pappus. For y is obtained as a function of x; that is,

$$y = y(x). \tag{22}$$

This is an example of an indeterminate construction problem. Associating a curve with its defining algebraic equation dramatically expanded the domain of mathematics, as Newton agreed when he compared modern mathematics to the practices of the Greeks: "[T]he moderns advancing yet much further have received into geometry all lines that can be expressed by equations" (Kline 1972, p. 271).

Optics

One of the simplest, but most important, laws of macroscopic optics is the law of refraction, discovered independently by Descartes and Snell (Shea

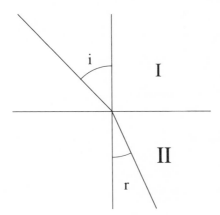

Figure 5. The refraction of light. From Kline 1972, p. 315.

1990, p. 149). Refraction is the phenomenon of light bending as it traverses the boundary from one medium to another when their densities differ (e.g., a stick in water seems bent). Descartes was the first to quantify it.

He proposed that the law of refraction is a ratio of sines (*CSMK*, 39; *AT*, I, 255):

$$\frac{\sin (i)}{\sin (r)} = \text{constant} \tag{23}$$

(see figure 5), where *i* is the angle of incidence of incoming rays, and *r* the angle of refraction of outgoing rays, both relative to a normal (i.e., a perpendicular line) constructed upon the refracting surface. The fact that the ratio of sines is constant depends upon the velocity of light in the two media. Descartes measured this index of refraction (i.e., the ratio) and obtained the almost accurate value of 4/3 for rays passing from air to water. (He subsequently used this magnitude to explain rainbows.) Once the index has been obtained by measurement at one incident angle, it may be confirmed by observation that the law of refraction (i.e., equation 23) holds for any incident angle. Measurements also allow confirmation that the law holds for any pair of differing materials (e.g., for glass, water, or air).

Descartes used his law of refraction to determine the anaclastic curve – the curve on which parallel rays focus to a point after traversing a refracting medium. This was a critical objective for optics, because knowledge of this curve makes it possible to grind lenses to a shape that produce clear images in telescopes, microscopes, and spectacles. It was known by the Greeks that

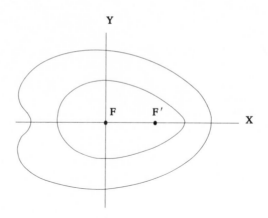

Figure 6. The ovals of Descartes. From Kline 1972, p. 316.

spherical lenses do not conform to an anaclastic curve. Optical instruments could be made by trial and error; but before Descartes, there was no general solution that could direct lens-making. Descartes found the desired curves, now called the "ovals of Descartes" (Descartes [1637] 1954, pp. 114–131). They are sketched in figure 6. The ovals are the locus of points P, whose distance from the foci, F and F', satisfy the defining equation

$$FP \pm nF'P = 2a, \tag{24}$$

where n and a are arbitrary real numbers except that $2a > FF'$. If this equation is expressed explicitly in terms of the axis variables, it becomes one of fourth degree in x and y in the general case. The ratio of the ovals defining distances FP and F'P is determined by the ratio of sines in the law of refraction.

Descartes knew these ratios, so he was able to solve the anaclastic problem. Knowing the anaclastic curve, he designed a grinding machine that would produce glass surfaces whose resolving power derived from the curve. He collaborated actively with the artisans and craftsmen who made these machines, exchanging letters and drawings.

Rainbows baffled Descartes' contemporaries, but Descartes was able to explain them, using his refraction law and a simple, but effective, experiment. Of course, some information was available to him already. We infer from rainbows seen in the spray of fountains that water droplets interact with light. Generalizing from rainbows in fountains to those in the sky, we infer that they, too, result from the interaction of light and water, as when rainbows are seen after rain. But the question is: How are rainbows made?

Descartes used a spherical glass of water as a substitute for a single drop of water. When he held the glass at arm's length with the sun at his back, he observed a flash of red light at an angle of approximately 42° subtended by rays passing from the sun to the glass, then to the eye. Rotating his arm while holding the glass on the surface of a cone whose apex coincided with his eye, he was able to maintain both the 42° angle and the observed flash of red light. Descartes' moving arm inscribed a conic surface. Now imagine that surface extended into the sky; there the goblet is "replaced" by a raindrop, which behaves analogously.

A rainbow occurs if there is an angle of 42° in the trajectory of the rays of light that pass from the sun through the refracting raindrops to the eye, for then all such drops lying on the surface of a cone whose apex coincides with the observing eye will be seen as falling within the rainbow. Why must the angle be 42°? Because of Descartes' (Snell's) law of refraction and because of the particular sine ratio of the interface between air and water, a ratio that Descartes knew experimentally to be approximately 4/3. His computation for the angle was based upon the simplest apposite geometrical assumption. It supposes that a solar ray entering a raindrop passes to an observing eye after it has been refracted twice, with one internal reflection in between. Descartes calculated the results for hundreds of examples, confirming by calculation and experiment that the values for the angle of refraction cluster around 42°. For "double" rainbows, we calculate the angle of refraction on the assumption that there are two refractions and two internal reflections. In this case the angle is 52°. Descartes' theory can be extended to predict multiple companion rainbows, simply by increasing the number of internal reflections. Laboratory experiments have confirmed multiple rainbows having as many as eighteen internal reflections. We may even take advantage of air travel to confirm the applicability of his theory to circular rainbows (Sears and Zemanski 1953, pp. 733–734).

Mechanics and Mechanism

Mechanism is the idea that qualitative differences in nature express the relations of a small set of physical variables. Descartes, along with several others (e.g., Galileo and Beekman), is responsible for some of the basic concepts of mechanics. Three of his ideas are fundamental. (i) He affirmed that a body in motion traverses a straight line in the absence of external forces (*CSM*, I, 241; *AT*, VIIIA, 63). (ii) He proposed that a body in equilibrium tends to maintain its state of motion, whether of rest or of movement at constant speed – this is an early statement of the law of inertia (*CSM*, I, 240; *AT*, VIIIA, 62). (iii) He recognized that forces acting on a body change its motion, and he postulated a net "motion" invariance constraining impact; thus he formulated – as no one had before – a conservation principle (*CSM*, I, 240, 242; *AT*, VIIIA, 61, (65)). Descartes proposed these ideas in the context of a larger program: his universal mechanism explained both the generation of individual mechanical systems (whether human organs or the solar system) and their current operation. These ideas were revolutionary. Looking back, Descartes' program violated the Aristotelian-Scholastic doctrine that things of a kind act distinctively because of their substantial forms, as flutes are different from horns. Looking forward, it anticipated, sometimes in detail, Newton's mechanics. Newton's first law, that the equilibrium state of a body at rest or in linear motion persists and is characterized by zero force, derives from Galileo, Beekman, and Descartes.

Descartes applied his mechanics in specific ways.

(*a*) He characterized the dynamics of impacting bodies as follows:

> When a moving body collides with another, if its power of continuing in a straight line is less than the resistance of the other body, it is deflected so that, while the quantity of motion is retained, the direction is altered; but if its power of continuing is greater than the resistance of the other body, it carries that body along with it, and loses a quantity of motion equal to that which it imparts to the other body. (*CSM*, I, 242; *AT*, VIIIA, [65])

There are specific applications of this statement in his impact rules. Their application is illustrated in figure 7. The first rule affirms that bodies of equal size and speed approaching one another along a line through their centers (before impact) retreat (after impact) along the same line, in opposite directions, with the same speeds. Rule 7, case *a*, affirms that when a body following another body is larger and is moving more quickly than the one ahead, the effect of impact is that the two bodies then move in tandem at the speed indicated. Each row in the figure can be interpreted in these same terms (i.e., with respect to size, speed, and direction). Rule 4 precludes a smaller body setting a larger one in motion and is therefore mistaken. The other rules, subtly modified, are correct: if the size, m, is reinterpreted to mean mass, and if the signs of v_2 in rules 2 and 3 are reversed, the rules are brought largely into conformity with the principle of conservation of mo-

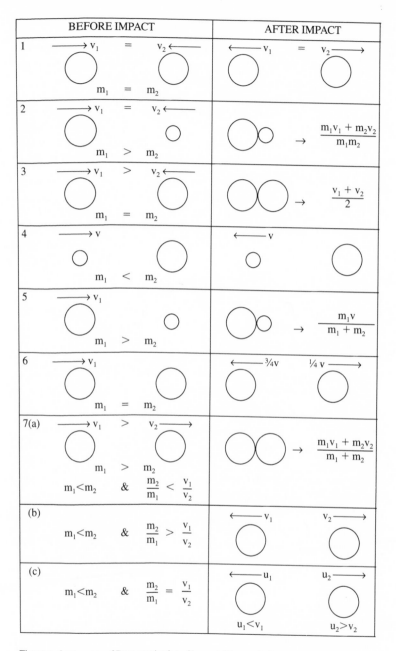

Figure 7. A summary of Descartes' rules of impact. The symbols *m* and *v* signify size and speed, respectively. From Shea 1990, p. 297.

mentum. The necessity of such changes was recognized by Huygens, who used the rules in his analysis of the percussion of pendulums, thereby determining that kinetic energy is conserved in elastic collisions. Huygens's treatment of percussion affected Newton's formulation of his third law: that bodies exert equal and opposite forces upon one another (Newton [1687] 1962; Huygens [1669] 1950, 172–173).

(b) Descartes' dynamics entail that all forces are impact forces associated with collision and exchange of motion. An outgrowth of this is Descartes' idea of heat, as he expressed it in *The World*:

> Now since it does not seem possible to conceive how one body could move another except through its own movement, I conclude that the body of the flame which acts upon the wood is composed of minute parts, which move about independently of one another with a very rapid and very violent motion. As they move about in this way they push against the parts of the bodies they are touching and move those which do not offer them too much resistance. I say that the flame's parts move about individually, for although many of them often work together to bring about a single effect, we see nevertheless that each of them acts on its own upon the bodies they touch. I say, too, that their motion is very rapid and very violent, for they are so minute that we cannot distinguish them by sight, and so they would not have the force they have to act upon the other bodies if the rapidity of their movement did not compensate for their lack of size. (*CSM*, I, 83; *AT*, XI, 8)

This description, essentially related to the motion of microscopic particles, suggests the modern concept of heat (Sears and Zemanski 1952, p. 426). It supposes that heat is energy in transfer across the boundary of a system in the presence of a temperature gradient at that boundary, where the temperature is a measure of kinetic energy (i.e., energy associated with microscopic motion). It is only as we recognize heat as a kind of energy that we can formulate the first law of thermodynamics: that energy is conserved.

(c) Vortices are another idea implied by Descartes' views regarding impact forces in a plenum. The motion of one thing in the absence of a vacuum requires a reciprocal motion in such other things as make way for it; and where the space is bounded, the motion is a vortex. Boyle exploited this idea when he constructed his theory of the "spring of air": the pressure of a gas, he said, is a function of the incessant motion of particles in the gas (Partington 1989, pp. 72–73). Newton's objections to vortices, as expressed in the second part of his *Principia*, helped him to justify his own theory of gravitation (Newton [1687] 1962, pp. 235–396). Later, when this aspect of Descartes' mechanics seemed defunct, Laplace and Kant resurrected the idea of vortices in speculating about the nebular formation of the solar system (Unsöld and and Baschek 1983, pp. 390–391).

(*d*) The case of zero force defines all situations of mechanical equilibrium. There are, for example, simple machines whose effectiveness depends upon mechanical advantage, including pulleys, inclined planes, and levers. Every such machine works on the principle of the lever. This principle holds that a force sufficient to lift a weight W through a given distance x will also lift a larger weight nW through a smaller distance x/n. (*CSMK*, 66–73; *AT*, I, 435–447).

(*e*) Modern physiology has its inception in Descartes' microphysics – change results from the collision of small bits of matter (corpuscles) – together with his claim that bodies are machines. Notice that Descartes' mechanist convictions were unaffected by his views about mind and its self-perception (as expressed in the *Meditations*):

> [W]e may find it hard to believe that the mere disposition of the bodily organs is sufficient to produce in us all the movements which are in no way determined by our thought. So I will now try to prove the point, and to give such a full account of the entire bodily machine that we will have no more reason to think that it is our soul which produces in it the movements which we know by experience are not controlled by our will than we have reason to think that there is a soul in a clock which makes it tell the time. (*CSM*, I, 315; *AT*, XI, 226)

An animal machine can perform, Descartes claimed, *everything* that we humans do (*AT*, XI, 185).[2] Or, more cautiously (as in the *Meditations*), the body is responsible for everything except consciousness, thought, and volition. These claims were supported by careful observations of bodily processes (e.g., of live and dead hearts [*CSM*, I, 316–319; *AT*, XI, 239–245]) and by applying mechanistic assumptions to imagined models of working, bodily parts (e.g., to impulses propagated from sensory organs through long nerves to the brain [*CSM*, I, 101; *AT*, XI, 141]).

It almost goes without saying that an effective physiology requires more than a theory about the interaction of corpuscles. We should not lose the forest for the trees, as happens if we forget that the architecture of reciprocally related, often hierarchically organized, semi-autonomous systems is as critical for body as the pervasive sameness of its molecular and metabolic processes. This is true not only of body's structure, but also of its evolution (e.g., of tissues and organs from a single, fertilized cell). Descartes was as preoccupied as we are by the task of explaining how the body's complex parts are generated by the dynamic relations of microparticles (*CSM*, I, 313).

Descartes was not the first to dissect human bodies for the purpose of trying to understand how they work. Galen, Fernel, Vesalius, Harvey, and others had already mapped the body and identified some of its principal functions. However, these earlier theorists and anatomists typically worked within the context of Galen's four humors – the idea that nature's four elementary, substantial forms (fire, earth, air, and water) are expressed in bodies as yellow bile, blood, phlegm, and black bile. Individual temperaments, they supposed, are dominated by one or another of these humors. These thinkers were also, more or less explicitly, Aristotelian teleologists: they described organs by specifying their purposes (e.g., we eat to save ourselves and reproduce to save our kind; we imagine and move to satisfy desire; we think for love of wisdom).

Descartes' mechanism eliminated both teleology and substantial forms. Body is a machine, subject only to mechanical forces. There is, for example, his "pneumatic" description of activity in the nervous system:

> If [a] fire . . . is close to [a] foot . . . , the tiny parts of the fire have the power to move the area of skin which they touch, thus pulling the tiny fibre . . . attached to it, and simultaneously opening the entrance to the pore . . . located by the point where this fibre terminates, just as when you pull one end of string you cause a bell hanging at the other end to ring. When the entrance to the tube . . . is opened in this way, the animal spirits [fine corpuscles] . . . enter and are transmitted, some to the muscles which serve to pull the foot away from the fire, some to the muscles which turn the eyes and head to look at it. (*CSM*, I, 101–102; *AT*, XI, 142–143)

The role that Descartes assigned to animal spirits – they were to be carriers of information – is credited nowadays to neuro-electrical impulses. This is typical of changes in physiological understanding since Descartes: our conception of the means is much refined; the directing, mechanical program is much the same (Hall 1975; vol. 1, pp. 250–264).

(*f*) We should expect that phenomena of one size will provide a useful basis for understanding phenomena of other sizes. Descartes exploited these analogies of scale. He explained the microscopic behavior of elements in the nervous system by citing the macroscopic behavior of mechanical "equipment" (*CSM*, I, 101–102; *AT*, XI, 142–143); he compared the solar system to macroscopic behaviors on earth (Cottingham 1993, p. 11). Descartes said of his analogies: "I compare only movements and movements, shapes and shapes, microscopic with macroscopic, thus differing only as two circles, one small, and one big" (*CSMK*, 122; *AT*, II, 368). Comparisons of this sort inspire the physical scale models used to study phenomena in almost every branch of science, including mechanics, electrodynamics, fluid dynamics, acoustics, explosives, and thermodynamics. Our modern practice has one advantage unknown to Descartes: for we know the equations of motion – the force laws – applicable to the particular domains compared or scaled.

These six issues (*a–f*) illustrate the larger point that Descartes' mechanics was a universal program for analysis and explanation. This is the astonishing gamble that scientific analysis will resolve the many apparent, qualitative differences, showing their inception in a geometrized, dynamic space. Newton, like every cosmologist who followed him, learned his confidence from Descartes. No matter that they disagreed about the relevant laws and the character of the things to which they apply. Each of these later thinkers could imagine that nature is generated and sustained – in every domain and on every scale – by the same constituent variables.

Three assumptions, described or implied above, support this universal mechanics. First is the idea that physical reality is exhausted by extension, as it is qualified and differentiated by magnitude, shape, and motion. Second is the idea that extension is divided into small regions of space (we would call them *atoms* but for Descartes' aversion to the idea that there are indivisible atoms in a void); we are to assume that every complex system is constructed from these elements. This implies that everything that happens in nature is the expression or result of the assembly, motion, and impact of such elements. Matter interacts with matter, so every level of organization, microscopic, macroscopic, or cosmological, expresses this pervasive mechanism. The only ultimate mechanism is that of impact. Descartes' rules for impact, constrained by conservation of motion, are the direct antecedent of our own. Modern rules for impact are generalized to equations of motion; impacts are generalized to functions for forces between particles; and conservation of motion is generalized to conservation laws of mass, energy, momentum, spin, charge, and so on. Descartes' affinities to our time – in conceptualization and even in language – are plain.

There is also this third assumption: that the relations of impacting bodies, hence every impact, can be represented mathematically. Descartes' formulation prefigures our own:

> I have resolved to quit only abstract geometry, that is to say, the consideration of questions which serve only to exercise the mind, and this, in order to study another kind of geometry, which has for its object the explanation of the phenomena of nature. (*CSMK*, 118–119; *AT*, II, 268)

Mathematicians sometimes explore abstract spaces without regard for the world. Descartes, by contrast, was practical: his mathematics was exactly suited to his mechanism, since geometry maps exactly matter that is only extension. There is an identical tension in our own mathematical thinking: how pure and independent of experimental application should mathematics be? Like Descartes, we seek to appease both sides. For we have this practical concern: where everything in nature is mechanical, nothing in it is exempt from our mathematical representations of it. We are satisfied when *some* of our mathematics is cogent to nature's processes and design.

Cartesian Legacies

Descartes' ideas have been, and are, used in various ways. Here are two developments in mathematics, two in optics, and five in mechanics. They are preceded by a comment about method and followed by a short list of consequential errors.

(i) The apriorism of the *Meditations*, with their emphasis on the truth of clear and distinct innate ideas, was foreign to Descartes' scientific work. This was true both before Galileo's censure and after it. Descartes was a hypothesizer. Given some phenomenon he did not understand, he invented stories intended to explain it. Where there were mathematical techniques suited to the task, he exploited them. Where not (e.g., his impact laws and vortex theory), he carried on with qualitative notions that had no obvious mathematical expression. Either way, he elaborated his hypotheses with attention to the empirical differences that would obtain if they were true. Or he affirmed a hypothesis because of its accurate empirical predictions even when he believed it false (i.e., the entities or relations posited do not exist) (*CSM*, I, 288–290; *AT*, VIIIA, 326–328). Wherever possible, he used his hypotheses in conjunction with experiments (i.e., not merely with observations already available): a hypothesis would direct the experiment while predicting the sensory effects it should generate. These three emphases – on hypothesis, experiment, and confirmation – made Descartes (like Galileo and Huygens) a model for the rest of us.

Philosophers are not mistaken in emphasizing Descartes' apriorism. It is rather that he was both an experimentalist *and* an apriorist – the one in regard to nature (extended substance), the other in regard to self-discovering, inspecting mind. The more relevant dispute for science is that which separates Descartes from Newton (and by implication Bacon). Does science advance by way of hypotheses that identify the conditions for a phenomenon (including its parts, causes, or laws)? Or should it imitate Newton's practice (or so he alleged) of reading nature's laws off the face of the data? Koyré suggests this précis of the difference:

> [T]he protracted struggle for and against Descartes and Newton transformed both of them into symbolic figures: the one, Newton, embodying the ideal of modern, progressive, and successful science, conscious of its limitations and firmly based upon experimental and experiential data which it subjected to precise mathematical treatment; the other, Descartes, symbol of a belated, reactionary – and fallacious – attempt to subject science to metaphysics, disregarding experience, precision, and measurement, and replacing them by fantastic, unproved, and unprovable hypotheses about the structure and behavior of matter. Or, even more simply, the one, Newton, representing the truth, and the other, Descartes, a subjective error. (Koyré 1965, pp. 55–56)

Newton described his method in this way:

> In experimental philosophy we are to look upon propositions inferred by general induction from phenomena as accurately or very nearly true, not withstanding any contrary hypotheses that may be imagined, til such time as other phenomena occur, by which they may either be made more accurate, or liable to exception. This rule we must follow, that the argument of induction may not be evaded by hypotheses. (Quoted by Koyré 1965, p. 268)

One is to discern regularities or functions in the data – though how this should be done remained uncertain. Subsequently, Kant argued that it is not done: mind, he said, projects order, even character, onto sensory data ([1781] 1965, pp. 65–238). We make Kant's point more simply: sensory data, we say, are overdetermined by the theories used to interpret them, meaning that our conceptualizations introduce characterizations and relations that are not present in the data alone. Seeing smoke and saying "Fire!," I claim more than I see. Though notice that I may also describe the data as steam, thereby implying an altogether different set of properties and relations.

The variability of possible interpretations, together with theory's overdetermination of data, vindicates Descartes' use of hypotheses, for there is, as he might have said, no sure way of knowing what causes the data have. But now, Kantians and Cartesians divide. Descartes believed that his hypotheses identify extra-experiential conditions for the data (i.e., parts, causes, or laws), whereas Kant supposed that no extra-experiential condition can be signified or thought: the only world that we can know or think is the one presented in experience; inferences to extra-experiential causes are illegitimate. Later formulations of Kant's views emphasize "curve-fitting": the best explanation, they say, is the one that fits the data to the simplest among contending interpretations, or the one that best coheres with doctrines already accepted. The line of development from Descartes' use of hypotheses runs, instead, through Peirce's notion of *abduction*: hypotheses identify the extra-experiential conditions for phenomena (Peirce 1931–35, vol. 5, pp. 113–127). Thus Descartes explained light as the centrifugal pressure of matter moving in vortices. His explanation was mistaken, but the form of his argument was identical to that explaining heat as the activity of molecules. We need to be careful, given this difference between Descartes and Kant, about using such slogans as "inference to the best explanation." It fails to distinguish between (Kantian) curve-fitting and (Cartesian) abduction.

What has become of Newton's view that we may read natural laws off the face of the data? It has few modern defenders among scientists or philosophers of science (Mill [1843] 1973; Whewell 1989), though it is congenial to apriorist philosophers such as Husserl ([1913] 1931, pp. 374–378).

(ii) Descartes' mathematics showed a firm sense that mathematical functions are ordered pairs (e.g., values on the x and y axes of a coordinate system). Equally, his mathematical practice was sensitive to the continuity properties of analytic functions. Together with analytic geometry, these notions helped to promote the invention – by Newton and Leibniz – of the calculus (Bell 1945, p. 141). Newton and Leibniz exploited two of Descartes' ideas: the algebraic representation of curves, using two variables (values from the x and y axes of coordinate systems), and a point considered by medieval mathematicians and clarified somewhat by Descartes, that there is an infinity of points (each one an "infinitesimal") between any two other points plotted on the same curve.

(iii) Descartes discovered a geometrical theorem which could have belonged to classical Greece, a theorem that is useful to contemporary topology, the mathematics of surfaces. Considering any regular polyhedron, such as the Platonic solids – tetrahedrons, octahedrons, cubes, dodecahedrons, and icosahedrons – it says that there is a relation among the number of vertices, P, edges, C, and faces, F, namely:

$$P - C + F = 2. \tag{25}$$

This is the Descartes–Euler formula (Boyer 1968, p. 336). It says that for every regular polyhedron the number of vertices plus the number of faces equals the number of edges plus two. Euler discovered the theorem independently, more than a hundred years after Descartes (Kline 1972, p. 1163). Critically for topology, he showed that the left-hand side of the equation is an invariant of the surface under topological (i.e., rubber sheet-like) distortions. This is called the *Euler characteristic* of the surface, χ: for a sphere, $\chi = 2$; for a torus (a doughnut-like shape), $\chi = 1$, and so forth. Surfaces with different Euler characteristics are topologically distinct and do not allow distortions into one another. Transformations of natural bodies, from one into another, are therefore limited.

An intimate geometrical relationship called "dualism" exists between pairs of polyhedrals having the same Euler characteristic and permuted P and F values. Using the Platonic solids as examples, we see that the tetrahedron is a dual of itself, the dodecahedron of the icosahedron, and so on.

Among the most interesting classes of molecules discovered recently are the carbon Fullerenes, C_N (where N is an integer), so named because their polyhedral shape resembles the architectural structures of Buckminster Fuller. Fullerenes, a previously unknown form of carbon, have a host of structural, chemical, and electronic properties useful to material science. The relationship of duality based upon the Descartes–Euler formula allows the geometrical prediction that boron Fullerenes, $B_N H_N$, are also viable. This inference is supported by quantum-mechanical calculations showing that these molecules would be energetically stable (Lipscomb and Massa 1992, p. 2297). These molecules would be as useful as their carbon analogues. Their synthesis, when achieved, will have been motivated by the Descartes–Euler formula.

(iv) Descartes was an early contributor to theories of light, though he wrongly believed that light is transmitted instantaneously (*CSM,* I, 153; *AT,* VI, 84). Its velocity has a finite value, first measured reasonably well by Roemer, using astronomical observations (viz., eclipses of Jupiter by its moons). Fizeau made successful terrestrial measurements of the velocity of light, as did Foucault. Highly accurate measurements were made by Michelson, giving a value of about 3×10^8 m./sec., in agreement with values obtainable by means of Maxwell's equations. Einsteinian relativity is predicated on a finite velocity for light (Hauser 1965, p. 449).

Descartes believed that light is pressure transmitted through the material plenum (*CSM,* I, 153–156; *AT,* VI, 84–93). The notion of transmitted pressure influenced Huygens, who showed that the known laws of reflection and refraction were consistent with the idea that light is a traveling wave. Newton held light to be corpuscular in nature; but the wave theory of light won out with the investigation of interference effects in the experiments of Fresnel, since they were not easily explained by a particle theory. The wave theory was further consolidated and confirmed when Young made measurements yielding the wavelengths of light. Maxwell's equations showed that light waves radiate from oscillating electrical charges and gave an expression for their velocity. Hertz succeeded in producing such Maxwell-equation waves, and the matter seemed settled. However, the particle theory was revived with Einstein's explanation of the photoelectric effect: he supposed that photons deliver energy to small localities, as would a particle. This view was supported by Compton's discovery that impacts of photons and electrons conserve momentum and kinetic energy in a manner familiar from two-particle collisions. Beginning with Heisenberg, Schrödinger, and Dirac, quantum mechanics asserts that photons, and matter generally, have these complementary features: their motion is wavelike, but energy is exchanged in the manner of impacting particles (Messiah 1961, p. 115).

(v) Descartes' scientific theorizing was often motivated by his practical concerns, as witnessed by his use of the anaclastic curve to design optical instruments capable of perfect image formation. This interest was shared by contemporaries and successors. Light microscopes, their lenses designed to the specifications of the anaclastic curves, were used by Hooke to discover large, biological cells (in cork, for example) and the insect parts that he copied into his notebooks. Subsequent, better light microscopes magnified still smaller cells and their parts. But those were early days for a trajectory that passes through our own time. Improving imaging is a priority for us. All manner of aberrations, chromatic, spherical, and astigmatic, have been discovered and reduced (Sears et al. 1980, pp. 672–694).

High-quality modern lenses are sometimes composites of many lenses. Aberrations that may be all but ineliminable from individual lenses are eliminated from such composites. We also avert such aberrations in other ways. For image formation is not limited to the refraction and focusing of visible light (i.e., light detectable by the human eye). We have devices that focus electromagnetic waves of wavelengths both longer and shorter than visible light: infrared and ultraviolet images are used routinely in many fields of science and engineering. At even smaller distances, electrons have been used in place of visible light, as when viruses are observed. The electron microscopes used to see them are designed so that magnetic fields of anaclastic curvature assume the role of the material lenses (e.g., of glass) known to Descartes. At the still smaller distances characteristic of atoms and molecules, images are formed by means of scattered x-rays. In this case, no material substance controls image formation. Instead, the role of the lens is played by an entirely mathematical process: a Fourier transform calculation. The anaclastic effect is calculated according to a rule which mimics mathematically the physical effect that a lens would have. In this way, the detailed geometry of molecules is routinely explored. It has been proposed that the Fourier transform method is also suited to the scale of the quantum-mechanical electronic orbitals associated with atomic and molecular positions. Image formation using accelerators – or, more accurately, "image formation," given this degree of extrapolation – is an active topic of research at even smaller scales (Glusker and Trueblood 1985; Clinton and Massa 1972).

There has been analogous progress in the application of Descartes' (and Snell's) refraction law to the design of telescopes. Galileo could see things – Saturn's moons, for example – that are relatively nearby. We see further, because telescopes, such as those at Kitt Peak, have glass lenses whose anaclastic curve is controlled over a diameter of several meters. The orbiting Hubble telescope, with its "blurred vision," is a different sort of example. The anaclastic curvature of its elements was damaged accidentally in the manufacturing process, and this was discovered only after the telescope had been placed in orbit. The aberrant focus was then corrected by means of additional lenses – spectacles in effect. The results fulfill our best hopes. They include the observation of whirling high-speed gases deep within a galaxy 50 million light-years away, the telltale sign of a black hole. Equally potent discoveries have been made by telescopes using wavelengths other than those of visible light, as with the observations of subtle variations in the infrared radiation left over from the "Big Bang" that initiated the universe (the COBE experiment) (Smoot and Davidson 1993).

Recall Descartes' program: "Give me extension and motion and I will remake the world." The mechanics he espoused, in theory and practice, has surely revised our understanding of the world.

(vi) Analytic geometry made the discovery of the calculus almost inevitable. Calculus, in turn, nourished investigations of mechanics. How? By supplying a means for formulating such notions as Newton's idea of acceleration, as implied by his second law, $F = ma$.

The mathematical resources for representing mechanical laws have been generalized. There are, for example, various ways to construct and represent coordinate systems. The second law is generally written in orthogonal Cartesian coordinates (see fig. 2). Other problems, which assume other symmetries, justify using other orthogonal sets of coordinates. Newton himself used polar coordinates for the representation of spherical problems. Lagrange and Hamilton transformed Newton's second law into other, information-equivalent differential equations (Hauser 1965, pp. 142–201). His equations of motion were subsequently generalized in various ways: relativistically in the special and general theory of relativity equations of Einstein and quantum-mechanically in the equations of Schrödinger and Heisenberg. Dirac's equation integrates special relativity with quantum mechanics; but no one, so far, has integrated general relativity with quantum mechanics. Here, in results achieved or merely anticipated, coordinate systems derived or generalized from Descartes' own are the basis for equations used to represent mechanical systems.

Notice that machine-like systems of reciprocally related parts are not the only ones represented by the differential (and integral) equations considered above. Virtually every system in nature is, or can be, investigated and understod by way of equations of motion that define its domain (e.g., Maxwell's equations in electrodynamics, the Navier–Stokes equations in hydrodynamics). This is further confirmation of Descartes' wager.

(vii) Rest, not motion, was the normal state of nature for Aristotle. Motion was displacement, so the paths of moving things were interpreted teleologically: sublunar things go up or down to their places of rest. Only celestial things were said to move naturally – in circles. This, too, is evidence that rest is the natural state of things, if we suppose that circular motion imitates rest by always returning things to their previous places.

Descartes, together with Galileo, Beekman, Huygens, and others, introduced the contrary view: that matter is naturally in motion, and that rest is merely one value of motion (viz., zero) (*CSM*, I, 93–94; *AT*, XI, 38–40). Inertia, for them, is the power of a body to maintain its state of motion. Newton adopted the Cartesian idea of inertia, expressing it in his first law: that bodies continue in uniform, rectilinear motion in the absence of forces. This formulation is assumed throughout the history of classical mechanics, without amendment. Only recently, with relativistic mechanics, has there been any change, it now being said that the measure of inertia (i.e., the mass of an object) is no longer a constant but is rather a function of the object's velocity. This is decisive only at velocities approaching that of light. Rockets and satellites are launched using laws that are classically mechanical.

Descartes supplied a comprehensive understanding of mechanical equilibrium, meaning bodies under zero force. For such bodies retain their state of motion: namely, rest. (Newton's first law also entails this result.) This is the domain of statics, of machines that perform in a state of equilibrium. These behaviors include the structural stability of suspension bridges, sub-oceanic tunnels, skyscrapers, submarines at maximal ocean depth, and earth-orbiting space stations.

(viii) Descartes opined that something in nature – quantity of motion was his candidate – is conserved. There are two histories implicit in this claim: one is the critical response to Descartes' formulation, then to the formulations of his successors; the other is the development of this idea in various domains, many of which Descartes never considered.

He remarked in *The World* that God preserves "each thing by a continuous action" (*CSM*, I, 96; *AT*, XI, 44). Presupposed is the notion that God imparts a sustained impulse to the created world. This idea is familiar from Plato and Aquinas (see n. 1). Descartes added some embellishments: God's immutability, hence his constancy, is one of his perfections. Having supplied a certain quantity of motion to the created world, he sustains it. But now a second question follows: Given size, speed, and directionality, which of these, and in what relation, does God conserve? Quantity of motion (size times speed) was Descartes' reasonable, but mistaken choice.

Huygens (after an experiment using two spheres hanging as pendulums) surmised that kinetic energy (a quantity proportional to mass and speed squared) is conserved when transferred from body to body on impact (1885–90, pp. 33–91). Leibniz proposed a thought-experiment which confirms the error of Descartes' formulation by invoking kinetic energy without impact. Descartes had assumed that equal quantities of motion (i.e., size times speed) have the same "power," but they do not. Suppose that a given unit of speed is required to raise a body with a given unit of size to some specified height. The quantity of motion thereby determined is equivalent to the quantity determined by raising a second body with units of speed and size equal in magnitude respectively to the units of size and speed in the first body. However, these two quantities of motion are not equal in "power." For if the two bodies are dropped, they fall through different distances, and achieve different speeds in accordance with Galileo's law of free fall (viz., the speed achieved is proportional to the square root of the distance fallen). One has more kinetic energy than the other, as it should not if the bodies have equal "power" because of having equal quantities of motion. Equal quantities of motion do not entail equal quantities of potential or kinetic energy. Descartes' principle is a formula for generating energy, not conserving it: we would be able, were it true, to multiply "power" by transferring the motion conserved in larger bodies to smaller ones. This would make it feasible to build perpetual motion machines (Leibniz [1675–1716] 1989, pp. 49–51). Leibniz has not faulted Descartes for failing to explain the transfer of kinetic energy during impact. Instead, he assumes that energy is conserved and shows that potential and kinetic energy would not be conserved if quantity of motion were conserved.

Leibniz's own formulation was tentative: he speculated that the quantity conserved is some product of size, as mass, and a power of velocity (speed with directionality). Newton confirmed that momentum, mv, is conserved. That this is so is entailed by his second law, $F = ma$, given the assumptions that the net external force on the colliding system is zero and that acceleration is zero. These assumptions are equivalent to the statement that momentum is a constant (i.e., is conserved). Newton, by correctly identifying the pertinent relationship (i.e., mv), also explained its conservation when transferred by impact.

This brief history has a philosophic moral. Descartes supposed that matter is extension, and that all the changes of matter can only be changes in one or more of its three variables: size, shape, and motion. A conservation principle for matter would have to join two or more of them. Why only them? Because Descartes, after Plato and before Hegel, affirms that the real is the rational and the rational is the real: nothing can happen in nature that is not already anticipated in our ideas of it, especially our geometrical ideas. A conservation principle, too, must be prefigured in our idea of extension. Yet, nothing that Descartes could find in geometrical ideas anticipates the idea of mass, or its cousins of his time, impenetrability or weight: they do not seem to be analyzable without remainder into features of extension.

Einstein inveighed against philosophers who "have had a harmful effect upon the progress of scientific thinking in removing certain fundamental concepts from the domain of empiricism, where they are under our control, to the intangible heights of the a priori" ([1922] 1953, p. 2). Descartes often used hypotheses to specify the conditions for observed phenomena; but his idea of matter is not so much a hypothesis as a consequence of his belief that matter is exhaustively intelligible by way of our innate geometrical ideas (i.e., of figure). Such notions as mass did not seem to be explicable in these terms. Einstein would eventually show that mass is a function of motion in a geometricized space (see next section); but his formulation exceeded anything that Descartes proposed or implied. None of it required Einstein to believe that the pertinent ideas are innate. He would probably have agreed that Descartes was sometimes an empiricist of convenience, meaning one who examined empirical data and inferred their alleged conditions (e.g., vortices) only when such hypotheses conformed to his idealized, and allegedly a priori, idea of matter.

The idea of conservation expressed Descartes' theological persuasion that something in nature is immutable. But why stop at one thing conserved: could there not be several? We confirm that energy, momentum, and angular momentum are conserved by discovering the coordinate symmetries of the phenomena inherent in the coordinate symmetries of the equations used to represent them – Noether's theorem (Kaku 1993, pp. 23–30). So conservation of momentum follows from invariance under translation in space. The pattern of explanation for these more recently discovered principles of conservation is straightforward: we locate invariant features of nature (e.g., translations and rotations in space, translations in time), rather than credit all the invariants to God's good will, perfection, or immutability.

(ix) Descartes is most inventive, albeit perplexing, when he argues that the geometry of space, hence of shapes and curves, is both the limiting and the formative condition for the interactions of matter. This emphasis upon a geometricized space is one of the abiding trajectories of our intellectual history. Plato's *Timaeus*, in which space is described as the geometricized "receptacle" in which all change occurs, is one early expression of this notion (1964, p. 1176). Descartes' ideas define the middle of its development. Einstein's theory of general relativity is its current end point.

Descartes supposed that matter is characterized entirely by extension and motion, and that the net motion of the material world is conserved. This led to his vortex theory and thereby to his claim that forces on bodies arise because the vortices in which they ride are swept into the vortices of other bodies (*CSM,* I, 237; *AT,* VIIIA, 58). Newton ([1687] 1962) demurred. Mass, he thought, is a factor distinct from space and geometry, since bodies are distributed in a space that is mostly empty. But if matter is not separable from space, is it even distinguishable from it? General relativity reintegrates matter into a geometricized space-time, masses being determined by curvatures in space (Berry 1976, p. 76). Is there more to matter than a thickening and bending of space-time? Koyré implied that there is: "Physics cannot be reduced to geometry – but attempts to so reduce it belong to its nature. Is not Einstein's theory of relativity an attempt to merge together matter and space, or better, to reduce matter to space?" (1965, p. 63, n. 1). This is unfinished business.

(x) Purging substantial forms and teleology from the understanding of human bodies has implications that still resonate among us. La Mettrie's *L'Homme machine* has become the theme of our self-understanding. This is apparent not only in medicine, but also in the funeral practices of those who dispose of dead bodies as they would of broken stoves or chairs. The moral implications are troubling; nor will they be resolved soon. Some other tensions in Descartes' conceptualization are more easily described.

One outcome of his program is the ease with which computer intelligence comes to be assimilated to human thinking. Though he usually supposed that intellect is not a bodily activity, Descartes did believe that activities such as remembering perceived qualities are bodily. We have come to accept that many or all mental activities are merely mechanical because of seeing these functions mimicked by physical systems (e.g., machines that calculate, recognize images, regulate themselves, write music, or learn). That we resist so little is testimony to the rhetorical success of Descartes' mechanical program.

A more technical dispute has also been resolved on the side favored by Descartes. He identified particular functions with specific organs. This is reasonable enough as regards eyes and ears; but it was speculative when Descartes sought a location within the brain for its interaction with mind. The singularity of the pineal gland and its position at the base of the brain recommended it as the likely site (*CSM,* I, 341; *AT,* XI, 354–355). Descartes' successors could forgive his mistake, while seeing it as confirmation of the Aristotelian idea that differentiation of functions presupposes differentiation of structures. This regulative principle has not always been confirmed experimentally: it has sometimes seemed (to Hughlings Jackson, for example) that brain functions are performed by whole sectors of the brain, or even by the brain as a whole. Current thinking endorses the view (of Gall and Broca) that brain functions (e.g., seeing, feeling, remembering) are localized (Brain 1962, pp . 84–86), with the proviso that effects occur because of the reciprocal relations of these specialized parts, a point that Descartes emphasized. See his representation of images projected onto the back of the eye, then onto projection areas of the brain (fig. 8) (*CSM,* I, 105; *AT,* XI, 175).

(xi) No matter that the idea of a universal mechanism is splendid; some of Descartes' formulations were mistaken. Here are three principal errors.

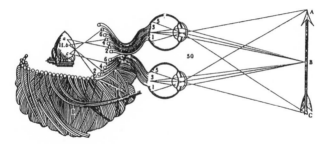

Figure 8. Transmission of an image. From *CSM*, I, 105; *AT*, XI, 175.

First, his ontology was wrong-headed. The vortex hypothesis excited Descartes because it supplied an explanation for motion at every scale, from large to small, including planetary motion, ocean tides, the magnetic field of the earth, and the weights of bodies at the earth's surface. But he failed to express the hypothesis mathematically, or to test it carefully. There is no reason to believe that vortices exist, given both Newton's objections to them and his more effective explanation of the phenomena at issue (Newton [1687] 1962, pp. 235–396).

The laws of Descartes' mechanics were also off the mark. His conservation law was mistaken: it is momentum, not quantity of motion (size times speed), that is conserved. His impact laws required revision, especially that implying that a smaller body can never move a larger one, because they assume that bodies are "completely separated not only from each other, but also from the rest of the world, [and] that they are absolutely rigid" (Koyré 1965, p. 78). This is Descartes' apriorism – his taste for idealization – sabotaging his empirical good sense.

Second, Descartes' emphases in analytic geometry were not always those confirmed by his successors. He obtained an expression for the slope of a curve, a result so beautiful, he said, that he hardly aspired to anything more. His contemporary, Fermat, obtained a different expression, as the limit of a ratio of infinitesimal quantities (Kline 1972, p. 345). Fermat's concept promoted, first, our understanding of the derivative in calculus, then its use in solving problems of optimization (i.e., finding maximum and minimum values that a function may obtain). It is impossible, Descartes supposed, to "rectify" curved lines ([1637] 1954, p. 91). Stymied by this belief, he did not explore the concepts that would lead to the integrals of calculus. He preferred problems of determinate construction (ibid., p. 13), even though problems of indeterminate construction were more important, because critical to the concept of function, hence to the association of curves with equations (ibid., p. 59). Is there a systematic reason for these errors? None is apparent.

Third, Descartes failed to recognize the importance of explanations that represent a phenomenon mathematically, even when no causes for it are at hand. He objected when Galileo favored such mathematical representations: "Everything Galileo says about bodies falling in empty space is built without foundation; he ought first to have determined the nature of weight" (Kline 1972, p. 333). One infers, though Descartes is perplexingly inconsistent in this regard (see the first error discussed above), that he feared apriorism in mathematical thinking, wanting empirical evidence of real-world causes to confirm mathematical representations.

These errors are serious, but they are more than offset by the many things, including ideas, program, and method, that Descartes got right. Cartesian science promised a comprehensive explanation of natural phenomena. Such explanation was to be forthcoming from the back-and-forth exchange of theory and experiment. The numerical calculations of the one were to match (within assignable errors) the numerical measurements of the other. Descartes the scientist was not always, or usually, the rabid apriorist described by philosophers.

NOTES

1. Descartes could have justified this reformulation by saying that it was required by his deeper understanding of nature and mathematics, not merely by his prudence. The earlier claim, formulated before 1633 and expressed in *The World*, was that "God continues to preserve [the world] in the same way that he created it" (*CSM,* I, 92; *AT,* X, 37). This view had two significant antecedents. Plato's *Timaeus* describes the impulse, imparted by the Demiurge, that starts motion within a receptacle (space), with the effect that an immutable, intelligible pattern achieves imperfect realization within the flux (our perceived, natural world) (Plato 1964, p. 1167). Aquinas affirmed that contingent beings presuppose the existence of one who is necessary, so that every motion presupposes the God who supports it ([1266–68] 1964, pp. 13–17). Both arguments were commonplace in cosmological thinking prior to Descartes. He could have accepted them without compromising his belief that all the specific determinants of natural phenomena are located within nature itself. However, these assumptions also permit the development they received after Galileo's censure, when God is again described as an active participant in nature. This role comes easily to him – without

regard for Descartes' anxiety – when analytic geometry has persuaded us that motion is a trajectory binding the discrete points mapped by coordinate systems. For those points, without God to sustain and bind them, seem disconnected. Hence the claim of the *Principles of Philosophy* that "the world is continually preserved through an action identical with its original act of creation. . . . [W]hen he created the world in the beginning God did not only impart various motions to different parts of the world, but also produced all the reciprocal impulses and transfers of motion between the parts" (*CSM*, I, 243; *AT*, VIIIA, 66). The later formulation seems a mere elaboration of the earlier one, but it is not: a remote, cosmological condition has become the hands-on Maker who generates and sustains coherent trajectories (i.e., motions) within the flux.

2. The last-quoted work was written in 1647–48, the *Meditations*, with their emphasis on the cogito, was published in 1641. Either Descartes held contradictory beliefs about mind–body interaction, or his beliefs changed. Either way, fewer than all, or no, bodily actions wait on Ryle's ghost-in-a-machine (Ryle 1960, pp. 11–24). The *Meditations* surely encouraged Ryle's interpretation. Our reason for ignoring the contrary, physiological side of Descartes' view needs explaining. Could it be our preference (in philosophy) for exotic views?

REFERENCES

Aquinas, Thomas. [1266–68] 1964. *Summa Theologiae*, trans. Timothy McDermott, vol. 11. New York: McGraw-Hill.

Bell, E. T. 1945. *The Development of Mathematics*. New York: McGraw-Hill.

Berry, Michael. 1976. *Principles of Cosmology and Gravitation*. Cambridge: Cambridge University Press.

Boyer, C. B. 1968. *The History of Mathematics*. New York: Wiley.

Brain, W. Russell. 1962. *Diseases of the Nervous System*. Oxford: Oxford University Press.

Clinton, W. L., and Massa, L. 1972. Determination of the Electron Density Matrix from X-ray Diffraction Data. *Physical Review Letters* 29, no. 20: 1363.

Cottingham, John. 1993. *A Descartes Dictionary*. Oxford: Blackwell.

Descartes, René. [1637] 1954. *The Geometry of René Descartes*. New York: Dover.

Einstein, Albert. [1922] 1953. *The Meaning of Relativity*. Princeton: Princeton University Press.

Glusker, J.P., and Trueblood, K. W. 1985. *Crystal Structure Analysis*. New York: Oxford University Press.

Hall, T. S. 1975. *History of General Physiology*, 2 vols. Chicago: University of Chicago Press.

Hauser, Walter. 1965. *Introduction to the Principles of Mechanics*. Reading, Mass.: Addison-Wesley.

Husserl, Edmund. [1913] 1931. *Ideas*, trans. W. R. Boyce Gibson. New York: Macmillan.

Huygens, Christian. 1669. Règles du mouvement dans la recontre de corps. *Journal des Scavans*, March.

――――. 1885–1950. *Oeuvres complètes de Huygens*, 22 vols. The Hague: M. Nijhoff. vol. 16, Société hollandaise de sciences. DLC.

Kaku, Michio. 1993. *Quantum Field Theory*. New York: Oxford University Press.

Kant, Immanuel. [1781] 1965. *Critique of Pure Reason*, trans. Norman Kemp-Smith. New York: St. Martin's Press.

Kline, Morris. 1972. *Mathematical Thought from Ancient to Modern Times*. Oxford: Oxford University Press.

Koyré, Alexandre. 1965. *Newtonian Studies*. Cambridge, Mass.: Harvard University Press.

Leibniz, G. W. [1675–1716] 1989. *Philosophical Essays*, ed. and trans. Robert Ariew and Daniel Garber. Indianapolis: Hackett.

Lipscomb, W. N., and Massa, L. 1992. Closo Boron Hydrides and Carbon Fullerenes. *Inorganic Chemistry* 31, no. 12: 2297–2299.

Messiah, Albert. 1961. *Quantum Mechanics*. Amsterdam: North-Holland Publishing Company.

Mill, John Stuart. [1843] 1973. *System of Logic*. Toronto: University of Toronto Press.

Newton, Isaac. [1687] 1962. *Mathematical Principles of Natural Philosophy and His System of the World*, trans. Andrew Motte. Berkeley: University of California Press.

Partington, J. R. 1989. *A Short History of Chemistry*. New York: Dover.

Peirce, Charles Sanders. 1931–35. *Collected Papers*, ed. Charles Hartshorne and Paul Weiss, 6 vols. Cambridge, Mass.: Harvard University Press.

Plato. 1964. *Collected Dialogues*, ed. Edith Hamilton and Huntington Cairns. New York: Pantheon.

Ryle, Gilbert. 1960. *The Concept of Mind*. London: Hutchinson and Company.

Sears, F. W., and Zemanski, M. W. 1952. *College Physics – Mechanics, Heat, and Sound*. Reading, Mass.: Addison-Wesley.

———, ———. 1953. *College Physics – Electricity, Magnetism, and Optics.* Reading, Mass.: Addison-Wesley.

———, ———, and Young, H. D. 1980. *College Physics.* Reading, Mass.: Addison-Wesley.

Shea, W. R. 1990. *The Magic of Numbers and Motion: The Scientific Career of René Descartes.* New York: Watson Publishing International.

Smoot, George, and Davidson, Keay. 1993. *Wrinkles in Time.* New York: Morrow.

Unsöld, A., and Baschek, B. 1983. *The New Cosmos.* New York: Springer-Verlag.

Whewell, William. 1989. *Theory of Scientific Method.* Indianapolis: Hackett.

Essay 6
Political Theory and Ethics

WILLIAM T. BLUHM

René Descartes did not write a politics. But the thought encapsulated in his cogito contains the seed from which the lineage of individualist liberal political theory has sprung. Despite his acid criticism of the *Meditations*, Thomas Hobbes displays in his own work a distinct affinity to Descartes. John Locke carries the line forward, followed by the political theorists of the French Enlightenment. The main development from then is through Jeremy Bentham to contemporary utilitarian theory.

Intellectual lineages develop through intellectual intercourse, which centrally involves critique, commentary, reflection, and dialogue. In the give-and-take of history, implications, reformulations, and modifications take place in a variety of ways that produce not only continuity but also diversity. The main line of an intellectual lineage is surrounded by collateral branches. This is certainly the case with Cartesianism. Transcendental moralists like Immanuel Kant and communitarians such as Rousseau, who rejected Cartesian ethical assumptions, share markedly Cartesian judgments about the nature of the real and the knowable, which significantly affect their political thought. It is also the case that while Friedrich Nietzsche led a revolt against Cartesian rationalism, he built the edifice of his thought on a very Cartesian conception of will. Nietzsche and postmodern philosophers do not repudiate Descartes; their work reveals instead anomalies inherent in the Cartesian world view, which threaten today to bring its long influence to a close. Whether these anomalies can be overcome by contemporary Cartesian theory and practice remains an open question.

The words *skeptic*, *individualist*, and *hedonist* specify the major qualities of the Cartesian self which inhabits the political theories of individualist liberalism, the chief Cartesian lineage. They derive from the answers Descartes gives to questions about what is real, what is knowable, and what is good. Descartes also was (ambivalently) both an egalitarian and an elitist. Let us reflect on the significance of these characteristics of his work.

Skeptic

Descartes' point of departure in theorizing a new canon of knowledge was radical doubt about everyday experience and everyday moral language. By contrast, Plato and Aristotle, whose thought constituted the foundation of the medieval world view that Descartes repudiated, accepted the meaningfulness of the common language as their point of departure. Philosophical innovator though he was, Plato remained strongly attached to traditional ideals of Greek *paideia* and saw his mission as an attempt to put those ideals on a rational basis. Similarly, Aristotle broke no revolutionary ground but sought rather to refine the Greek ideal of action according to the mean and to develop the concept of prudence as the Greeks practiced it; and likewise with the Scholastics who succeeded them as the Christian synthesis of faith and reason emerged. All took as their point of departure communally based moral agreement.

Descartes, however, stressed his detachedness, his merely provisional acceptance of the moral culture in which he had been bred. "I did naught but roam hither and thither, trying to be a spectator rather than an actor in all the comedies the world displays," he wrote (19; *CSM*, I, 125; *AT*, VI, 28). He rejected the elaborate structure of learning of the Scholastics as oppressive prejudice. The conflict that had arisen with the Reformation had destroyed the credibility of the Thomistic theological and philosophical synthesis for him. And the success of a new natural science based on a mechanical understanding of causation had undermined Aristotelian physics. Philosophy over the centuries had provided nothing which was not in dispute and consequently doubtful, wrote Descartes. Moreover, the ethical writings of the ancients were nothing but "palaces most superb and magnificent, which are yet built on sand and mud alone" (7; *CSM*, I, 114, 115; *AT*, VI, 8). All alleged knowledge of the world and of principles of action had to be rejected.

Individualist

Descartes sought a starting point for his philosophizing in isolation from society and communal norms. This was his famous cogito – the idea that he could ground his first evident truth, that he existed, on the evidence of his thinking. He judged that he "might assume, as a general rule, that the things which we conceive very clearly and distinctly are all true" (22; *CSM*, I, 127; *AT*, VI, 33). In a surface argument he appeared to find a criterion of clarity and distinctness in a very traditional proof of the existence of God. But, as we read, we realize that this substantive idea is not his criterion; he has already left tradition by the wayside. It is rather the formal character of the proof that is important: mathematics and logic furnish Descartes with his criterion for clarity, and it is mathematics that is central to his new method of knowing. (Locke, Leibniz, and d'Holbach thought that Descartes did not mean his proofs of God's existence in the *Discourse* and *Meditations* to be taken seriously by reform-minded intellectuals. They were there only to satisfy the demands of censorious authority for orthodoxy. In our time, Gilson, Maritain, Jaspers, Heidegger, and Caton are among those who share this view [Caton 1973, p. 11]. In another place I have analyzed what I take to be deliberate subterfuge on Descartes' part in presenting numerous flawed proofs of the existence of God. As Charles Adams put it, they were "a flag to cover the goods, the physics" [quoted ibid.]. See also Bluhm 1984, chap. 2.)

Descartes arrived at the minimal, fundamental truth of his existence curled up by himself in soliloquy in the corner of a warm room. How different from Plato's search for knowledge through dialogue and dialectic – social methods of knowing. From his initial point of self-certainty, Descartes moved out to read the "great book of nature" (*le grand livre du monde*) – extended body – and also inward through his "soul" (*âme*), or mind, to create a new structure of reliable knowledge. Knowledge of body would constitute a new physics, that of mind a new psychology. But body and mind would be united in each enterprise. For without the judging mind, how could there be knowledge of bodily motion? And without sensations from the world of body, where would the mind acquire data to judge and act upon?

Descartes radically confined the beginnings of all knowledge to the individual. And its end as well. For the object of the new knowledge was not contemplation, knowledge for its own sake, but for the sake of power. He wrote that his scientific experiments had satisfied him "that it is possible to attain knowledge which is very useful in life, and that, instead of that speculative philosophy which is taught in the Schools we may find a practical philosophy by means of which we may render ourselves the masters and possessors of nature" (38; *CSM*, I, 142–143; *AT*, VI, 62). Psychology – the inquiry into mind – would yield both a true understanding of human values and a method for achieving those values based on self-mastery. Physics – the inquiry into body – would produce an understanding of the mechanical processes of nature, which could then be manipulated to maximize the satisfaction of individual desires.

Hedonist

Descartes presented the results of his psychological inquiries in his last published work, *The Passions of the Soul* (1649). In this, as in all his writings, he broke with the past. The ancients have left us little information about the passions, he wrote, "and for the most part . . . implausible" (*CSM*, I, 328; *AT*, XI, 32). He expounded his own doctrine in 212 "articles." The passions (there are six primary ones: wonder, love, hatred, desire, joy, and sadness) are aroused by stimuli to our nervous system, either from some external object that affects "our outer senses" or from some movement of "our inner appetites." The function of the passions is to help the soul will things that nature has determined are useful to us. They "contribute to actions which may serve to preserve the body, or render it in some way more perfect" (*CSM*, I, 376; *AT*, XI, 430). Most efficacious are joy and sadness. Sadness, which proceeds from pain, is of special importance, because it prevents imprudent actions that might destroy us. Preservation is the fundamental good. Thus we have a formulation of the hedonistic calculus of pleasure and pain, which was to become the primary theory for expounding the nature of human values in the liberal tradition of political theory. Articles 139–143, which he devoted to a discussion of the passions "in so far as they belong to the soul" rather than the body, reveal themselves on analysis as empty words intended to satisfy the ecclesiastical censor. Cartesian psychology equates the good with desire (*CSM*, I, 377–379; *AT*, XI, 432–436).

But to be fully good, desire must be rational. We should seek alone to satisfy those desires that "depend only on us" – that is, only those goods that are within our power to acquire. This is not a Stoic doctrine of resignation, however, because Descartes has shown us in the *Discourse* how to manipulate the laws of nature ("providence," understood as determinate principles of cause and effect) through science. Thus in article 144 he wrote that "the mistake we ordinarily make in this regard is never that we desire too much; it is rather that we desire too little." In proceeding to the satisfaction of desire, we should act on the best information available and order our preferences (sort out the less useful desires). Descartes called this procedure "pursuing virtue," which he defined as "[never] failing to do something [one] judges to be the best" (*CSM*, I, 382; *AT*, XI, 442).

In moving from self to other, Descartes presented no theory of shared symbols and meanings, no theory of family or other communal association. But he did have a doctrine for the treatment of others. We should be generous to them and judge them as capable of "virtuous will" (or "free will," i.e., self-control) as we judge ourselves to be. (Self-control was for Descartes the only ground for praise or blame.) His moral doctrine is thus one of enlightened self-interest for all mankind, understood as an aggregate of autonomous individuals (*CSM*, I, 384–385; *AT,* XI, 446–448).

In the *Discourse* Descartes presented yet another rule of enlightened interest: that which obliges us to promote as far as possible the general good of mankind. But how can we derive such a rule from the sensationalist psychology that alone grounds Descartes' moral theory? We arrive at it descriptively. Since pleasure is what is really desired by all as good, and pain is evil, then clearly it follows that it is in the interest of us all to maximize the amount of pleasure in the world. Descartes has anticipated Bentham by more than a hundred years (38; *CSM*, I, 142; *AT,* VI, 62).

Execution of the rule of the maximization of pleasure is in the hands of utilitarian technocrats. For it is science that points the way to the good. In the *Discourse* Descartes has foreseen, in a technological vision, the future happiness of mankind. Application of his method would make possible "the invention of an infinity of arts and crafts which enable us to enjoy without any trouble the fruits of the earth and all the good things which are to be found there." It would also promote the conservation of "health, which is without doubt the chief blessing and the foundation of all other blessings in this life." He even foresaw the genetic enhancement of desirable traits: "[I]f it is possible to find a means of rendering men wiser and cleverer than they have hitherto been, I believe that it is in medicine that it must be sought." Through medicine it might also be possible to free us of "an infinity of maladies both of body and of mind, and even also possibly of the infirmities of age" (38; *CSM*, I, 143; *AT,* VI, 62).

Egalitarian/Elitist

The *Discourse* opens with the idea that "Good sense is of all things in the world the most equally distributed . . . [T]he power of forming a good judgment and of distinguishing the true from the false, which is properly speaking what is called Good Sense or Reason, is by nature equal in all men" (3; *CSM*, I, 111; *AT,* VI, 1–2). Differences in opinion, he goes on, are due not to different abilities, but to different methods. The problem of reliable knowledge is therefore to be solved not by developing an intellectual aristocracy but by cultivating a sound scientific method for scholarly direction. Descartes' egalitarianism is also revealed in his *Passions of the*

Soul, in which he calls for equal esteem to be paid to all men on the basis of their common capacity for enlightened self-interest.

We also find prominently displayed in Descartes' writings a contrasting admiration for the preeminent mind. In the *Discourse* he observes that there is "less perfection in works composed of several portions, and carried out by the hands of various masters than in those on which one individual alone has worked." And he goes on to adduce examples from architecture, city planning, and politics. "I believe that if Sparta was very flourishing in former times, this was . . . because [her laws] being drawn up by one individual, they all tended towards the same end" (9; *CSM*, I, 116–117; *AT*, VI, 11–12). There is also no doubt that Descartes saw himself as a kind of legislator, setting forth a new way of ideas that would lead from oppressive ignorance to the reign of free enlightened reason. Nowhere does Descartes resolve the tension between his egalitarianism and his elitism. We also find this tension displayed repeatedly in the Cartesian lineage, especially in the work of Hobbes, Rousseau, the French utilitarians, and Bentham. Here, then, is the Cartesian self: skeptic, individualist, hedonist, and ambivalently egalitarian/elitist.

Thomas Hobbes

A contemporary of Descartes, Hobbes was the first philosopher to insert this self in a political setting: "the war of all against all." (Despite his disagreements with Descartes, as evidenced by his contributions to the *Objections* that were published along with *Meditations*, Hobbes shared many of Descartes' views about human nature. In 1637 he received a copy of the *Discourse* from Sir Kenelm Digby, shortly after its first publication and three years before the publication of his first work on politics, *The Elements of Law*. Both Descartes and Hobbes were early exponents of a mechanical conception of nature. See Reik 1977, p. 78.) In so doing, Hobbes drew together two aspects of the Cartesian theory of motivation that Descartes had left unconnected. Descartes first, and Hobbes after him, held out for a sensationalist theory of human perception and behavior. Both understood good and evil in terms of pleasure and pain. It was Descartes who first argued for the peculiar saliency of pain and fear in prompting us to action aimed at self-preservation, the fundamental human good. But he also assumed the universality of enlightened self-interest, including an ability of humankind to be "generous" to one another.

Perhaps it was the chaotic times of the English Civil War that led Hobbes to judge that in a social setting from which the institution of government has been removed – a "state of nature" – the passion for "power after power" dominates human behavior. Each person, vaingloriously trusting in his own strength and cleverness, sets out to subjugate others and to use them in any manner whatsoever "for the preservation of his own Nature; that is to say, of his own Life" (Hobbes [1651] 1968, p. 189). Transmuting a formerly moral concept, directed to the free will (*jus naturale*, natural right), into a quasi-physical principle (like the natural laws described by scientists), Hobbes defined the right of nature as a liberty to act. Like physical particles moving freely in space until stopped by an outside force, human beings move freely in political space until halted by the power of another. Only when he experiences the fear of violent death, perhaps from wounds suffered in battle, does a person come to reason – to a recognition of the need to limit his aggressive drive (his right of nature) in order to preserve his life. Thus fear engenders the willingness to live and let live, the Cartesian ability to be "generous" to others. The recognition takes the form of the mutual adoption of "the Laws of Nature" (*leges naturales*), which Hobbes terms "precepts of reason," as a constitution for civil society: "That every man ought to endeavour Peace, as far as he has hope of obtaining it. . . . That a man be willing, when others are so too, as farreforth, as for Peace, and defence of himselfe he shall think it necessary, to lay down this right to all things; and be contented with so much liberty against other men, as he would allow other men against himselfe" (ibid., p. 190).

Hobbes also understood the tenuous character of reason after it has been generated. Given the power of human vainglory, the right of nature tends to reassert itself once initial fear has been allayed. And then the "war of all against all" returns. "For Covenants, without the Sword, are but Words, and of no strength to secure a man at all" (ibid., p. 223). A Leviathan power is required constantly to generate the healthy fear that keeps reason alive and operative.

But at this point Hobbes faced a dilemma. In his logical Cartesian model, no limit could be placed by principals on their agent. The latter's power must be absolute to be adequate to the task set before him; therefore he must stand outside the contract of government, as a neutral enforcer, whose right of nature remains complete. He must also be sovereign author of all public principles of right – of the law. For only a liberty to do anything whatsoever for self-preservation is a right by nature. Public right must therefore consist of rules of law laid down by a sovereign, emanating from his will. They ought, indeed, to implement Hobbes's reasonable "Laws of Nature"; but only the sovereign could be allowed to interpret what these laws might require. Without him, they are precepts merely. Here is the elitist face of Hobbesian theory – an elitism of legal necessity.

Since human beings, for Hobbes, constitute by nature no moral community, share no principles of comity and right by which to order their common life, their "representative," the sovereign, cannot be held responsible to them. They are compelled to trust him to act for their good. They agree to suspend their own right of nature and authorize all his acts (ibid., p. 269). But since he too is a human being (or an assembly of human beings), how can they safely do so? The threat of arbitrary government by the agent appointed to secure peace and preservation looms forever on the horizon.

Additionally, Hobbes thought that for many men vainglorious behavior might be invincible to fear, especially if they felt unprotected by the sovereign. Rebellion is implicit in the "reserve clause" that Hobbes included in his model contract for the abatement of the right of nature (ibid., p. 192). He therefore envisaged that "in case a great many men . . . together have . . . resisted the Sovereign Power unjustly . . . for which every one of them expecteth death, whether have they not the Liberty then to joyn together, and assist and defend one another? Certainly they have" (ibid., p. 270). Under such circumstances, the sovereign would fall, and men would be back in a state of nature and in a new war of all against all. Thus the Hobbesian political model cycles endlessly, from dictatorship to anarchy and back again.

Hobbes, the skeptic, the individualist, the hedonist, and the egalitarian/ elitist – the Cartesian self – was also a liberal. Radical freedom is the natural condition of mankind, and although it can be limited politically to insure peace and the security of persons and property, liberty should abound in all other things. Hobbesian man is free to build his home and educate his children where and how he will, to engage freely in economic activity, and to think whatever thoughts he will (though he may not always be free to express his thoughts). As a Cartesian self, he is also engaged in science, commerce, and the utilitarian quest for comfortable, even abundant, living. But the political "if" is a large one. The Cartesian model contains no concept of natural community, no concept of human sharing. Hobbesian society must remain a mere aggregate of individuals – vainglorious rather than generous individuals – for whom peace and preservation remain will-o'-the-wisps, always beyond sure grasp. In a recurrent war of all against all there is

no place for industry; because the fruit thereof is uncertain and consequently no Culture of the Earth; no Navigation, nor use of commodities
that may be imported by Sea; no commodious Building; no Instruments
of moving and removing such things as require much force; no Knowledge of the face of the Earth; no account of Time; no Arts; no Letters; no
Society; and which is worst of all continual feare, and danger of violent
death; and the life of man, solitary, poore, nasty, brutish; and short.
(ibid., p. 186)

John Locke

The next philosopher to embrace the Cartesian self, in his model of human
nature, was Locke. But he found a way to modify it so as to make some kind
of community possible, the thing so critically lacking in the Hobbesian
social contract. Man in a state of nature was capable of moral education,
thought Locke, capable of internalizing the law of nature, "which obliges
everyone . . . that being all equal and independent [not] to harm another in
his life, health, liberty or possessions" (Locke [1690] 1980, p. 9). This
could be accomplished by teaching Christian moral principles, principles
that all denominations could agree upon. Central to that teaching should be
the fear of God. Not a human sovereign, but a punishing God is the proper
sanction of the law of nature for self-interested men.

Locke set forth this doctrine in detail in *The Reasonableness of Chris-
tianity.*

The greatest part of mankind want leisure or capacity for demonstration;
nor can they carry a train of proofs, which in that way they must always
depend upon for conviction, and cannot be required to assent to, until
they see the demonstration . . . The greatest part cannot know and
therefore they must believe . . . The instruction of the people were best
still to be left to the precepts and principles of the gospel. (*Works*, vol. 6,
p. 146; cited in Aarsleff 1969, p. 132)

It had for him the status of a wholesome myth, like Plato's "Noble Lie,"
without which the war of all against all could not be overcome (see Bluhm
et al. 1980, pp. 414–438). In his *Second Treatise of Government*, Locke
envisaged a society imbued with law of nature principles whose "moral
majority" is able to act together to keep its elected rulers, its agents for the
guarantee of peace and the security of property, also obedient to the law of

nature. He designed a system of legal institutions to guarantee constitutional responsibility, and when these fail, a right of revolution to bring arrogant officials back under the law.

Thus Locke, through the device of moral community, was able to solve the problem of free government and to articulate a constitutionalist theory that is still influential today in the liberal democratic world. It is significant, however, that he had to go beyond the Cartesian model of human nature to accomplish this, for in a purely Cartesian world there is no community; there are only aggregated individuals. Locke had to reach back into the tradition that Descartes had rejected to solve the problem. He did so by adapting the medieval notion of church as community to a newly pluralist society. According to Locke's formula, Protestant denominations could form such a community despite theological and organizational differences, though Catholics and atheists had to be excluded. But in our own time, the Lockean system is wearing thin. As social pluralism advances and church membership declines, Cartesian skepticism is on the increase, and the social order of the technological city of which Descartes dreamed is in process of disintegration. Can a purely Cartesian society sustain free government?

Enlightenment: French Utilitarian Thought

From seventeenth-century England, the extension of the Cartesian lineage moved back to France. Influenced directly by Descartes but also through the reception of Lockean ideas, the *philosophes* of the French Enlightenment developed still further the Cartesian heritage. Taking issue with an earlier scholarship that ascribed to Enlightenment philosophy an exaggerated originality, Peter Schoules has recently argued that the Enlightenment "did little more than widely disseminate an inherited idea," of which Descartes was author. "Enlightenment thought," he writes, "was preoccupied with human freedom. It was preoccupied with freedom from prejudice and from political and social oppression, with freedom from drudgery, pain, and anxiety. It was equally interested in mastery, and hence in the power which scientific knowledge was supposed to give to humanity, for it was believed that scientific knowledge would allow each person to become master of his destiny." *Freedom, mastery,* and *progress* were its watchwords. And it was Descartes who first systematically canvased the three as a philosophical ensemble (Schoules 1989, pp. 3, 4).

In his surface argument Descartes explicitly denied a revolutionary intent: "I cannot in any way approve," he wrote, "of those turbulent and unrestful spirits who, being called neither by birth nor fortune to the management of public affairs, never fail to have always in their minds some new reforms." His own intention, he disarmingly wrote, was solely "to reform my own opinion and to build on a foundation which is entirely my own" (11; *CSM*, I, 118; *AT*, VI, 14–15). In his provisional morality Descartes espoused a maxim that enjoined him to cleave to the laws and customs of his own country. By contrast, the philosophes directly attacked established institutions and boldly opposed *les lumières*, the light of reason, to oppressive custom. Denis Diderot, editor of the *Encyclopédie* wrote in 1762: "We are promoting a revolution in men's minds to free them from prejudice" (quoted by Woloch 1982, p. 235). And it was the *Encyclopédie*, the joint work of the philosophes, which became their public landmark. A hundred specialists in all the fields of the new knowledge which Descartes had both cultivated and prophesied, authored twenty-eight volumes designed "to change the general way of thinking" (Woloch 1982, p. 241). The *Encyclopédie* abounded in social critique and in schemes for social, educational, economic, and political reform. One of its contributors, Claude Adrien Helvétius, a leading member of a group of French utilitarians, was to be a primary transmitter of the Cartesian legacy to Jeremy Bentham. Elie Halévy writes that it is "impossible to exaggerate the extent of [the] influence [of his book *De L'Esprit*] throughout Europe at the time of its appearance," and that the "first to submit to it was Bentham" (Halévy 1928, p. 18).

If Descartes evaluated the new knowledge that proceeded from the use of his method in terms of its utility, Helvétius took the idea one step further and set up a hierarchy of the sciences, ordered in terms of their utility (ibid., p. 19). Drawing on Descartes' sensationalism as developed by Locke, he also made important inferences from the idea of the equal distribution of "bon sens." One was that all knowledge proceeds from environmental stimuli, and that differences in education account for differences in outlook, talent, and mental capacity. To preserve the original equality of understanding, all human beings are entitled to equal rights, especially equality of educational opportunity.

Helvétius also developed an important gloss on Descartes' rule about promoting "the general good of mankind." Differences in education not only produce different minds; they also account for different and conflicting interests. Since conflicting interests cannot be summed, they must be artificially reduced to an identity through a system of rewards and penalties. And this is the work of the legislator, who for Helvétius was the enlightened monarch.

The excellence of laws depends on the uniformity of the views of the legislator, and on the interdependence of the laws themselves. But in order to establish this interdependence, it must be possible to *reduce all the laws to some simple principle*, such as *the principle of the utility of the public*, that is to say, of the greatest number of men subject to the same form of government; a principle whose full extent and fruitfulness are known to no one; *a principle which embraces the whole of morals and of legislation*. (*De L'Esprit*, quoted by Halévy 1928, p. 21)

We see here clearly reflected in the thought of Helvétius the egalitarian/ elitist ambivalence which characterizes the Cartesian self. J. L. Talmon views the role of Helvétius's "legislator" as a root of modern totalitarianism (1960, p. 35).

The most complete expression of French utilitarianism is the work of the Baron d'Holbach, also a contributor to the *Encyclopédie*. His home served as an intellectual center for the philosophes of the second part of the eighteenth century (Cobban 1960, p. 128). In his *Christianisme dévoilé* (1767) d'Holbach openly expounded the atheism that Descartes had carefully hidden under "nonproofs" of the existence of God. Following Hobbes, he also swept aside the paradoxes of Cartesian dualism and reduced reality to a frank materialism. In his *Système de la nature* (1770) d'Holbach described the human soul as an obscure function of the body and argued that it could be studied anatomically. His materialist reductionism made morals a branch of physics. Human behavior was subject to universal scientific laws along with the rest of reality (Cobban 1960, p. 129). These laws he expounded as rational principles of social utility. The happiness of mankind rests on "the eternal and invariable relations which subsist between beings of the human species living in society, and which will subsist as long as men and society do" (quoted in Cobban 1960, p. 129). He agreed with Helvétius that these relations require regulation if happiness is to be assured. Human beings must be brought to cooperate with one another for their own good. But d'Holbach perceived the problem of effecting this cooperation as much more complex than did Helvétius. Nor was he willing to resort to authoritarian means to achieve it. His doctrine on the matter resembles that of Locke: he understands the advantages of society as consisting in "liberty, property, and security" and is in favor of negative restraints on governmental power

(Cobban 1960, pp. 165, 166). D'Holbach is an opponent of despotism in all its forms. "Since government ony derives its authority from society, and is only established for the good of society, it is evident that society can revoke this authority when its interest so demands" (quoted in ibid., p. 166). Like Descartes, d'Holbach was an optimist regarding human rationality, however; he believed in progress. Diderot, Helvétius, and d'Holbach had nothing to offer on the problem of community. Their reliance was wholly on Cartesian rationality to establish the good society.

Collateral Cartesianism: Rousseau

The Romantic countercurrent to Enlightenment rationalism inaugurated by Jean Jacques Rousseau, deviant though it was from the main line of Cartesian liberalism, nevertheless remained within the ambit of Cartesian philosophy. In Rousseau and his intellectual descendants we encounter a collateral Cartesianism.

Rousseau's "natural man" is an extreme version of the Cartesian individualist. He does not desire freedom under a rationally apprehended law of nature which would secure natural rights to person and property. Rather, he craves independence – the independence of a state of nature that resembles the original condition of mankind as Rousseau envisioned it. It is the wild freedom of the solitary beast, who has not yet come to share the society of other human beings. He has no language and lives by instinct, without reason. Rousseau has here presented a logical transposition of Descartes' solipsistic cogito from the realm of thought to that of feeling. This "natural" condition constituted for Rousseau the standard of freedom (*Discourse on Inequality*, in Rousseau 1987, pp. 40, 46).

Original man, like the natural man of Hobbes and Locke, is a self-interested individual concerned with preservation. He is not rapacious, however, but gentle, and is even compassionate towards others when he sees them in trouble. Perhaps this is an affective variation on Descartes's rationalist "generosity." But, like Descartes, Rousseau comes to no teleological conclusion about natural sociality. With Descartes, he rejects all reference to Scholastic final causes.

> [M]editating on the first and most simple operations of the human soul, I believe I perceive in it two principles that are prior to reason, of which one makes us ardently interested in our well-being and our self-preservation, and the other inspires in us a natural repugnance to seeing

any sentient being, especially our fellow man, perish or suffer. It is from the conjunction and combination that our mind is in a position to make regarding these two principles, without the need for introducing that of sociability, that all the rules of natural right appear to me to flow. [*Discourse on Inequality*, in Rousseau 1987, p. 35]

The political problem for Rousseau was how to secure independence for persons who today are compelled to live in society. He proffered it in Cartesian fashion, in language resembling that employed in geometry: "Find a form of association which defends and protects with all common forces the person and goods of each associate, and by means of which each one, while uniting with all, nevertheless obeys only himself and remains as free as before?" (*The Social Contract*, ibid., p. 148). The solution follows as an inference from the qualities Rousseau assigned to his version of the Cartesian self and its "natural" condition. It is the solution of the social contract that gives rise to a "General Will." The clauses of the contract are reducible

to a single one, namely the total alienation of each associate, together with all of his rights to the entire community. For first of all, since each person gives himself whole and entire, the condition is equal for everyone; and since the condition is equal for everyone, no one has an interest in making it burdensome for others. (Ibid., p. 148)

The difficulty with Rousseau's solution is that it requires natural man to be denatured as a pure Cartesian individual and then renatured as a citizen, a communal being. Without the community of the "General Will," individuals will be dominated by whatever combination of private wills is able to manipulate the public order. Rousseau has worked through the logic of atomistic society to the conclusion that it is incompatible with both constitutional liberty and independence of will. More is required than a Lockean community of faith that furnishes a divine enforcer of natural rights. What is required is a charismatic legislator to remake the fundamental stuff of human nature.

He who dares to undertake the establishment of a people should feel that he is, so to speak, in a position to change human nature, to transform each individual (who by himself is a perfect and solitary whole), into a part of a larger whole from which this individual receives, in a sense, his life and his being; to alter man's constitution in order to strengthen it; to substitute a partial and moral existence for the physical and independent existence we have all received from nature. (Ibid., p. 163)

Rousseau's paradoxical conclusion points to an inherent contradiction in the logic of Cartesian freedom. The only way to realize the values of Cartesian individuals is to reduce the individual to his opposite, the communal being of shared interest and will. Community is thus incompatible with the idea of a Cartesian self.

If Locke reached back to tradition for a concept of community to ground constitutional freedom, Rousseau reached forward to the national ideal. It was from his *Contrat social* that the nationalists of the French Revolution drew inspiration and argument for their passionate defense of *La Patrie*, the social cradle of the "Rights of Man." The later experience of liberal nationalism in France, Britain, and the United States and, more briefly, in Italy and Germany seemed to demonstrate the ability of the idea of a "nation" to supply the conceptual gap in the Cartesian model, Rousseau's paradox (contradiction?) nothwithstanding. But with the advent of totalitarian nationalism in the 1930s and subsequent global conflict, the contradiction in the Rousseauistic model began to work itself out existentially in world politics. The fragmenting experience of the 1990s, which has seen the dismantling of Yugoslavia and the Soviet Union as empires, does not give hope for political reintegration in freedom.

Collateral Cartesianism: Kant

In his *Grounding for the Metaphysics of Morals* and in a series of essays on political history, especially "Perpetual Peace," Immanuel Kant attempted to inject into the Cartesian paradigm a conception of inherent right as a standard of human action and thereby to transmute the Cartesian concept of technical progress into one of moral development. Avoiding a retreat into the Scholastic tradition, he attempted to find a principle of right within the assumptions of the Cartesian model. He accomplished this by reflecting on Descartes' concepts of free will and reason, which led him to dual noumenal and phenomenal ways of perceiving the world. For human autonomy to be established – the reality of free will – the human person must be able to act without determination by the phenomenal order of mechanical causation. Were this not possible, the Hobbesian reduction of Cartesian dualism would be correct. Mind and will would simply be computer-like entities. Kant argued that free will is real, but only as a moral will. Human beings, he held, believe that inherent right is a meaningful idea, and that when we act in accordance with the idea of right, we are free, because in so doing we act independently of determination by the passions – either our own or those of others.

The minimal idea of right that Kant could defend in a Cartesian universe was that of the categorical imperative: our actions are right if the maxims underlying them are universalizable as laws of nature. Thus "right" signifies action according to universal laws autonomously originated by free persons. This constitutes an analogue in the noumenal world to the rationality of universal physical laws in the phenomenal world. The physical and moral realms both operate according to universal laws (the core idea of "reason"). In the first, the laws are given externally to objects in motion. In the second, they are legislated by autonomous wills for human guidance, constrained only by the idea of what it is to be a law.

The second formulation of the categorical imperative is Kant's moral equivalent of Cartesian "generosity." "Act in such a way that you treat humanity, whether in your own person or in the person of another, always at the same time as an end and never simply as a means" (Kant [1785] 1981, p. 36). This formula implies the establishment of a "kingdom of ends" as the goal of history. Politically, this requires the creation of an order of republican governments federated in an organization resembling today's United Nations. In such a society the "mechanism of nature" would be employed by moral politicians to establish republican institutions of government universally, so that all human beings would be treated as ends in themselves – that is, as free persons.

Kant did not see a need for moral community to achieve universal constitutional liberty and independence in a world of federated republics; they could be achieved simply through the "mechanism of nature" (the rational play of the passions). But in predicting the movement of history in "Perpetual Peace," he wrote that its culmination in perpetual peace was *certain* only if people acted according to the principle of right.

Autonomous nations would be the vehicles of such an evolution, according to Kant. He defined *nation* in the second preliminary article of his proposed treaty of perpetual peace as a "society of men whom no other than the nation itself can command and dispose of. Since . . . each nation has its own roots, to incorporate it into another nation as a graft, denies its existence as a moral person, turns it into a thing, and this contradicts the concept of the original contract, without which a people [*Volk*] has no rights" (Kant [1795] 1983, p. 108). Kant presented no objective criteria for nationhood, however; his idea might rather be said to imply the process of infinite fragmentation that is our present experience of the politics of nationalism.

Culmination of the Major Line: Benthamite Utilitarianism

While Kantian ethics retains vitality in the West today – it is a fine philosophical justification for the United Nations Organization – a purer Cartesianism informs our urbanization and democratization, and especially the technological and commercial dynamics of our time: that of Benthamite utilitarianism. The development of this line of thought is historically unbroken from Bentham to contemporary utilitarian philosophy. Along with Kantianism, it constitutes one of the two chief ethical systems of our day. It also underlies the theories of major contemporary schools of economics and political science and informs the world of practice in both the private and the pubic sectors, in the guise of cost–benefit analysis.

With Bentham the conceptions of contract, state of nature, and natural right give place to the pure language of Cartesian utilitarianism. The first sentences of his major work on politics, *An Introduction to the Principles of Morals and Legislation*, restate the central theme of *The Passions of the Soul* boldly and succinctly. They also tie together that theme and the practical ameliorative aims of the *Discourse*.

> Nature has placed mankind under the governance of two sovereign masters, *pain* and *pleasure*. It is for them alone to point out what we ought to do, as well as to determine what we shall do. On the one hand the standard of right and wrong, on the other the chain of causes and effects, are fastened to their throne. . . . The *principle of utility* recognizes this subjection, and assumes it for the foundation of that system, the object of which is to rear the fabric of felicity by the hands of reason and of law. Systems which attempt to question it, deal in sounds instead of sense, in caprice instead of reason, in darkness instead of light. (Bentham [1789] 1970, p. 11)

By utility, Bentham meant that property in an object "whereby it tends to produce benefit, advantage, pleasure, good, or happiness . . . to the party whose interest is considered" (ibid., p. 12). To him, these were all synonyms. Something could be said to be in an individual's interest if it added to "the sum total of his pleasure" or diminished "the sum total of his pain" (ibid.).

Like Descartes, Bentham had no concept of community as a shared good or a shared system of values. Nevertheless, he employed the word, noting that its meaning "is often lost." He defined it as a "fictitious *body*, composed of individual persons who are considered as constituting as it were its members." The interest of a community, he claimed, was simply "the sum of the interests of the several members who compose it" (ibid.). Moving to the public order, Bentham argued that a governmental policy might be deemed conformable to the principle of utility if its tendency "to augment the happiness of the community is greater than any which it has to diminish it" (ibid., p. 13).

Talk of good and bad in this way implied the possibility of precise measurement. To make this possible, Bentham tried to develop a quantitative scale of pleasure and pain in the form of a "felicific calculus" which took into account the propinquity, duration, intensity, certainty, fecundity, purity, and extent of pleasures and pains. This raised the question of interpersonal comparisons of utility, a subject which is still hotly debated by utilitarians. How do we compare the views of individuals about what gives pleasure and pain and their senses of intensity, fecundity, and so forth? There was also the problem of how to sum social pleasures and pains in the face of conflicting interests and values. However the calculation was to be made, Bentham insisted on strict equality among individuals in casting up the greatest quantity of social good. Each was to count for one and one only, regardless of rank or social status: Bentham as democrat.

Bentham held out both for a natural identity of interests and for a need in some spheres of action of their artificial identification by the agency of government. On the one hand, he subscribed to Adam Smith's doctrine of economic liberalism, which depends on the idea that egoistic individuals pursuing their private interests, by means of an invisible hand working through the division of labor and free exchange, produce the greatest happiness. The Philosophical Radicals, a Benthamite party in the British Parliament which took its stand on this theory, promoted policies of free trade in nineteenth-century Britain. Today's elimination of national boundaries to increase the advantages of trade through such organizations as the European Union (EU) and the North Atlantic Free Trade Association (NAFTA) is simply a contemporary extension of the idea, a logical inference from Cartesian individualism.

The free market cannot in Benthamite opinion do everything, however. Interests may conflict and need to be reconciled with each other artificially. In this case Bentham entertained a variety of policies, policies to incorporate the egalitarian/elitist ambivalence we noted in the thought of Descartes and others in the Cartesian lineage we have been reviewing. In his early work, Bentham took an elitist turn. A reforming absolute ruler might be an effective instrument for rationalizing and equalizing the law. The superior mind that stands above the pains and pleasures of the citizenry in order to measure them also takes the form of the expert administrator and dispassionate social scientist. This might be Bentham himself, recommending a utilitarian code of penal law based on his felicific calculus. Today it might be the policy analyst, researching public attitudes to health care reform and devising policies to maximize social efficiency.

Along with this elitist concept of government in the figure of the "legislator" goes a collectivist, majoritarian concept which points in the opposite direction to the *laissez-faire* principle. For social utility, not individual liberty, was the governing criterion in Bentham's political theory. James Steintrager argues that "recent scholarship . . . has pointed to the fact that Bentham's followers played an important role in such reforms as the Factory Act and the Poor Law, which sent England on the road toward a centralized welfare state." Bentham's *Constitutional Code*, written between 1820 and 1832 and taken as a model for reform by the Philosophical Radicals, was a detailed blueprint for state collectivism (Steintrager 1977, pp. 65, 66). This irony points up the contradiction between the libertarianism implicit in Descartes' individualism and the collectivist welfare liberalism implicit in his utilitarianism.

As he grew older, Bentham discovered that monarchs and oligarchs were obstacles rather than instruments of utilitarian reform. The democratic side of his thought came to the fore in a late-blooming passion for extension of the franchise. He came to see that the enactment of penal reform and other measures of utilitarian policy required first the reform of Parliament toward greater popular participation.

Cartesian Political Culture Today: The European Union and the Problem of Moral Community

To judge the present vitality of Cartesian political theory, we must move from philosophical statement to the world of political action. The ethos of the Cartesian self without admixture of alien ideas is almost perfectly incorporated today in the political culture and structures of the European Union. These reveal both the strengths and the weaknesses of the Cartesian political legacy to our time. (The paragraphs that follow represent a condensation of ideas originally presented in Bluhm 1993.)

The Treaty of Rome incorporated all three Benthamite methods for aggregating interests. The inauguration of a free European market by removal of tariffs among member sovereign states and by the adoption of measures which would gradually allow free movement of labor and capital across national borders bodes well for an ever fuller realization of the

Cartesian dream of generalized abundance. But there also had to be policies to reconcile divergent interests, which called for the creation of an expert "harmonizer," the European Commission, a supranational executive. Provision for the creation of a European Parliament embodied the third Benthamite mode, that of democratic aggregation. The EU thus came to incorporate Cartesian individualism and libertarianism, along with both its technical elitism and its egalitarianism.

The experience of the European Union displays the tensions among the various characteristics of the Cartesian self, in particular between its technocratic and democratic elements. Altiero Spinelli has written vividly of the great faith in the powers of administrative institutions among the functionaries of the European Commission and of their "technocratic indifference" to politics. He discovered that the Commission reacted "suspiciously and fastidiously to intrusions of the political world upon well-ordered administrative activity" (1966, pp. 16, 72).

Beginning as merely a consultative body, the European Parliament is gradually acquiring substantial power and authority vis-à-vis the Commission. In a recent year, thirty-two of forty-nine amendments to legislative proposals passed by the Parliament were accepted by the Commission. The Parliament also wields power over the Union's administrative budget. The institution of a parliamentary question period has obliged the Council of Ministers to develop public positions on significant issues. And the direct election of members in the component states has caused political parties in these states to develop European policies. The result has been the gradual development of a genuine European public opinion – which Bentham regarded as the most powerful agency for aggregating a general interest.

The strength of the EU lies in its capacity for increasing both the material welfare of Europeans and the number of institutional safeguards of a large array of individual economic, social, and political rights. Its weakness lies in its strictly utilitarian character, its lack of definition as a community with shared moral purposes. Moral authority, as well as legal sovereignty, for better or worse, still rests with the national entities which comprise the Union. Further, the governments of these states still largely monopolize the "high policy" areas of defense and foreign affairs. Peacekeeping efforts by the Union, as in war-torn former Yugoslavia, have been a failure. The EU does not have the will to act like a state with strategic interests and moral responsibilities. Then, too, a united Germany is the most powerful state in the Union. Fear has been mounting recently that German national interests may not always be compatible with those of the Union. During times of recession, as in 1993, even progress toward economic unity can be threatened by resurgent nationalism, such as that which prevented the merger of the Swedish Volvo and French Renault corporations.

The European Union is thus a community only in the restricted Benthamite sense of an area in which individual utilities are aggregated by a variety of processes. The Union faces a standing dilemma as to which additional states should be admitted. What is "Europe"? No concept exists whereby its boundaries can be defined, because utilitarianism is essentially cosmopolitan. There is no organizational concept between the nation and the world in Benthamite philosophy. "Nation," as we have seen, has no theoretical ground, only a sentimental one. And the potential of nationalist feeling for political disintegration seems to increase daily, especially during periods of economic distress. The central problem for the European Union is thus precisely that of Cartesian society as such: namely, the absence of a viable concept of moral community. The Cartesian self is not a communal animal.

Utilitarian Progress or Nihilism?

The problematic of a society of Cartesian selves is also illustrated by the incipient disintegration of the modern city. In Western industrial states, violence is increasingly rampant, especially among the underclass who have not shared in the prosperity produced by Cartesian technology. In changing Communist and Third World societies, enormous economic and social dislocations have been caused by efforts to shift to a free market economy from failed socialist and traditional economies. Since Cartesianism incorporates no concept of moral community, traditional communities of faith (churches) and of blood (family, nation) have been called on to fill the gap. But their ability to do so has become ever more questionable. Main-line churches are in decline, and at the fringes morbid caricatures of spiritual movements, such as the Jonestown settlement and the Koreshan compound in Waco, have appeared. The family is weakening as a foundational institution, and everywhere concern for the decay of "values" is voiced. Nationalism has become strident, bellicose, and politically destructive.

Friedrich Nietzsche

This last philosophical voice in the Cartesian lineage prophesies two possibilities for the future: transcendence of our present nihilism in the direction of a radically new age of "The Overman" or catastrophe. Nietzsche's philosophy is grounded in the idea expressed by Descartes in *The Passions of the Soul* that "the will is by its nature so free that it can never be constrained" (*CSM*, I, 343; *AT,* XI, 359). Peter Schoules has argued that in Descartes' view each of us "has the first word and the last word in the matter of determining what is and what is not to be accepted as truth." Freedom to doubt, not the cogito, is Descartes' Archimedean point (Schoules 1989, pp. 38, 45, 51). For the Cartesian philosophers whose work we have reviewed, free will meant resignation to determination by the objective order of reason. It also seems to have meant this for Descartes. But Nietzsche presents a quite different, but just as logical, conclusion: on Descartes' assumptions, to embrace reason – as an objective, universal order beyond the self – is an act of faith. As Hiram Caton has pointed out, Descartes' method adds nothing to the indubitability of mathematical and logical truth. Only an act of will can affirm the validity of the whole body of evidence (Caton 1973, p. 125).

This line of thought opens up the possibility that it is our fiat that creates the world: "Nothing is true and everything is permitted!" In *The Genealogy of Morals* Nietzsche wrote: "Though the world perish, let there be philosophy, the philosopher, *me*" (1968, p. 544). This is his nihilistic conclusion of a reflection on self-existence as fundamental truth. It dissolves the public world of community and moral authority, just as we experience that dissolution today. It completes the nihilism inherent in the characteristics of the Cartesian self. Nietzsche embraced the conclusion both as prophecy and as his own will. He thought, according to Tracy Strong,

> that the structures holding society and life together . . . have slowly broken down over the evolution of the West to such an extent that they are now only maintained by various moral, epistemological, and political strongarm techniques. If they are to be replaced with new foundations, they will have to be shattered. This task, which Nietzsche sets himself, can only be accomplished by breaking that which still holds culture together. Nietzsche is willing to risk all on the desperate gamble that, with proper preparation (that is why he writes), a transvaluation may be accomplished, once the genealogical chains of the past are definitely shattered. As such, the enterprise might be thought to be political; through volition and domination it seeks to replace one form of existence by another. (Strong 1975, p. 187)

In the completion of nihilism, in a final leveling and atomization of society, Nietzsche foresaw the possibility of a new nobility of "Overmen" who would create a new civilization – "free, *very* free spirits," energetic, creative, self-disciplined, with a will to power. Scholars will continue to argue for a long time about whether Nietzsche saw these "Overmen" as an entire society of independent individuals or a new conquering elite. Whatever the truth of the matter, the "Overman" would have one defining characteristic: he would know that no objective order of the world is given; he or she would have to create order from his or her own will. The alternative to Nietzsche's view is chaos or finding a new way of ideas. The philosophical task of a new way would be to join freedom and science to rational moral community.

REFERENCES

Aarsleff, Hans. 1969. The State of Nature and the Nature of Man in Locke. In *John Locke, Problems and Perspectives*, ed. John W. Yolton, pp. 99–136. London: Cambridge University Press.

Bentham, Jeremy. [1789] 1970. *An Introduction to the Principles of Morals and Legislation*. London: Athlone.

Bluhm, William T., et al. 1980. Locke's Idea of God: Rational Truth or Political Myth? *Journal of Politics* 42: 414–438.

——. 1984. *Force or Freedom?: The Paradox in Modern Political Thought*. New Haven: Yale University Press.

——. 1993. Toward 1992: Utilitarianism as the Ideology of Europe. *History of European Ideas* 16, nos. 4–6: 487–494.

Caton, Hiram. 1973. *The Origin of Subjectivity*. New Haven: Yale University Press.

Cobban, Alfred. 1960. *In Search of Humanity: The Role of the Enlightenment in Modern History*. New York: Braziller.

Halévy, Elie. 1928. *The Growth of Philosophic Radicalism*, trans. Mary Morris. New York: Macmillan.

Hobbes, Thomas. [1651] 1968. *Leviathan*. London: Penguin.

Kant, Immanuel. [1785] 1981. *Groundwork for the Metaphysics of Morals*, trans. J. W. Ellington. Indianapolis: Hackett.

——. [1795] 1983. *Perpetual Peace and Other Essays*, trans. Ted Humphrey. Indianapolis: Hackett.

Locke, John. [1690] 1980. *Second Treatise of Government*. Indianapolis: Hackett.

Mintz, Samuel I. 1962. *The Hunting of Leviathan*. Cambridge: Cambridge University Press.

Nietzsche, Friedrich. 1968. *Basic Writings*, trans. and ed. Walter Kaufman. New York: Random House.

Reik, Miriam. 1977. *The Golden Lands of Thomas Hobbes.* Detroit: Wayne State University Press.

Rousseau, Jean-Jacques. 1987. *The Basic Political Writings*, trans. O. A. Cress. Indianapolis: Hackett.

Schoules, Peter. 1989. *Descartes and the Enlightenment.* Kingston and Montreal: McGill-Queens University Press.

Spinelli, Altiero. 1966. *The Eurocrats: Conflict and Crisis in the European Community*, trans. C. E. Harris. Baltimore: Johns Hopkins University Press.

Steintrager, James. 1977. *Bentham.* Ithaca: Cornell University Press.

Strong, Tracy. 1975. *Friedrich Nietzsche and the Politics of Transfiguration.* Berkeley: University of California Press.

Talmon, J. L. 1960. *The Origins of Totalitarian Democracy.* New York: Praeger.

Woloch, Isser. 1982. *Eighteenth-Century Europe: Tradition and Progress 1715–1789.* New York: W. W. Norton.

Essay 7
Psychoanalysis

DAVID WEISSMAN

Many practices thrive as arts long before theorists have explained their efficacy: there were steam engines and bridges before engineers could explain how they work or stand. Psychoanalysts have emphasized their scientific credentials so fiercely that we may ignore the success of clinical practices that carry on without the burden of theory. Theory may come later. This was the sequence when anxiety and odd behavior were observed and treated before Freud had described and explained them. Those earlier treatments were often elaborate – think of rituals liberating victims from demonic possession. Still, they could not have enduring, therapeutic effect, because mental illness is not treated to any depth without an accurate theory of its development and causes. Bits of theory and comment (e.g., Plato's remarks about dreams and Augustine's report of a boy's embarrassed jealousy when he sees his mother nursing someone else's child) have been available for centuries, but none promoted effective therapy until mental life was seen to have an integrity of its own, one that is distinct from social conditions (e.g., poverty) and from the body (e.g., stomachaches).

Cartesian dualism separates mind from its context, thereby enabling us to distinguish the activities and symptoms pertinent to mind from those relating to our circumstances or bodies. Plato too emphasized the separateness of soul and body, but nous is active intellect grasping the Forms. There is no provision for self-perception – nous does not say, *I* am, *I* exist. Cartesian minds, separate from bodies but also distinct from one another, are a more congenial site for personalized attitudes and ailments. Each of us has a body; so each of us is a mind.

Mind's Structure

The structure that Descartes ascribed to mind may be represented as two acts of awareness focused by some content (see fig. 9). In the figure, *a* is any

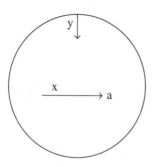

Figure 9.

content of awareness, *x* any act of first-order awareness, whether perceiving, conceiving, feeling, or willing, and *y* is second-order, reflexive awareness. Every *a* and every *x* are accessible to *y*: but more, each of them *is* only if it is or can be perceived by *y*. For nothing is if there is not evidence sufficient to justify affirming that it is. Only *y*, second-order reflexive awareness, can testify authoritatively that there is some *a* or *x*. Equally, there is each *y*'s affirmation, with evidence to support it, that *y* is: I am, I exist, each *y* declares. What does *I* signify? Just the structure of the self-discovered thinking subject, meaning the relationship of *a*, *x*, and *y*.

Descartes supposed that every thinker is challenged in three ways: by external threats or inducements to its associated body, by bodily passions that mind perceives as dangerous or foolish, and by the obscurity of its ideas. Will, as much as thought or perception, is a critical faculty in each case: we resolve to avoid bodily harm or enhance bodily well-being; we suppress inappropriate desires; we are careful not to affirm or deny obscure ideas. These expressions of mind's resolve imply three topics that are critical for psychoanalytic theory: object relations, impulse control, and the opposition of public and private meanings.

Object Relations

Mind relates directly to its associated body, and indirectly to other bodies. Where every body is a mode of the one extended substance, an alteration in any mode resonates in every direction, affecting remote bodies. These effects sometimes register as percepts in the minds joined to these bodies. Each thinker responds after estimating that the effects are good or bad for its interests (i.e., for the interests of this coupled mind and body). Or mind anticipates body's needs and directs its interactions with other things, including other people.

Descartes described these relations under two headings: mind's relation to the body associated with it and the instrumental use of or flight from things deemed good or bad for one's mind and body. Relations of both sorts are secured by actions that express our moral sense. But here, Descartes' responses are odd. He professes an exaggerated regard for the classic virtues, including generosity, loyalty, and friendship; yet the prudence he commends is justified principally by self-interest, not by sympathy or care. Descartes says little or nothing that would imply mind's emotional dependence on other thinkers. Even friendship is justified in terms that are formal and remote:

> [S]ince we cannot equally love all those in whom we observe equal worth, I think that our only obligation is to esteem them equally, and since the chief good of life is friendship, we are right to prefer those to which we are joined by secret inclinations, provided we also see worth in them. Moreover, when these secret inclinations are aroused by something in the mind, and not by something in the body, I think they should always be followed. The principal criterion by which they can be known is that those which come from the mind are reciprocated, which is often not the case in the others. (*CSMK*, 323; *AT,* V, 58)

Recall that the sixth *Meditation* restores our belief in all the significant things doubted in the first one, but that nothing is said there regarding the thinker's renewed beliefs about relations to his family and friends. This is less curious if we remember that Descartes said nothing of these beliefs in the first *Meditation.* Where nothing was doubted, there is nothing to restore. One may explain that sympathy for others is ignored in both places because Descartes' concern is knowledge, not feeling. But this is only half right: both *Meditations*, the first and the last, concern object relations. Affect is a way of expressing one's beliefs about other people and things: it expresses the conviction that they accept or reject us. Descartes ignores affect. The thinker he describes is emotionally inert.

This emotional isolation reinforces the separation entailed by the categorial difference between mind and body: mind's relation to any material object, its own body included, is problematic. Descartes affirms mind's control of its body in the sixth *Meditation* – God would not sabotage the belief that we have this control. But the force of his argument inclines the other way: each thinker's autonomy and reserve preclude relations with other things, especially other people. Leibniz confirms our mutual isolation when he argues that each thinker is a windowless monad ([1675–1716] 1989, p. 214). Object relations – excepting that to God – are delusions promoted by the coherence of experience, not by real interactions. It only *seems* that we have easy access – in thought or feeling – to one another. Kant's transcendental egos and Schopenhauer's thrashing wills are equally singular. Still, Descartes hardly needs support from Kant or Schopenhauer. His cogito is already isolated, its principle virtue being its ability to calculate and pursue its advantage. Descartes may espouse heroic virtues for the cogito, but there is little trace of fellow feeling in them (e.g., one is to be generous out of regard for one's own perfection, not out of sympathy for those one helps [*CSM*, I, 384; *AT,* XI, 446–447]). Equally, the thinker is to be moral, but only because one "transfer[s] the care one previously took of oneself to the preservation of this whole" (*CSMK*, 311; *AT,* IV, 611).

We can test this reading of Descartes with a question provoked by contemporary psychoanalytic theory: Is the autonomy of the cogito breached in any way by the introjections that Heinz Kohut (1978, pp. 99–100, 125–126) describes as "self-objects." These are the internalized representations of parents or friends whose empathy we feel and for whom we act. Nothing in the cogito, Leibniz's monads, or Kant's transcendental egos is evidence of either this mutually penetrating empathy or the idealizations that form as we nourish our memories of it. Cartesian self-identity is formed from the inside out, never from empathic intrusions that are incorporated as part of oneself.

Can an ego be as self-sufficient as Descartes requires? Hegel's description of the master-slave relation ([1807] 1967, pp. 228–240) is evidence that something is missing in the cogito and its heirs. We identify this missing nuance by comparing the two notions of sociality discussed in essay 3. One notion requires that each will bend to laws, whether or not other people accept any particular law and whether or not we engage other people: we stop at red lights even if no other car is in sight. The other idea affirms that sociality is reciprocity in both action and feeling (see Kohlberg 1981 and Gilligan 1982). Sociality of the first sort has limited application, because there are no laws prescribing the fine grain of most interpersonal relations. No law prescribes what friends shall do together; no law dictates subject matters for the conversations of therapists and their patients. The relation binding patients and therapists, with its mix of feeling and idealization, creates a new self-object in the patient: the patient can respond to the therapist's empathic support, recover censored feelings and experiences, and explore new ways to think, feel, and act. Talk therapy could not succeed if there were no sociality – and no talk – of this other kind.

The cogito engaged by other people and things is thereby enlarged. Rather than defend our rigid autonomy, we make ourselves permeable to others. They, in turn, are doubled: there are the people to whom we relate and the representations of them – the self-objects – that are creatures of memory, idealization, and play. These doubles exist, ambiguously, in the intermediate space that Winnicott describes (1971, pp. 53–64), the space in which imagination reworks our perceptions and memories of real people for our own purposes. We relate to these people in ways skewed by our distortions. Someone who acts as I hope he will confirms my idea of him; failing to do that, he betrays me. But then I am confused: should I blame him or my idealization of him? Either way, my incorporation of relevant others shapes my understanding and behavior by fixing my values and aims. I prize or fault myself as I imagine they would judge me. Descartes' cogito atrophies for want of these significant others; or it turns grandiose, seeing others as shells onto which to project the image of its own virtues.

Impulse Control

Descartes supposed that we conquer bodily impulses by using will to direct or suppress them. Will is informed by criteria of good and evil and by the knowledge of truths (*CSM*, I, 347; *AT,* XI, 368). Ideas of good and evil coupled with truths about body's circumstances (the good and the true are joined as prudence) are sufficient to tune and harmonize body's drives. We are to assume, with Plato, that the passions have a natural cycle, so that controlling them is easy once their natural rhythm is discovered. We discern this by turning in upon ourselves, clarifying, regulating, and directing our passions so that they are expressed in ways that satisfy personal needs, customs, and laws. This is Descartes' description of will under the control of self-perception (*CSM*, I, 335; *AT,* XI, 343). It recalls Peirce's emphasis on self-controlled self-control (1934, vol. 5, p. 296). Notice Descartes' assumption that conscious discipline of the passions does not generate frustration or conflict within us, just as the well-tuned piano does not fight back, subverting the pianist by forcing dissonances into the music played. Think of Kohut's suggestion that the drives of a "firm" self are placated without frustration, and that frustrated drives are the disintegration products – and symptoms – of a dissolving self (1978, pp. 69–83). Plato made the same point when he said that the citizens of a luxurious state become sick if the internal harmonies of their lives are overwhelmed by the goods that inflame their appetites. (1964, p. 619).

Freud emphasizes that drives are dominant and innate, just as sexuality is innate and easily aroused, and that frustration and guilt are experienced when drives are confounded or felt strongly (1966–74, vol. 19, pp. 45–47). Kohut, following Plato and Descartes, believes that unruly drives and feelings are evidence that a disintegrating self has not established the rhythm and focus appropriate to its appetites. Are we frustrated, irascible, and liable to excess? If so, we suffer from appetites that have not been trained for the reliable, cyclic expression appropriate to bodily appetites. But our anxiety and frustration are the result of bad training, not evidence of un-appeasable appetites. This dispute remains unresolved, though both sides agree that drives that are fractious (from birth or because of disintegration), arouse guilt, and are repressed.

Public and Private Meanings

Is there a moral difference between idiosyncrasy and illness? Or should these two be conflated so as to stand together against an idealized standard of meanings that are public and universal? Freud's concern for neurotic meanings (1966–74, vols. 4–5, 6), like Nietzsche's anguish for the creative outsider ([1901] 1969, pp. 196, 484, 508–509), is paradoxical: the meanings are idiosyncratic, but Nietzsche and Freud will tell us about them – or the artists, original thinkers, and neurotics will do that for themselves – making publicly comprehensible what was otherwise singular and private. The patient who starts in idiosyncrasy is to be changed by making himself intelligible to himself, as to the rest of us, by way of behaviors, thoughts, and feelings that we can recognize as healthy because they are like our own. This is cure by exposure, cure by universalizability. Like Wittgenstein's distaste for private languages (1966, pp. 97–104), it is anticipated by Descartes' (and Plato's) emphasis on meanings which are common to all the members of an intellectual community (or language-game): illness is idiosyncrasy, because idiosyncrasies are unintelligible to the rest of us. Counting ourselves healthy because we communicate easily with one another, we make our meanings normative. Anyone who would join us, anyone who would speak to us, must speak as we do, understand as we understand. This formulation is only slightly misleading: it makes communicability the reason for making public meanings standard, though Descartes would have said that communication is possible because each thinker entertains the same luminous ideas: perceiving essences is the condition for communicating about them. Lacan makes the similar point that the analyst helps the patient to locate his singular *parole* in the context of a universal *langue* (1968, pp. 51, 57, 85).

Clarity and distinctness, this implies, are Descartes' standard for the health of minds whose virtue is their cognitive power: idiosyncratic meanings evaporate – or are superseded – when each of us achieves understanding and knowledge of the same essences (the Forms), or as we learn the social meanings of our generation or community. But this too is paradoxical, for it entails that I lose whatever is distinctive in the perception that I am, since what I am is a thinker distinguished by my private meanings. Does it follow that I recover and sustain a distinctive personal identity only as I retreat into obscurity and distortion? There is no accord among psychoanalysts about the answer to this question. Jung's ([1936–55] 1959) inherited racial memories imply a standard of public conformity and health: R. D. Laing's (1966) *The Divided Self* speaks for the idiosyncrasies that other people call madness.

Development

Descartes believed that mind is almost complete at the moment of its self-discovery. All its ideas are innate, all its powers present and conspicuous. Mind's development has only the vector described above: from idiosyncrasy and obscurity to universality and clarity. Thinkers do have animal needs – for food and sleep – but they learn to satisfy them moderately, so that mind's intellectual development is unimpeded by chronic, chafing desires. Mental development has, for Descartes, these two aspects only, the one intellectual, the other practical. It follows that children are junior adults, having the mental structure of adults and the same raw capacity for moderation and intellectual clarity, even if they are confused, having not yet discovered the difference between mind and body (*CSM*, II, 297; *AT*, VII, 441). Development is the record of this self-discovery and control of the parts revealed, though control of the two parts is not concurrent: we learn to control our bodies before we have control of our minds. Will is the instrument of control; this is the faculty that disciplines appetite and understanding. The uses of will are, however, difficult in adults and children. For children must learn to will correctly before they know why this control is desirable. All of us do, or can, perceive the reasons for controlling our-selves, so that eventually we do, or can, achieve moderation and under-standing, goodness and truth.

Descartes seems never to have realized that mind's evolution is more than learning to clarify ideas or inhibit appetites. The child errs in ways that the adult avoids. A philosopher, says Descartes, "should never rely on the senses, that is, on the ill-considered judgements of his childhood, in prefer-ence to his mature powers of reason" (*CSM*, I, 222; *AT,* VIIIA, 39). Chil-dren, this implies, are adults in potency, but not yet in act. This is half right: children do become adults. But childhood may also be a time apart, a time for cultivating imagination, spontaneity, feelings, skills, and relations. Each of these is a resource for adulthood, but also a good in itself, a good that may be lost or repressed in adulthood. Children are not miniature adults, as few people before Freud understood.

Consciousness-Unconsciousness

There is no place in Descartes' thinking for the unconscious, unless we suppose that body – and every other mechanism – is unconscious, trivially, because it is not conscious. Compare Freud and his successors: the uncon-scious, as they describe it, is coupled to, but set against, consciousness, not mechanism. We have, therefore, this pair of questions: Why is there nothing in Descartes' understanding of consciousness that implies the possibility of the unconscious? What aspect of consciousness is, for Freud, evidence of the unconscious?

Descartes' rejection of the unconscious derives from his views about knowledge and existence: nothing can be said to be if the evidence for its being is not sufficient to support our claim to know it. The unconscious could be known to exist only if we could know it through (consciously) inspecting it. But then it would be false to itself, in having been pierced by consciousness. Alternatively, the unconscious is not directly inspected, is not known to exist, and therefore does not exist. Sartre follows this logic precisely, concluding that "Existential psychoanalysis rejects the hypothe-sis of the unconscious; it makes the psychic act co-extensive with con-sciousness" ([1943] 1969, p. 728).

One imagines Descartes or Sartre supplementing this epistemological argument with a phenomenological description: consciousness, they might say, is an efflorescence that fills and defines our mental space. Nothing that is not visible within this space can be known, but, equally, anything think-able, hence visible, can be known. So Kant posited a world of things-in-themselves, declaring them noumenal and unknowable, while Hegel countered that such things are brought into consciousness, so confirming their possible existence, merely by thinking them. Similarly, matters not presently conscious but stored as memories may be recalled. Such things as noumena and memories exist conditionally, in that they can be made the objects of awareness. Where are they when currently uninspected? We invent a question-begging locution, saying that they are "preconscious." Or we agree with Leibniz that consciousness allows for degrees of intensity, so that there is always this more or less luminous space in which to locate things whose existence depends upon their being perceived.

This Cartesian consciousness may be characterized in one of several ways. Describing it as the illumination of a mental space, like a lantern at night, we say that it fades into darkness at the edges. Or we say that consciousness is a beam of attention or intention surrounded by penumbral light. These metaphors emphasize that the borders of consciousness are less consequential than the intensity of the center. There is a similar implication in the idea that consciousness emerges at a threshold of intensity or organization, one that occurs when certain physiological conditions are satisfied: when these conditions fail, we are drowsy or we sleep. Light is most intense at its center or source; equally, higher-order cognitive work requires that we be alert and focused, not merely awake.

Every such metaphor or hypothesis identifies consciousness with the intensity of inner light, and each concedes that the light is less focused at the margins. But is this so? Does consciousness merely fade at the edges, or is it extinguished for some reason that is not apparent within consciousness itself? The metaphysical and epistemological arguments canvased above would justify saying, after Berkeley and Sartre, that there are no phenomena affecting consciousness from a position beyond it: esse est percipi.

Freud thought otherwise. He never supposed that mind, let alone the ambient world, ends at the borders of self-awareness. Indeed, less of mind is conscious than unconscious, since mind's organizing, executive functions – ego – and drives – id – are usually unconscious (1966–74, vol. 19, pp. 17–18). This hypothesis needs explaining. Why are some things conscious when others are not? Freud answers by describing the boundaries of consciousness in a way that differs from the alternatives mentioned. Consciousness is not a luminous space or beam that shades into darkness. It has limits fixed by the censorship or repression – mind's executive (ego) functions – of drives that arouse anxiety: think of sexual desires that are abhorrent in the thinker's culture. Rather than being all of mind, consciousness has borders, borders that are barriers.

These limits are a dynamic, seismic fault: current perceptions mix with ego-endorsed thoughts and desires on one side, censored drives energize us from the other side. Freud revised Descartes' views in order to provide for activities and structures that are more often unconscious than conscious. These include drives that are repressed because they are dangerous, given learned social conventions or mind's estimate of its self-interest and circumstances. Also included are learned but unconsidered strategies for satisfying mind's interests, memories of all sorts, and learned but unexamined formations of drives and habits. Freud emphasized that the greater part of mental activity and structure is never available for inspection. Like icebergs, they are mostly out of sight, though it is anxiety, not bulk, that explains the submergence – the suppression – of hurtful memories, socially censured passions, and the defenses against them. Appetites and drives often pass the barrier, as we are conscious of being thirsty. But id, meaning the array of instinctual drives, is never inspectable all at once, because one cannot attend to all one's appetites simultaneously, and because some appetites are repressed, when learned social behaviors – Superego – teach us to curb public displays of vanity or sexuality (Freud 1966–74, vol. 19, p. 35). Ego is the set of functions that mediates between our drives and socially sanctioned ways of satisfying them (ibid., p. 56). Each of us develops complex strategies for solving this opposition, for establishing coherence within ourselves and viable relations with other people and things. But none of us can list or survey all the features of this intrapsychic posture. Ego, as much as id, is mostly out of sight (Freud 1966–74, vol. 22, p. 69).

This altered model has consequences for all mind's principal features and relations. *Object relations* are transformed, because each of the three factors in Freud's structural model refers beyond itself to things external to the mind. The drives constitutive of id require satisfaction by goods or services that mind and body alone cannot provide. Superego is the embodiment of rules and standards learned from other people. Ego mediates between insistent drives and the circumstances that oppose us. We cannot satisfy any of these interests unless we use our wits to influence other people and things.

Impulse control is more problematic than Descartes (or Plato) supposed, because drives are not moderated or harmonized easily. Hunger is cyclical – we are successively hungry, satisfied, quiescent, then hungry again – but sexuality may have us permanently on edge, forever tempted to do what social rules proscribe. Impulse control is these two things: learned styles of gratification that satisfy both bodily needs and societal rules; and the repression or redirection of drives that cannot be satisfied in the raw form desired, because either the means are unavailable or the rules forbid it.

Development is more complex than Descartes believed, for three reasons. First is the need to develop three powers, not only the two he emphasized. We learn, he said, to control or cultivate feelings – the preferred passions are wonder, love, sadness, and joy (*CSM*, I, 350–351; *AT,* XI, 373–376) – and to make true judgments. Freud added that feelings and instincts (e.g., sexuality) also develop. Second is this difference in the notions of cause appropriate to these two conceptions of development. Development is teleological for Descartes; its critical cause is formal for Freud. We grow toward self-discipline and rationality in the first, we are shaped and directed by a genetic template in the second, as infancy, childhood, adolescence, and adulthood are successive, genetically programmed formations (Freud 1966–74, vol. 16, p. 303–319). Each stage intrudes new obstacles and opportunities, so development becomes incrementally more complex. A baby does not fend for itself; a toddler does. Drives that were quiescent in the latency period – from age six or seven to ten – turn rabid in adolescence. Third, mental development as Descartes describes it occurs entirely within consciousness. It is, for Freud, the transfer of control from largely unconscious, instinctual drives to conscious ego. The consciousness that was once overrun by drives or circumstances learns to coordinate its interests both with drives made (partly) conscious and with the demands of other people and things.

The development that Freud describes has a product: namely, a more or less viable cognitive-affective posture (Weissman 1989, pp. 179–204, and 1993, pp. 101–123). This posture is unique. Like the distinctively gnarled roots and trunk of a tree, it embodies and records each person's distinctive resolution of these three competing interests – instinct, circumstances, and understanding and self-control. The balance is always somewhat impaired, because the complex of issues to be coordinated exceeds perfect understanding or effective control (including control of all the significant consequences). Or there is a strain within us, like a wound that has healed badly. We have overlaid or grown around – compensated for – conflicts and frustrations that once stymied us, though we are less effective than we might otherwise be because of our accommodation to them. This tension may be slight and tolerable, so we are able to satisfy other people and ourselves. Or we usually cope but are less effective than we want to be because we are actively conflicted, in ourselves or with others. Or, for any of several reasons, the product of development is less firm and reliable. Something chronic or adventitious has disrupted us, or something in us is uncommonly weak or excessive. Perhaps, some misdirected drive (e.g., a grievance or passion) was nursed and satisfied out of all reasonable proportion while other needs languished. Or we had no caretakers to idealize, so we never learned to like ourselves. Or our self-objects were cruel in themselves or distorted by us, so we are vicious and disreputable. Anxious or grandiose, misinterpreting every situation and opportunity, we are angry and frustrated everywhere and always. It is less important now that we are very smart, and that all our ideas are clear and distinct.

Selfhood

Cartesian selfhood is unified by the cogito's self-reflection: I am one by virtue of my unifying self-perception. By contrast, consciousness cannot unify the Freudian self, because there is only limited access to matters that are unconscious: some of them are fiercely repressed, whereas others, including strategies of thought or action, are inferred from the behaviors they regulate. The unity of the Freudian self is a point of contention. How is it unified? Indeed, *is* it unified? Let us defer consideration of the Freudian *how* while we consider Kohut's affirmation that the self is unitary.

Freud is obliged to identify a self in the midst of its parts, some of which are out of touch with each other (as feelings or drives may be isolated by repression). Kohut remarks that the self is an "encompassing superordinated configuration" (1978, p. 97). It includes ambitions, skills, and ideals, each related to the others by way of the "energic tension arc (from nuclear ambitions via nuclear talents and skills to nuclear idealized goals) that persists throughout each person's lifetime" (ibid., p. 178). The result is a " 'nuclear self' . . . an independent center of initiative and perception" (ibid., pp. 177–178). What unifies this self? The internal, unifying process is not fully specified, though Kohut supposes that self-objects, the remembered and idealized caretakers, have a principal role in making the self forceful and coherent (ibid., pp. 85–87). Their love and demands nourish its self-esteem and standards: "The child that is to survive psychologically is born into an empathic responsive human milieu (of self-objects) just as he is born into an atmosphere that contains an optimal amount of oxygen" (ibid., p. 85).

This is remarkable when compared to the views of Descartes and Leibniz, because it implies that the cohesion of the self is the product of its object relations. These are human relations of dependence, encouragement, and

idealization. Whereas Freud's characterization of development is sometimes mechanical (the child passes through a succession of preordained
stages) and monadic (infantile, anal, and genital periods occur irrespective
of external circumstances), Kohut's is always relational: the child will not
acquire a firm, resilient self if it is not loved, if it does not have caretakers
like Winnicott's "good enough mother" (1990, p. 179).

Kohut supposes that the self is created in the process of responding to,
while internalizing, the idealized models of empathic others. Someone who
was deprived of these relations may be incapable of therapy. For therapy
requires transference (Freud 1966–74, vol. 16, pp. 439–447) – a pathway
for empathy from the therapist, trust and idealization from the patient –
though transference cannot be established if a patient has no experience of
giving or receiving feeling. Kohut emphasizes these features of the transference, while suggesting that Freud may not have valued them enough:
there cannot be an empathic bridge between patient and therapist if each
person's psychological development is largely monadic, and if therapists
rarely enter into the reveries of their patients. Transference of a Freudian
kind risks becoming a one-way street: the patient reflects and talks, address-
ing himself or the void, just as Descartes' letters often seem to have been
written for their author. Kohut responds that the therapist's empathy nour-
ishes the patient, making therapy possible (Kohut 1978, p. 251).

Hence these questions: How directly do we engage one another in
thought and feeling? How critical are these reciprocities for our psychic
development? How vital is it that the dynamic of these early encounters be
mimicked in therapy? We have Descartes and Freud on one side, Winnicott
and Kohut on the other (ibid., p. 173n).

Dualism

Consider this Freudian statement of the question regarding mind's unity:
namely, how are consciousness and the unconscious, or ego, id, and superego unified? Freud believed that these are coordinated states or activities of
human bodies (1966–74, vol. 1, pp. 283–397). Accordingly, mind's unity is
a function of body's physiological integration. This is increasingly plausible, as we speculate that consciousness is the state of a hierarchically organized, neural network having some least level of perceptual inputs (i.e.,
consciousness lapses as the perceptual organs shut down).

This account of mind's unity is unsettling, because it renounces the
dualism from which psychoanalysis has profited so much. For there was no

science or medical art of the mind as long as mind's symptoms could not be distinguished from the consequences of social position or bodily states. Psychoanalysis was created when mind seemed autonomous: this was the historical condition for establishing an independent science with a unique domain in which to practice its therapy. Do we cut the ground from beneath psychoanalytic theory and treatment by supposing that mind's unity is supplied by the very body from which Descartes distinguished it?

This question preoccupies contemporary psychoanalysts and psychiatrists, drug companies, and the agencies that pay for medical care. Talk therapy is expensive; pills are cheap. Why pay for years of therapy when (crude) comparative studies suggest that talk therapy is no more effective in the long term than no therapy (but see Dawes 1994). This skepticism is reinforced by the mystery of talk therapies – how do they work? Freudian theory, like dualism itself, seems otiose. Is it?

Freud assumed that mind is the activity of a material system. But there was and is no practical, near-term hope of translating conceptualizations appropriate to complex mental phenomena into the terms of molecular biology or even physiology. We cannot explain, just now, awareness of qualitative difference – red as different from green. Mechanistic explanation is all the more anomalous when applied to the self-awareness that issues in altered self-control. Freud had to choose: restrict himself to mechanistic theory and say nothing of mind, or invent a vocabulary useful for describing and treating mental disorders, while supposing that the words are only place-markers for mechanistic concepts that may be introduced some time in the future. Psychoanalysis flourished when Freud (1929) chose explanatory cogency and the fiction that mind is operationally autonomous.[1] But there is this hidden cost: organic medicine is explicitly materialistic. All its descriptions, explanations, and therapies are rooted in the body's anatomy and functions. Psychoanalysis purchased its independence by separating itself from the vocabulary and tide of modern medicine. Now, as materialism overtakes the mind, psychoanalysis finds itself unintelligible to the rest of the medical community. The mind it defended now seems a phantom with no life apart from Freud's exotic jargon.

This exile may not be permanent. For nothing precludes the translation of psychoanalytic concepts into the language of a mechanistic theory. There are only these three caveats. First is the proviso that this language be richer than anything currently available: there must be a place in it for words signifying phenomena – consciousness, for example – that almost no one denies, however difficult it is to explain their generation in a material system. Second, describing mind in physical terms effects a reduction of concepts, not things; consciousness (like life) is not eliminated just because our notion of it is enlarged to specify its necessary and sufficient material conditions. Third, the notions thus translated must not ascribe to mind properties that no material system could have. This point is difficult, because of the lingering persuasion that some principal mental activities or states (consciousness, thought, and intentionality, for example) cannot have exclusively material conditions. Here are some rudimentary hypotheses that justify thinking otherwise.

Complexity in organized systems of neurons precludes the ready access of every neuronal cluster to the signals passing through every other one. Suppose that consciousness is generated in a cluster or clusters having some least degree of hierarchical organization. Consciousness there is consistent with the absence of consciousness in other clusters. Distinguish now between the signals – the information – passing through these networks and the material character of the neurons themselves. We could describe both things as unconscious, though doing so is significant only when the matters designated could be conscious, as signals and stored information may rise to consciousness, though the internal architecture of the clusters does not.

Predicates, such as *thought* and *intentionality*, have typically been defined ostensively by reference to conscious experience. But they are not senseless when applied to activities that are not now, and may never be, conscious. For awareness is not a condition for much that is represented, calculated, and interpreted, as information-processing machines do all three without being conscious. It is also plausible that we have a rich but unconscious intentional life. Imagine someone who organizes her affairs to avoid situations like that of a childhood humiliation. Repressing her memories, she takes care never to make herself vulnerable in that way, with the result that her behavior is oddly routinized, for reasons she does not understand.

Why is it that access to our thoughts and intentions is so restricted? Consciousness has a very narrow span: it is usually reserved to matters of current urgency or random attention, not to everything at once or even to everything sequentially. Still, the eye of the storm is less than all of it. Each person's developmental path is a weave of initiatives, experiences, and interpretations. These shape consciousness without appearing within it. Repression hides the evidence of crippled solutions. Efficient design hides the rest.

Notice that these hypotheses are still inadequate to the practice of psychoanalysis. For it is no good telling the analyst that his patients' defenses are only the material or organizational features of a physical system. The analyst requires a conceptualization sufficient to direct his treatment.

Amended Freudian theory is his only conceptual resource when the available physical models are too programmatic or vague.

Could psychoanalysis satisfy its need for theory (while easing itself into conformity with organic, materialist, medical practice) by identifying mind with mindlike systems such as information-processing machines? Freudians should object that doing this would ignore two critical aspects of mind: namely, its attitudes and its functional integrity. Attitudes combine affect with interpretation and preference: we differentiate and favor something or distinguish and reject it. Hierarchically organized clusters of attitudes, most of them unconscious, are created in us as we develop a psychic identity. Programmed computers do not have attitudes; that explains their bland efficiency. They cannot be paradigms for psychoanalysis, because we humans use information in the ways prescribed by attitudes. It is usually conflicts among these attitudes, not failures of representation or calculation, that make us sick. Identifying, then altering, attitudes is a principal objective as we struggle to control ourselves.

It follows that programmed computers are drastically deficient as models of unitary selves. They could not be selves even if they were conscious, because selfhood in us is a complex of information, attitudes, drives, and learned strategies, not of information and calculation only: we apply the strategies to satisfy drives in ways prescribed by the attitudes. This mix of factors achieves a particular design in each of us because of our developmental history: this is our cognitive-affective balance. Descartes cleared a space in which to examine this complex result; but this space, rather than being all of mind, is only a point of access – a window – to the structure below. No one is surprised that the view is obscure, or that tapping on the glass often fails to alter the things inside.

A Saltant Lineage

How should we explain the 250-year gap between Descartes' *Meditations* and Freudian theory? The difference between Cartesian and Freudian consciousness, the one fading at the edges (like penumbral light), the other circumscribed by repression, is clearly anticipated in Plato's remarks about dreaming. There was, however, a different, more potent story about the mechanism bounding consciousness in the years that separate Descartes and Freud. Thinkers distracted by this barrier had little time for more classical questions about appetite, self-knowledge, and self-control.

There is a glimmering of this mechanism in the difference, implied by

Descartes, between consciousness and self-consciousness: a thinker who is conscious in any way is also aware of being conscious. Kant embellishes this distinction, creating from it the difference between the empirical and the transcendental ego. Empirical consciousness is unified by the transcendental unity of apperception, so every moment stands in some temporal relation (simultaneous, before, or after) to every other. This inferred difference has two effects. First, self-consciousness limits consciousness, while being inaccessible to direct self-inspection. We know of it only as we infer to this extra-experiential condition for the unity of experience. We exceed the barrier between these two modes of consciousness (Kant alleged) only as we pass from our awareness of desire to self-conscious, rational control of the will. How is this exemption to be explained? Why should mind not be accessible to itself, as Hegel said, wherever thought steps beyond its bounding condition at the moment of identifying it: seeing a line, I see both sides of the space it divides. Kant would have rejected the metaphor: the boundary between consciousness and self-consciousness is not a line or a window frame such that one stands on one side while seeing the other. We do infer the transcendental, unifying conditions for phenomena unified in space and time, but we cannot look through the one to see the other. There is no access to the unifying transcendental ego from the empirical ego. Second, the empirical ego – Descartes' *I am* – is only the feeling or impression of *I* that accompanies all my experiences. This I and these experiences are the montage created by the unifying, schematizing transcendental ego. They are insubstantial, with no depth that self-reflection could expose. Descartes, this implies, has misled us in thinking that his "I am, I exist," marks the discovery of a substantial self. He has located us among the appearances, thereby misidentifying us. It was thought that Kant had done better. He decoupled consciousness from self-consciousness and located substantiality in the self-consciousness that he described as a "transcendental ego." Nothing in this transcendental self could be idiopathic, because every transcendental ego unifies experience, because the categories of understanding used to make experience are common to every thinker, and because every rational thinker suppresses self-interested desires in favor of maxims that are universalizable. None of these tasks qualifies this subject for self-reflection. It acts without having to scrutinize or explain itself, even to itself.

This is the complex claim that had to be disavowed before mind could be characterized as Freud proposed. Three changes were required. Kant's rigid distinction between consciousness unified and unifying self-consciousness had to be rejected. It was rejected, in part because Kant himself quickly repudiated the idea of mind's inaccessibility to itself (in the *Critique of Practical Reason*), in part because ordinary experience confirms Descartes' view that mind is typically or always self-aware. The demands of ethics and self-control had to be reformulated so that the principal considerations were not arrogated to a domain of transcendental rigor and self-denial. The task of joining satisfaction to self-control had to be recovered by ordinary men and women in touch with themselves. Bentham's empirical ethics, with its emphasis on pleasure and pain, learning, and habit, is an example of the demythologizing theory required. Someone needed to reaffirm, as Schopenhauer did, that passion (i.e., the will to satisfy desire) is the energizing ground of all experience, including the desire for understanding and self-control.

Freud joined these three considerations. Thought is coupled to passion within a unitary subject able to know, alter, and control itself. This subject has a developmental history, a structure (i.e., character), reciprocal relations with other people and things, and access to its own depths. Freud's ontology is naturalistic, his point of view Cartesian. That I am is perceived and assumed. What have I become, and why? Once baffled by my own habits and feelings, I become clear and distinct to myself.

NOTE

1. Freud realized as early as 1900 that explanations in psychoanalysis require the introduction of notions different from, or additional to, those available to physiology: "If we adopt the method of interpreting dreams which I have indicated here, we shall find that dreams really have a meaning and are far from being the expression of a fragmentary activity of the brain, as the authorities have claimed. *When the work of interpretation has been completed, we perceive that a dream is the fulfillment of a wish*" (Freud 1966–74, vol. 4, p. 121). Passages like this one imply that Freud's dualism was sometimes ontological, not methodological.

REFERENCES

Dawes, Robyn. 1994. *House of Cards: The Collapse of Modern Psychotherapy.* New York: Free Press.

Freud, Sigmund. 1929. Unpublished letter to G. S. Viereck, 6 Nov., in Pierpont Morgan Library, New York (accession no. MA 4794).

———. 1966–74. *The Standard Edition of the Complete Psychological Works of Sigmund Freud*, 24 vols. London: Hogarth Press.

Gilligan, Carol. 1982. *In a Different Voice.* Cambridge, Mass.: Harvard University Press.

Hegel, G. W. F. [1807] 1967. *Phenomenology of Mind,* trans. J. B. Baillie. New York: Harper and Row.

Jung, C. G. [1936–55] 1959. *The Archetypes and the Collective Unconscious,* trans. R. F. C. Hull. New York: Pantheon.

Kohlberg, Lawrence. 1981. *The Philosophy of Moral Development.* San Francisco: Harper and Row.

Kohut, Heinz. 1978. *The Restoration of the Self.* New York: International University Press.

Lacan, Jacques. 1968. *Speech and Language in Psychoanalysis,* trans. Anthony Wilden. Baltimore: Johns Hopkins University Press.

Laing, R. D. 1966. *The Divided Self.* Harmondsworth: Penguin.

Leibniz, G. W. [1675–1716] 1989. *G. W. Leibniz: Philosophical Essays,* trans. Roger Ariew and Daniel Garber. Indianapolis: Hackett.

Nietzsche, Friedrich. [1901] 1969. *The Will to Power,* trans. Walter Kaufmann and R. J. Hollingdale. New York: Random House.

Peirce, C. S. 1934. *Collected Papers,* vol. 5 ed. Charles Hartshorne and Paul Weiss. Cambridge, Mass.: Harvard University Press.

Plato. 1964. *Collected Dialogues,* ed. Ruth Hamilton and Huntington Cairns. New York: Pantheon.

Sartre, Jean-Paul. [1943] 1969. *Being and Nothingness,* trans. Hazel Barnes. New York: Washington Square Press.

Weissman, David. 1989. *Hypothesis and the Spiral of Reflection.* Albany: State University of New York Press.

———. 1993. *Truth's Debt to Value.* New Haven: Yale University Press.

Winnicott, D. W. 1971. *Playing and Reality.* London: Routledge.

———. 1990. *Home Is Where We Start From.* New York: Norton.

Wittgenstein, Ludwig. 1966. *Philosophical Investigations,* trans. G. E. M. Anscombe. New York: Macmillan.

Essay 8
Literature and the Arts

THOMAS PAVEL

When investigating the legacy of Descartes' philosophy, it is natural to look for traces of his influence throughout the culture of the period, literature and the arts included. Since his thought had such an extraordinary impact upon metaphysics and theology on the one hand and scientific research on the other, could it have failed to leave its imprint on the artistic and literary world? The question is legitimate, and its answer, predictably enough, is that it could not. But this conclusion is not easily reached, and on my way to it I will examine and challenge a few unwarranted assumptions about the Cartesian lineage in French high culture.

Descartes and French Classicism

A prevalent mind-set ascribes some kind of pervasive national spirit to French culture as a whole, one whose core quality is Cartesianism. This commonplace is shared by cultural analysts, journalists, and travel-guide writers alike. Orderly French gardens, for instance, so different from their English romantic counterparts, are thought to instantiate a basic French drive for method, reason, and symmetry. French neoclassical architectural achievements, such as Mansart's Versailles and Perrault's design for the colonnade of the Louvre, as well as the successes of French urbanism (e.g., the Place de la Concorde in Paris, the city center designs of Rennes and Dijon) are deemed to express the same impulse for rational rigor as does Descartes' philosophy. The same goes for literature and music. On this view, which assumes that culture is an expressive activity, and homogeneously expressive at that, Descartes is the most typically French of all philosophers, because he incarnates the French ideal of order and method.

An alternative way of looking at the impact of Cartesianism on French culture restricts it to seventeenth-century art and literature, on the assumption that cultural periods, rather than national cultures, are the site of expressive homogeneity. If, in addition, human thought is believed to propel history, and if great thinkers are granted a greater role in shaping this history than lesser ones, the way is prepared for the widespread notion that the essence of a period is defined by the ideas of its greatest thinker. Being a contemporary of a figure of Descartes' stature then entails being subject to his philosophy: French neoclassicist art and literature must thus be explained in Cartesian terms.

More modestly, and without taking for granted a link between Descartes and the essence of his historical period, it has been surmised that French seventeenth-century art and literature were influenced, at least, by ideas that became widely known throughout Europe soon after the publication of his *Meditations*. It is true that French neoclassicist writers and aestheticians relentlessly stress the primary of reason in art and literature. Like Descartes, they praise common sense and are deeply suspicious of extravagance – preferences which would seem to signal Descartes' visibility and prestige in seventeenth-century France. And although Descartes failed to develop a full-blown aesthetics himself, Boileau's *Art poétique*, whose precepts correspond to those of Descartes' philosophy (reason, clarity, unity, identity, simplicity, absolution perfection, and method), would constitute a *de facto* aesthetic manifestation of Cartesianism.[1] In our time, Luc Ferry (1993) has suggested that the origins of modern aesthetics lie in the rivalry between reason and the heart, the former represented by the rationalist, Cartesian poetics of Boileau, the latter by the sentimental aesthetics of Père Bouhours and Abbé Dubos.

I am not sure that these views fully capture the dynamics of seventeenth-century aesthetics or of Descartes' influences on literature and the arts. As I will argue, the idea that Descartes crucially influenced seventeenth-century aesthetics and literature has no real basis; in fact, a fortiori, belief in the existence of a homogeneous seventeenth century whose essence is expressed by Descartes' thought, along with the conviction that the French national spirit is profoundly Cartesian, must be abandoned. The Cartesian lineage, I submit, is present in French, as well as European, literature and art, but in ways that are at once less obvious and more pervasive.

In seventeenth-century France, the classicist literary and artistic doctrine was deeply indebted to the work of Italian theoreticians of the sixteenth century, who promoted a mixture of Neoplatonic aesthetics and Aristotelian poetics. Italian poeticians and their French disciples shared a set of convictions on the nature, or essence, of things, on perfection, and on beauty. Insofar as the particular nature of each thing is revealed by the end it serves, essence and finality are closely linked. Perfection resides in conformity with one's nature, and beauty, which consists in agreement between the parts and the whole, is the perceptible aspect of perfection. As animals endowed with reason, humans perceive a multiplicity of appearances, from which they infer the end and essence of each object. Holistic and teleological, this view was particularly sensitive to the place of humans in the great chain of being. The ideal of these theoreticians was to bring art and poetry into harmony with the requirements of our physical and moral environment as closely and as successfully as possible.[2]

With regard to the physical environment, classicist doctrine was concerned with the characteristics of human perception and was impressed by the earlier discovery of the laws of perspective. In their quest for the perfect optical illusion, Italian painters of the fifteenth century had proved that, with the help of projective geometry and aerial perspective, they could design a pictorial space that stimulates the human eye in the same way that natural space does (White 1967). Equally important, these theoreticians sought to perfect their explicit knowledge of our moral environment. On a classicist view, moral perception is as dependent on our species' particular position in the world as is physical perception. Human conduct obeys general rules insofar as our desires, vices, and virtues lead to predictable behavior; conversely, the external symptoms of our moral characteristics are easily interpretable. These general rules are the object of rhetoric, a discipline which emphasizes well-known facts and recognizable features. The aesthetic pleasure approved of by classicism – in Boileau's formula, "Rien n'est beau que le vrai" (Nothing but the truth is beautiful) – is the rhetorical pleasure that accompanies our recognition of familiar characters, stories, attitudes, ideas, and styles. The feeling it stimulates is the joy of inhabiting that corner of the universe which is reserved for us humans (Lenoble 1969; Tocanne 1978).

It is therefore not surprising that the notion of truth – taken to mean "the recognition of the habitual" – occupies a central place in classicist doctrine, or that this notion is linked with that of verisimilitude, a somewhat weaker concept.[3] Truth is the ideal of art whenever the latter aims at faithfully representing the appearance or moral content of the world inhabited by human beings. And, as the importance of verisimilitude indicates, truth is pursued only insofar as it is already accessible to the inhabitants of this world, by virtue of their natural perceptual and moral endowment. Neither the painter nor the poet aspires to reveal insights which are new, unexpected, or inaccessible to common sense; all their efforts aim, on the contrary, to capture truth as their contemporaries already know it.

The emphasis on nature and reason thus indicates not so much adoption of the new Cartesian metaphysics by classicist theoreticians as their eagerness to promote an art that highlights the *easy recognition of the familiar.* As Jean Mesnard (1992) puts it, "what Boileau called 'reason' or 'common sense' is a search for truth, an interest in verisimilitude, a respect for nature, and a precision of language. 'Reason' here is not opposed to 'sensibility' but to 'imagination' insofar as imagination generates irreality." Left to its own devices, imagination would soon move away from the natural point of view, which is grounded in the coincidence between the spectator's position and the place assigned to our species in the universe. Without this coincidence, the entire edifice of classicist aesthetics would collapse.[4]

By contrast, the most striking feature of Descartes' philosophy is that it detaches the human mind from its natural habitat and projects it into a new intellectual space whence it closely attains to God's view of the world. For Descartes, the human being is not just a social animal: it belongs to a species that is at once immersed in the world and radically divorced from it. The idea that reflective consciousness is the first source of absolute evidence and thus serves as the foundation for certain knowledge, an idea found in the *Meditations*, would have puzzled Aristotle; and despite Descartes' persuasive presentation, it was not noticed – let alone developed – by Aristotle's classicist disciples, in whose view any certainty we may reach in this world is the product of patient cooperation between the mind and the senses. Moreover, although – as is well known – Descartes' dualism inaugurated the modern reign of subjectivity, and although its legacy informed Kantian philosophy and modern idealism, dualism was originally designed to solve a problem that concerned philosophers interested in experimental science: how to explain the extraordinary convergence between geometry and mechanics. Galileo's mechanics drew attention to the remarkable fact that mathematics, an abstract discovery of the human intellect, accurately represents not only the movement of incorruptible astral bodies, but also that in the terrestrial domain. The visible universe thus acquired an unprecedented unity, and the human mind – without the help of revelation – was found capable of discovering the laws God followed in creating the material world. The relevance of mathematics to terrestrial mechanics placed the human mind in the same league as God's mind: infinitely far, that is, from the world.

For Descartes, as dual beings, humans are immersed in the world, but this immersion is of a peculiar kind, since the material world in its unity is reducible to a handful of properties such as extension, shape, and movement. Corporeality is fully exhausted by the mathematical study of these properties, and the luxuriant world of appearances turns out to be nothing more than a sensorial encoding of mathematical laws which govern the world.[5] Since God has granted us the ability to discover these laws, however, the aim of knowledge is to go beyond the sensorial encoding – that is, beyond the realm of appearances – to grasp the universal *mathesis*.

The astonishing arrogance of these claims was sensed by Gassendi ([1641] 1972) who, defending an epistemology less realist than that of Descartes, insisted that we humans have no way of knowing what goes on in God's mind. Malebranche ([1696] 1992) by contrast, embraced Descartes' hyperrealism and pushed it to its limits, concluding that our mind not only has access to the mathematical laws governing the universe, but sees these truths in God himself (pp. 688–690). Thus, in the Descartes–Malebranche line of the idealist tradition, the human mind, on the way to winning its epistemological autonomy, lingers in the vicinity of God's mind, as if it needed to absorb his infinite power by osmosis.

Nothing could be further from the position of classicist writers and theoreticians than such philosophical hubris. Boileau demanded that poetry stay away from anything which is not warranted by everyday reason, common sense, experience, and moderation. Corneille's *Trois Discours sur le poème dramatique* ([1660] 1987) are a rich mine of empirical, commonsensical remarks about the craft of the playwright, none of which depend on Descartes. As for painters, their discovery of artificial perspective had two consequences, both anticipating, as it were, Descartes' mathematization of the physical world. One is that paintings became easier to interpret visually. Although the human eye is certainly capable of correcting the geometric imperfections of Byzantine frescoes, and those of Giotto for that matter, the effort required to interpret the visual clues of Masaccio's *Trinity* (in Santa Maria Novella) is much less. Spatial information flows smoothly, and the viewer enjoys the comfort and pleasure of perceiving a credible section of his world virtually without effort. Artificial perspective reinforces the viewer's sense of belonging to a well-determined niche in the existing universe, his or her best chance of achieving an accurate representation of this world consisting in understanding the way in which it reveals itself. This attitude contrasts with Descartes' determination to free the human mind from its enslavement to appearances and to reach an understanding of the material world independent of our position within it. The other consequence is that, although mathematical reasoning plays as much of a role in artificial perspective as in Cartesian physics, the difference between these uses is significant: whereas for Renaissance painters the purpose of optical geometry was to describe the regularities of our perception of appearances and thus to glorify the visible world, Descartes' physics aims to see through the world of appearances and reduce it to its mathematical underpinnings.

A Romance Hero

Although they may have little to do with French neoclassicism, the links between Cartesian thought, literature, and the arts continue a much older tradition, on the one hand, and herald an aesthetic movement which blossomed fully only some centuries later, on the other. A student of the Jesuits, Descartes had learned his rhetoric well and, as a writer of what today we would call nonfiction, was unusually effective. His *Discourse on Method* was the first successful work of philosophy to be written in readable, cogent French. Distancing himself from the loose, rambling style of his predecessor Montaigne, Descartes modeled his prose on a popular narrative genre, that of the spiritual autobiography.[6] In the *Discourse*, and later in the *Meditations*, philosophical arguments are introduced in the guise of an autobiographical narrative. As presented in the *Discourse*, Descartes' life consists primarily of epistemological rather than spiritual events, yet its main moments correspond to those in a religious story of sin and conversion. Like St. Augustine's *Confessions*, the *Discourse* speaks of childhood and youthful experiences, of its author learning the ways of the world, and of a moment of revelation thanks to which earlier errors are abandoned and the path of truth selected. The story mixes confidence in the present with a healthy dose of skepticism. Descartes is a modernist: "our century seemed to me as flourishing, and as fertile in great minds, as any which had preceded" (5; *CSM*, I, 113; *AT*, VI, 5). Yet the wealth of knowledge he acquired in school left him dissatisfied. The more popular disciplines – history, languages, and eloquence – easily led to frivolity, while mathematics, a solidly built discipline, had too few applications. As for philosophy, it was the least certain of all disciplines: instead of teaching the truth about each topic, it offered a multitude of opinions, all false. The great book of the world which he set out to study taught him that human opinions are as diverse and uncertain as those of philosophers, and that skepticism is therefore the only appropriate stance.

The turning point in this narrative was the period of solitude when Descartes was in Germany during the winter of 1619–20. Although the *Discourse* omits the central episode in his conversion to philosophy – the night of 10–11 November 1619, with its sequence of three symbolic dreams – the narrator makes it clear that all his ideas are rooted in discoveries he made at that time. The metaphor used for his progress in the reformation of philosophy, that of a man "who walks alone and in the twilight" (12; *CSM*, I, 119; *AT*, VI, 16), has strong religious overtones. And if God is not present at the beginning of the journey, Descartes' proof of his existence is close to a revelation, albeit a philosophical rather than a spiritual one.

Spiritual autobiographies are themselves subgenres of a larger literary family, that of the quest romance. A quest romance narrates the progress of its protagonist from weakness to strength, ignorance to knowledge, obscurity to glory. The main character of a quest romance passes through three stages: he must first qualify as a hero, then accomplish a difficult feat, and finally gain public recognition for his achievement. At each step, his readiness is measured by a test imposed on him by the outside world, which he passes successfully, with the help of Providence.[7] Thus, in the folktale type known as "the dragon-slayer," the hero, usually the youngest son of a king, undergoes a qualifying test at the hands of his father, who thereupon entrusts him with his weapons and his horse; the hero then defeats the dragon and frees the young princess; finally, against the claims of his rivals, he is recognized as her liberator. All along, the hero benefits from the help and advice of supernatural actors who side with him against his enemies (Aarne and Thompson 1961). This type of tale, whose plot has been traced back to archaic initiation rites, provided the human imagination with one of its most productive narrative schemata. It became virtually indispensable for narratives of foundation, whether social, religious, or, as in Descartes' case, epistemological. It informs the Greek novel and the baroque romance and in seventeenth-century France provides the narrative core of the lengthy and immensely successful romances of La Calprenède, Gomberville, and Madeleine de Scudéry.

Descartes, the French knight who sets out at a brisk pace to conquer the world of knowledge, tells a story similar to those of the Greek novels and baroque romances idolized by early seventeenth-century readers. He sees himself in the realm of science as the equivalent of the great romance heroes who perform every feat imaginable solely with their own strength, guided by the light of Providence. Solely with their own strength: "One of the first of the considerations that occurred to me was that there is very often less perfection in works . . . carried out by the hands of various masters, than in those on which one individual alone has worked" (9; *CSM*, I, 116; *AT,* VI, 11). Just as Polexandre or Artamène, heroes of popular romances by Gomberville and Madeleine de Scudéry, defeat every enemy in sight by virtue of their own unsurpassable valor, Descartes is convinced that he will be able to find the way to every truth on his own, with the sole help of his natural inner light. This brings us to the help of Providence: all romance heroes trust their lucky star, and rightly so. They are never betrayed by

Providence in any crucial meeting with their adversaries, and if these adventures periodically include reversals of fortune, the latter always function as tests of patience and perseverance. Similarly, Descartes's quest for truth is informed, from its very inception, by proof of God's existence. In both the *Discourse* and the *Meditations*, as soon as the foundation of certainty is established ("I think, therefore I am"), its first application is the discovery of a hidden link between human mind and an infinite Being.

Many epic and romance heroes, like Aeneas, father of Rome, and Artamène, founder of the Persian Empire, end up by establishing great empires, and the successful completion of their story is merely the starting point for a grand collective project. Descartes' quest for truth is likewise divided into two stages, the first being the quest proper, the phase accomplished by the hero alone, which leads to the discovery of the principles of science, the second, significantly enough, being a collective enterprise. The "principal fruit of these Principles is that by cultivating them we may discover many truths which I have not expounded, and thus, passing little by little from one to another, acquire in time a perfect knowledge of the whole philosophy and attain to the highest degree of wisdom" (*CSM*, I, 188; *AT,* IX(2), 18). The Quest romance thus culminates in a progressive utopia.

The Cartesian Legacy in Literature:
The Secularization of the Self

Descartes' philosophy did indeed have an impact on French classicism, one might argue, but *retroactively.* Over time, his insistence on clarity and distinctness as criteria for correct thought came to be seen as analogous to the classicists' revulsion for fuzzy expression. The Cartesian reverence for the faculty of human attention (even more conspicuous in Malebranche's writings than in Descartes' own) appeared, when considered from the vantage point of our century, to echo the classicists' emphasis on conscious control over the powers of imagination. A Romantic writer would reject demands for rational control over oneself, while a Modernist painter would feel alienated by requirements for both clarity and distinctness. Yet the Cartesian heritage – or at least its saltant lineage, to use David Weissman's suggestive term (p. 112) – had a stronger impact on the development of first-person narratives, on Romanticism and on Modernism, than on Descartes' artistic contemporaries.

The great baroque romances are narrated in the third person as if to suggest that the hero of the quest and his progress may be freely inspected by the community. As the narrative unfolds, the hero is often kept in the dark about his own birth, his future destiny, and his chances of success; but once he becomes aware of his strength and learns to trust Providence, his point of view blends smoothly into that of the narrative as a whole. The baroque hero enjoys no idiosyncratic inner life, because he does not need any: his tribulations and successes, his loneliness and integration into the community, all take place according to the latter's norms, which also govern the cosmic order. To be understood, the destiny of the quest hero does not need to be presented from the hero's internal perspective, but can be expressed in the normative language of the community. Hence both the majesty of the baroque novel and its lack of appeal to modern readers, who have lost the habit of seeing themselves as part of a universal normative order.

While Descartes' philosophical romance shares many traits with the baroque romance, it borrows the technique of first-person narration from the spiritual autobiography. Descartes' narrative inventiveness becomes apparent when one realizes that in the sixteenth and seventeenth centuries, narratives in the first person were a rarity. In accordance with the Augustinian tradition, humans were seen as fallen beings, powerless against temptation, sometimes capable of discovering the good, but never able to resist evil on their own, hence unable to overcome their native wickedness without the help of divine grace. Seen from inside, human life thus offered a rather depressing spectacle of frailty and corruption. The subjective perspective of the first-person narrative was that of a sinner who would either become the target of divine grace or remain a wrongdoer indifferent to religious and moral norms.[8] Accordingly, there were two major ways to depict real life in the first person: spiritual autobiography and the picaresque novel, a genre invented in sixteenth-century Spain.[9] A spiritual autobiography would recount how God had rescued the narrator from a life of sin, whereas a novel would focus on the main character's miserable life, bereft of God's manifest intervention. Looking inside themselves, early modern narrators could discover only the power of grace and the misery of sin; thus they had the choice of emulating either Augustine's *Confessions* or *The Life of Lazarillo de Tormes*.

Descartes' *Discourse on Method* and *Meditations*, in breaking with this constraint, contemplate and recount from within the ordeals of a quest protagonist. The *persona* who undertakes the philosophical adventures narrated in these texts resembles neither the sensitive converts saved by grace who are the heroes of Augustine's *Confessions* and its numerous imitations, nor the irredeemable rascals of Lazarillo de Tormes's ilk. He is not a fallen being who, if he follows his own impulses, is certain to persist in a life of crime. In his first-person narratives, Descartes, like a baroque romance hero, exercises full mastery over his own virtue; all he shares with sinners and saints is an internal perspective on his own activities. It is undoubtedly this peculiar alliance between the inner gaze and the strength of the soul that made Descartes' *Discourse* and *Meditations* at once so unexpected and so persuasive.

The Cartesian subject has all the energy of the modern philosophical subject, who is ready to defy authority and discover epistemological certainty within itself, yet is endowed with a personal voice, as if the epistemological adventures undertaken were of a moral or spiritual nature. They were not; and from the *Discourse* on, Descartes made a special effort to emphasize the moral and religious neutrality of his story. Uninterested in theological speculation, preaching submission to existing religious authorities and prevailing moral norms, Descartes put his newly invented device, a first-person narrative that has to do neither with eternal salvation nor with the misery of sin, in the service of strictly metaphysical musings. In a voice as seductive as those of great saints and great sinners, Descartes speaks of such dry topics as philosophical doubt, the grasping of the first subjective certainty ("I think, therefore I am"), proof of God's existence, and the division of the world into extended and nonextended substances. The metaphysical drama becomes deeply moving, as if it were a story of morality, sin, and grace. Descartes' use of first-person narrative makes epistemological progress look as desirable as personal salvation.

Each component in this powerful mixture was influential. Thanks to Descartes' narrative technique, philosophical speculation inherited all the pathos of narratives of religious salvation. If epistemology and metaphysics can become the object of a story as uplifting as St. Augustine's *Confessions*, the obvious conclusion is that solitary epistemological and metaphysical speculation constitutes a human activity as lofty as, and perhaps even loftier than, religious dialogue with God. The relegation of religion to the role of *ancilla philosophiae*, which later became the mark of Spinozan, Kantian, and Hegelian idealism, might not have been possible without Descartes first *showing* how a soliloquy can deal with a philosophical topic, yet not lose any of the highly dramatic effects typical of salvation narratives. Moreover, Descartes' story created a new narrative device, one which could be called "the self-assured inner voice," which represents the stylistic counterpart of the confidence in the powers of the human intellect shown by seventeenth-century rationalists and eighteenth-century partisans of the Enlightenment.

The literary consequences of these elements – the supremacy of philosophical over religious concerns and the self-assured inner voice – took form only gradually. Throughout the seventeenth century and during the first half of the eighteenth, most narratives in the first person, like their picaresque predecessors, carried the same age-old message about the frailty and corruption of the self. This message could be conveyed by the "low" realism of a Daniel Defoe, whose Moll Flanders and Roxana are presented as compulsive sinners and, as such, as typical incarnations of our fallen nature, or it could be couched in the medium style (*style moyen*) of moralist prose, as in Abbé Prevost's *Manon Lescaut*, whose narrator and main character, the Chevalier Des Grieux, is the epitome of gullibility and weakness. The theme of these first-person narratives is the characters' inability to rise to the norms of their communities; the main character's discourse is a confession of guilt.

Virtuous characters who have no need to feel ashamed of their behavior gradually start to speak in the first person. Since her behavior is in full accordance with the moral norms of her community, Richardson's Pamela, unlike Defoe's Moll Flanders, does not whisper her adventurous life into the compassionate ear of the reader; she proudly proclaims her moral conformity in letters to her parents. A more complex case, Richardson's Clarissa, demonstrates at once an independence from her family's authority *and* high moral standards. Clarissa's self-assured voice conveys a new sense of moral autonomy, although the values she embraces are in large part traditional. But the turning point is Rousseau's *La Nouvelle Héloïse* and his *Confessions*. Here, to the amazement of contemporary readers, the self-assured narrative voice is used to assert the right of humans to be their own moral legislators and judges. In *La Nouvelle Héloïse*, Saint-Preux and Julie deliberate and decide in favor of free love, in accordance with the principle that moral law is dictated by the human heart. Whereas Descartes' *Meditations* adapted first-person spiritual autobiography so as to let it express the power of the subject in metaphysics, Rousseau generalized this power to include morality.[10] Rousseau's and Richardson's epistolary novels created a new type of first-person narrative: stories told by individuals who feel that they, and only they, are their own moral and social judges.

Benjamin Constant's *Adolphe*, a later example, is the story of a young man who has a scandalous affair with an older woman whom he does not love. Adolphe's behavior to Ellénore demonstrates as much weakness as that of the Chevalier des Grieux in *Manon Lescaut*, yet Adolphe, true Rousseauist as he is, condemns himself not so much in the name of socially accepted standards as in the name of his right and duty to determine his own standards of behavior. All Romantic characters suffering from the *mal de siècle*, along with all Balzac's strong men, inherit this right and duty. In this regard, they are all descendants of Descartes' self-assured inner voice, through the Rousseauist assertion of moral self-judgment.

Rousseau's moral version of the Cartesian self exercised a powerful influence on French Romantic poetry, especially on Victor Hugo, Alphonse de Lamartine, and Alfred de Vigny. The nineteenth-century French critic Ferdinand Brunetière (1898) noted that Romantic poetry originates in the transformation of an obsolete literary genre, the sermon. Part of the *belles lettres* until the separation between literature and rhetoric in the nineteenth century, sermons withdrew from the literary scene, leaving behind a need to ponder majestically the spiritual destiny of humans. This need was fulfilled by Romantic poetry. If Brunetière is right, nineteenth-century poetry carried the Cartesian abduction and secularization of religious narrative and Rousseau's self-righteous inner voice one step further. The self, which from the time of Augustine was the site of intimate congress between man and God, became, in the wake of the *Meditations* and of Rousseau's writings, the self-assured judge of both knowledge and morality. Romantic poetry clothes spiritual reflection in secular garb. It thus resonates, consciously or unconsciously, with Descartes' *Meditations*. In the work of Victor Hugo and Alphonse de Lamartine, the poet's subjectivity becomes the measure of all things, just as the solitary thinker in Descartes' *Meditations* alternately summons and dismisses the world of appearances, eternal truths, and even God himself. Lamartine's *Méditations* and Hugo's visionary poems *Dieu* and *La Fin de Satan* would be difficult to imagine had not Descartes previously empowered the self, separating it from the rest of the cosmic order and setting it up as examiner and judge of the world.

Philosophical and Literary Critiques of the Cartesian Self

Successful as they were, Descartes' secularization of the self and its Rousseauist extension to moral notions did not go unchallenged in philosophy and literature. The philosophical pride in Descartes' first-person narrative soon came under attack. Kierkegaard's subjective philosophy attempted to bring philosophical narrative back to its religious origins. Since philosophical speculation is a first-person activity, and since the only genuinely important story that needs to be told in the first person is that of personal salvation, the objectivity achieved by the German idealist tradition, in particular by Hegel's phenomenology, is illusory. Subjectivity can be dealt with only in stories of personal anxiety, despair, and perhaps salvation, a set of experiences which Kierkegaard and his followers, notably Karl Barth, cast in a religious framework, but which his twentieth-century descendants, among whom Heidegger and Sartre were the most influential, transposed to a secular framework.

Dostoevski reacted along similar lines to the heroic self-determination of Romantic and realist heroes. For Dostoevski, characters who, in the wake of Descartes and Rousseau, aspire to take knowledge and morality in their own hands represent the epitome of ignorance and evil. In *Crime and Punishment*, Raskolnikov, in a demonic caricature of Saint-Preux and Julie's self-indulgence, decides to kill an innocent old woman. In *The Possessed*, Peter Verkhovensky, leader of a secret revolutionary society, orders his followers to assassinate Shatov, an innocent comrade. Just as Raskolnikov's crime is thought to help him assert his true freedom, so the collective murder, Verkhovensky assumes, will harden the revolutionary resolve of his followers. Dostoevski's point is that in both cases the opposite happens. The sense of guilt that overcomes Raskolnikov after the crime reveals that man is not his own moral arbiter. And shortly after the execution of Shatov, the revolutionaries, demoralized by fear and remorse, abandon their struggle. Rediscovery of the old sense that we depend on an exterior, perhaps transcendent, moral order subverts the self-assurance of the narratorial voice. Just as for Kierkegaard inner life resounds with fear and trembling, so in Dostoevski the collapse of modern moral autonomy leads to the creation of a new type of narrator: weak, confused, rambling, and unreliable, utterly lacking in self-assurance and ready to renege on the little he knows.

Opposition to the Cartesian subject with its self-assured voice also came from other quarters, not just from those who held religious views of human imperfection. French realism discovered its own version of the frail ego and carefully examined its tedious existence. In Flaubert's novels, the main characters are as frivolous and easy to corrupt as those of pre-Rousseauist fiction, only less remarkable. Madame Bovary is a Roxana without glamor. Frédéric, in *L'Education sentimentale*, is as weak as the Chevalier des Grieux, but lacks the latter's naive sincerity. None of Flaubert's characters possess the vitality of Balzac's young heroes, of a Félix de Vandenesse, an Henri de Marsay, a Delphine de Nucingen; nor are they as evil as Lucien de Rubempré or Vautrin. Far from ruling over their own lives, Flaubert's characters are, like picaros, borne alone by circumstances and by their own whims. But unlike picaros, who know fully the nature of their trespasses and the limits of their power, Flaubert's heroes spend their lives under the illusion that they create their own norms and draw up their own life plans. They act as if they were morally autonomous beings, while in fact they instantiate only imperfection and emptiness. Their perspective on their own inner life has no truth and little interest, except insofar as the author is aware of their self-deception and debunks it for the reader's benefit.

The dialectic of a character's illusory inner life and an author's ironic presentation of it is captured by the device of free indirect discourse, a device brought to perfection by Flaubert. In such discourse, a thought or an impression attributed to a character is narrated in the third person by the author-narrator in a style which attempts to capture the free flow of inner speech. Thus the reader is not quite sure whether the originator of the sentences couched in free indirect discourse is the character or the author-narrator.[11] In the following passage from Flaubert's *Madame Bovary* (1857), Emma's husband is described in a third-person passage which reflects Emma's own doubts about him: "Un homme . . . ne devrait-il pas tout connaître, exceller en activités multiples, vous initier aux énergies de la passion, aux raffinements de la vie, à tous les mystères? Mai il n'enseignait rien, celui-là, ne savait rien, ne souhaitait rien" (p. 328) (A man, surely, should know about everything in a multitude of activities, introduce you to passion in all its force, to life in all its grace, initiate you into all mysteries! But this one had nothing to teach; knew nothing, wanted nothing. [p. 54]). The reported thoughts and feelings, while clearly experienced by the character, acquire an additional layer of ironic distance, as if the author-narrator were commenting, *sotto voce*, on their inauthenticity and spuriousness. The philosophical implication of this technique is that the Cartesian subject and its Rousseauist offspring represent strong – all too strong – idealizations of the actual functioning of human subjectivity.

Flaubert's realism and Dostoevski's visionary prose thus converge in emphasizing the weak links between human thought and human action. Flaubert's characters do not know exactly why they are doing certain things, or what moral consequences will result from their decisions. Free indirect discourse shows how hollow and self-deceptive their deliberations are, and how little these characters know of their own motives. Dostoevski's heroes are objects of obscure impulses and base desires, whose strength they neither recognize nor want to recognize. The main character in *Notes from the Underground* is a compelling example of an individual whose uplifting conscious discourse is relentlessly contradicted by the depravity of his unconscious motivations. In describing such phenomena, nineteenth-century narrative prose undermined belief in a Cartesian or Rousseauist self and foreshadowed Nietzsche and Freud's analyses of unconscious motivation.

A further innovation made possible by the development of free indirect discourse is the exploration of sensory experience beyond the limits of a character's linguistic awareness. All the first-person narratives mentioned until now observe the implicit rule that the subject is a reliable observer of his or her own inner life and has no difficulty describing it in everyday language. On this assumption, conversion from a first-person to a third-person narrative and vice versa should always be possible. Take, for example, an inner monologue of Julien Sorel, in Stendhal's *The Red and the Black* (1830): "Julien voulait à toute force être honnête homme jusqu'à la fin envers cette pauvre fille qu'il avait si étrangement compromise; mais à chaque instant l'amour effréné qu'il avait pour Madame de Rênal l'emportait" (p. 694) (Julien wanted intensely to behave decently to the end towards this poor young woman whom he had compromised in such strange circumstances; but on every occasion, the passionate love he felt for Madame de Renal would win out [my translation]). A transposition of this passage into first-person narrative would be entirely convincing: "I want to behave decently to the end towards this poor young woman whom I have compromised in such strange circumstances." Like picaros and Rousseauist characters, Julien Sorel uses everyday language when speaking of moral behavior, whether such behavior is in accordance with the norms of the community or with his own norms, based on a reasoning that can be made fully explicit. As long as the self is assumed to be the locus where moral debates take place (as in the religious tradition), where epistemological decisions are made (as in the Cartesian tradition), and where humans establish the moral law (as in the Rousseauist tradition), private thoughts can be as clearly articulated as public ones and can, accordingly, always be expressed aloud. The first-person narrative, be it that of Augustine, Descartes, Moll Flanders, or Rousseau, could at any point become a soliloquy, if not a publicly recited monologue. In all these traditions, the self is the site of strategic, epistemological, and moral deliberation. It is like a deliberation chamber, rather than an absolute origin of thought and language.

Free indirect discourse, by contrast, in making possible the representation of nonlinguistic elements through inner speech, suggests a new organization of the self. The windows of the deliberation chamber open, letting in a world of sensations, memories, and diffuse desires over which the self has no effective linguistic control. A sentence like Flaubert's "Une immensité bleuâtre l'entourait; les sommets du sentiment étincelaient sous sa pensée" (1857, p. 439) (A misty-blue immensity lay about her; she saw the sparkling peaks of sentiment beneath her [p. 175]) suggests a narrator writing about Emma Bovary's inner life in terms inaccessible to Emma herself. Indeed, one cannot imagine her uttering the first-person equivalent of the above sentence: "A misty-blue immensity lies about me; I see the sparkling peaks of sentiment beneath me." One cannot read such a passage without thinking of Wilhelm Dilthey's criticism of classical idealism for its neglect of non-rational experience. Dilthey's defense of a fuller view of human beings, one that includes sensory and affective experience, pleads in philosophical terms for an expansion beyond the limits of rational discourse and is analogous to narrative's celebration of nonlinguistic human awareness.[12]

In our century, narrative prose has continued to explore these three types of critique, expanding existential subjectivism, playing up the role of the unconscious, and refining techniques for describing nonlinguistic awareness. Existential subjectivism, both religious and secular, has yielded a rich literary progeny in the twentieth century. The gloomy first-person narratives of Bernanos and Sartre, representing as they do a return to the principle that the inner gaze sees only weakness and corruption, cannot be understood apart from the context of resistance to the Cartesian model of first-person heroic narration. The role of the unconscious is the object of much twentieth-century American prose, Faulkner's in particular, as well as of the French *nouveau roman*. Proust and Joyce each develop a non-Cartesian, non-Rousseauist analysis of self-awareness, incorporating a wealth of sensorial cues, hidden memories, instinctive reflexes, and non-logical discourse.

Thus, for one and a half centuries, philosophers and prose-writers have been busy either refuting the Cartesian and Rousseauist idea of the self head on or expanding it through the exploration of semi-conscious or unconscious aspects of subjectivity. Since the Romantics, no serious prose-writer has attempted to represent a Cartesian or a Rousseauist self in all its heroic glory. It is somewhat ironic, then, that, under the influence of thinkers like Jacques Lacan and Jacques Derrida, contemporary literary critics seem both convinced that logocentrism rules the world, including the literary world, and eager to refute the Cartesian unity of the self. But in fact, far from representing a new, unanticipated development, these recent critiques of the unified self have been made possible by the long-term trends noted above, Lacanian psychoanalysis being dependent on both Nietzsche and Freud's critique of consciousness, and Derrida's metaphysical speculations having their roots in Heidegger's ontology, which in turn depends on both Nietzsche and Kierkegaard's critique of rationalism.

Descartes and Modern Art

If Descartes' thought had such resonance in nineteenth- and twentieth-century prose, its impact on modernist art was even stronger, however belated.[13] Descartes's conviction that the material world can be reduced to extension, shape, and movement and described in purely mathematical terms is profoundly disturbing to painters, since it implies that everything they represent belongs to a superficial – possibly illusory – layer of reality. I suggested above that the discovery of the formal nature of artificial perspective in fifteenth-century Italy prevented Descartes' ideas on the subject from having an immediate impact on the visual arts. The fact that geometry was applied to optics long before it conquered terrestrial mechanics made Descartes' revolutionary work appear less surprising to painters than to physicists and metaphysicians. For two centuries painters had known that reality conforms to rigorous mathematical rules; and although in the seventeenth century the amount of geometry needed in perspective had become a topic of heated debate, until the end of the nineteenth century a painting's basic fidelity to the world of appearances was never put in question (Kemp, 1990, pp. 119–131).

Descartes' "derealization" of appearances[14] was something so contrary to the solid world of common sense that for a long time visual artists did not even give it a thought. As Descartes himself foresaw in the Preface to his *Principles of Philosophy*, it would be "many centuries . . . until all the truths which may be deduced from these principles [were] so deduced" (*CSM*, I, 189–190; *AT,* IX(2), 20). But by the second half of the nineteenth century, modern science had managed to come up with a fully credible account of how the world of appearances may be reduced to a set of mathematical relations.

At this point, art finally took an interest in the demolition of sensory appearances. Nonfigurative painting rebelled against what had always been the natural habitat of visual art: the human environment seen through human eyes. The cubists in France, the futurists in Italy, Kandinsky and the suprematists in Russia, all attempted to go beyond the thin film of the phenomenal world and grasp something that the human eye always fails to see: the hidden geometry of objects (Braque), the schemata of movement through space (Boccioni), and, most ambitious of all, the hidden essence of the world (Malevich). This project was also undertaken in sculpture at around the same time, with Brancusi searching for the geometric patterns that underlie natural shapes. Soon, virtually all twentieth-century visual art joined the struggle against appearance, leaving the task of imitating the visible world to a minority of contemptible practitioners: Nazis, socialist realists, and commercial artists.[15]

Modernist poetry followed suit. Reneging on its age-old alliance with rhetoric, poetry ceased to imitate human discourse, searching instead for deeper levels of intelligibility. An increasingly subjective relationship with language led modernist poets to reject all existing conventions and constraints upon their art. The freedom thus gained was used to explore the hidden face of language and to evoke inexpressible features of the world. Note that such a rebellion against the world of appearances is quite different from the expansion of sensory awareness sought by Flaubert, Proust, and Joyce, as well as from the exploration of unconscious motivations in nineteenth- and twentieth-century narrative prose. This dissimilarity may explain why narrative prose has not felt it necessary to emulate the radical moves of modernist painting and poetry: instead of demoting sensory appearances, narrative prose was – and still is – busy reflecting on the weakness, depth, and sensuality of the self.

The difference between modernist art and the Cartesian demolition of appearances is that Descartes displayed infinite caution at every step. If he postulated a radically dissimilar structure behind the perceptible world, it was only because he was able, with the help of rigorous mathematical argumentation, to make full sense of that structure. He cast doubt upon the fragile certainties of the human realm in the name of a clearer, more rational representation of the universe. Modernism, by contrast, rejected the world of appearances without having first secured a firm grip on its hidden form. Could modernist artists have proceeded otherwise? Probably not. The Cartesian revolution, taken to its logical limits by science, had left visual art with a stark choice: either to stay faithful to a naive view of the world – the classicist solution – and lose touch with the evolving intellectual landscape, or to emulate the Cartesian rejection of appearances, only to be left without an object of its own. By selecting the latter option and attempting to sever the visual links between humans and their world, twentieth-century visual arts have embarked on a dangerous journey toward self-destruction. Is there a way out of this impasse? It is difficult to say. Supposing that practitioners of the visual arts notice at some point that the demolition of appearances is not their true mission, modern narrative prose, with its sensitivity to the predicament of the modern self and its relationship to sensory experience, might provide painters and sculptors with a successful model for meeting the challenge of the Cartesian legacy.[16]

NOTES

1. See Krantz 1882. A more moderate variety of the same claim has been made popular by Lanson (1906) and adopted by numerous literary

historians, e.g., Lombard (1913). For a refutation of Krantz's thesis, see Abercrombie 1936.

2. Bray 1927 is the best survey of classicist literary theory. For an original description of the classicist model, see Shenningham 1992, pp. 37–77. Lacoste 1986 is a perceptive presentation of the classicist notion of ideal beauty (pp. 52–79).

3. Bray 1927, pp. 191–214; Corneille [1660] 1987, 142–173.

4. A similar argument has been succinctly expressed by Henri Busson (1948, p. 73): "Les classiques sont cartésiens . . . par une évolution parallèle de la pensée et de l'art français vers la simplicité et la clarté; mais les principes de l'art classique sont bien plus anciens que ceux de Descartes et ils ont été plus longs à élaborer" (Neoclassicism looks Cartesian because of a parallel evolution of French art and thought towards simplicity and clarity; yet the principles of neoclassicist art are much older than those of Descartes and took a longer time to develop). See also the persuasive argumentation of Zuber (1992).

5. Marion 1986 and 1992. On the role of mathematics in Descartes' philosophy, see Brunschvicq [1927] 1951, pp. 11–54.

6. Roksenberg-Rorty 1986; for Descartes' rhetoric, see Lyons 1986 and Fumaroli 1988.

7. These notions have been developed by Propp (1928) and Greimas (1970).

8. The continuity of the Augustinian tradition of self-examination is the object of two illuminating studies by Pierre Courcelle (1950, 1963).

9. I leave aside a third possibility, the allegorical story, which recounts the initiation of the narrator into the mysteries of love (e.g., *Hypneroto-machia Poliphili* by Francesco Colonna [1499], translated into French by Jean Martin in 1546), since this genre makes no claim to realist representation.

10. To be sure, as Charles Taylor (1989) reminds us, Rousseau speaks the language of the heart, in opposition to the rationalism of Descartes (pp. 355–367). Yet, just as Descartes' first-person narrative conveyed a sense of epistemological self-reliance, so Rousseau's sentimental "I" radiates moral self-reliance.

11. For a comprehensive discussion of the notion, see Pascal 1977, pp. 8–32. According to Cohn 1978, free indirect speech is a species of "narrated monologue," a technique characterized by "the seamless junction between narrated monologues and their narrative contexts" (p. 103).

12. The discussion of this topic is taken from Pavel 1992, pp. 17–28.

13. Alquié (1965) argues that surrealist poetry rediscovers the Cartesian cogito (pp. 68–73).

14. The term is borrowed from Alquié 1965.

15. Besançon (1994) traces the ancestors of modern nonfigurative painting back to Plato's philosophy and to Byzantine theological disputes over the representation of the Godhead. Yet, when motivated by respect for the Godhead, iconoclasm simply turns away from the representation of sensory appearances and instead encourages sophisticated decorative art. By contrast, twentieth-century nonfigurative art takes an aggressively adversarial stand toward sensory appearances, whose rejection becomes one of its esssential themes.

16. I wish to thank David Weissman for his generous criticisms and suggestions and Joshua Landy and Jean van Altena for their patience in editing my English.

REFERENCES

Aarne, Antti, and Thompson Stith. 1961. *The Types of Folktale: A Classification and Bibliography*. Helsinki: Academia Scientiarum Fenica.

Abercrombie, Nigel. 1936. Cartesianism and Classicism. *Modern Language Review* 31: 358–376.

Alquié, Ferdinand. 1965. *The Philosophy of Surrealism*, trans. Bernard Waldrop. Ann Arbor: University of Michigan Press.

Besançon, Alain. 1994. *L'Image interdite: une histoire intellectuelle de l'iconoclasme*. Paris: Fayard.

Bray, René. 1927. *La Formation de la doctrine classique en France*. Dijon: Darantière.

Brunetière, Ferdinand. 1898. *L'Evolution des genres dans l'histoire de la littérature*. Paris: Hachette.

Brunschvicq, Léon. [1927] 1951. Mathématique et métaphysique chez Descartes. In *Ecrits philosophiques*, vol. 1, pp. 11–54. Paris: Presses Universitaires de France.

Busson, Henri. 1948. *Religion de classiques (1660–1685)*. Paris: Presses Universitaires de France.

Cohn, Dorrit. 1978. *Transparent Minds: Narrative Modes for Presenting Consciousness in Fiction*. Princeton: Princeton University Press.

Corneille, Pierre. [1660] 1987. *Trois Discours sur le poème dramatique*. In *Oeuvres complètes*, ed. Georges Couton, vol. 3. Paris: Gallimard.

Courcelle, Pierre. 1950. *Recherches sur les Confessions de Saint Augustin*. Paris: E. de Boccard.

——. 1963. *Les Confessions de Saint Augustin dans la tradition littéraire. Antécédents et postérité.* Paris: Etudes augustiniennes.

Ferry, Luc. 1993. *Homo Aestheticus: The Invention of Taste in the Democratic Age,* trans. R. de Loaiza. Chicago: University of Chicago Press.

Flaubert, Gustave. [1857] 1951. *Madame Bovary.* In *Oeuvres,* Bibliothèque de la Pléiade, vol. 1: 291–611. Paris: Gallimard. English trans. by Alan Russell. Harmondsworth: Penguin, 1950.

Fumaroli, Marc. 1988. *Ego Scriptor:* rhétorique et philosophie dans le *Discours de la méthode.* In *Problématique de la réception du Discours de la méthode,* ed. H. Méchoulan, pp. 31–46. Paris: Vrin.

Gassendi, Pierre. [1641] 1972. *Rebuttals against Descartes.* In *Selected Works,* ed. Craig B. Brush. New York: Johnson Reprint.

Greimas, A. J. 1970. *Du sens.* Paris: Seuil.

Kemp, Martin. 1990. *The Science of Art: Optical Themes in Western Art from Brunelleschi to Seurat.* New Haven: Yale University Press.

Krantz, Emile. 1882. *Essai sur l'esthétique de Descartes étudiée dans les rapports de la doctrine cartésienne avec la littérature classique française au XVIIe siècle.* Paris: Germer Baillère.

Lacoste, Jean. 1986. *L'Idée de beau.* Paris: Bordas.

Lanson, Gustave. 1906. *Boileau.* Paris: Hachette.

Lenoble, Robert. 1969. *Histoire de l'idée de nature.* Paris: Albin Michel.

Lombard, A. 1913. *L'Abbé du Bos, un initiateur de la pensée moderne.* Paris: Hachette.

Lyons, John. 1986. Rhétorique du discours cartésien. *Cahiers de littérature du XVIIe siècle* 8: 125–147.

Malebranche, Nicholas. [1696] 1992. *Entretiens sur la métaphysique, sur la religion et sur la mort.* In *Oeuvres,* ed. Geneviève Rodis-Lewis, vol. 2: 649–967. Paris: Gallimard.

Marion, Jean-Luc. 1986. *Le Prisme métaphysique de Descartes.* Paris: Presses Universitaires de France.

——. 1992. Cartesian Metaphysics and the Role of Simple Natures. In *The Cambridge Companion to Descartes,* ed. John Cottingham, pp. 000–000. Cambridge: Cambridge University Press.

Mesnard, Jean. 1992. Le Classicisme français et l'expression de la sensibilité. In *Culture du XVIIe siècle. Enquêtes et synthèses,* pp. 487–496. Paris: Presses Universitaires de France.

Pascal, Roy. 1977. *The Dual Voice: Free Indirect Speech and Its Functioning in the Nineteenth-Century European Novel.* Manchester: Manchester University Press.

Pavel, Thomas. 1992. "Between History and Fiction: On Dorrit Cohn's Poetics of Fiction. In *Never-ending Stories: Toward a Critical Narratology*, ed. Ann Fehn, Ingeborg Hoesterey, and Maria Tatar, pp. 17–28. Princeton: Princeton University Press.

Propp, Vladimir. [1928] 1968. *The Morphology of the Folktale*, trans. L. Scott, rev. Louis A. Wagner. Austin: University of Texas Press.

Roksenberg-Rorty, Amélie. 1986. The Structure of Descartes' *Meditations*. In *Essays on Descartes' Meditations*, ed. Roksenberg-Rorty, pp. 1–20. Berkeley: University of California Press.

Shenningham, Marc. 1992. *Introduction à la philosophie esthétique*. Paris: Payot.

Stendhal. 1830. *Le Rouge et le noir*. In *Romans et nouvelles*. Bibliothèque de la Pléiade, vol. 1. Paris: Gallimard.

Taylor, Charles. 1989. *The Sources of the Self: The Making of Modern Identity*. Cambridge, Mass.: Harvard University Press.

Tocanne, Bernard. 1978. *L'Idée de nature en France dans la second moitié du XVIIe siècle*. Paris: Klincksieck.

White, John. 1967. *The Birth and Rebirth of Pictorial Space*. London: Faber.

Zuber, Roger. 1992. Introduction to R. Zuber et al., *Littérature française du XVIIe siècle*. Paris: Presses Universitaires de France.

Essay 9
Descartes in Our Time

DAVID WEISSMAN

Think of Descartes in his nightgown, warmed by the fire in his bedroom grate, uncertain that he sees clearly by its light. The *Meditations* record Descartes' ascent from this evocation of Plato's cave. Descartes was a Platonist – with a difference. He agreed that knowledge is more than true opinion, and that it is achieved when its objects are intuited, not merely hypothesized or inferred. Like Plato, he supposed that the material world is intelligible in itself and intelligible to us who think about it, because matter is a geometrically configured space, and because relations in the material world are discerned by a mind properly sensitized to its innate geometrical ideas. Descartes separated himself from Plato when he asked this other question: What is the mind that knows? Plato's answer exalts us – as in the *Phaedo* – by identifying reason with world soul, though doing so strips us of the individuality we value in ourselves. Descartes' response is distinctive, because he particularized and personalized nous: I am, I exist, he said, by virtue of my thinking. Why substitute an individual knower for the world soul? Because Descartes had Augustine and Calvin as his examples: one who said that divinity and thought are personalized, the other that conscience is individual and self-affirming.

Descartes and Kant

Descartes' influence is pervasive among us, but his role is disguised by Kant's constructivism. It displaces Descartes' assumption that ideas represent the features of a world which mind acknowledges but does not make. Consider the three questions cited at the beginning of essay 3: What are we? What is the world? What is our place in it? These questions, together with a fourth one – What is it good to do or be? – are the agenda for civilized reflection. We organize ourselves to supply viable answers, as when engineers and medical schools act in the name of the good, and novelists or physicists tell us what and where we are. Aristotle would find nothing amiss in either the questions or this division of labor. Descartes would object that something vital is missing, namely, a fifth question: How can we know that our answers to the previous four are good ones? His influence is conspicuous wherever thought or practice is rejiggered so that this fifth question is the decisive one.

It would have been reasonable to hear this last question as a warning: Take care that your answers to the other four questions are defensible. But Descartes, like Plato, supposed that the chasm between knowledge and true opinion is so wide that no one who misses the one should take satisfaction in the other. Demanding caution, he usually insisted that no answer is acceptable if it falls short of necessary truth. Uncertain that our answers are good enough, we – temporarily – stop asking the questions. They can be revived when the necessary and sufficient conditions for meaning and truth are known and satisfied.

It was plausible in medieval times that we humans should regard ourselves in naturalistic terms: we are, it seems, specially endowed animals living in a world we alter but do not make. Now, we rethink our nature and our place in the world in terms prescribed by the fifth question. How far can we advance beyond the circle of mind's awareness without losing the certainty of our judgments? For there is no certainty to judgments regarding things that are separate from our minds: there is a gap between them and us, so our claims about them may be distorted or mistaken. Realizing that we cannot guarantee the truth of judgments whose referents do not lie within the mind, we say that the only things existing are those that are, or can be, set before our inspecting minds, as percepts, thoughts, or words.

Consciousness is ephemeral, as someone drifting into sleep resembles a flickering light bulb. Is Descartes' logical defensiveness, his demand that there be rigorous standards for meaning and truth, not sabotaged by the mind's own weakness? No, say Descartes and his successors: mind is most feeble when it is identified as the active principle of a corruptible body. Let mind be self-sufficient, as it is when the cogito achieves its apotheosis in Kant's transcendental unity of apperception. Minds once humiliated by their imperfections are reconceived as world-makers. What world do they make? The only one that matters for us thinkers: the one revealed to perception. This is a world whose organizing principles, its laws, are rules deployed to schematize sensory data. For remember Descartes' remark about our percept of the sun: seeing a small, flat disk, we construe it as evidence of a vastly larger body. How do we know what this percept signifies? By introducing the concept used – as a rule – to interpret it. Equally, we say what *man* or *woman* signifies by citing rules that prescribe behaviors acceptable in boys or girls. Knowing the world experienced is unexpectedly simple: it requires that mind know itself, including both the thinkable experience that qualifies it and the rules used to construct this experience. Retiring into ourselves, we answer the questions that were temporarily put aside. We learn that mind, once thought to be passive to the world perceived, is the agent that schematizes experience, thereby making the only world we can think or know.

Each thinker also perceives him or herself, including mind's structure, especially its desires. How shall we satisfy them when our high standards for knowledge have made us skeptical about everything whose existence is independent of our thinking? Let mind have the full measure of the autonomy claimed for it when Kant and Fichte elaborated on the cogito, producing the transcendental ego: let this ego contrive the experiences – the world – whereby its desires are satisfied. How? By using either conceptual systems to create thinkable worlds or rules to construct social systems in which each actor knows his or her role, identity, and rights.

What am I? What is the world? What is my place in it? Only now do we discover that the questions are perverse. For the world is in me and has only the character prescribed by my interests. The often modest, passive mind that Descartes described has turned grandiose. Too bad that having so much power assures my isolation. For other thinkers are invisible when I cannot be aware of them as I am of myself: social relations are formal, because driven by laws, or make-believe. Why should I limit the power for satisfying myself when knowledge of other thinkers is speculative or precluded? Self-concern is the only value prescribed by the things I know: looking for others, I can see and sympathize with them only as I reach out to grasp the reflection of myself. Think of quarrels between men and women or competing ethnic groups: you create an identity for me, as I do for you. Mutual opposition and incomprehension are guaranteed. There is only this one qualification: I can share a world with others if we use the same rules, for then our worlds are the same, and each one discovers the same things – these rules – when reflecting upon him or herself.

Do we recognize ourselves in this Kantian transformation of the Cartesian demand that we be perpetually self-regarding, self-confirming, always sure? Could it be that these preoccupations make us sick? Surely, they explain our inability to imagine community as more than an aggregate of individuals or factions. We discover that the individualism precious to Descartes and Kant distorts our self-perception: we are to be self-creating, without regard for the reciprocal relations binding us to other people or things, excepting only the people who use our rules to create worlds that dovetail with our own. Nature stands outside this circle of thought-created meanings and things, hence our contempt for that paradigmatic thing-in-itself, the nature we pollute because it exists only as we conceive it useful to ourselves.

Is everything, whether physical or political, "constructed" for our purposes? Kant recoils at this point: other transcendental egos are not our constructions; the maxims directing each person's behavior must satisfy the categorical imperative. But this is the defective sociality described in essay 3. It is satisfied when each person or group wills a universalizable maxim, though each thinker's maxim could be so different from every other that acting on it would isolate him. We get sociality without practical reciprocity between individuals or groups of them. Formally socialized, we are effectively alone. Only the members of factions – people who share a set of world-making rules – avoid this isolation. Descartes is (mis)represented in our time by this mix of Kantian persuasions. For there would be no transcendental ego had there been no cogito.

Logicism

A second effect of Descartes' ideas is more narrowly academic. This is the emphasis on *rigor*. There are two lineages for which this is a cardinal virtue, both deriving from Descartes' emphasis on knowledge. One is the line from his analytic geometry to Leibniz, Newton, and modern mathematical science. Descartes transformed the disciplinary matrix in which the mathematical and mechanical sciences are pursued. Pythagoras and Plato had said that space has an intrinsic geometric form; Ptolemy, Copernicus, Kepler, and Galileo explored it. There was, however, no effective way of representing this form until Descartes invented analytic geometry. The significance of this invention cannot be exaggerated. Nor should anything obscure the order of determination: we demand rigor in the formulation and relations of scientific representations so that scientific theory will be adequate to the mathematical character of the things represented. Cartesian metaphysics conditions this aspect of Cartesian method.

The other of these lineages passes through Descartes' *Rules* to Locke and Hume, then to Frege, Russell, Wittgenstein's *Tractatus*, and Carnap and his heirs. This lineage demands that meaning and truth be exhibited on the face of thoughts or sentences or it establishes formal criteria for the truth of sentences organized as systems. Rigor here is independent of the concern for rigor in science, though we philosophers would be less confident that rules and formal structures are the solution to most problems in epistemology and metaphysics if we did not aspire to be fellow travelers in rigor, doing in our place what physicists do in theirs. There are, for example, three dominant views in the philosophy of mathematics, formalism, logicism, and intuitionism. Their advocates agree that mathematics is a formal system, not a representation of mathematical properties in nature or an extrapolation from them to constructed properties and relations. Rigor and these constructions so dominate our thinking that we forget the metaphysical assumption – nature's geometrical form – that provoked Descartes' invention of analytic geometry. We no longer care that rigor in our theories is valuable, principally, if it guarantees precision to the thoughts or sentences representing the mathematical character of matter itself. Why ignore this motivation? Because Descartes also taught us this other emphasis: we worry that mathematics may become slippery and opaque if it is not reduced to elementary formal truths or conventions and the systems constructed upon them.

What promotes the autonomy of concepts and rules? It derives from the mind's own autonomy and from the consideration that concepts and rules are distinguishable and separable from extra-mental states of affairs. What is the evidence for this autonomy? Just the fact that concepts and rules may be formulated or discovered within thought itself, then entertained without regard for whether the matters signified obtain or not in the extra-mental world. Think of formal grammarians, ordinary-language analysts, or modal logicians proving their theorems about God or possible worlds. How do they explain themselves? "We are doing *conceptual* analysis, not empirical science."

The rationale for their attitude is Descartes' own. What can we know with certainty? Only concepts and the logic used to organize them, as we have the simples described in the *Rules*, then the principles used to compound them. Knowledge of these concepts and constructs, like knowledge of the rules, is a priori. We are to achieve it in a space in which philosophic discipline concedes nothing to the rigor of scientific theories, for the latter, however, systematic, are never more than hypotheses: they could be mistaken. Descartes and his successors promise to do better: claiming direct inspection of ideas and rules in which nothing is hidden, reporting only what they see or do, they make no mistakes.

One may believe, as inscriptionists do, that concepts and rules have no reality apart from marks or sounds and the habits for using them. But this is the careful emendation of an attitude more classically Cartesian. The older view affirms – as Husserl, Frege, Russell, the early Wittgenstein, and Austin agree – that the thoughts, words, or percepts rigorously organized are entertained in a mental ether (e.g., by Husserl's transcendental ego or Wittgenstein's metaphysical subject). This is the intuitionism common to Descartes' heirs. It underwrites their claim to certainty and control. For there is no gap between mind and its contents, hence no obscuring mist and nothing to attenuate our command of the things themselves.

We often credit Descartes with having put an end to the Scholastic era in philosophy. But this is true only insofar as his physics repudiated substantial forms and final causes. It is false as regards the Scholastic taste for apriorist, conceptual analyses. Descartes' *Rules*, then Kant's analytic of concepts, energizes these logical reflections with a force that exceeds every precedent but Aristotle's *Prior* and *Posterior Analytics*. Descartes' heirs are the many philosophers who will not concede that they may be confuted by the evidence of some extra-mental state of affairs.

These thinkers would probably hesitate if asked about our place in the world, for their opinion is unsettled. It moves back and forth between Plato and Kant. On the one side, mind observes its concepts without making them – as Husserl, Frege, Moore, ordinary-language analysts, and some logicians of possible worlds believe. On the other side are thinkers like Nietzsche and the later Wittgenstein who suppose that concepts and rules are the products of a mind at play: a concept or rule is no more sacrosanct than a tune; hum it whatever way you like. One can imagine Plato and the *Rules* reasserting the authority of fixed rules and forms over the conventions generated by conceptual play. But how far could this go? Might there be a priori dicta regarding essences, religious truths, and moral prescriptions? This would be evidence for the revival among us of a different, though related, scholasticism.

Foundationalism

One hears that foundationalism is dead. Is it? Foundationalism is normally understood as a claim about knowledge: namely, that we avoid an infinite regress of justifying assumptions only if one (or more) is known to be true without a justifier anterior to itself. Other knowledge claims can then be constructed or derived from this one. This requirement can be satisfied in either of two ways: either the claim said to be true unconditionally is a logically necessary truth, or the matter affirmed as a ground for knowledge is validated by a comprehensive, faultless intuition. Clarity and distinctness – Descartes' test for truth – may be construed in either way. Sometimes this is the formula requiring that no idea count as clear and distinct if its negation is not a contradiction – this is the standard appropriate to geometry. More often, clarity and distinctness signify that an idea is distinguished from every other – its clarity – while apprehended as having a specific, logically consistent content – its distinctness.

Foundationalism is these two things. First is the *ontological* claim that mind is the ground of truth because truth is achieved as mind apprehends the matters set before it: truth is disclosure. Second is the *epistemological* claim that content of a particular kind is the ground on which other truths are constructed. It is not required that this latter ground be innate; we require only that it be susceptible to comprehensive inspection and that it support the derivation or construction of other contents or vehicles for truth. The cogito, as ontological foundation, is a mine of possible grounds, including mind's existence, structure, percepts, ideas (e.g., thoughts, propositions, or sentences), rules, and will. Each of these has been the epistemological foundation preferred by some faction of Descartes' successors.

Foundationalism of both sorts thrives in our time. Mind affirms itself as ontological ground in literature, psychology, and politics, as in philosophy. For mind is the crucible in which systems are constructed and experience schematized. This ontological foundationalism is especially conspicuous among Kantian pragmatists. They repeatedly advise us that the world as we know it is only the product of thought or language, though little or nothing is said of the minds that create or use these conceptual systems.

W. V. O. Quine undermined one sort of epistemological foundationalism by diluting Carnap's distinction between synthetic observation reports, and analytic truths or syntactic rules (Quine 1961, pp. 20–46). Carnap had supposed that observation reports are foundational, and that theoretical terms are defined or introduced by way of them. Higher-order hypotheses, containing these terms and confirmed by observation reports, were to be constructed upon this foundation by application of syntactic rules (Carnap 1969). Quine challenged this formulation by arguing from two sides: rules used to construct a system of sentences are not empirically neutral (e.g., construction rules in geometry make tacit assumptions about the homogeneity or curvature of space); substantive – factual or empirical – terms are not exempt from the prescriptive effects of organizing rules (e.g., geometry's basic concepts, including *line* and *angle*, are understood in terms decreed by interpretive rules). There are only some idealized cases (e.g., algebraic rules and raw feels) where rules and substantives are not mutually penetrating. But then it follows that our perceptions of the world are nearly always biased by the rules that inflect our thought or talk. These rules are like treacle: we can never get our minds free of them as we consider and characterize the data.

Carnap's distinction between observation reports and the higher-order terms and sentences constructed from them repeats the distinction in Descartes' *Rules* between simple ideas and the complex ideas created when deductive rules are used to join the simples (e.g., as in geometry). Quine's objection – that sentences are neither purely analytic nor purely synthetic – reformulates Kant's doctrine that some propositions are synthetic a priori truths: they join otherwise unrelated contents in the way of synthetic truths, while having the regulative force of a priori rules. The dispute between Carnap and Quine is a reprise of that earlier difference. This is no terminal assault on foundationalism. Quine has criticized one candidate for the role of epistemological ground – oberservation reports – while recommending that we replace it by another: organizing ideas or rules. Either way, something is constructed on a foundation: hierarchically ordered systems of hypotheses are mounted on observation reports, or experience is founded on the rules used to project qualities and relations onto sensory data. Mind survives as ontological ground whether we tell one story or the other: it is affected by sensory data before it constructs the abstract systems whose empirical meaning and truth derive from the data; or it creates experience by using conceptual systems to project differences and relations onto sensory data.

Is there an alternative to foundationalism? Someone remarking that Plato's Forms are the first epistemological ground and the inspiration for almost every subsequent theory of knowledge may despair. But there *is* an alternative. The pre-Socratics applied it when they inferred from the phenomena observed to their conditions – love and hate, or water. Descartes used it too.

He usually relied on the inspection of innate ideas, supported by God's guarantee for knowledge of things existing apart from the mind. But sometimes, perhaps chastened by trying to use the method of the *Rules* to explain physical phenomena that do not reduce to complexes constructed from inspectable simples, he proposed a different method: we explain phenomena by inferring from them to their hypothesized conditions, including causes, constituents, or laws (39–40; *CSM*, I, 144, 288; *AT,* VI, 64; *AT,* VIIIA, 326). Proposing one or another explanation for physical events, we check the empirical data: are they such as would occur if the conditions specified by our hypotheses were to obtain? Never mind that these hypotheses are representational and probabilistic: we cannot guarantee that what we see is smoke from a fire, not steam from a hot pipe. It is enough that our hypotheses explain and predict the events observed. Apriorism is renounced as Descartes anticipates Peirce's "abductive" method (Peirce 1934, vol. 5, pp. 113–127; Weissman 1989, pp. 27–28 and 73–137).

Can abduction break through the heavy weave of conceptual systems to extra-conceptual states of affairs? It can, though not by enabling thought to slip away from itself, thereby achieving a neutral point of view between the world and our ideas of it. Abduction gives us traction in the world by testably identifying the conditions for the matters observed. Someone speculating about the cause of vapor seen coming from a window, may be able to predict some other perceivable effects: predicting and seeing flames, for example, probably eliminates the hypothesis that this is water vaporized by a hot pipe. Are smoke, pipes, flames, and steam precipitates of our conceptual systems? Has thinking created them? Descartes and Peirce agree that these are conditions we discover and sometimes manipulate. They are not created merely by our thinking them.

Many philosophers distrust hypotheses, however well confirmed by empirical or conceptual evidence, because hypotheses are speculative and fallible. We are to suppose that knowledge by acquaintance – knowledge achieved as we are directly affected – is the only reliable basis for belief. Knowledge remote from its object because of being representational or instrumental (e.g., information communicated over a noisy telephone line) seems less authentic, less sure. Perhaps we dread the separation of knowledge from control, because of fearing that we shall be unable to change things known in ways appropriate to our interests: they may resist or turn against us. Losing control of them, we risk losing command of ourselves. Compare the objects or systems mind constructs and inspects: they invite control.

Suppose that most of the things known are not the mind's own qualifications and products; we know other people as well as our own somatic states. Are we less rational or reasonable because understanding is separated from its objects by natural and conventional signs – percepts and words? We are accustomed to thinking that hypotheses supply information about things remote from us – as space probes do – so, curiously, doubts about the hypothetical method are more intense when the issue is knowledge and control of ourselves.

Peirce supposed that knowledge of all the mind's states, including percepts and sensations, is only hypothetical, there being no mental organ or power for the direct perception of anything (1965, vol. 5, pp. 135–155). Someone who resists Peirce, denying that he needs hypotheses to identify his pleasures and pains, may admit that he requires them to identify attitudes and motives that are known only as they are inferred from his behavior. For this part of mental activity (decisive for personality, action, and value, but too little emphasized by Descartes) is largely beyond the range of easy identification and control. The elusiveness of attitude is confounding for anyone who believes that mental contents and acts are always available to self-controlling self-reflection. Think of blood rushing from a cut: we grab the limb and press the wound closed. Mind, we believe, also has direct access to, and control of, its own states. This assumption is mistaken if any fraction of mind's activities is only known inferentially by way of representations. For some acts may be misrepresented, whereas others are inaccessible because of being unrepresented. Mind risks losing track of itself.

There is this offsetting benefit: foundationalism collapses. The method of hypothesis – Peirce's abduction – averts the need for epistemological foundationalism by supplying testable claims about states of affairs. Ontological foundationalism dissolves because there is no reason to found a constructed world upon mind's existence: we use hypotheses to know things whose existence and character are independent of our own. Mind's own acts, hypothesizing included, are known inferentially, by way of their effects.

Materialism

Suppose that the "I think, I am" is stripped of its powers for world-making. What is left? There are, to start, the many finite minds, each one replete with its valorizing attitudes and its percepts of colors, tastes, and sounds, most of them caused by things perceived. This qualitative diversity is quixotic and embarrassing if Descartes was right about matter, for we thinkers are deluded: nature itself is a barren, but dynamic, geometricized space-time, with no place in it for either values or the qualities we enjoy. Is Kant's idealism only his way of saving the decorations and virtues of our lives from the charge that they are secondary properties and conceits?

Descartes would have straightened our backs: there are, he said, two kinds of created substances, finite minds and extended matter, each autonomous and each qualified in ways appropriate to itself. This is only temporary relief. For Descartes also said that every material thing, human bodies included, is a machine. He encouraged both engineers and physiologists, and they demonstrate, by way of theory and the machines they build, that two aspects of thought which he stressed – representation and calculation –

are the activities of physical systems. Only awareness is safe, just now, from explanation in physical terms. Suppose that it, too, is shown to have exclusively physical conditions. Minds would still be the active fissures wherein bodies deliberate, care, and invent; specifying the physical basis for consciousness would not make it disappear. Still, we would feel devalued. For we have convinced ourselves that the worth of our intellectual, moral, and aesthetic lives derives from the autonomy of our minds made in God's image. Are we not less dignified, less responsible for the things we do, if our nature is only material?

How shall we choose between these contrary notions of man-in-the-world: one as it makes us responsible for the worlds we experience, the other as it locates us among the rabbits, weeds, and stones? Are we world-makers? Is the world knowable only as it exists in us? Or do we live in nature as its creatures? Descartes is the unintended sponsor of these mutually exclusive alternatives. Our schizoid uncertainty is a remote consequence of his complex but unitary thesis being fractured because of skepticism about God, its guarantor. Matter was thereby reduced to an idea, so minds cast adrift from material things were obliged to find the whole basis for intelligibility within themselves. This was also an opportunity, for mind may be spontaneous and free if there is no matter to constrain it. Where is the middle way? How shall we find our way back into nature without having to concede that qualitative diversity, freedom, and value are delusions?

Marking off the differences between Descartes and Kant is a useful beginning. Kant supposed that nature is thinkable and known only as it is schematized in ways that satisfy our interests, with the result that nature is unspecifiable – it has no identity or integrity – apart from schematizations driven by our interests. Kant's transformation of the cogito claims infinite freedom for our projects and for the promise that we can satisfy any consistent desire. But Kant has promised too much: no one makes worlds. Think of disparate tribes. Must each be permanently unintelligible to the other except as the other creates a role and value for it within a conceptual system and world congenial to itself? Are tennis and baseball different "worlds," so that either is unintelligible to those who play only the other? Descartes is more plausible. He never confused thinking with world-making: we do represent the world, and sometimes we alter it, but never does thinking by itself create the world known. Plato, Kant, Hegel, and Bergson supposed that knowledge is imperfect unless we participate in the known, as happens if we think, do, or make it. The identity of knower and known is, on this telling, the condition for truth. Descartes is more detached: understanding what geese do and why they do it does not require that one be a goose.

Cartesian selfhood, the private domain reserved to understanding, imagination, and self-reflection, compares to the depersonalized Kantian ego. The place that Descartes describes is a region of self-discovery and resolve, a staging ground for art, hypotheses, argument, and action. Most everything we prize about ourselves is centered there. This self is, nevertheless, precarious. For how shall we reconcile Descartes' ahistorical, extra-natural claims about mental life with our deflated status as creatures having a nature that is, perhaps, exclusively material? Material creatures have a developmental history; their every feature is the effect of some antecedent condition, whether physical, social, or psychological. Descartes made us self-affirming, but autonomy, intellectual or moral, is a delusion if all of us are drenched with the same information, biases, and techniques. Each thinker – however unique the mix of habits and information – is a ripple in this common sea. Descartes' piety – real or feigned – saved him from having to address this issue. Skepticism about his dualist answer makes us responsible for another.

I suggest this one: not believing, or doubting, that our worth is an expression of God's esteem, we value our human selves. Living as pockets of self-regulating complexity within the physical manifold, we do justice to one another and to our habitat. Our virtues are those encouraged by Descartes, including loyalty to family and friends, good citizenship, temperance, and prudence. (*CSMK*, 266; *AT,* IV, 292–293). Pursuing the plan of our lives, we prize affiliation and reciprocity. Acknowledging our place in a world we do not make, we shape and decorate a space for ourselves, in words, colors, law, and stone.

Are we too self-absorbed? No one looks after others or oneself without being somewhat monadic. Vulnerability – to climate, war, thugs, or disease – intensifies our preoccupation. But self-concern is hard to sustain amidst the rush of other people, each with a trajectory different from our own. More subverting are the novelists and filmmakers who mock our Cartesian integrity by assembling the disjointed perceptions and attitudes of incongruous standpoints, ascribing them all to a single name or body (Kohut 1978, p. 286). Is the impulsive violence of these characters evidence that there is no power of deliberation and control in us? Is each of us merely an aggregate with only contiguity or succession, but no moral center, to join the parts? Think of a dissonant phrase, thoughtlessly variant, as it drones interminably – by rule or chance – from a synthesizer; imagine angry bees, mindlessly stinging one another. Are these the deeper truths about us? Our self-conviction is secure only as we reestablish our worth on grounds that do not require mind's categorial separation from matter.

We have Descartes both behind and before us. His idea of an abiding, reflecting self is our sanctuary. His humility before God is an analogue of the modesty appropriate to our place in nature. Yet, Descartes' divided ontology – mind's firmest defense – collapses upon itself. Is there a naturalistic interpretation of the cogito? Or is the life of the mind terminated, because Cartesian mechanism has cannibalized Cartesian mind?

REFERENCES

Carnap, Rudolf. 1969. *The Logical Structure of the World*, trans. Rolf A. George. Berkeley: University of California Press.

Kohut, Heinz. 1978. *The Restoration of the Self*. New York: International Universities Press.

Peirce, Charles Sanders. 1934. vol 5. *Collected Papers*, ed. Charles Hartshorne and Paul Weiss. Cambridge, Mass.: Harvard University Press.

Quine, W. V. O. 1961. *From a Logical Point of View*. New York: Harper and Row.

Weissman, David. 1989. *Hypothesis and the Spiral of Reflection*. Albany: State University of New York Press.

Rethinking the Western Tradition

Discourse on the Method and Meditations on First Philosophy

RENÉ DESCARTES

Edited by David Weissman,

with essays by William T. Bluhm, Lou Massa, Thomas Pavel, John F. Post, Stephen Toulmin, and David Weissman

Descartes' ideas not only changed the course of Western philosophy but also led to or transformed the fields of metaphysics, epistemology, physics and mathematics, political theory and ethics, psychoanalysis, and literature and the arts. This book reprints Descartes' major works, *Discourse on the Method* and *Meditations* and presents essays by leading scholars that explore his contributions in each of those fields and place his ideas in the context of his time and our own. There are chapters by David Weissman on metaphysics and psychoanalysis, John Post on epistemology, Lou Massa on physics and mathematics, William T. Bluhm on politics and ethics, and Thomas Pavel on literature and art. These essays are accompanied by others by David Weissman and by Stephen Toulmin that introduce the idea of intellectual lineages, discuss the period in which Descartes wrote, and reexamine the premises of his philosophy in light of contemporary philosophical, political, and social thinking.

David Weissman is professor of philosophy at the City College of the City University of New York. William T. Bluhm is professor of political science emeritus at the University of Rochester. Lou Massa is professor of chemistry and physics at Hunter College and the Graduate School of the City University of New York. Thomas Pavel is professor of French and comparative literature at Princeton University. John F. Post is professor of philosophy at Vanderbilt University. Stephen Toulmin is Henry Luce Professor at the Center for Multi-ethnic and Transnational Studies at the University of Southern California.

RETHINKING THE WESTERN TRADITION